FRONTIERS OF ACCESS TO LIBRARY MATERIALS
No. 1

FRONTIERS OF ACCESS TO LIBRARY MATERIALS

Sheila S. Intner, Series Editor

No. 1 Barbra Buckner Higginbotham and Sally Bowdoin. *Access versus Assets: A Comprehensive Guide to Resource Sharing for Academic Librarians*

ACCESS versus ASSETS

A Comprehensive Guide to Resource Sharing for Academic Librarians

**Barbra Buckner Higginbotham
Sally Bowdoin**

American Library Association
Chicago and London 1993

025.62
H63a

Composed by Alexander Graphics on Datalogics
   in Melior and Optima

Printed on 50-pound Glatfelter, a pH-neutral stock,
   and bound in B-grade Arrestox cloth by
   Braun-Brumfield, Inc.

The paper used in this publication meets the minimum requirements of American National Standard for Information Sciences—Permanence of Paper for Printed Library Materials, ANSI Z39.48-1984. ∞

Library of Congress Cataloging-in-Publication Data

Higginbotham, Barbra Buckner.
    Access versus assets : a comprehensive guide to resource sharing for academic librarians / by Barbra B. Higginbotham and Sally Bowdoin.
      p. cm.
    Includes bibliographical references and index.
    ISBN 0-8389-0607-9
    1. Interlibrary loans—United States. 2. Document delivery—United States. I. Bowdoin, Sally. II. Title.
Z713.5.U6H54 1993
025.6'2--dc20   93-16601

Copyright © 1993 by the American Library Association. All rights reserved except those which may be granted by Sections 107 and 108 of the Copyright Revision Act of 1976.

Printed in the United States of America.

95 94 93   5 4 3 2 1

For Hal and John

CONTENTS

Chapter 1
    Introduction   1

Chapter 2
    A Point of Embarkation: "What's Past Is Prologue"   7

Chapter 3
    Cooperative Relationships: "We Band of Brothers"   31

Chapter 4
    Reciprocal Agreements: "He That Runs May Read"   68

Chapter 5
    Interlending: "Friends Share All Things"   77

Chapter 6
    Commercial Document Suppliers: "For All We Take We Must Pay, But the Price Is Cruel High"   144

Chapter 7
    Approaches to Document Delivery: "Deliberate Speed, Majestic Instancy"   201

Chapter 8
    Making Decisions for Access: "A Mighty Maze! But Not without a Plan"   249

Chapter 9
    Shaping Our Future: "Such Stuff As Dreams Are Made On"   292

Appendix
    Case Studies in Resource Sharing   331

Bibliography   359

Index   379

CHAPTER 1

Introduction

I. Access versus Assets: Scope and Purpose 1

II. Definitions 2

III. A Comprehensive Approach to Access and Delivery Options 3

IV. Costs, Evaluation, and Decision Making 4

V. Coverage of Related Topics 5

VI. Information Ethics: "Free" versus "Fee" 5

Access versus Assets: Scope and Purpose

At their most basic, the collections of all academic libraries meet the instructional and research needs of undergraduates. Larger college and university libraries may either partially or, in the case of some very large university collections, almost completely support the scholarly activity of graduate students and faculty. *Access versus Assets* does not specifically concern itself with these substantial university library collections; while its counsel will be useful to larger institutions, to public libraries, or indeed to any library attempting to meet a portion of its readers' needs through access rather than acquisition, it is aimed at the professional staff, faculty, and graduate students of the many colleges and universities attempting to support graduate work and faculty research with collection development budgets inadequate to the task.

Robert F. Munn speaks persuasively to the hearts of college librarians: "Somehow, the problems of the major research libraries are starting to be regarded as universals. So, too, are the proposed solutions to these problems."[1] But we who staff small- and medium-sized academic libraries must be very careful about taking comfort in these words, now ten years old. If we can convince ourselves, as Munn wrote then, that those who require broad access to scholarly materials are affiliated with the seventy-plus research universities of this country, then we can turn away from any serious pursuit of access: our institutions will have been tested and disqualified. If, however, we believe that contemporary educational descriptors (emphasis on publishing and research, whatever the institution's size or special mission, for example) and the negative economic climate have come to dictate resource sharing in every academic library, we will have to agree that time has altered Munn's contentions and we are not off the hook: we have now inherited many of the problems that a decade ago confronted only research libraries.

Definitions

Much of the terminology associated with interlending and resource sharing confuses rather than clarifies our understanding of the options. "Access" is a loosely used and often misunderstood word. Not so very long ago, we equated the term "access" with "circulation"; the "access services librarian" was the person in charge of circulation, and perhaps some related services such as library information or the reserves collection. With the creation of the Commission on Preservation and Access, we grew even more baffled: what exactly was the meaning of the "access" part of this national body's name, and how did it fit in with our existing understanding of the term? Then, we began to read in the library press about "access versus ownership," and such concepts as "temporary" and "permanent" acquisition. Confusion reigned.

Authors of lengthy articles that attempted to differentiate among library consortia, networks, and cooperatives further muddied the taxonomic waters: must librarians trouble themselves with such demarcations? Then there are those who have insisted that "interlibrary loan" is at best a mid-twentieth-century expression: since no one returns photocopies, which typically constitute over 50 percent of "loans," how can the library unit providing these surrogates have the word *loan* in its title? A variety of alternatives to "interlibrary loan," none entirely satisfactory and each serving to create further bewilderment, was offered; among these are "resource sharing" and "document delivery" (but does the latter indicate the entire procedure, or just the delivery portion?). When the commercial sector began to involve itself in providing copies of unowned items, the plot thickened even further: some termed these services "commercial," others "fee-based," while still others limited "fee-based" to the description of services for which libraries themselves made a charge.

It is not the purpose of *Access versus Assets* to settle such semantic questions. In fact, while striving for clarity, the authors prefer also to fend off boredom by using terms such as "resource sharing" and "interlending" quite broadly, so that they include not only the acquisition of originals, but also of surrogates, and not just lending and borrowing library-to-library, but also the use of commercial document services: after all, while some progressive institutions may have renamed "interlibrary loan" the "access center" or "document delivery unit," most of us still see "interlibrary loan" on our organization charts, despite the many access approaches that unit may now embrace.

Similarly, unless the individual chapters clearly differentiate between one term and another, we will use interchangeably "consortium," "cooperative," "network," and the like; neither will we trouble ourselves or our readers by making fine distinctions between "fee-based" and "commercial" document services. The only semantic absolute in *Access versus Assets* is the consistent use of the term "access" to mean "access to that which one does not own," rather than access to local collections.

A Comprehensive Approach to Access and Delivery Options

Academic librarians everywhere know that self-sufficiency, if indeed it ever flourished, today is dead. We are turning toward access, but some of us may be doing so less purposefully, cost-effectively, and efficiently than we might, because we have not considered all of the available options in an organized fashion, concluding by making those arrangements which best meet our readers' needs. This book describes and explores a broad range of approaches academic librarians can use to provide their readers with access to information that exists outside the walls of the local library. While the library collections of larger libraries doubtless go further in meeting the needs of advanced scholarship, this book may contain some access ideas as yet untried or inadequately tested even in these more comprehensive settings.

Within the context of an information ethic that must transcend our contemporary ability to purchase, *Access versus Assets* can be a useful decision-making tool for libraries and consortia considering an imposing array of access options. Put most simply, this book guides librarians and faculty in locating wanted materials and then arranging access to them. It provides hard information about obtaining what the reader requests; identifying and evaluating productive resource sharing or consortial arrangements; access approaches; and delivery options.

This book assumes the local availability of (or the desire to implement) some form of interlending automation, such as access to one of the bibliographic utilities' interlibrary loan modules, or perhaps an electronic mail messaging system. For the library not yet automated, there is a wealth of advice and information that can lead to the informed selection of productive electronic approaches to resource sharing.

Costs, Evaluation, and Decision Making

Access versus Assets also identifies the cost centers associated with each approach (copyright and other fees, staff time, equipment, communication charges), as well as the advantages and disadvantages of each method. For example, perhaps commercial document delivery is found to be fast, but expensive; in some cases interlibrary loans can be obtained without direct payment of fees, but arranging these loans is often time-intensive. If an approach will only show promise under certain circumstances (the success of telefacsimile and scanning is dependent on the existence of a body of logical partners), these are identified.

Evaluation and balance are the most important themes of *Access versus Assets*. This book suggests how librarians can evaluate and assign costs to individual approaches to access, such as interlending and commercial document supply. It illustrates how a library might determine which mix of components its own access program will contain (under what circumstances might a library choose one access method over another, when several are available?) and explains how to develop a budget that includes the costs of all the elements in a comprehensive access program.

Access versus Assets does not directly concern itself with cost-reduction techniques, although some of the suggested approaches may involve cost cutting or result in cost savings. The intent, however, is to identify the most efficient and economical approaches to access, the most effective balance of collection and access dollars. If the counsel in this book is enthusiastically applied, it will result in increased business for the interlending or access unit: the aim here is not simply the redirection of existing transactions (the reader used to get this off the shelf, but the library canceled it, so she now requests it through interlibrary loan), but the generation of new activity: readers will seek access to materials the local library does not own in greater numbers than ever before.

The application of these techniques will increase the speed and scope of the local interlending unit, build the campus's confidence in resource sharing, and transfigure the typical ILL client from a man or woman in an information crisis to one who simply needs timely access to a range of remotely held materials: business will grow. These pages will not recommend access as a substitute for assets, but rather an economic, informed, and reasonable balance between the two concepts.

Coverage of Related Topics

This handbook becomes useful the moment someone determines that a request for unowned materials is a legitimate one that the staff will move to fill. Much advice is available elsewhere on preliminary and related topics, such as how to determine which materials one should purchase and which, instead, one should "access," and the issue of whether the requested item is appropriate and useful to the reader's research, or whether something in the local collection will do just as well. Similarly, topics that relate more directly to ownership than to access (coordinated collection development, storage centers, CD-ROM or other electronic full-text data available in the local library) are treated only briefly, if at all. *Access versus Assets* should be used in conjunction with Virginia Boucher's *Interlibrary Loan Practices Handbook*, and is not intended in any way to supplant the detailed and practical information on finding locations, the interlibrary loan interview, copyright issues, and other important topics there contained.[2]

Information Ethics: "Free" versus "Fee"

A great deal has already been written about contemporary issues of access "ethics." Among the most interesting are the questions of information excess, ownership, and equity (sometimes characterized as "free" or "universal" access to information). The library's responsibility to provide access to that which its readers require, whether owned or unowned, is this book's major ethical tenet. While the costs associated with ownership have spurred interest in interlending, there are also significant costs associated with resource sharing. Unless a library understands these costs and is willing to pay them, its access program will not succeed: in the present economic climate, few institutions are willing to be large net lenders and most insist on a certain balance of trade among themselves and their resource sharing partners. *Access versus Assets* helps libraries understand and calculate the several costs associated with access; it shapes the twin issues of imposing charges on one's readers and other libraries and outlines the questions every institution should consider. Someone must pay, and the decision of who is left to the local library.

Neither a paean to technology nor its absence, this guide simply describes and discusses any academic library's access options within the twin contexts of speed and cost. Academic librarians recognize that there is a need to improve various aspects of contemporary access, whether by establishing an electronic "national union catalog," speeding document delivery, or through many other means; the final chapter of *Access versus Assets* speculates on how new information-delivery technologies are likely to change our present set of resource sharing concerns. However, this book is basically a "what to do 'til the doctor comes" guide to access approaches and delivery mechanisms, strongly grounded in the way things are, rather than the way things should or will be. It reflects the recognition that, while we should all work for change, at the same time we must live and work in the present, and (for the sakes of our readers) as effectively as we can.

Notes

1. Robert F. Munn, "Collection Development vs. Resource Sharing," *Journal of Academic Librarianship* 8 (Jan. 1983): 352.
2. Virginia Boucher, *Interlibrary Loan Practices Handbook* (Chicago: American Library Association, 1984).

CHAPTER 2

A Point of Embarkation

What's Past Is Prologue
(Shakespeare, *The Tempest*, II, i)

I. The Demise of Self-Sufficiency   7
  A. Declining Library Budgets   8
  B. The Growth of Scholarly Publication   8
  C. Rising Journal Prices   9

II. The Growth of Cooperation and Interlending   10

III. The Impact of Technology   12
  A. The Bibliographic Utilities   12
  B. New Information Sources and Formats   12
  C. Shared Catalogs and Catalog Gateways   13
  D. Other Electronic Information Resources   14

IV. The Hidden Costs of Ownership   15

V. The Uneasiness of the Academic Librarian   16

VI. The Role of Local Collections   16

VII. The Viability of Resource Sharing   17
  A. The Attitudes of Librarians   17
  B. The Attitudes of Faculty   19
  C. The Academic Library: Autonomy or Dependency?   21

VIII. Modifying Institutional Attitudes   21

IX. Selecting for Use   23
  A. The Pittsburgh Study   23
  B. The DePauw Study   25
  C. Analysis of Collection Use: An Obsolete Pastime?   26

X. Today's Access Options   26

The Demise of Self-Sufficiency

Academic librarians and the faculty and graduate students whom they serve acknowledged some time ago that most institutions can no longer acquire all the materials serious scholarship demands. In 1976 Richard De Gennaro commented:

> Powerful inflationary trends on the one hand, coupled with increasingly effective technological and resource-sharing capabilities on the other hand, are causing all academic research libraries to undergo a fundamental reassessment and reorientation of their traditional collection development goals and service strategies as they make the painful transition from the affluent sixties to the austere seventies and eighties.[1]

If the seventies and eighties could be characterized as "austere," what of the nineties? What are the specific forces that seem to muffle what Patricia Battin called "the siren song of institutional autonomy and self-sufficient collection standards"?[2]

Declining Library Budgets

Robert F. Munn believes that "academic librarians clearly perceive themselves to be in a Time of Trouble. There is general agreement as to the cause of the trouble—a disastrous combination of soaring costs and static or declining budgets."[3] Certainly the declining academic library budget is a major factor in the demise of self-sufficiency; the lack of growth in funding for library acquisitions makes it difficult to keep up with inflation, much less with the increased output of information.[4] Addressing a group of New York City librarians in April 1992, Thomas J. Michalak remarked that any new money for libraries will likely be used to offset inflation, rather than to increase purchasing power.[5]

The Growth of Scholarly Publication

Contrasting the annual output of scholarship to contemporary buying power, librarians find that even the largest research institutions can purchase only 5 to 10 percent of the world's publishing output.[6] Journal literature is particularly problematic; there has been an increase worldwide in the number of scholarly, scientific, and technical journals, and a well-known library educator concedes that "the universe of materials is so large that libraries, in a sense, cannot even cover basic needs."[7] The problem is compounded as existing serials grow large and bulky:

> Simultaneously, the increasing clustering of specialists whose areas divide and subdivide makes a journal's contents too heterogeneous to appeal to a single population of readers. At this point, the journal "twigs," becoming two or more discrete publications directed to more specialized audiences.[8]

There is also the demand from new quarters for serial literature: for some time, scientists have been heavily dependent on journals; now, librarians observe the heightened use of periodicals by scholars in the social sciences and the humanities.

In the July 1991 issue of *College & Research Libraries* Paul Metz and Paul M. Gherman examine this great increase in scientific and scholarly productivity:

> The number of abstracts in physics alone leapt from 24,000 in 1962 to 143,000 in 1988. With the number of physicists doubling and their per capita productivity growing, the number of *Physics Review* pages quintupled in the same period. According to *Ulrich's*, more than 133,000 periodicals are now in print; that is more than twice the roughly 60,000 listed in 1978.[9]

Robin Downes, the University of Houston's librarian, points to similar jumps in research output:

> It took 32 years to reach the first million abstracts published in *Chemical Abstracts*, 18 years to reach the second million, the third million in 8 years, the fourth in 5 years, and the fifth million was reached in only 3 years. Publishers also point out correctly that new subdisciplines appear with increasing frequency, each with its cadre of journals and professional society affiliations.[10]

Despite these compelling figures, academic librarians have had little success in convincing college and university administrators that this swift increase in the knowledge base calls for a different distribution of the institution's budgetary resources.[11]

Rising Journal Prices

Perhaps the two events that have most strongly dictated the shift of emphasis from ownership to access are the spiraling costs of journal subscriptions and the decline of the American dollar in the foreign markets where many scholarly periodicals are published. Writing in *Library Journal*, Harold Billings observed:

> The journals problem is, of course, simply a part of our total information system crisis. It reflects an increase in scholars and scholarship, the continually growing rush of information and knowledge, the devastation wrought by inflation, dollar devaluation and at least a few greedy publishers, and the insidious diminishment of financial support for higher education.[12]

At the same time library budgets are shrinking, subscription prices are rising at rates considerably more accelerated than the

Consumer Price Index; this has proven to be a volatile combination. In the decade between 1980 and 1990, the average cost of research journals increased 160 percent, a trend that is likely to continue.[13] In the summer of 1991 Paul E. Peters expressed alarm about "the skyrocketing costs of library materials." During the previous three years serials expenditures of the 119 members of the Association of Research Libraries (ARL) had risen by 53 percent, but the number of serial titles purchased dropped by 1 percent. "No matter how you cut these facts," Peters concludes, "they add up to the same thing: much less information is being obtained for much more money."[14] A library thinking to add subscriptions by canceling existing journals is often dismayed to find that it must drop several older periodicals in order to buy one new one: new titles typically cost substantially more than older ones.

Librarians have also voiced concern about the impact of escalating journal costs on the collecting of monographs: during the same three-year period mentioned above, spending for books increased by 19 percent, yet the number of volumes purchased fell 16 percent. It seems that monograph acquisition rates are plunging to such low levels that the book collections of many academic libraries may soon be suitable only for undergraduate use.[15]

The Growth of Cooperation and Interlending

While academic libraries have always cooperated with one another "after their fashion," of late the absolute necessity (versus the desirability) of authentic interdependence has become clear. Comparing contemporary and past levels of collection growth, librarians conclude that the time of building giant research collections is past. Returning to the ideas of Patricia Battin, "The inability of individual institutions to continue to acquire and house comprehensive book collections at traditional levels is beyond dispute. We are not now collecting with the same depth or breadth as our predecessors."[16]

One of the sharpest signs of increased cooperation has been the considerable growth of interlending. ARL statistics show that between 1985-86 and 1990-91 the number of faculty on ARL campuses increased 16 percent and the number of students grew 10 percent. However, interlibrary borrowing increased 47 percent and lending rose 45 percent during the same period. Perhaps this contrast is less surprising when one considers that the number of serial titles purchased by ARL libraries dropped 2 percent, the number of books 15 percent.

Taking a slightly different approach, one ARL member underscores the enormous difference between increases in circulation traffic (41 percent, over an eleven-year period), reference requests (117 percent), and interlibrary borrowing (a whopping 274 percent). Similarly, Hugh C. Atkinson describes an ILL borrowing pattern at the University of Illinois that jumped from between six thousand and eight thousand items per year to (a mere five years later) fifty thousand items annually. The volume of interlending will probably continue to increase, and perhaps in large jolts rather than in a smooth, predictable, linear fashion.[17]

There is evidence that interlending volume in smaller academic libraries may be growing at rates that compare to if not exceed those of the ARL libraries. Susan K. Martin observes that, with the implementation of the OCLC ILL subsystem, smaller libraries began to experience an increase in their lending traffic. Before the days of easy access to the holdings of more modest institutions, many would-be borrowers found larger libraries to be more profitable sources. But, since smaller institutions often catalog books more quickly than larger libraries, and their interlibrary loan operations sometimes operate more efficiently, these factors now make their collections popular "targets" for borrowing requests.[18] This is not to say that most smaller libraries have become net lenders, but rather that the number of requests they receive has significantly increased.

Library networks and consortia other than the Association of Research Libraries report similar leaps in interlending. In the comparatively brief history of the Network of Alabama Academic Libraries (NAAL), founded in 1984, interlibrary loan has increased network-wide 400 percent. During the three-year period from 1987–88 through 1990–91, libraries in the SUNY/OCLC network saw interlending rise 30.52 percent, while cataloging activity increased only 9.23 percent.[19] Like the ARL statistics cited above, these figures show that interlibrary borrowing and lending are clearly outstripping the volume of other library services; it also indicates a sobering ratio between new acquisitions and resource sharing.

What does the future hold for resource sharing through interlibrary loan? There is no expert who anticipates anything but further growth. Clifford A. Lynch, examining the Internet, the improved access to information it offers, and the coming National Research and Education Network (NREN), concludes that these powerful "information highways" will generate enormous increases in the use of interlibrary loan and document delivery systems.[20] Richard M. Dougherty echoes this belief:

We must, I believe, be prepared to accommodate further growth in the volume of lending/borrowing as more libraries convert bibliographic records into machine-readable form and contribute them to bibliographic databases. And growth in the volume of transactions will probably continue until demand is saturated or until demand exceeds our capacity to deliver materials in a timely manner.[21]

A panel of librarians assembled by OCLC to caucus about a broad range of interlending issues could only concur: focus group members agreed that interlending activity will continue to expand, propelled by factors such as greater reader sophistication, growth in the number of information databases, and technological progress.[22]

The Impact of Technology

Library budgets are down and the rate of publishing is up; buying power has been lessened by materials costs that far exceed general inflation, as well as the weakness of the American dollar; thus interlending has soared. But does this complete the tale? Far from it: there are several other reasons why academic libraries both borrow and lend at levels that seem to know no cap.

The Bibliographic Utilities

First, the existence of the bibliographic utilities—OCLC (Online Computer Library Center), RLIN (Research Libraries Information Network), and WLN (Western Library Network)— simplified interlending: even though librarians continued to complete and mail ALA forms to distant collections, the process of verifying citations and identifying locations was greatly simplified. Later, some libraries made OCLC or RLIN terminals publicly accessible, increasing their readers' awareness of other institutions' materials. With the advent of the utilities' automated interlibrary loan modules, the process of requesting materials became much more efficient, and some have argued that this served to increase volume, perhaps because of the positive impact on librarians' attitudes toward interlending.

New Information Sources and Formats

Alternative formats (such as audio, video, and electronic information resources) now compete for the dollars once shared by books and journals; academic librarians need pause only briefly to recall the difficulty, scarcely five years ago, of finding money for CD-ROM subscriptions and equipment. But CD-ROMs and their more mature cousin, the online search, are culpable in the present interlending crisis for more reasons than that they siphon dollars from other areas of the materials budget. Their greatest contribution is that they raise the reader's consciousness of the vast universe of published materials, only a tiny fraction of which the local library will own.

William Arms and Thomas J. Michalak, speaking of Carnegie Mellon's experiences, note the enormous impact of CD-ROM indexes on interlibrary loan requests, a jump of 70 percent in a recent three-year period during which this new technology was introduced and gained a strong footing in the library's service program. Michalak observes that paper-based periodical indexes never created the demand for journal literature that CD-ROMs have generated: if they had, our print indexes would have been in tatters. He suggests that readers like the ease and flexibility of CD-ROM searching so much that electronically available data may drive that which is not electronic from the marketplace.[23]

Shared Catalogs and Catalog Gateways

Most libraries experienced a similar phenomenon when the online catalog was introduced: just as journal indexes on CD-ROM have driven up the demand for periodical literature and interlending, online catalogs (easier to use and more powerful than the card or microform catalogs that preceded them) caused circulation to jump. Now in some academic settings the electronic catalog (online or CD-ROM) shows it can also affect interlending activity; this typically happens in one of two ways.

The shared or multiple institution catalog that contains the book and journal holdings of several libraries will certainly increase the demand for items that are not locally owned. Of course, this is the whole point of such projects: to promote resource sharing among a discrete group of institutions. Even when a catalog includes the materials of a single institution, when that college or university has more than one library, the demand for intra-institutional loans (which could be viewed as a sort of interlibrary lending, depending on local policy) will increase.

The Internet, a powerful linkage of regional supercomputer networks around the country, now provides any institution that can connect with it the ability to access several hundred library catalogs scattered from coast to coast. Similarly, powerful software like NOTIS's PACLink and PACLoan permit readers in one library to search the catalogs of remote institutions and, seeing what materials they hold, to place borrowing requests directly from their local online catalogs, independent of the assistance of the local interlibrary loan office.[24] These gateways to other libraries' catalogs can only increase faculty and student interest in materials available outside their local libraries. Contemplating these developments, Sheila T. Dowd comments:

> Librarians are increasingly aware of other libraries' resources, and increasingly inclined to view them as an extension of their own collections . . . library users are increasingly prone to expect that the library will get a publication for them if it doesn't own it.[25]

Other Electronic Information Resources

Some libraries have begun to make periodical indexes available through their online catalogs; readers simply indicate whether they wish to search the catalog or the periodical indexes. Several vendors make their indexes available on tapes, which can be mounted on the same computer that holds the library's catalog; in the best cases, readers use the same commands to search both the catalog and the indexes, and there is an indication as to whether the local library owns the journal in question.

These indexes (still rather new) have had much the same impact on interlending as those of CD-ROM—it is likely their impact will be even greater, because the reader's ease of access (certainly key to the use of any service) is greater: instead of leaving one machine (the catalog terminal) and logging onto another (the CD-ROM workstation), the student or faculty member can meet his or her needs using a single piece of equipment. There are also online periodical indexes that stand alone, unlinked to the catalog, and indexes tied to document supply services; chapter 6 fully describes these products. The point to be made here, as Atkinson commented, is the enormous impact on resource sharing of "the awareness of how little we have in any given library." Continuing this thought, he writes:

> The recognition of how much there is, how much is needed, and how little we are providing produces a willingness to approach networking, not just as a nice additional service, but as one of the fundamental parts of library activity.[26]

In their chapter on interlibrary loan in the *Operations Handbook for the Small Academic Library*, Marilyn E. Miller and Patricia R. Guyette emphasize the impact of this heightened access to bibliographic data on smaller college and university libraries:

> The small academic library may well find that its access to information sources through computer-based literature-search services increases its interlibrary borrowing activity, especially for serial requests. Students today are highly computer literate, and they gravitate toward whatever information can be found using computers.[27]

For all these reasons, interlibrary loan units report that request volume has grown and continues to grow. There is no reason to suspect that this condition will alter in the near future.

The Hidden Costs of Ownership

There are several facts of modern library life that make access especially appealing to library managers. Jay K. Lucker, Paul E. Peters, and Harold Billings all cite the space required to house library collections and the already overcrowded condition of most academic libraries.[28] Another librarian sums up the issue in this way:

> Not only are library materials themselves expensive, the space to house them is also more costly than ever. It can cost up to $125 per square foot to construct prime library space. What institution will be able to afford the housing for vast collections in the future?[29]

But the commitment to subscriptions (and, to a certain extent, to books) goes far beyond space: there are also the costly issues of selection and acquisition, processing, shelving, circulation, and preservation. Billings cites the expenses of "record keeping, claiming, binding, preservation, security-stripping, housing, circulation, etc.; capital costs, operational costs, computing and telecommunications costs."[30] In a journal aimed at helping faculty and campus administrators understand important library issues, Marcia Tuttle emphasizes the obligation a library assumes when it places a journal subscription:

> Unlike purchasing a book, subscribing to a journal is not a one-time expenditure; it is a long-term commitment for a library. . . . If journals are retained in microform, the cost of storage cabinets, mechanical equipment, and maintenance

must also be included. . . . The receipt, availability, and location of journals must all be recorded to ensure patron access. Maintaining these records, whether manually or online, requires funding for personnel and equipment.[31]

One could add to all of these costs those of computer space (presumably, the library's catalog is automated) and telecommunications.

The Uneasiness of the Academic Librarian

This environment has caused serious concern among academic librarians who recognize that, even though the library cannot afford to own certain materials, it is nonetheless still obligated to meet the information needs of its faculty and students, wherever the books and journals they want actually reside: ethics prohibit an information policy whose practice confines itself to what is locally owned.

Thus, a great number of academic librarians find themselves in an awkward position: there is no institution that does not require its faculty to conduct research and publish, and even relatively small colleges and universities often have graduate programs whose students' information needs are similar to those of faculty. Yet, it is difficult (one could say, impossible) for a library of even one to two million monographic and periodical volumes, much less one of a few hundred thousand, to satisfy such demands through self-sufficiency.

The Role of Local Collections

Despite a difficult economy, larger college and university libraries may either partially or, in the case of some very large university collections, almost completely support the scholarly activity of graduate students and faculty. At their most basic, however, the collections of all academic libraries meet the instructional and research needs of the undergraduate population. This is unlikely to change; as Munn writes, "For the foreseeable future, each institution will continue to be responsible for the provision of undergraduate requirements. No network now envisaged will enable institutions to shift to others the cost of providing instructional material."[32] Furthermore, as academic librarians we know that undergraduates approach their work rather differently from graduate students and faculty: often they are looking for three books and six articles on a given topic, their need is immediate, and they stop as soon as the required number of resources has been met. Access to other collections will probably be a very incomplete solution to the needs of college students.

The Viability of Resource Sharing

Despite the seeming inevitability of resource sharing, depending on the collections of other libraries or commercial suppliers to meet some group of information needs creates its own set of anxieties, and it is best to acknowledge and address these rather than ignore them. As Dougherty asks, "How effective is resource sharing as a way of supporting local academic programs? Or, put another way, can collections located at colleague institutions serve as satisfactory substitutes for local collections?"[33] There are several issues to be considered.

The Attitudes of Librarians

In the days before the OCLC ILL subsystem, when requests to borrow were typed on ALA forms and sent through the U.S. mail, interlibrary loan librarians trained those who consumed their services to be patient; a successful transaction was one that resulted in the eventual delivery of the wanted item, no matter how much time was required. Cautions such as "at least a month" were typically given. When the major utilities introduced automated request systems and consortia developed effective delivery services, some librarians shortened their warnings accordingly: "It will take at least two weeks," was commonly heard.

Nevertheless, the added speed offered by telefacsimile, electronic messaging, a broad range of commercial services, and excellent air and ground delivery systems has not changed the approach of some library professionals, who continue to believe that there is no great need for haste, and that patient readers will be grateful for the document, whenever it arrives. In other cases, librarians may not be convinced of the value of commercial document delivery services, perhaps because they believe information should be supplied 'free," or because the introduction of such services will call for certain local procedural changes.

The experience of City University of New York librarians with commercial document supply services, whose costs were completely subsidized by the university's Office of Academic Affairs, points sharply to the degree to which local library "culture" influences degree of use. Despite the fact that use of the services was "free," libraries whose interlending operations were noted for their aggressiveness in meeting readers' needs, those serving traditionally "vocal" faculties, and those with forceful directors made significantly greater use of these document suppliers than did libraries with more conventional interlibrary loan units. Here, staff seemed reluctant to raise the expectations of students and faculty, whom they had so carefully trained over time to wait. This seems to support library educator Herbert S. White's image of traditional interlending:

> Library users inevitably find completely unexpected my question of whether or not they consider loan delays to be unreasonable. "However long it takes" is the definition of reasonable. We have trained our users to be passive.[34]

When local collections met the large majority of local needs and interlibrary borrowing was an infrequent event, perhaps the standard for success ("We got it, eventually") was not such a bad one. But, as libraries' success in satisfying their readers with materials from their own collections declines, the importance of efficiency grows. Unless librarians place considerable emphasis on delivery speed, thereby building readers' confidence in the effectiveness of access to remote collections, all but the most desperate faculty and students will avoid the interlibrary loan unit; they will scoff at access as a viable substitute for ownership. Dougherty's counsel is sound: "Substantive change in faculty attitudes toward dependency on collections owned by others is not likely to occur until libraries can implement programs that increase the real or perceived effectiveness of document delivery systems."[35]

There is another major reason why librarians may resist a strong institutional emphasis on access. Marcia Tuttle's comments bear on the views of librarians, faculty, and academic administrators:

> Big is important to Americans; it's one of our favorite standards. We want bigger cars, bigger homes, bigger academic departments. The standard for libraries is no different. The perceived value of a library is based on quantitative measures: those owning the largest numbers of books or journals are usually considered the best. . . . In times of tight budgets and high prices it is unfortunate that size is the measure of quality in libraries.[36]

Until all members of the academic community can accept a new standard for measuring the quality of the library, one which emphasizes effective delivery of wanted information, wherever it resides, it is unlikely that what some have called the "access model" will succeed. This presents a depressing scenario, one in which local collections cannot meet any significant portion of readers' demands, yet a solid and aggressive commitment to access has not been made; librarians, faculty, students, and administrators alike will be frustrated and miserable as they continue to strive toward the unattainable "ownership model."

It seems worthwhile to note here that access (interlending or the use of commercial services) is not yet perfect and there is still much improvement to be made. As Allen Kent points out, we will devote our energies to making resource sharing more efficient once we are completely convinced of its superiority to the old model of self-sufficiency:

> The cost-effectiveness of resource sharing is diminished at present because it has to run in parallel with systems working toward self-sufficiency. As more integrated systems of resource sharing develop, more benefits can be realized from redistributed responsibilities and resources.[37]

Battin's views are similar:

> Many of our consortium and cooperative activities of the past have made the fundamental mistake of attempting to share resources without giving up our basic notion of the autonomous organization of libraries.... We have discovered that we cannot meet the increased demand by simple exploitation of the existing sharing mechanisms. We must consider today, not the sharing of resources, but the sharing of dependencies.[38]

The Attitudes of Faculty

A short ten years ago Joe A. Hewitt wrote:

> Users of research libraries appear inclined to use off-site materials only when these materials are of unquestioned relevance and high presumed need. Thus, an operationally critical level of dependency on materials sharing may not come about until ... there is a disastrous decline in materials budgets which leaves research library collections inadequate to provide basic support to their primary clienteles.[39]

Today, one could easily argue that the condition Hewitt describes has come to pass, not just in research libraries, but in academic libraries of all sizes. One faculty attitude often shared by librarians and other members of the academic community ("big is best") has been mentioned above; there are several related and no less commonly held ideas. One academic librarian observes:

> In no institution will a substantial shift of resources away from collection development go unnoticed; in only a few will it be applauded. . . . A reduction in emphasis on local collections is not likely to be popular with most scholars. Faculty members . . . may agree, as a theoretical proposition, that programs designed to make more effective use of resources are desirable. However, there is little evidence that they are prepared to endure much inconvenience, let alone make any real sacrifices. Faculty members are far more likely to oppose [resource sharing programs] as threats to established and comfortable patterns.[40]

Allen Kent, whose collection use study at the University of Pittsburgh fifteen years ago created a furor among faculty, is also well qualified to describe their concerns:

> If all libraries turn to resource sharing, none will have books to lend; if resource sharing proves unworkable, the library will be even further behind; the major defects with resource sharing proposals are that the technology and organization structures are not presently available to provide a level of service comparable to that available today with existing [local] methods.[41]

Today, these charges seem fairly easy to answer. Resource sharing and the use of commercial document delivery services do not release any academic library from its responsibility to continue to develop its collections. Conversely, an increasing emphasis on access should require that libraries examine their readers' needs more closely than ever before, in order to be certain that each acquisition dollar is spent to purchase those materials that are likely to be most needed. As for the fear that the failure of resource sharing will place libraries even further behind (presumably, in collection building), when one compares the costs of access to those of ownership (which only begin, as noted above, with the purchase price of the book or journal) this seems all but impossible.

Today's electronic table of contents and indexing/abstracting services provide a view of the scholarly universe that more closely approximates local, on-the-shelf, browsable access than anything heretofore available; when combined with effective delivery mechanisms, in some cases they can certainly substitute for ownership. Thus, it remains for librarians to provide access to remote materials without generating the "inconvenience" and "real sacrifices" faculty may fear are part and parcel to resource sharing.

The Academic Library: Autonomy or Dependency?

It has been argued that resource sharing must finally fail, because academic libraries are far from autonomous:

> For some reason, many librarians insist on writing about academic libraries as if they were largely autonomous units with very considerable freedom to establish their own goals. One would suppose from reading the literature that at least the larger libraries are not integral parts of their institutions but rather essentially free-floating organizations able to do whatever seems to them to be in the public interest.[42]

Librarians, then, ought not be the decision makers when the choice is made between an access or an ownership model: rather the college or university's faculty and administrators must decide whether available resources will be directed primarily at collection building or resource sharing. This idea may appear to be a crafty one, but it is actually very similar to one of the issues Kent cites above (what if resource sharing fails, and the library is further behind than ever?). Certainly, academic libraries are not autonomous; however, we can say with equal certainty that no library will opt for a model that is completely based on either access or ownership. Instead, the one that will best serve an academic community will combine both elements; because access is so much less costly than assets, an institution will find it necessary to forego very little collection building in order to engage in quite a bit of highly effective interlending and fee-based access.

Modifying Institutional Attitudes

Richard M. Dougherty poses the question, "How will one convince faculty to tolerate the transition from the traditional library to one in which there is a greater balance between ownership (local collections) and access (acquisition on demand from other sources) to information?"[43] When it comes to educating readers for resource sharing, small- and medium-sized academic libraries may have an important advantage. Unlike faculty and students affiliated with large research institutions, their clientele well understands that one cannot buy everything; some degree of reliance on other collections is probably already a fact of life. When one considers the number of books and journals not present in the local collection, and the wealth of new material a successful interlending program will provide, it seems likely that support for access can be built.

Here as in almost every aspect of life, nothing succeeds like success. A library will build faculty and student confidence in the effectiveness of access programs only by actually providing rapid delivery of wanted materials; all the glamorous promises one might make for the service will do little to promote its use, compared to the business that positive word-of-mouth will generate. Several librarians have observed that the most politic moment to implement an effective access program is before journal cancellations are mandated: if faculty have already seen that the library can quickly get them what they need, there will be fewer difficulties when subscriptions must be cut. Carolyn Dusenbury and William Post, writing about the University of California at Chico's successful reliance on Berkeley's collections, report:

> This has been very beneficial politically with the faculty as Chico has gone through the painful process of reducing subscriptions.... Some departments were quite adamant that cancellations would cripple research. The institutional will to support research was questioned.... By demonstrating that we could provide reasonable access and delivery of materials, these departments, while not entirely sanguine about the currently proposed cancellation project, have raised much less fuss about it. The contribution to library-faculty goodwill alone has made the agreement worth the investment.[44]

There is probably no way we can completely compensate readers for the lack of "serendipity" with which local access is often associated, and it is difficult to answer a faculty member's contention that the perfect resource is often discovered when, going to the shelf for one book, he or she instead finds another. Ten years ago Hewitt commented:

> There are critical differences in terms of use between materials available on site and those which must be provided through interlibrary loan, however bibliographically accessible these may be. Materials available only from remote sites cannot be used for current awareness, browsing, and screening large amounts of material for relevance to a given need.... Sharing of materials cannot be presented as an alternative which is equal to providing materials on site, in terms of service to users.[45]

While we must still partly agree with Hewitt's observations (no one would argue that access is a perfect substitute for ownership), in the past ten years technologic advances in indexing, abstracting, and table of contents services (such as those offered by CARL and OCLC) have made it possible to give readers at least a vivid illusion that they can browse and screen a great deal of current information, despite its being remotely held. A decade later, Dusenbury and Post neatly answer Hewitt's contentions:

> Is there a downside to such an arrangement? Yes. The research community at Chico has lost the ability to browse journals and to engage in the serendipitous discovery of related but relevant information. The ordering of articles based on a citation does not have the *a priori* benefit of actually previewing the material. The mitigating factor is that because of the mere quantity of information available, faculty simply cannot browse through everything that might be relevant. More and more they are seeking known items based on the research of others or "current contents," so relying on Berkeley is not as disruptive to exploration as it might have been.[46]

Selecting for Use

Allen Kent is not the only advocate of collection use studies; Paul E. Peters, Bernard H. Holicky, Thomas J. Galvin, and Larry Hardesty, as well as librarians at both the University of California at Riverside and the University of Tennessee at Knoxville, have expressed concern about the underutilization of academic library collections.[47] While Kent may have begun his famous and hotly protested study at the University of Pittsburgh with an eye to justifying greater dependency on resource sharing (his sharpest critics say his conclusions were already written before the study was begun), in today's environment where some degree of reliance on remote materials is all but impossible to avoid, collection use studies seem desirable insofar as they provide guidance to selectors who are allocating scarce collection development dollars. Kent argues that, as shrinking collecting budgets force a greater degree of dependence on remote collections, it becomes more important than ever to spend whatever is available for acquisitions of titles that will be used.[48]

The Pittsburgh Study

Perhaps it would be well to say a word or two about what the Pittsburgh study found. Working from data collected by the university library's automated circulation system between 1969 and 1975, Kent and Galvin concluded that any book purchased during this period had a chance slightly better than one in two of ever circulating. When a book did not circulate during the first two years of ownership, its chances of being borrowed were reduced to one in four. If a minimum of two circulations was used as a criteria for a cost-effective acquisitions program, 54 percent of what was acquired would not have been bought.[49] The Pittsburgh study was even more damning in its examination of journal use:

> Preliminary results of the journal use study suggest that the effect of aging is even more pronounced in the use of journals than in the use of books and monographs. . . . The question is, can research libraries continue to afford to purchase material that is not likely to be used?[50]

Galvin and Kent suggest that librarians have failed to do a better job of focusing their collecting habits because they lack sufficient "predictive data" to do so: "It is not particularly helpful for a bibliographer to know that ten percent of the titles selected will satisfy ninety percent of client demand for materials in a given discipline, unless we can determine which ten percent."[51] To improve the circulation "hit rate," they argue that selectors can make use of data generated by circulation systems. "The results, combined with detailed examination of mean acquisition costs, should make possible the identification of those LC classes that are 'high risk' and relatively 'low risk' from the standpoint of book ordering."[52] Certainly, a greater degree of predictability would be desirable.

Many faculty questioned the methodology and the conclusions of the Pittsburgh study and predicted dire outcomes for any library that would be guided by them:

> Researchers can manage when the percentage of materials which must be obtained by interlibrary loan or from storage is small. As the percentage grows, research soon becomes impossible. The developers may do grave damage to our research libraries by their insistent promotional activities on behalf of materials sharing. They simply do not begin to explain what might be the consequences, the social costs, or the shifts they recommend. The natural consequence of the impairment of our library environment will be the impairment of our research and teaching.[53]

The study was attacked on the most basic grounds possible: that the chief methodology used—the interpretation of circulation data—could not and did not satisfactorily measure the use of the library's collections. Librarians reminded readers and one another that academic library collections are built to satisfy not just today's readers, but also the scholars and students of tomorrow. However, even if both of these contentions are true (and we certainly will not debate the second one), they do not diminish Kent's idea that collection use data can be very helpful in shaping selectors' decisions.

The DePauw Study

The Pittsburgh study (whose methodology is described in its final report) was replicated at smaller DePauw University. Without commenting on the adequacy of the approach for a research library, Larry Hardesty suggested that "recorded circulation statistics may be more appropriate for measuring the undergraduate use of a college library."[54] In the DePauw study, where each book included was physically examined, a clear relationship was found between circulation data and the in-house use of books: "It soon became evident that books with no recorded circulation also had remained virtually untouched within the library. Their pages were unsmudged and their spines creaked as they were opened."[55]

One might think that the books in a college library, fewer in number and for that reason perhaps more painstakingly selected than those for a research library, would receive a higher level of use. However, Hardesty found otherwise: "At both schools, approximately 20 to 30 percent of the books accounted for 80 percent of the total circulation."[56] Do such findings indicate that the libraries studied are buying too many books, and that their materials budgets should be reduced? Not at all: an analysis of the honors theses of a group of DePauw students showed that half the titles cited were from other libraries. "The problem may not be that too many books are being acquired, but that the wrong books are being acquired."[57]

The DePauw study suggested that careful selection could influence collection use. Among its more intriguing findings were that books received as gifts circulated less frequently than books that were purchased, and books selected by librarians were used more often than those selected by faculty.[58] Bernard H. Holicky recommends that, as the small academic library cannot avoid resource sharing, its director should arm him or herself with collection use data and present it to faculty, students, and campus administrators. "These data will serve, at worst, as insurance against the charge that the library's [collecting] policies are based on caprice and, at best, will bring an understanding of the reasons for change."[59]

Analysis of Collection Use: An Obsolete Pastime?

The Kent study was conducted in the mid-1970s; Hardesty applied its methodology at DePauw a few years later, and Holicky's piece was published in 1984. With the exception of the work done at Riverside and Knoxville (mentioned above), not a great deal about use studies has since appeared in the library press. Critics' questions about the validity of Kent's conclusions have never been successfully resolved, nor can they be. Is the under-utilization of academic library collections the result of "faulty acquisitions," or rather "the unpredictability of scholarly curiosity"?[60] If the latter, is the situation therefore virtually incorrectable? Is it inevitable today that we will rely to some extent on access, not just in low-use disciplines, but in almost every area in which we collect? Are such studies then passé, a waste of time, redundant in light of today's very persuasive economic and publishing climates? Yes and no.

Perhaps Holicky's approach is the more practical one—to gather use data in order to justify continuing to collect in some areas, while relying more heavily on access in others—and makes the most sense. Realistically, collection use studies like that performed at Pitt have probably gone the same way as collection inventories: they are time-consuming exercises that today's short-staffed academic library can scarcely imagine conducting, whatever the perceived value of the resulting data.

But libraries are still conducting use studies, though not perhaps ones as complex as Kent's and Galvin's, and they seem to serve their purposes very well. One of the more interesting continues at California State University at San Bernardino where a study locally designed by collection development officer Marty Bloomberg consists of something as simple but effective as posting a number of very large "do not reshelve" signs throughout the stacks, and hiring a cadre of student workers to collect journal volumes left lying about on reading tables, compare them to a list of periodical titles, and check them off. The results have been used to support San Bernardino's decision to cancel less frequently used titles and provide access (rather than ownership) to them. The message? Use studies still have their place, but their structure and purpose will probably be somewhat different from those of the late 1970s.

Today's Access Options

Perhaps today's access theme could be characterized as "choice." In terms of getting materials for readers that they want but that the local library does not own, academic librarians have many more alternatives than were available even five years ago. Approaches include borrowing from other libraries, on-site access to other collections, and a growing array of commercial or fee-based document services from which one can purchase articles and other materials. The choice of delivery mechanisms seems equally broad: the U.S. mail, air or ground courier services, telefacsimile, and scanning are among the available options. The final chapter in this book, which suggests how new models for information delivery may alter our present set of access concerns, indicates that delivery options will continue to improve and expand.

The scenery has been painted, and the canvas is now complete: dwindling budgets, the mounting costs of library materials, and readers' heightened awareness of information wealth have contributed to what some call the crisis in interlending. But the drama that now unfolds need not be a tragedy: as academic librarians, we can assume whatever roles we want, and thus govern the outcome of the play. We can continue to operate interlending units that were probably adequate in their scope and goals twenty years ago, and watch our readers fall further and further behind in meeting their information needs. Or, through effective resource sharing, we can seize the moment and save the day, despite a dismal economic climate and spiraling publication patterns. The choice is ours.

Notes

1. Richard De Gennaro, "The Libraries in Transition," *University of Pennsylvania Almanac* (Feb. 10, 1976): 305.
2. Patricia Battin, "Research Libraries in the Network Environment," *Journal of Academic Librarianship* 6 (May 1980): 68.
3. Munn, "Collection Development," 352.
4. Jay K. Lucker, "Electronic Journal Publishing and Libraries," in *Prospects for Improving Document Delivery: Minutes of the 101st Meeting, October 13–14, Arlington, Virginia*, ed. Nicola Daval (Washington, D.C.: ARL, 1983), 11.
5. Thomas J. Michalak, "The Impact of Table of Contents on Document Delivery in Libraries," Address, New Approaches to Document Delivery, a seminar sponsored by the Interlibrary Loan Roundtable of the Library Association of the City University of New York (LACUNY), New York City, Apr. 10, 1992.
6. Sarah C. Michalak, "Visions for the Future on Resource Sharing," *PNLA Quarterly* 52 (Spring 1988): 4; Richard M. Dougherty, "A Conceptual Framework for Organizing Resource Sharing and Shared Collection Development Programs," *Journal of Academic*

Librarianship 14 (Nov. 1988): 289; Ruth J. Patrick, *Guidelines for Library Cooperation: Development of Academic Library Consortia* (Santa Monica, Calif.: System Development Corporation, 1972), 3.

7. Lucker, "Electronic Journal Publishing," 11; Dougherty, "A Conceptual Framework," 289.
8. Paul Metz and Paul M. Gherman, "Serials Pricing and the Role of the Electronic Journal," *College & Research Libraries* 52 (July 1991): 316.
9. Ibid., 315.
10. Robin Downes, "Resource Sharing and New Information Technology—An Idea Whose Time Has Come," *Journal of Library Administration* 10, no. 1 (1989): 121.
11. Ibid.
12. Harold Billings, "The Bionic Library," *Library Journal* 116 (Oct. 15, 1991): 38.
13. Sharon J. Rogers and Charlene S. Hurt, "How Scholarly Communication Should Work in the 21st Century," *College & Research Libraries* 51 (Jan. 1990): 8.
14. Paul E. Peters, "Networked Information Resources and Services: Next Steps," *CAUSE/EFFECT* 14 (Summer 1991): 36.
15. Ibid.; Downes, "Resource Sharing," 120.
16. Battin, "Research Libraries," 71.
17. Kendon Stubbs, "Supply and Demand in ARL Libraries, 1985–86—1990–91," Graph, 1992; James H. Sweetland and Darlene E. Weingand, "Interlibrary Loan Transaction Fees in a Major Research Library: They Don't Stop the Borrowers," *Library and Information Science Research* 12, no. 1 (1990): 91; Hugh C. Atkinson, "Policies and Controversies," in *Prospects for Improving Document Delivery: Minutes of the 101st Meeting, October 13–14, Arlington, Virginia)*, ed. Nicola Daval (Washington, D.C.: ARL, 1983), 16.
18. Susan K. Martin, "Delivery Systems: Hurry Up and Wait," in *Online Catalogs, Online Reference, Proceedings of a Library and Information Technology Association Preconference Institute, June 23–24, 1983, Los Angeles*, ed. Brian Aveney and Brett Butler (Chicago: American Library Association, 1984), 166.
19. Sue O. Medina, "Improving Document Delivery in a Statewide Network," *Journal of Interlibrary Loan & Information Supply* 2, no. 3 (1992): 7–14; David N. Forsythe, "Acquisitions or Access: A Changing Pattern," *SOL: Messages from SUNY/OCLC Network* 4 (May-June 1991): 2.
20. Clifford A. Lynch and Cecilia M. Preston, "Internet Access to Information Resources," in *Annual Review of Information Science and Technology*, vol. 25, ed. Martha E. Williams (Amsterdam: Elsevier, 1990), 266.
21. Dougherty, "A Conceptual Framework," 288.
22. OCLC, "Interlibrary Loan Discussion Panel: Final Report," Unpublished report, Oct. 1990, vi.

23. William Arms and Thomas J. Michalak, "Carnegie Mellon University," in *Campus Strategies for Libraries and Electronic Information*, ed. Caroline Arms, EDUCOM Strategies Series on Information Technology (Bedford, Mass.: Digital Press, 1990), 258; Michalak, "Impact."
24. NOTIS Systems, Inc., "PACLink and Z39.50 Implementation," Press release, Apr. 23, 1991; NOTIS Systems, Inc., "PACLink ILL Patron Interface," Press release, June 18, 1991, revised Sept. 25, 1991. Prepared by Sara Randall.
25. Sheila T. Dowd, "Library Cooperation: Methods, Models to Aid Information Access," *Journal of Library Administration* 12, no. 3 (1990): 76.
26. Hugh C. Atkinson, "Atkinson on Networks," *American Libraries* 18 (June 1987): 439.
27. Marilyn E. Miller and Patricia R. Guyette, "Interlibrary Loan," in *Operations Handbook for the Small Academic Library*, ed. Gerard B. McCabe (New York: Greenwood Press, 1989), 110.
28. Lucker, "Electronic Journal Publishing," 11; Peters, "Networked Information Resources," 36; Billings, "The Bionic Library," 41.
29. Michalak, "Visions," 4.
30. Billings, "The Bionic Library," 41.
31. Marcia Tuttle, "Journal Information: Ownership and Access," *Library Issues* 10 (Sept. 1989): 1.
32. Munn, "Collection Development," 352.
33. Dougherty, "A Conceptual Framework," 289.
34. Herbert S. White, "Interlibrary Loan: An Old Idea in a New Setting," *Library Journal* 112 (July 1987): 53.
35. Dougherty, "A Conceptual Framework," 289.
36. Tuttle, "Journal Information," 1.
37. Allen Kent, "The Goals of Resource Sharing in Libraries," in *Library Resource Sharing: Proceedings of the 1976 Conference on Resource Sharing in Libraries, Pittsburgh, Pennsylvania*, ed. Allen Kent and Thomas J. Galvin (New York: Marcel Dekker, 1977), 27.
38. Battin, "Research Libraries," 70.
39. Joe A. Hewitt, "Interlibrary Cooperation," in *Academic Librarianship Yesterday, Today, and Tomorrow*, ed. Robert D. Stueart (New York: Neal Schuman, 1982), 114.
40. Munn, "Collection Development," 352–53.
41. Allen Kent, and others, *Use Study of Library Materials: The University of Pittsburgh Study* (New York: Marcel Dekker, 1979); Kent, "The Goals of Resource Sharing," 27.
42. Robert F. Munn, "Cooperation Will Not Save Us," *Journal of Academic Librarianship* 12 (July 1986): 167.
43. Richard M. Dougherty and Carol Hughes, *Preferred Futures for Libraries: A Summary of Six Workshops with University Provosts and Library Directors* (Mountain View, Calif.: The Research Libraries Group, 1991), 14.

44. Carolyn Dusenbury and William Post, "Subscribing to a Research Collection," Unpublished report, Apr. 1991, 12.
45. Hewitt, "Interlibrary Cooperation," 110–11.
46. Dusenbury and Post, "Subscribing," 12.
47. Peters, "Networked Information Resources," 36; Bernard H. Holicky, "Collection Development vs. Resource Sharing: The View from the Small Academic Library," *Journal of Academic Librarianship* 10 (July 1984): 146–47; Thomas J. Galvin and Allen Kent, "Use of a University Library Collection: A Progress Report on the Pittsburgh Study," *Library Journal* 102 (Nov. 15, 1977): 2317–20; Larry Hardesty, "Use of Library Materials at a Small Liberal Arts College," *Library Research* 3 (Fall 1981): 261–82; Jeff Selth, Nancy Koller, and Peter Briscoe, "The Use of Books within the Library," *College & Research Libraries* 53 (May 1992): 197–205; William A. Britten and Judith D. Webster, "Comparing Characteristics of Highly Circulated Titles for Demand-Driven Collection Development," *College & Research Libraries* 53 (May 1992): 239–48.
48. Kent, "The Goals of Resource Sharing," 31.
49. June L. Engle and Sue O. Medina, eds., *Issues in Cooperative Collection Development, SOLINET Resource Sharing and Networks Support Program, March 11, 1986* (Atlanta, Ga.: SOLINET, 1986), 14.
50. Galvin and Kent, "Use of a University Library Collection," 2320.
51. Ibid., 2317.
52. Ibid., 2319.
53. Murdo J. MacLeod and Casimir Barkowski, "Report on the Study of Library Use at Pitt by Professor Allen Kent, et al. (A Pittsburgh Reply)," ED 178 100 (July 1979), 46.
54. Hardesty, "Use of Library Materials," 262.
55. Ibid., 264–65.
56. Ibid., 270.
57. Ibid., 272.
58. Ibid., 278.
59. Holicky, "Collection Development vs. Resource Sharing," 147.
60. Hardesty, "Use of Library Materials," 276.

CHAPTER 3

Cooperative Relationships

We Band of Brothers
(Shakespeare, *Henry V*, IV, iii)

I. Cooperative, Consortium, Network, or Association: What's the Difference? 34

II. Cooperatives Come in All Shapes and Sizes 35
   A. Geography 35
   B. Function 36
   C. Library Type 36
   D. Political Structure 36
   E. Materials Type 37
   F. The "Impure" Cooperative 37

III. Library Cooperatives: What to Look For 38
   A. Are the Library's Goals and Needs Similar to Those of the Consortium? 38
   B. Is Resource Sharing a Top Consortial Priority? 38
   C. Are the Collections of the Other Members of Interest to Local Readers? 39
   D. Are Effective Shared Computing and Telecommunications Technologies in Place? 40
   E. Does the Library Have Access to Its Partners' Holdings? 41
      1. Shared Catalogs 41
      2. Separate and Linked Catalogs 42
      3. Catalogs Available via the Internet 42
   F. Is There Geographic Proximity among Members? 43
   G. Are Effective Document Delivery Mechanisms in Place? 44
   H. Is the Consortium Stable and Are Membership Costs Reasonable? 44
   I. Is There Effective Support for All Services Offered? 45
   J. Will the Library Have a Voice in Consortial Governance? 45
   K. Can the Library Deliver What Membership Requires? 45
   L. Is There a Commitment to Coordinated Collection Development? 46

IV. The New Phenomenon of the "Miniature" Cooperative 49

V. Evaluating and Costing Consortium Memberships 51

A. Does Resource Sharing Save Money? 52
B. The "Greater Good": Valid or Passé as a Motive for Cooperation? 52
C. Taking the Measure of Membership Benefits versus Membership Costs 53
   1. Mutual Benefit or Economic Equity 55
   2. Costs and Monetary Savings 59
   3. Computer and Telecommunications Technologies 60
   4. Extending the Total Resources Available to Readers 61
   5. Interlibrary Loan Efficiencies 61
   6. Reciprocal Access and Borrowing 61
   7. Miscellaneous Benefits 62

VI. Establishing a Library Cooperative 62

VII. Cooperation: Is It Worth All This Trouble? 63

That libraries band together in groups—consortia, cooperatives, associations, networks—to accomplish collaboratively what they cannot do (or cannot do as well or as cost-effectively) individually is not a new idea. One can scarcely find a library that does not belong to at least one cooperative, and most belong to several, each membership perhaps serving a different purpose. No academic librarian will discount the political value of such associations: when he or she asks the campus administration for more money, it is always helpful to demonstrate that the library is already fully engaged in resource sharing. And, as local dollars become harder to come by, we begin to look closely at those cooperative arrangements, seeking to make them more profitable than they may have proven in the past. Some librarians have begun to view resource sharing agreements as virtual "insurance policies": if productive agreements and procedures are already in place, when the economy worsens it will be less painful for both librarians and faculty to cancel subscriptions.

Bernard H. Holicky points out that administrators of major research libraries do much of the writing on networking and resource sharing; thus, the problems of the research libraries have come to be regarded as "universals."[1] One can only add, "correctly so": today, there is no such thing as a self-sufficient academic library, however large or small. During the 1970s and 1980s, this country consciously turned aside from what Richard De Gennaro terms "a single monolithic national network embracing all libraries and providing all types of services," rejecting both a national periodicals center and the idea of the Library of Congress or any other single entity as a sole provider of technical services.[2] Patricia Battin explains how "the old unities have been fragmented and destroyed by the new technology":

> First, we lost the architectural unification of the all-inclusive building. Next went the idea of a single, comprehensive, self-contained collection. Then, true to form, we turned to the concept of a single, all-embracing computerized network to which we would all belong and which would replace the vanished security of our old unities.[3]

Thus, many academic libraries find themselves spread out across several buildings, meeting readers' needs with materials from many sources (local as well as remotely held collections), and entering into a number of cooperative arrangements (local, state, multistate, or national), for an even greater number of reasons (interlending, reciprocal access, continuing education, preservation, and so forth): we have accepted the fact that no one building, collection, or network affiliation can meet all our readers' needs. Joe A. Hewitt agrees with Battin that library economics demands a cooperative approach:

> An attempt should be made to identify reliable alternative sources for materials no longer to be collected, perhaps with associated arrangements for priority handing of requests and extended loan periods. These arrangements serve to reduce to some degree the gap in service between owning materials and depending on the resources of other libraries.[4]

This chapter will suggest some approaches academic libraries can use to identify and evaluate consortial arrangements that enable productive resource sharing; it will not concern itself with other potential benefits and aspects of association membership, such as continuing education, cataloging, or preservation, or with forming a consortium where one does not already exist. (Ruth J. Patrick's book *Guidelines for Library Cooperation: Development of Academic Library Consortia* gives excellent and thorough advice for those wishing to start their own library cooperatives; however, she advises that one begin by ascertaining whether existing consortia can provide the benefits the library seeks.[5] Paul H. Mosher and Marcia Pankake's article "A Guide to Coordinated and Cooperative Collection Development" is also good reading for libraries wishing to develop their own agreements, especially ones with coordinated collecting elements.)[6]

Cooperative, Consortium, Network, or Association: What's the Difference?

In this book the terms library network, consortium, partnership, association, system, cooperative, and all similar expressions are used interchangeably, as convenient terms for describing a group of libraries. While many authors have differentiated among these words and phrases (Donald B. Simpson feels a cooperative may be less "self-serving" than a consortium; Vernon E. Palmour and Nancy K. Roderer developed elaborate definitions for each group, depending on its particular geographic, political, technologic, or other features), our focus is a different one, and we will not.[7] It will be useful, however, to look at a common definition that all these library groups can share.

Palmour and Roderer suggest that library groups, consortia, cooperatives, and so forth represent "the organizational arrangements for achieving a variety of resource sharing objectives."[8] Mosher and Pankake speak of "a community of two or more libraries which have formally agreed to coordinate, cooperate in, or consolidate certain functions."[9] Sheila T. Dowd calls resource sharing arrangements "programs which endeavor to improve clients' access to information by defining and identifying existing resources, and devising delivery systems."[10] A modest combination of these explanations is adequate to the task at hand: a library cooperative is a group of at least two libraries whose members have agreed to engage in resource sharing, whether by interlending, reciprocal borrowing, or related means.

Perhaps we should also take a closer look at the term "resource sharing." Allen Kent says that resource sharing means the sharing of a function or functions by a number of libraries:

> The goals are to provide a positive net effect: 1) on the library user in terms of access to more materials or services; and/or 2) on the library budget in terms of providing level service at less cost, increased service at level cost, or much more service at less cost than if undertaken individually. These goals should be realized without harm to the missions of participating libraries, although their methods of operation invariably must be adjusted. Similarly, the goals are realizable only with some changes in the habits of users.[11]

For our purposes, Kent's definition will do nicely: when resource sharing is effective, readers have access to more materials than they previously enjoyed; the library will benefit as it offers valuable services more cost-effectively. However, certain behavioral adjustments will be required, for both the library and the reader.

Cooperatives Come in All Shapes and Sizes

A library cooperative can be two libraries, or two thousand; the members may be a few blocks apart, or on opposite coasts. They may be libraries of a particular type (research; academic; public; school), or they may be a multitype group whose members have joined forces to accomplish some very particular goal. There is scarcely a resource sharing pundit to be found who has not attempted to divide all library consortia into some half-dozen neat categories. Merging and distilling the thinking of several of these experts, one can identify several bases on which cooperatives are formed.

Geography

Sometimes libraries form cooperatives simply because they are near one another, often regardless of what type libraries (academic; public; school) they may be; such associations take good advantage of what one librarian calls "a kind of 'natural information district.'"[12] One example is the Houston Area Research Library Consortium:

> A key to its potential success is the multi-type membership, with two medical libraries in which strong biological science collections are supported, plus a number of equally strong collections in other member libraries in engineering, natural sciences, and physical sciences.... Taken together the eight libraries have a well balanced book and journal collection of over seven million volumes.[13]

Ruth J. Patrick suggests that consortia whose members are geographically close benefit from easy telephone and face-to-face communication; member privileges often include reciprocal borrowing and expanded interlibrary loan programs, including features such as delivery services, semester loans, and more generous lending policies.[14]

Libraries may also associate themselves geopolitically, often because they are remote from one another, scattered across a large, sparsely populated area that shares unified governance.

Fred M. Heath gives a good example of this sort of association when he describes the coordinated collection development that has been done by Alaskan libraries during the past ten years.[15]

Function

When libraries group themselves together in order to perform cooperatively a given activity (interlending; collection development; cataloging; preservation), we might call this a consortium based on function.[16] Few consortia are functionally "pure," and most endeavor to support multiple operations (cooperative cataloging and coordinated collection development, for example). However, as telefacsimile and optical scanning have made distance between libraries largely irrelevant for purposes of exchanging journal literature, we have also seen the emergence of the "sole purpose" library cooperative. Examples include the interlending agreements between Canadian universities such as Alberta and Regina, and Alberta and New Brunswick, which are supported by scanning and telefacsimile equipment.

Library Type

Sometimes libraries of a given type band together for cooperative purposes; these could be academic libraries, public libraries, military libraries, and so forth. Examples include the Washington Research Library Consortium, the "Oberlin Group," and the FEDLINK libraries. "Library type" is an especially popular and productive model for academic institutions; as Miller and Guyette point out, while college and university libraries share with other library types, academic institutions borrow primarily from one another.[17] Library cooperatives based on "type" are often appealing because member institutions typically have similar collections, readers (faculty and students; lawyers; medical professionals), and organizational patterns.

Political Structure

Library consortia may be local, regional, intrastate, interstate, national, or international. For example, all libraries (regardless of type) in a given region, state, or country might form a network to meet common goals. Such groups include the New York Metropolitan Reference and Research Library Agency (METRO), regional networks like SOLINET and AMIGOS, and the Network of Alabama Academic Libraries (NAAL). Often such consortia are also called multitype library systems, if they include academic, special, public, and school libraries within a given political structure.

Edward M. Walters calls these groups based on political structure "authority sanctioned networks" because they are created and sustained by government agencies such as a state legislature; this definition may not fit the regional networks quite so well as it does many local and state associations of libraries.[18] As Susan K. Martin points out, many times libraries have no choice but to participate in such consortia—indeed, the structure of the parent institution may impose membership; as an example, she cites the University of California system, with nine separate campuses and nine university librarians.[19] However, even in situations in which cooperation may be prescribed, there is often much local autonomy, and libraries should look carefully at what is mandated, and what is voluntary, even in "politically structured" consortia.

Materials Type

Sometimes medical, law, music, or other libraries that collect similar materials will form a cooperative. These libraries may exist in different cities and states, and may represent different institutional types (academic and hospital, or research and corporate, for instance). Examples include the fourteen land grant institutions now participating in the North Carolina State University Digitized Document Transmission Project (NCSU DDTP), all collecting heavily in the field of agriculture, and the Regional Medical Library System.

The "Impure" Cooperative

As these examples illustrate, there are very few consortia that fit into only one category: most combine elements from several, though one feature may hold sway over the others. For example, the eighteen libraries of the City University of New York, located in the five boroughs of New York City, joined by political structure, possessing like collections, and cooperating primarily for resource sharing, could be said to fit each of the associational categories listed above. Thus, these classes are useful in that they help us organize our thinking about consortia and the bases on which these can be formed, but at the same time they show us the value of flexibility when we consider cooperative arrangements.

Library Cooperatives: What to Look For

It seems fair to say that many libraries fail to understand or take advantage of the full array of benefits available to them through the networks to which they belong; this is doubly unfortunate, because in most cases their membership fees are supporting these underutilized services. Correspondingly, when a library considers new resource sharing arrangements, it may easily fail to look for certain valuable features. Some specifics against which we can test existing or potential cooperative arrangements, particularly as these support resource sharing, can be helpful.

Are the Library's Goals and Needs Similar to Those of the Consortium?

Heath speaks of "an elusive concept that may be best described as a sense of common purpose."[20] This is most likely to exist when the services available through the consortium are valued and supported by each member of the cooperative; as Joe A. Hewitt and John S. Shipman suggest, without similar commitments, close cooperation is difficult or impossible.[21]

Is Resource Sharing a Top Consortial Priority?

Look carefully to see what sorts of resource sharing programs are supported by the system. Are there generous provisions for on-site access to members' collections? Do participants provide one another with free interlibrary loans? What other special privileges will members of the consortium receive when sharing with one another? For example, each library might agree to give priority to filling other members' borrowing requests, to lend restricted materials like microforms, or to participate in a shared delivery system.

One measure of any system's commitment to resource sharing are its interlibrary loan fill rates and turnaround time. In some cases (for instance, if all members use the same utility or mechanism for interlending) it will be possible to get this information from the network's administrative staff. It is also worthwhile to look closely at the cooperative's provisions for reciprocal access: will all readers receive the same privileges, or are there restrictions for certain categories (undergraduates, perhaps)? Are there provisions for both reading and borrowing? How generous are the loan periods?

A library should also ascertain whether its readers will receive the same services from other participants that it will supply to their faculty and students. Sometimes libraries enter consortial agreements only to find that they are driving down a one-way street: while they are providing free interlibrary loans and on-site access to clienteles from other institutions, they find bills for photocopying services in their own mailboxes and learn that their readers are being turned away from other libraries' doors. This is not to suggest that complete reciprocity in every benefit must exist for membership in a system to be worthwhile: often one member or another does not participate in a specific program, or participates to a greater or lesser extent. A library may agree to lend books free of charge, for example, but charge for photocopies; it may allow reciprocal borrowing for faculty from other institutions, but not for their students.

The larger a given cooperative and the more diverse its membership, the more likely it is that such disparities will exist. Each library should acquaint itself fully with the benefits that will accrue to its readers, and then judge whether any "inequity" in the distribution of privileges is so substantial that it makes membership unproductive. Of course, one will also want to consider whether the potential for being exploited is strong: it is one thing if those libraries that are unwilling to extend free loans and on-site access are also unlikely to deluge one with borrowing requests and their own information-hungry readers, but quite another if the local library judges that this is a real possibility.

A library may decide that participation in a particular system is valuable, even though reciprocal access and interlending are limited in some fashion; a careful comparison of the needs of one's readers to the services that membership conveys is the important thing. The match may a good one, even when it stops somewhere short of *carte blanche*.

Are the Collections of the Other Members of Interest to Local Readers?

There are a number of ways in which a library can assess the collections of other participants in a consortium. Many systems have sponsored collection assessment projects whose results may be revealing. In the absence of standardized assessments, cooperatives often compile informal, more subjective descriptions of their members' collecting strengths. In some cases (as when participants share a catalog or bibliographic utility) a library contemplating joining a network can search its borrowing requests from the last twelve to twenty-four months against the common catalog or utility, and actually determine what percentage of these the members could have filled. And, since studies indicate that much of what any library borrows is material it could have been expected to select (in other words, the missing materials fall within the library's collecting profile), a useful though less scientific approach is to examine the degree programs and demographic profiles of member institutions; if these are similar to one's own, there is a good chance their collections could be of considerable interest.[22]

Collection overlap data can also help identify productive resource sharing partners. A consultant's analysis of the holdings of a group of Louisiana libraries determined that there is no large-scale duplication among libraries in that state. During the period studied, more than 80 percent of the records added to the statewide database were unique; only eight titles of the 72,335 submitted were held by as many as nine of the sixteen participating public and academic libraries. The consultant concluded that access to the collections of other libraries expands not only the number of copies available, but the number of titles as well.[23]

Similarly, studies of university libraries in Illinois showed that collection overlap rarely exceeds 50 percent, indicating that resource sharing partnerships among such institutions are quite worthwhile.[24] Collection assessments conducted among the members of NAAL also demonstrate a high degree of uniqueness, 51 percent. Such studies were used to reassure the Alabama legislature that its support of NAAL's resource sharing program would indeed be cost-effective.[25]

Although most interlibrary loan codes prohibit borrowing titles included in the local collection, it is a fact of library life that many institutions seek to secure through ILL items they own but which for some reason (binding, loss, charged to another reader) are unavailable at the time they are wanted. Some consortia explicitly permit such borrowing; in other cases, libraries make such requests, despite existing prohibitions. Hugh C. Atkinson, writing of the University of Illinois libraries, observed that over 50 percent of the materials borrowed are items Illinois owns, but that are inaccessible when they are requested. He goes on to say that collection overlap studies often show a surprising lack of duplication among the collections of similar institutions, reinforcing the idea that like libraries may make good resource sharing partners.[26]

Are Effective Shared Computing and Telecommunications Technologies in Place?

When we examine the history of resource sharing, we may be too quick to assign early failures to lack of institutional commitment, perhaps because libraries were wealthier then and there was less economic impetus to share. However, Heath suggests that the absence of effective communications capabilities ensured the relative unproductiveness of earlier cooperative efforts. He recommends that libraries look carefully to see whether all consortium members enjoy what he terms "a shared starting point in the new automated environment."[27] No matter how useful other collections may be, if one cannot identify what partners hold, participation in the system is worth very little.

Does the Library Have Access to Its Partners' Holdings?

There are at least three different types of access to one's partners' holdings. Everyone is probably familiar with the print or microform catalog and union list of serials. A step above this (in terms of ease of access) is a shared utility. Many consortia (NAAL, the states of New York and North Carolina) support retrospective conversion projects for member libraries, striving to get everyone's holdings into the same utility as quickly as possible; such projects make an excellent first priority for solid resource sharing. In today's economic environment, when many libraries annually cancel several thousand dollars worth of journal subscriptions, online versus printed access to partners' holdings is very desirable; printed lists become dated far too quickly, leading to considerable frustration for borrowers and librarians.

Shared Catalogs

Joe A. Hewitt points out that the most effective resource sharing calls for something beyond a shared bibliographic utility: common or linked local catalogs are highly desirable.[28] Whether online or on CD-ROM, these catalogs are important because they enable not just librarians but also readers to see the holdings (and sometimes the circulation data) of other libraries, promoting the tendency to view other collections very much like one's own. This provides a significantly greater consortial membership value, and probably a higher membership cost. (Such projects require substantial commitments of staff and financial resources; Richard Boss estimated the cost of linking the online public access catalogs (OPACs) of Michigan's publicly funded college and university libraries at $600,000.[29])

MELVYL, the shared catalog of the University of California libraries, and the CARL system in Colorado are two examples; several others appear in the appendix to this book. Illinois' ILLINET/LCS system has the extra benefit of permitting readers to place their own interlibrary loan requests for books, direct from an online catalog terminal, rather than making a trip to the interlibrary loan office or the library that actually holds the wanted item. Shortly after the implementation of this feature, the number of books borrowed from other libraries by readers at the Urbana-Champaign campus jumped to 10 percent of the library's total circulation; a more typical figure for interlibrary borrowing is 1 to 2 percent of aggregate circulation.[30] It seems clear that, the more obstacles we can remove from interlibrary borrowing, the more frequently this service will be used.

Separate and Linked Catalogs

A somewhat unequal peer to the shared catalog is the separate catalog one can access easily. Some libraries place terminals or microcomputers dedicated to a partner's integrated library system near their own OPAC, as did the University of Tennessee at Knoxville and Vanderbilt during their IRIS project; stacks of interlibrary loan request forms were kept nearby.[31] A neater arrangement is that enabled by Florida's College Center for Library Automation (CCLA), where a shared catalog of the state's twenty-eight public community colleges allows readers to "toggle" into the catalog of the state university libraries (the two union catalogs are provided by different vendors).[32] Similarly, the purpose of NOTIS's PACLink software is to allow readers at one NOTIS installation to menu into the remote catalogs of other NOTIS libraries. PACLink and its sister, PACLoan, also offer a patron-initiated interlibrary loan feature, one more powerful than Illinois' LCS system. Using PACLoan, a reader can then request either a book or a journal article from a remote library.[33]

Catalogs Available via the Internet

A "poor relation" of the arrangements described above is the Internet's array of library catalogs. While many academic libraries already use the Internet, and many more will gain access as time passes, taking advantage of its resources takes time and training. Suffice it to say that this "network of networks," described more fully in the chapters on delivery mechanisms and the future, connects a number of physical networks located across the United States and in other countries, allowing those who can access it to utilize free of charge many different library catalogs. Thus, someone at the University of California at Berkeley can log into the catalog of the City University of New York and search it as if he or she were a local reader.

There is no common command language for these catalogs, and the interested party requires unique instructions for accessing each one. If a desired item is located, the reader must still go to the interlibrary loan office to obtain it, and it may well be that the local library has no resource sharing agreement with the distant one. Nonetheless, some libraries have produced guides to Internet catalogs for their readers; the Columbia University Libraries calls its publication "Searching Library Catalogs over the Internet." Less than four pages in length, it explains that the cost of the search is that of a local telephone call, how to determine which catalogs are available, how to connect to a catalog, and how to disconnect. Caveats include the fact that some institutions restrict access to parts of their catalog (generally, periodical indexes licensed only for local use) to their own readers, and the slowness of response time, particularly during the afternoon when there is likely to be considerable activity, whatever the time zone. For the reader's convenience, a reference department electronic mail address is provided for those who have questions.[34]

Is There Geographic Proximity among Members?

Today, when certain types of delivery mechanisms are in place (telefacsimile; scanning), geographic proximity is of little importance, especially when the Internet (accessible, as mentioned above, for the price of a local telephone call) rather than commercial telephone lines is used for transmission. The scanning technology that enables Canada's University of New Brunswick to request journal articles through the Internet from the considerably larger University of Alberta is a good example of agreements in which great distances present no barriers, either in terms of time or money.

However, in many instances one's partners' nearness is very important. Many of the factors that can make coordinated acquisitions programs succeed also apply to other types of resource sharing:

> The collections of neighboring institutions to which users have direct access and special borrowing privileges, and which may be connected by daily delivery services, can play a role similar to the collections of the home library.[35]

Arrangements like those among Duke, the University of North Carolina, and North Carolina State, and the college libraries that make up LIBRAS, certainly would not exist were the institutions not located near one another. Reciprocal access and borrowing privileges, while possible—as in the Research Libraries Group's (RLG) nonresident program—when libraries are distant, generally will flourish when the institutions are an easy walk, bus ride, subway trip, or automobile drive away. Likewise, many delivery mechanisms (the U.S. Postal Service; courier services such as Federal Express and United Parcel Service) work most effectively when the sender and receiver are near to each other.

The University of Pennsylvania, a member of RLG, reports that it prefers partners like Princeton, Cornell, and Yale, from whom it can receive materials by UPS (RLG's preferred courier service) much more quickly than it can from libraries located in the western part of the country; because the state of Pennsylvania has a very effective shared delivery system, Penn also finds Pennsylvania State University (a non-RLG library) an efficient partner.

Are Effective Document Delivery Mechanisms in Place?

Heath suggests that resource sharing agreements should include "clear reference to member obligations in terms of document delivery."[36] It is certainly true that, even if our partners' collections are highly useful, and we are also able to peruse their holdings with ease, without effective delivery mechanisms the consortial relationship is of little worth. The variety of delivery systems is wide and interesting. Large cooperatives with nationwide membership like RLG use telefacsimile, scanning, and UPS, eliminating or reducing the impact of distance. Several states (Illinois, Pennsylvania, Connecticut) have statewide delivery programs. Some regional cooperatives (METRO in New York) also sponsor delivery systems. It is not uncommon for larger libraries to receive more "stops" per week than do smaller ones, or several "stops" per institution, in the case of multiple libraries.

Is the Consortium Stable and Are Membership Costs Reasonable?

In a list of a half-dozen characteristics of successful library systems, Heath includes stable sources of funding.[37] Richard De Gennaro comments on the need to keep careful watch over consortial costs, lest increases begin to erode the value of membership:

> The establishment and growth of library networks, bibliographic utilities, and service centers in the decade of the 1970's has been a remarkable success story, but with that success comes a problem. The problem now is to keep the growth of the

network budgets and staffs within reasonable limits so that the administrative overhead costs do not exceed the value of the benefits that individual libraries may realize from network participation. Networks are like our libraries and other bureaucracies; they have a natural tendency to increase their staffs without commensurate increases in productivity.[38]

Every library system should make available its financial statements (showing income sources and allocations), both to members and prospective members; a consortium's annual report often includes such data. Additionally, the membership agreement should clearly spell out the extent of each participant's financial commitments or obligations.[39]

Is There Effective Support for All Services Offered?

Donald B. Simpson suggests that the cooperative's procedures and communication paths should be simple, clearly documented, and efficient.[40] A prospective member of any consortium should talk with its administrative staff, as well as staff in constituent institutions, to ensure that adequate support exists for all programs, particularly those that make membership most compelling (a shared catalog or delivery system, for example).

Will the Library Have a Voice in Consortial Governance?

In any cooperative, decisions must be made. These can range from topics of some interest and importance (salary increases for the system's staff; a change in the faculty loan period enforced by a shared catalog; the admission of new members) to those of enormous concern and corresponding cost (whether to add capacity to an existing integrated library system, or select and implement a new one). A library should understand its ability to influence or make such decisions, and be satisfied with that role. Further, the governing structure of the cooperative and each library's part in it should be described in the membership agreement.[41]

Can the Library Deliver What Membership Requires?

This is a critical question, one that goes far beyond membership fees; it can be very difficult to answer. Just as a library interests itself in the benefits it will receive from consortial membership, so must it consider the impact of dispensing similar privileges to its partners and their readers. To what extent will the provision of access or borrowing privileges for a group of new readers tax existing staff and resources? How large will this new clientele be? Will the number of requests to lend shoot up as a result of membership? If so, will the additional access local readers gain to the collections of others offset this new burden, and will it be necessary to add staff to interlibrary loan?

One can attempt to answer some of these questions by talking with other network members (especially newer ones) and exploring their experiences. Common sense may dictate some of the answers; if a much smaller institution is within easy walking distance, it stands to reason that on-site use of one's collections by its clientele will probably be heavy. The question then becomes, would such use be onerous? Depending on a cooperative's fee structures, if a prospective member genuinely questions its ability to meet its obligations, it may be possible and beneficial to negotiate an initial, finite, experimental affiliation. It is also possible that the consortium has certain "load-balancing" policies in effect to protect larger or centrally located libraries from an immoderate number of requests for service.

Is There a Commitment to Coordinated Collection Development?

A university librarian commented that "one of the most important results of . . . economic pressures will be even closer relationships between resource sharing and collection development librarians than have existed before."[42] The positive relationship between coordinated (collaborative; cooperative) collection development and resource sharing has become a common theme. Richard M. Dougherty believes that the former helps strengthen the latter:

> If scholars are to have even a chance to gain access to the full range of materials of possible value to them, the only strategy of promise seems to be cooperative collection development. One underlying assumption of RLG is that none of its members, from the largest to the smallest, can collect all materials that its scholars might need or demand. . . . Through careful planning, it should be possible to coordinate collection development to increase the number of titles available and, through well-designed, shared collection resource programs, minimize the delay and inconvenience of securing publications needed by the library user.[43]

Hugh C. Atkinson saw a cause-and-effect relationship between increases in interlending and coordinated collection development:

> The success of ILL is producing a demand for other forms of networking such as cooperative collection development. As we borrow or buy more, coordinated collection development becomes more important—we have to be sure somebody (and somebody who's committed to keeping it) owns it.[44]

Today, as seemingly endless journal cancellations lead to greater reliance on commercial document delivery services, we are beset by a creeping fear that the commercial sector may one day elect to discard that which is no longer profitable; thus, we take quite seriously Atkinson's enjoinder that someone (presumably, some library) must retain subscriptions to important titles.

As much as ten years ago Joe A. Hewitt outlined some of the benefits of membership in a consortium that is committed to coordinated collection development:

> Coordinated collection development is necessary for an intentional transition to greater dependency on resource sharing, for several reasons.... An attempt should be made to identify reliable alternative sources for materials no longer to be collected, perhaps with associated arrangements for priority handling of requests and extended loan periods. These arrangements serve to reduce to some degree the gap in service between owning materials and depending on the resources of other libraries. More important, however, the scrutiny of collections and collection-development policies involved in developing such agreements insures an orderly and systematic transition to greater dependence on resource sharing, and specific resource-sharing arrangements can become operable factors in selection decisions.[45]

Today, most libraries would be delighted if they needed to depend on resource sharing only for "materials no longer to be collected." Still, Hewitt's counsel about the relationships between resource sharing and collaborative collection development is good, and there is certainly a place for the latter in our collecting policies and profiles. Indeed, Dougherty's notion that shared collection development programs ought not "intrude unnecessarily into local collection development programs" seems like a charming midcentury anachronism: in today's economic climate, the role of such agreements must be clearly spelled out in our collecting policies, else our acquisition patterns will look like something akin to a Swiss cheese.

The critics of cooperative collection development have a great deal of truth on their sides; these collaborative programs can be highly complex, affected as they are by such diverse forces as faculty attitudes, collection "status," funding, document delivery mechanisms, and institutional autonomy. For example, it seems clear that, insofar as any library's collections mirror its curriculum and its faculty's research interests, the institution may have limited control over what it collects. What of the new scholar or program requiring materials no longer collected and assigned to a resource sharing partner? What happens when shifts in funding or reader interests dictate new collecting emphases which may conflict with assigned cooperative collecting responsibilities?

In a very real sense, a library entering into a coordinated collecting agreement may be making promises that it ultimately cannot keep. When a library makes a commitment to continue to build collections in areas of historic strength, it has some chance of meeting its obligation to its partners. When such commitments are endorsed at the highest levels in the library, if not the parent institution, they have an even better chance of succeeding. Otherwise, there is a good possibility they will gradually be displaced by local exigencies or self-interest.

Having said all of this, yet still convinced of the value (some would say, the necessity) of coordinated collection development as a critical underpinning for resource sharing, we can examine how such programs typically relate to resource sharing agreements, the topic of this chapter. Depending on the nature of a library consortium, cooperative collection development may simply occur as a matter of course. The Houston Area Research Library Consortium is a good example, consisting as it does of two medical libraries with strong biological sciences collections, and equally strong collections in other member libraries in engineering, natural sciences, and physical sciences: rather than the product of systematic planning, cooperative collection development is the natural result of the cooperative's makeup.[46]

In a paper summarizing the results of their study of cooperative collection development programs among research libraries, Hewitt and Shipman explain that many cooperative collection development agreements are strengthened by interlending and document delivery programs, as well as borrowing privileges for partners' students and faculty:

> Cooperative collection development tends to be viewed as the logical outgrowth of other programs such as reciprocal borrowing, special interlibrary loan agreements, and joint network development. Few consortia were identified which exist exclusively for the purpose of developing and operating programs of cooperative collection development.[47]

It seems that if faculty and students are truly to rely on the "collections of strangers" to meet some portion of their needs, effective interlending and document delivery services are absolutely essential: how can one consider a neighboring college's collection to be an extension of the home library unless materials from it can be identified easily and supplied quickly? Faculty are more likely to have confidence in the outcomes of coordinated collection development if the partners to the agreement share a catalog; when a reader can see the holdings of other libraries, materials the local library has foregone in favor of resource sharing, he or she will feel more sanguine about access to the titles in question. If the local catalog cannot include all the records of partners in shared collection development, it should at least include those for materials in the "cooperative" areas.

Geography is something to consider when one thinks of cooperative collection development. Such arrangements may be more successful (and more politically palatable) when libraries are close to one another, because of the ease and benefits of reciprocal access, and the viability of shared or linked catalogs. However, coordinated collection development programs with broad geographic bases (like that of RLG) do exist and one might examine their benefits. When excellent delivery systems are in place (scanning, telefacsimile, courier service) and the local reader can easily determine which materials are remotely held, arrangements like RLG's can succeed.

The New Phenomenon of the "Miniature" Cooperative

In the 1960s when academic libraries often felt as rich as Croesus, and even in the decade and a half that followed, as funding began first to dwindle then to plunge, we viewed consortial arrangements and interlending far more broadly than we can today. Then, libraries often borrowed randomly from other institutions that participated in the same bibliographic utility; today, the concept that "OCLC is my consortium" no longer works for most libraries that are seeking closer, smaller, special arrangements. Libraries may well belong to very large systems like OCLC, RLG, and many state networks, but many are looking to meet a large part of their resource sharing needs as members of much smaller groups, groups that sometimes consist of only two or three other libraries.

In some cases, libraries are discovering that it is inefficient to treat all partners in these larger cooperatives the same way; in others, they find that the volume of requests they receive is so great that they simply cannot treat all comers equally. Increasingly, libraries are looking to develop partnerships with a small number of institutions whose collections can meet a large percentage of their borrowing needs, and to enhance these arrangements by according special privileges (including speed of delivery) to one another. It is not so much that libraries cease lending to and borrowing from institutions outside these "miniature" cooperatives (which are often formal or informal subsets of larger consortial relationships), but that they lend to them only after they have satisfied the needs of their closer partners, and perhaps under less expansive conditions.

These small consortia may or may not be formalized by explicit agreements; in some cases (as when a larger library system of which each institution is a member requires "equal" sharing among all members) partners may even be loathe to acknowledge their existence. The similarities and differences among these miniature cooperatives also suggest a number of categories into which such arrangements may fall. Sometimes a group of smaller academic libraries band together to meet each other's needs; examples include NOVANET, a Canadian consortium of seven colleges and universities that share an automated catalog, the CTW Library Consortium (which includes Connecticut College, Trinity College, and Wesleyan University) whose members also share a catalog, and LIBRAS, a group of Chicago-area academic libraries.

In other instances, large and small libraries join together for resource sharing. In arrangements like that between California State University at Chico and the University of California at Berkeley, money may change hands in return for a smaller institution's access to the collections of a larger one; similarly, the first year of an agreement among James Madison University, the University of Virginia, and Virginia Tech has been completely funded by James Madison, the smaller of the three and therefore, presumably, the largest beneficiary. In other "unequal" partnerships (those between the Canadian universities of New Brunswick and Regina with the much larger Alberta), interlending is done at no charge.

In describing such arrangements, it is often said that the smaller library "subscribes" to the collections of the larger one. This is both handy terminology and a useful analogy, since most of these projects were designed to provide access to journal literature. There are also many examples of larger academic libraries (Duke, the University of North Carolina at Chapel Hill, and North Carolina State; the University of Michigan and Michigan State) forming small, very productive partnerships for resource sharing.

An appendix to this book provides more examples and details of library systems of all types, including these miniature consortia.

It is clear that the smaller, highly productive library cooperative is one of the strongest trends in contemporary resource sharing. How does one reconcile this practice with what many may think of as the "Illinois model," one in which a large number of libraries interlend, and the emphasis is on sharing a combined wealth among many partners? Certainly the shared automated catalog with its patron-initiated interlibrary loan capability, coupled with a "no charge" policy and good statewide delivery system, has strengthened the Illinois system for resource sharing. In fiscal year 1991-92, however, severe budgetary cuts were made to the state's resource sharing program, suggesting the very real possibility that "the fiscal realities of cooperation may necessitate some sort of cost recovery policies."[48] It will be interesting to see whether interlending in Illinois reshapes itself in the near term, and whether the absence of financial subsidies changes forever the system influenced (if not governed) by Hugh C. Atkinson's philosophy of resource sharing.

Evaluating and Costing Consortium Memberships

Very few library cooperatives suggest means by which their constituents can evaluate or assign costs to the benefits that accrue from participation, or the delivery of services to other institutions that membership mandates. Based on a survey of 125 academic library consortia, Ruth J. Patrick observes:

> The most often used evaluative technique consisted of informal feedback from library personnel participating in consortium activities (66 percent), and from the ultimate users of the services (49 percent). More formal methods of evaluation were less frequently used: for example, analyses of cost and usage statistics (29 percent); operations research analysis such as work flow, cost effectiveness tradeoffs, etc. (13 percent); and formal surveys of the ultimate users of consortium services (10 percent).[49]

Patrick goes on to observe that informal feedback has its limitations, as it is dependent on those librarians who take the time to make their feelings (either negative or positive) known.

Certainly, the costs of belonging to a cooperative go far beyond that of the membership fee: there are also the expenses associated with rendering services to other participants and the question of whether these expenses will be adequately offset by services received. Perhaps the most critical issue is what provisions the cooperative makes to guard against extreme economic imbalances among its members.

How, then, are we to gauge the price and the privileges of consortium membership? Perhaps it may be worthwhile at this juncture to review some of the reasons why libraries join cooperatives. Donald B. Simpson suggests three common motives:

> First is that cooperatives can enhance the quality of services that a library provides its clientele. They can offer a number of effective resource sharing services to their libraries. . . . The second reason relates to the altruistic nature of the library profession. Sharing is good and working together seems to be the professionally right thing to do. . . . Thirdly, despite the many local pressures on libraries to be self sufficient, librarians strongly believe in resource sharing as a means to reduce their libraries costs. . . . In each case, or some combination of two or all three of the reasons, the decision of "Is it worth it?" is based on comparing the costs with the values just as any consumer would do when buying something.[50]

Does Resource Sharing Save Money?

Most would agree with Simpson's first suggestion, that cooperatives enhance the quality of services that a library provides its clientele. However, many will question the soundness of the second and third reasons he advances. Library administrators seriously doubt whether resource sharing (with its own associated transaction costs) saves actual dollars. Charles B. Lowry suggests that librarians who fail to examine closely the costs of cooperative endeavors are naive at best and irresponsible at worst.[51] One could find that the cost of membership exceeds that of benefits.

The "Greater Good": Valid or Passé as a Motive for Cooperation?

Simpson's suggestion that libraries join cooperatives because of the altruistic nature of the profession and the belief that "sharing is good" has come under forceful fire in the present harsh economic climate; the notions of resource sharing as "a general good" and the " 'human right' of universal access to information" no longer elicit the widespread sympathy and head nodding they once did.[52] Paul M. Gherman suggests that many institutions (perhaps those whose resources are most heavily taxed by the demands of their weaker fellows) no longer subscribe to the concept of a resource sharing "noblesse oblige":

> There is increasing recognition that information has value, is a commodity, and that there are specific and inherent costs in all aspects of its storage, access and delivery.... As this realization takes hold, networking becomes more an economic decision than one of "apple pie and motherhood." Accordingly, the goal of "the greatest good for the greatest number" is tempered by the recognition that nothing is free, by the desire to avoid exploitative imbalances of services between libraries, and by a preference for contractual or cost-based transactions over open-ended moral commitment.[53]

Herbert S. White observes that resource sharing has often failed when borrowers have attempted "to bludgeon lenders with a club of moral suasion." He continues with a strong political metaphor:

> Our attitude comes from acceptance of interlibrary loan not as a pragmatic commodity, but as a moral precept. "From each according to his ability to each according to his need," is a quote from Karl Marx. Librarians might be surprised to recognize to what extent this philosophy serves to define the interlibrary loan process for us. I find nothing terrible in this realization, because socialist doctrine always sounds much better than it works.[54]

White's analogy, apt in 1987 when he created it, is even more relevant today.

Taking the Measure of Membership Benefits versus Membership Costs

At a time when there is less tolerance within academic administrations and state legislatures for libraries' almost endless appetite for more dollars, resource sharing has become a popular necessity. However, it is important to prevent such commitments from reducing the services available to local readers. Allen Kent and James G. Williams both caution that we should not provide materials and services to other libraries and their clienteles if to do so is not cost-beneficial in terms of the materials and services provided in return; an unfavorable "balance of trade" can harm local interests.[55] And, we must not lose sight of the costs associated with memberships in library systems; there will be a strong need to balance the costs that participation adds to the library budget with the benefits or values it adds to local services.[56]

A library consortium should be able to provide cost data to members and prospective members; this can be helpful in determining value. Many libraries would find helpful a questionnaire like the "Value of METRO Membership," which this New York group published in its newsletter. This worksheet was designed for three purposes: to remind members of all services available from the consortium; to assist them in determining the value of each service, depending on degree of use, as well as the total value of membership; and to help libraries justify system participation to their administrations.[57]

Even when the cooperatives to which we belong do not provide such helpful tools, we are certainly free to list the services we use and assign a value to each. For example, if a distributor typically charges $75 to rent a film, and if there is no charge for this service through our consortium, and we borrowed fifty films from member libraries in any given year, we can value that service at $3,750. Or, if membership entitles us to a given number of free Regional Medical Library coupons, we can easily assign a value to this service.

Conversely, we can also enumerate and assess the costs of the services that membership requires us to provide, although such costs can often be more difficult to define and break out. Nonetheless, if we will take the time, it is possible to identify all loans we made to network members, and to assign a cost to such activity, based on the amount of staff time and other direct costs required. All that will then remain is to compare the two sums, the costs of services received versus services rendered, and hope that the first equals if not outweighs the second. As Lowry suggests, "The question becomes, 'is the cost outweighed by the benefit?'"

Another way of looking at things may be to follow Lowry's question with another: could the same benefits be achieved independently and, if so, what would they cost outside of a consortial arrangement? Or, within a consortial arrangement other than this one? (It is wise and perfectly permissible to do "comparison shopping" among cooperatives that offer similar benefits.) On those occasions (which one hopes will be rare) when costs seem to outweigh benefits, a library must consider how to adjust either its levels of use or service, or whether to resign from the system. Here, one would certainly examine alternatives and the associated costs.

What specific economic factors will we consider when assessing the value of our consortial relationships? Heath suggests that "accurate studies are probably feasible only when specific activities are analyzed" and recommends examining the features of successful cooperatives and cataloging the factors that work.[58] We can also identify a number of specific economic benefits that can be used to test the value of resource sharing arrangements, either substantively or philosophically.

Mutual Benefit or Economic Equity

It may seem strange to begin with one of the most amorphous measurements of consortial value; however, no one wishes to be exploited, so perhaps it is fitting to start by looking at exploitation's countersign, the issue of mutual economic benefit. Not all librarians are as concerned about equity in resource sharing as others. Hugh C. Atkinson put his own distinctive twist on the issue:

> The first and most important thing librarians should keep in mind when dealing with networks is that it is not necessary for outcomes, products, and uses of networks to be the results of an equal system, but rather that the network be valuable to each of the participants. Equity is not the goal—results are. Frankly, I don't care how many items are borrowed from us, assuming, of course, that we do not seriously interfere with their use by our students and faculty. . . . My point is that one should not try to reach some kind of theoretical balance of fairness, but to build a network that will provide, by its services and arrangements, the library activities that will satisfy each of the participants, although not necessarily in the same way.[59]

Dougherty and Heath support Atkinson: while it is important that cooperative resource sharing arrangements be perceived as mutually beneficial, this does not mean that complete parity is essential; all members do not have to benefit equally, but all must benefit.[60] The advantages that contribute to a perception of equity may also take many forms. For example, resource sharing may enable a library to engage in more selective acquisition, give it certain political leverage, or demonstrate service commitments needed to obtain grants and other types of financial support.[61]

There is something to be said for this flexible, less exacting approach to mutual benefit. Certainly, few would wish to belong to the "Eye for an Eye and Tooth for a Tooth Library Cooperative." Most libraries also understand that they may be net providers of some services and net consumers of others, and that they will find a consortium membership valuable based on the sum of its parts rather than the value or costs associated with any single service. However, over the past five years, as interlending has escalated, more and more net lenders have ceased to comfort themselves with the virtue of their positions. Today, most libraries find it fair and proper to insist on a clear economic benefit from membership in any cooperative.

In December 1989, OCLC sponsored a focus group for eight library administrators from around the country; the purpose was the discussion of a variety of issues relating to interlibrary loan.

One of the concerns identified was the desirability of eliminating the "lending burden" felt by many institutions. "In theory," the participants felt, "interlibrary loan service is a reciprocal relationship that should offer a balance of benefits to all participants."

> The opportunity to borrow should "reimburse" lenders for their time and effort. When the balance of interlibrary loan activity shifts toward significant net lending or borrowing, concerns about fairness increase. A net lender may begin to wonder whether its interlibrary lending is adequately "reimbursed" through the "currency" of reciprocal borrowing and may feel that the institution deserves additional compensation in harder currency (dollars, credits, coupons) to recompense its extra effort.[62]

The participants suggested that the OCLC ILL subsystem might be modified so that net lenders' symbols are automatically transferred to the end of any lending string (system-administered load leveling), and that libraries in the same resource sharing system could "settle up" financially at the end of each year, thanks to automated bookkeeping systems. It might be desirable to add a fund-accounting feature to the OCLC interlibrary loan module, to facilitate this financial reconciliation; presumably, net borrowers would be billed so much per net borrowing transaction, and net lenders would be reimbursed accordingly.[63] Such ideas show that library administrators are concerned with the desirability of mutual benefit and how we might attain it. One library manager recommends that costs be apportioned equitably among participants, and that no consortium "demand disproportionate sacrifice from any member." Equity, she suggests, is one of the major factors that makes consortial agreements appealing.[64]

Each library must decide for itself how it will define "mutual benefit" for purposes of evaluating cooperative arrangements. Some institutions will look for "balance of trade" assurances before joining a system; such provisions may be either automated or manual. James G. Williams suggests that load-leveling algorithms be added to computerized interlending systems; rather than the borrower choosing from where the desired item will be borrowed, the system would make loan choices based on borrowing and lending data.[65] This concept and its many variations (including the idea that each library in a consortium be permitted to borrow no more than it lends, or no more than X percent above what it lends) are not new; Williams's idea dates from 1977. As yet, such automated controls do not exist on any large scale.

A more common approach to enforcing mutual benefit is financially compensating net lenders. The state of Virginia mandates that publicly funded institutions lend free of charge. It ameliorates this requirement by reimbursing net lenders, although when a study validated the cost of lending at $6 to $8, the state declined to raise its reimbursement rate above the existing $3. Until July 1991, when fiscal exigency intervened, Illinois compensated its four research and reference center libraries (responsible for a huge percentage of the total loans within the state); in some cases, these funds not only supported the operating costs of interlibrary loan services but also supported some collection development and service enhancements.[66] Even more generous, NAAL reimburses members for both borrowing and lending.[67]

A good test of the fairness and broader implications of a library's conduct under any agreement is to ask oneself, "What would happen if everyone did as I am doing?" It is worthwhile remembering that no service is truly free: someone pays for everything, and it is natural to wish to carry one's share of the collective responsibility. Every college and university allows so many dollars-per-student for library services; the "net consumer" in any cooperative whose membership includes a number of academic libraries may wish to compare its administration's allocation to those of other participants, and make a strong case on the home campus for less dependency and stronger local support. Likewise, libraries that find themselves frequently exceeding copyright limitations should be able to make a persuasive appeal for better funding.

In short, it is no longer either fair or safe to fall back upon the "poor relation" view of consortium participation. Borrowing from others compels not only the expenditure of partners' staff time, but also wear and tear on their materials and equipment (photocopiers, telefacsimile machines, scanners). One can see clear signs that net lenders are becoming sensitive to the potential costliness of their positions, and that many libraries are moving toward smaller, more fruitful sharing relationships, lending to preferred partners first and others second, if at all. Thus, it is to every library's benefit to identify partnerships that are not only productive but also equitable, lest it be left with no partners at all.

If it is a given that a consortium should be something more than a program designed to "take from the rich to give to the poor" in which some participants clearly fall into one category or another and that reciprocity is valuable, the InfoDash program of

Polytechnic University (PU, Brooklyn, N.Y.) is an interesting example of an entrepreneurial and highly successful document delivery service that from time to time causes certain frictions between PU and the institutions whose collections it utilizes. PU's student runners or "dashers" gain access to almost every library in the New York metropolitan area by virtue of the University's membership in a large local multitype library system, METRO. There, they pull journal volumes from the shelves and photocopy articles wanted by Polytechnic's readers, to the tune of fifteen thousand to eighteen thousand per year.

Polytechnic feels strongly that its program does nothing to increase the capital costs of the libraries it uses; it invites other institutions to utilize its collection of about one thousand journal titles in the same way it uses theirs and offers to provide each library with data on the number of articles obtained from its collections, should the institution wish to include them in its annual interlibrary loan report. Many institutions have little or no objection to the InfoDash program; given the choice of having "dashers" come to their libraries or filling PU's interlibrary loan requests, they prefer the former. For a number of reasons, however, other libraries find the program troubling.

Those who consider the program a type of interlibrary loan point out that a library subscribing to one thousand journals but processing fifteen thousand to eighteen thousand journal articles a year must not be meeting the basic requirement for the utilization of ILL, that is, the maintenance of collections that satisfy one's readers' basic needs. Others point out that the argument that it is better to host the "dashers" than to fill thousands of ILL requests from PU is irrelevant: it would be impossible for Polytechnic to fill the same number of interlibrary loans from the same group of libraries at the same speed with the same cost: the University would be forced to find another solution, one requiring an expenditure of more of its own resources and less dependence on those of others.

Clearly larger "targets" are more profitable for PU's student messengers: big libraries have larger collections, and more articles can be obtained from a single large location. Some of these institutions believe that their student fees for library materials and services are subsidizing students at Polytechnic; they also comment on the wear on their journals caused by PU's photocopying, and the reshelving that is generated. Although the student messengers are trained to be inconspicuous, they are not always as successful as they might be; information services staff at the libraries they patronize sometimes complain about time spent teaching them to use local catalogs and union lists.

Who is right and who is wrong here? PU's program has been in place for a number of years, and what tensions exist are clearly insufficient to have any serious impact on InfoDash. Richard Sweeney, Polytechnic's director, has created a program that serves his readers exceptionally well; the University's administrators certainly are impressed by its low costs and effectiveness. Sweeney has suggested on several occasions that METRO institutionalize his program for the benefit of all its members; we'll pay CARL UnCover or UMI, he points out: why not become our own broker? He seems cooperative and committed to sharing, yet those tensions remain, along with the feeling that Polytechnic is somehow taking advantage of its peers.

Rather than asking who is right and who is wrong, perhaps a more productive question would be, what is going to happen here? It is unlikely that Polytechnic will drop its InfoDash program—indeed, it has plans for improvements, such as completing a database of libraries and journal holdings that will generate routing slips suggesting the most productive sources, and mounting *Current Contents* on the university network, enabling readers to "circle" wanted articles and forward their selections to the library. It seems more likely that the libraries whose collections Polytechnic uses will become, like libraries everywhere, harder and harder pressed to meet their readers' needs from local collections. As they examine the costs of expanded interlibrary loan operations and commercial document services, PU's program may appear more appealing and quite cost-effective. It seems likely that Polytechnic's program may represent a temporary imbalance in resource sharing in New York metropolitan libraries, one that is likely to be rectified as the program is eventually broadened to include more if not all METRO members.

Costs and Monetary Savings

In evaluating membership in any cooperative, the library should examine the charges it makes for services, the method used for determining these charges, and the importance of charges as a source of consortial income. Among the types of fees to be considered are those for membership, access to a delivery service, and interlibrary loans. A library should also examine indirect costs: has the institution added staff to its interlending unit, for example, as a result of participating in the consortium? What of the postage, telefacsimile, and supply costs associated with lending?

A library should also explore whether the cost of benefits received from membership in a consortium is competitive with alternative approaches to obtaining these same benefits; these might include commercial document delivery services or purchasing materials for the local collection rather than borrowing them.[68] Here, other costs associated with ownership should also be considered: housing, processing, preservation, binding, and so forth. Ease of access under the various scenarios should also be assessed: when one owns a book or journal, it may be on the shelf at the time it is wanted and instantaneously available (it may also be lost or charged out or mutilated). Can alternative methods of access provide convenience similar to that provided by the system in question, or local ownership? What is the relative value of such convenience?

If a library joins a given consortium, will it be able to realize immediate cost savings by canceling certain journal subscriptions and relying on other collections? Some institutions have reported that such cancellations more than pay for the cost of membership. Similarly, if a library previously paid for photocopies or books obtained through interlibrary loan and the cooperative offers such services free of charge, it can easily figure the value of this aspect of membership, balancing the value of copies provided and received without charge, and adjusting for the cost of issuing invoices and checks, if one previously charged or was charged.

When an institution can determine its costs both to lend and to borrow (perhaps it has applied RLG's Interlibrary Loan Cost Study), comparing these to the volume of both activities will serve as a good indication of one aspect of consortium membership.[69] (It is important to remember that system membership conveys the dual privileges of lending and of borrowing.) If there is a coordinated collection development program, libraries can assess whether the consortium's membership fee exceeds or is less than the value of the materials it would otherwise have felt it necessary to purchase.

Computer and Telecommunications Technologies

Although it is now fifteen years old, James G. Williams's article "Performance Criteria and Evaluation for a Library Resource Sharing Network" is required reading for those wishing to do a detailed evaluation of a library system's computer and telecommunications technologies.[70] Vernon E. Palmour and Nancy K. Roderer, relying heavily on Williams, observe that "as networking activities have increased substantially in size and scope in recent years, attempts to determine, in some measure, the value of these activities have also increased." Among the evaluation factors they recommend are reliability, flexibility, accessibility, availability, efficiency, effectiveness, and quality control.[71] One could add speed and performance time frames ("The major technical concern for a resource sharing system is the ability to perform reliably at peak load processing time") to these criteria.[72]

If as a result of network membership the library shares in an automated integrated library system, calculating the economic benefit of this benefit should be rather straightforward; in some cases, the cooperative may have already done these computations as part of the justification for a shared system. Certainly, with a bit of research, one can figure the costs (hardware, software, staffing) if such a system were locally funded and maintained, and the costs associated with the shared operation should be easy to obtain from the consortium's administrative staff. More difficult to assess will be the added benefit of the shared catalog itself.

There are a number of other criteria for measuring the value of membership in a library consortium, which may be described more briefly.

Extending the Total Resources Available to Readers

If a library can figure the extent of collection overlap, or safely presume it to be low, it can gauge the number of additional items to which membership provides access.

Interlibrary Loan Efficiencies

There are a number of important and effective measurements that can be applied to interlending. What is the consortium's requirement (or, absent a requirement, record) for delivering requested materials? If interlibrary loan "clearinghouse" services are offered (either for obtaining loans or location information) and the library takes advantage of them, it should also attempt to value these services in some way. Likewise, one might calculate the cost and value of any delivery services the cooperative provides; this should be fairly simple, since the network doubtless has information on the annual cost of the service, as well as the annual number of stops made, enabling a simple calculation of local value to be made. Much greater detail on evaluating interlending arrangements appears in the following chapter.

Reciprocal Access and Borrowing

If the members of the consortium have a shared circulation system, it may be possible to determine the number of loans made to partners' faculty and students, either aggregately or by individual institutions; this can serve as some measure of the increased use of the collections (and, by extrapolation, other library services) generated by consortium participation, while also enabling the home library to ascertain the extent to which its readers' horizons have been broadened by membership in the cooperative. Alternatively, through a survey of the charges that some academic libraries make for access or borrowing, one may be able to assign a base value to such a benefit, then multiply it by the number of times a local reader took advantage of gratis access to such a library.

Miscellaneous Benefits

Some costs and benefits will be difficult if not impossible to assess. Among these may be the "social" value of union catalogs, whatever their format. (On the other hand, as mentioned above, the cost savings associated with a shared catalog versus an independently funded and supported system are comparatively easy to assess.) Some of the equipment necessary to resource sharing (telefacsimile or scanning equipment, for example) may be available through the consortium at group rates; here again, cost savings will be simple to calculate. Likewise, the cooperative may offer discount rates for commercial document supply services, by virtue of establishing large deposit accounts on members' behalf; it will be easy to assess the difference between the rate the consortium can negotiate and what local costs would have been.

Establishing a Library Cooperative

With any luck, such an undertaking will not be necessary: a library will identify existing consortia in which memberships will be productive; an analysis of one's borrowing and lending patterns may indicate the effectiveness of relationships that have yet to be established.[73] Ruth J. Patrick's *Guidelines for Library Cooperation: Development of Academic Library Consortia* is required reading for those wishing to build their own cooperatives. (Additionally or alternatively, one could contact one of the libraries listed in the appendix of cooperative examples.) Patrick describes four stages or phases in the development of a consortium: exploratory, planning, development, and operation and evaluation. She also discusses the particulars of a long list of potential cooperative activities, including collaborative development of resources, and resource sharing. Her book includes many sample documents one might wish to use as points of embarkation for consortial agreements. *Guidelines for Library Cooperation* proceeds step by step, from calling the first exploratory meeting among potential participants, to evaluating the consortium's effectiveness after its programs have been implemented. It offers a variety of organizational and governance structures and also covers such practical topics as physical facilities, how to hire a system director, and implementation schedules.

Cooperation: Is It Worth All This Trouble?

In 1987, shortly before his death, Hugh C. Atkinson counseled us after this fashion:

> Libraries must start doing something with interlibrary activity and multitype systems, and not just planning and worrying. We should not be afraid to fail. We will never have absolute guarantees of success, and it is only through attempting to provide better library service that we will in fact improve our libraries and their services.[74]

Patricia Battin, another advocate of risk taking, often speaks of what she calls the "80 percent solution": any program we feel has the potential to address 80 percent of our needs is one we should be willing to try; if we insist on the 100 percent solution before taking action, action may never come. When considering collaborative arrangements with other institutions, she urges that we go even somewhat beyond resource sharing, to what she terms "resource dependencies":

> Many of our consortia and cooperative activities of the past have made the fundamental mistake of attempting to share resources without giving up our basic notion of the autonomous organization of libraries.... When resources are not equal to the demand, dependencies replace resources in the sharing equation. We have discovered we can no longer meet the increased demand by simple exploitation of the existing sharing mechanisms. We must consider today, not the sharing of resources, but the sharing of dependencies.[75]

In the past, libraries may have joined cooperatives fairly casually, with little thought for the actual benefits or responsibilities associated with membership; the goal was more "mom, the American flag, and apple pie" than any serious interest in productivity. If we found we were getting a great deal more than we were dispensing, perhaps we felt smug: after all, wasn't resource sharing a modern tale of Robin Hood, and weren't we therefore deserving? If the reverse proved to be true and we were giving far more than we were receiving, we may have comforted ourselves with the "blessedness" of our position.

Economic reality has invalidated both of these extreme positions, and the heavy net borrower would do well to look for more equitable and creative solutions to meeting its readers needs, as it seems certain that its benefactors will soon begin limiting their largesse. Today, "mutual benefit" if not "equity" is the name of the game and, as the models described in the appendix show, in some cases equity costs money. There is no such thing as the "perfect" library consortium: here, as in many aspects of life, "perfection" is quite subjective. However, by applying the tests suggested in this chapter, every academic library should be able to identify one or more cooperatives whose services meet its particular needs and in which membership will significantly increase local readers' access to information.

Notes

1. Holicky, "Collection Development vs. Resource Sharing," 146.
2. Richard De Gennaro, "From Monopoly to Competition: The Changing Library Network Scene," *Library Journal* (June 1, 1979): 1217.
3. Battin, "Research Libraries," 72.
4. Joe A. Hewitt and John S. Shipman, "Cooperative Collection Development among Research Libraries in the Age of Networking: Report of a Survey of ARL Libraries," in *Advances in Library Automation and Networking*, vol. 1, ed. Joe A. Hewitt (Greenwich, Conn.: JAI Press, 1987), 190; Hewitt, "Interlibrary Cooperation," 112.
5. Patrick, *Guidelines*, 28.
6. Paul H. Mosher and Marcia Pankake, "A Guide to Coordinated and Cooperative Collection Development," *Library Resources & Technical Services* 27 (Oct.-Dec. 1983): 417–31.
7. Donald B. Simpson, "Library Consortia and Access to Information: Costs and Cost Justification," *Journal of Library Administration* 12, no. 3 (1990): 85; Vernon E. Palmour and Nancy K. Roderer, "Library Resource Sharing through Networks," in *Annual Review of Information Science and Technology*, vol. 13, ed. Martha E. Williams (White Plains, N.Y.: Knowledge Industry Pubs., 1978), 147.
8. Palmour and Roderer, "Library Resource Sharing," 147.
9. Mosher and Pankake, "Guide," 419.
10. Dowd, "Library Cooperation," 67.
11. Kent, "The Goals of Resource Sharing," 15.
12. Edward M. Walters, "The Issues and Needs of a Local Library Consortium," *Journal of Library Administration* 8, no. 3–4 (1987): 22.

13. Downes, "Resource Sharing," 118–19.
14. Patrick, *Guidelines*, 30.
15. Fred M. Heath, "Library Cooperative Activity: Common Characteristics of Successful Efforts," in *Operations Handbook for the Small Academic Library*, ed. Gerard B. McCabe (New York: Greenwood Press, 1989), 39.
16. Simpson, "Library Consortia," 86.
17. Miller and Guyette, "Interlibrary Loan," 111.
18. Walters, "Issues and Needs," 21.
19. Susan K. Martin, "Technology and Cooperation: The Behaviors of Networking," *Library Journal* 112 (Oct. 1, 1987): 43.
20. Heath, "Library Cooperative Activity," 40.
21. Hewitt and Shipman, "Cooperative Collection Development," 199.
22. Dougherty, "A Conceptual Framework," 288.
23. Information Systems Consultants, Inc., *Document Delivery in the United States: A Report to the Council on Library Resources* (Washington, D.C.: ISCI, 1983), 7.
24. Downes, "Resource Sharing," 118.
25. Fred M. Heath, "An Assessment of Education Holdings in Alabama Academic Libraries: A Collection Analysis Project," Unpublished report, Apr. 1990, 7.
26. Atkinson, "Atkinson on Networks," 437.
27. Heath, "Library Cooperative Activity," 40.
28. Hewitt, "Interlibrary Cooperation," 99.
29. Information Systems Consultants, Inc., "Resource Sharing among Michigan's Publicly Assisted University Libraries," Unpublished report, Jan. 18, 1991, IV–5.
30. William G. Potter, "Readers in Search of Authors: The Changing Face of the Middleman," *Wilson Library Bulletin* 60 (Apr. 1986): 23.
31. Linda L. Phillips, "IRIS: University of Tennessee, Knoxville/Vanderbilt University Joint-Use Program, October 1988–December 1990: Final Performance Report," 3–4.
32. Joan Blair, "The Library in the Information Revolution," *Library Administration & Management* 6 (Spring 1992): 73.
33. NOTIS Systems, Inc., "PACLink ILL Patron Interface."
34. Columbia University Libraries, "Searching Library Catalogs over the Internet," Guide, Oct. 1991. Similarly, *Search Sheets for OPACs on the Internet* (by Marcia Klinger Henry, Linda Keenan, and Michael Reagan, California State University at Northridge) provides help in accessing 25 OPACs available through the Internet (Westport, Conn.: Meckler, 1992).
35. Hewitt, "Interlibrary Cooperation," 114.
36. Heath, "Library Cooperative Activity," 43.
37. Ibid., 40.
38. De Gennaro, "From Monopoly to Competition," 1217.
39. Heath, "Library Cooperative Activity," 43.

40. Simpson, "Library Consortia," 87–88.
41. Heath, "Library Cooperative Activity," 43.
42. Michalak, "Visions," 4.
43. Dougherty, "A Conceptual Framework," 289, 291.
44. Atkinson, "Atkinson on Networks," 439.
45. Hewitt, "Interlibrary Cooperation," 112.
46. Downes, "Resource Sharing," 118.
47. Hewitt and Shipman, "Cooperative Collection Development," 199.
48. Bernard G. Sloan, "Resource Sharing in Times of Retrenchment," *Library Administration & Management* 6 (Winter 1992): 28.
49. Patrick, *Guidelines*, 153.
50. Simpson, "Library Consortia," 86–87.
51. Charles B. Lowry, "Resource Sharing or Cost Shifting: The Unequal Burden of Cooperative Cataloging and ILL in Network," *College & Research Libraries* 51 (Jan. 1990): 11–19.
52. Heath, "Library Cooperative Activity," 30, 29.
53. Paul M. Gherman, "Vision and Reality: The Research Libraries and Networking," *Journal of Library Administration* 8, no. 3–4 (1987): 52.
54. White, "Interlibrary Loan," 54, 53.
55. James G. Williams, "Performance Criteria and Evaluation for a Library Resource Sharing Network," in *Library Resource Sharing: Proceedings of the 1976 Conference on Resource Sharing in Libraries, Pittsburgh, Pennsylvania*, ed. Allen Kent and Thomas J. Galvin (New York: Marcel Dekker, 1977), 227; Kent, "The Goals of Resource Sharing," 29.
56. Simpson, "Library Consortia," 83–84.
57. "Value of METRO Membership 1987–88," *For Reference*, no. 187 (Sept. 1988): 3–5.
58. Heath, "Library Cooperative Activity," 31.
59. Atkinson, "Atkinson on Networks," 432.
60. Dougherty, "A Conceptual Framework," 288; Heath, "Library Cooperative Activity," 44.
61. Danuta A. Nitecki, "Impact of an Online Circulation System on Interlibrary Services," *Special Libraries* 73 (Jan. 1982): 11.
62. OCLC, "Interlibrary Loan," vi.
63. Ibid., 5–6.
64. Dowd, "Library Cooperation," 70.
65. Williams, "Performance Criteria," 248.
66. Nitecki, "Impact," 6.
67. Sue O. Medina, "Tracking Success in a Statewide Academic Network," Unpublished paper, 1992, 1.
68. Kent, "The Goals of Resource Sharing," 30.
69. Research Libraries Group, Inc., "Research Libraries Group Interlibrary Loan Cost Study," Introductory material and worksheets, July 1991.

70. Williams, "Performance Criteria," 225–77.
71. Palmour and Roderer, "Library Resource Sharing," 163–64.
72. Williams, "Performance Criteria," 230.
73. Carol Burroughs, "Who Can Stop the Lemmings? Fees for Resource Sharing: An Overview and an Option," *PNLA Quarterly* 52 (Spring 1988): 7.
74. Atkinson, "Atkinson on Networks," 439.
75. Battin, "Research Libraries," 70.

CHAPTER 4

Reciprocal Agreements

He That Runs May Read
(Cowper, *Tirocinium*)

I. The Reciprocal Access Agreement 69

II. Reciprocal Reading and Borrowing: When and Why? 69
   A. Issues of Economics and Quantity 69
   B. Access to Noncirculating Materials 70
   C. Other Benefits for Readers 70

III. Who Should Be Eligible for Reciprocal Access? 71

IV. Other Ways of Delimiting Access 71

V. Monitoring Reciprocal Agreements 72

VI. The Delinquent Borrower 73

VII. Making On-Site Reading and Borrowing Easy and Appealing 73

VIII. Buying and Selling Privileges: Models and Choices 74

IX. Evaluating Reciprocal Access Agreements 75

Reciprocal access is the stuff that interlibrary loan librarians' dreams are made of: the reader gets the materials he or she needs, and both the local library and the partner institution that has agreed to provide on-site access to its collections are spared the labor associated with processing an interlibrary loan. Certainly some work is generated for the host institution, whose staff must review visitors' credentials and assist them in locating materials; however, most libraries agree that this work is small when compared to that of processing a request to borrow material through interlibrary loan.

Information Systems Consultants, Inc. (ISCI) defines reciprocal borrowing (also called "direct loan") in this way:

> Reciprocal borrowing is the movement of patrons, rather than library materials. At a minimum, it involves protocols gov-

erning access to collections, but it may include agreement to issue a borrower card good at libraries other than one's "home" library.[1]

One can think of reciprocal reading (which provides for on-site use of materials rather than borrowing) similarly.

The Reciprocal Access Agreement

"Reciprocal," of course, means "mutual," but it does not necessarily mean "free." Indeed, money does sometimes change hands and partnerships should be interpreted broadly rather than narrowly, enabling the most effective use of such arrangements. There are two basic types of reciprocal access arrangements: in the first, partners agree to provide a set of on-site services (reading; borrowing) free of charge to one another's readers. In the second, one partner agrees to pay what another charges for a like set of services. While we may prefer the free services, as we shall see, those for which we pay can also be quite valuable.

Reciprocal Reading and Borrowing: When and Why?

Issues of Economics and Quantity

Virginia Boucher suggests that reciprocal reading and borrowing are always less expensive than circulating materials through interlibrary loan.[2] This implies that the library's access unit should offer this alternative to interlending, whenever it is geographically feasible and either free of charge or reasonably priced. For example, even if a large neighboring collection charges for reading or borrowing cards, when a student or faculty member needs access to a quantity of material, the local library may find it less expensive to purchase access for a period of time than to process a large number of interlibrary loan requests; this can be especially true if the host collection also imposes fees for interlending.

Ruth J. Patrick's survey of resource sharing among 125 academic libraries showed that 78 percent of the institutions offered reciprocal access of some kind to other collections.[3] ISCI provides some guidance for the library that fears entering a reciprocal agreement, which includes on-site borrowing; a study which the consulting group performed for Michigan's publicly funded academic institutions suggests that a library that lends to unaffiliated readers need have no concern about their stripping the collection of its resources, unless the number of loans exceeds 3 percent of the host library's annual circulation.[4] Parenthetically, ISCI might have added, "a very unlikely event." Reciprocal access agreements can also provide for library services beyond reading and borrowing—reference service or the use of electronic information resources, for example. While such privileges may not relate directly to resource sharing, they may be interesting "value added" aspects for any reciprocal agreement.

Access to Noncirculating Materials

When a reader needs to work with rare or valuable materials, bulky or fragile items, titles in high demand at the potential lending institution, material subject to circulation restrictions, or items that could be impossible to replace, on-site access is a valuable alternative to interlending. Sometimes a lender will agree to provide a reproduction of such material (a copy of a microfiche journal article; a service copy of a microfilm master negative); at other times, the reader may prefer to work with the original and on-site access will be a better solution.[5]

Other Benefits for Readers

Ruth J. Patrick suggests additional ways in which readers benefit from on-site access to other libraries' collections:

> Reciprocity was of special benefit to commuting students, who are now permitted to use libraries closer to their homes. Another benefit is that it enables junior college students to become acquainted with the facilities of colleges or universities they may be considering for further study. Also, in some cases a user can obtain a book he needs more quickly if he goes directly to the lending library than if he were to wait for the material to be conveyed via interlibrary loan.[6]

ISCI describes Indiana's similar response to on-site access to other libraries' collections:

> What limited statistical data is available ... documents much more frequent movement of patrons than materials. When faced with the choice of driving to an [sic] another institution where the material is known to be available or waiting one or two weeks, Indiana's faculty and students get in the car five times as often as they seek interlibrary loans.[7]

Of course, distance and the willingness to jump into one's car are highly localized concepts: in a large metropolitan area like Chicago where people do not necessarily maintain private automobiles, taking public transportation from Northwestern University to the University of Chicago may be very unappealing, even though it could result in more rapid access to wanted materials. On the other hand, in communities where busses and subways have had little impact on citizens' transportation habits, an hour's drive to borrow from another library may seem quite reasonable.

Who Should Be Eligible for Reciprocal Access?

Most reciprocal access programs specify eligible reader populations—faculty, graduate students, undergraduates, staff, and so forth; once these are established, participating institutions generally grant every qualified reader the same privileges. In some programs, only one category of reader may be eligible—faculty, for example; in others, various groups are accorded different levels of access (perhaps faculty are permitted to borrow, while students may only read; or, faculty are granted unlimited borrowing, while students may have no more than ten books on loan at any given time). The models are almost endless.

When privileges are differentiated by type of reader, it is useful for local campus identification cards to indicate academic status ("faculty"; "Ph.D. student"); when this is not a practice of the home institution or local terminology does not correspond with the categories established by the group, the same thing can be accomplished by affixing a special descriptive sticker of some sort.

Other Ways of Delimiting Access

Reader population is only one way to define on-site access privileges; there are many others. RLG offers faculty of member institutions two different levels of reciprocal privileges, depending on whether the host collections are in the same geographic area as the visitor's institution ("resident" access—Columbia University's faculty using New York University's collections, for example) or in a different location ("nonresident" access—Yale's faculty using Berkeley's collections). Still other reciprocal programs are subject-based: a group of libraries decides to provide on-site access to each other's readers for the use of science and technology collections, for example.

In some library systems, each member decides what type of on-site access it will offer; if there is a system directory, libraries' reciprocal reading and borrowing policies are generally included with their listings. METRO is an example of such a cooperative. For reading access, members decide whether they will accept broad subject referrals ("Please allow Professor Black to use physics journals and monographs") or more restricted referrals for specific books or journals; METRO's referral cards are colored coded, so that host libraries can quickly differentiate between a subject and an item-specific request.[8] Members are allowed to delimit on-site access to their collections in other ways as well, including by the number of visits per semester or the length of time (a day, a week, a semester) for which a referral is good.

Monitoring Reciprocal Agreements

Every library should monitor the services it provides to other institutions' readers. Some libraries may want to include such data in their ILL activity reports, with the intent of reflecting more accurately collection use by unaffiliated borrowers. Certainly the local library will want to ensure that such borrowing is not depriving local readers of access to their home collection, either broadly (following ISCI's "3 percent" guideline) or in specific subject areas (computer science; dance). Automated circulation systems can often be used to define borrower categories and analyze borrowing activity by reader group. If a library has multiple reciprocal borrowing agreements, it may want to establish a separate borrower category for each one.

It will be useful for libraries participating in the same reciprocal access program to define, maintain, and exchange certain access information—the number of unaffiliated readers who made use of reading or borrowing privileges during any given period, perhaps further broken down by academic status (faculty, student, staff). If such information can be maintained library by library (as with NOVANET, a Halifax-based consortium of seven Canadian academic libraries using a shared integrated library system), so much the better: one institution can then identify the borrowing activity of each of several consortium members.

If a library begins to fear reciprocal borrowing agreements may be harming the interests of local readers, frank discussions with partner libraries are in order; perhaps these will yield some solution. It will be useful, through the presentation of circulation data, to demonstrate the type of materials unaffiliated readers are borrowing.

The library should also examine the use its readers have made of reciprocal privileges, to determine whether borrowing from its collections by unaffiliated readers is satisfactorily offset by the degree to which local readers are availing themselves of partners' materials. If a troubling inequity actually exists, several solutions are possible, though each may well result in a similar restriction on local reader's access privileges in partner institutions. The library can choose to suspend the privileges of certain "overzealous" reader groups (undergraduates, for example). Alternately, the number of books unaffiliated readers may borrow can be limited.

The Delinquent Borrower

Every reciprocal access agreement should include provisions for who pays the bill when materials are lost, never returned, or kept long overdue. There are several administrative models that can be considered, but the most common calls for the reader's parent institution to reimburse the host library for all costs, which it may or may not choose to attempt to recover. Libraries in a reciprocal access arrangement must also decide to whom overdues and bills for lost materials will initially be sent—the delinquent reader or the library itself?

Where automated circulation systems are in place, there is usually the facility to block borrowing privileges when certain delinquency thresholds are reached; where there exists no such quick ability to stop abuse, libraries offering reciprocal access may wish to issue special identification cards to eligible readers, perhaps to be presented along with a local campus ID and good only for a specific period of time (a month; a semester); dated stickers for the local ID are an effective alternative, and either approach provides an opportunity to review the visiting reader's access record before reaccording him or her privileges.

Making On-Site Reading and Borrowing Easy and Appealing

Readers will be more amenable to traveling to use materials they need, rather than waiting for the materials to reach the local campus through ILL, if reciprocal access privileges are easy to understand and use. If on-site access is to substitute for local collections in any meaningful way, the associated procedures must be almost as simple as those used by local readers for reading and borrowing. If the local reader need only show his or her campus ID card to gain admission to the library, persons entitled to reciprocal access should be required to do no more, or as little more as possible: certainly he or she should not be subjected to a complicated procedure for assessing credentials or issuing special identification cards.

The local library can also encourage the use of other collections by making it easy for readers to identify them, their locations, and hours of service. Each library should be able to supply its readers with such information, perhaps in the form of a flyer listing library names, addresses (including relevant public transportation information), telephone numbers, hours of service, requirements for use, and information about physical access and other services for persons with disabilities. Ruth J. Patrick notes that several consortia publish handbooks that provide readers with basic information about using members' collections.[9]

Buying and Selling Privileges: Models and Choices

Many libraries sell on-site access to unaffiliated readers, and there are almost as many models for such arrangements. A library typically charges different prices for reading and borrowing; the cost of these privileges may be further broken down by time period—a month, a semester, a calendar year. In some cases, larger blocks of reading or borrowing time are discounted (a borrowing card good for one month may sell for $50, for example, whereas one good for six months may sell for $225). Some libraries charge individuals who purchase cards one price, and institutions another price; in some cases, individuals get a lower rate, in others organizations are favored.

Under certain circumstances a library might decide to purchase a card for a local reader; perhaps he or she has long-term and extensive research needs that can be met by a neighboring collection. Alternately, a library could negotiate an annual fee for either reading or borrowing access for all members of a particular reader group (faculty, for example). The smaller an institution's faculty is, the more feasible and cost-effective such an arrangement might be; local access to the host library's catalog will be a very useful adjunct to such on-site privileges.

An interesting phenomenon that seems to be gaining in popularity is some libraries' willingness to sell "group" cards that can be used by any reader affiliated with the purchasing institution.

Such cards are typically lent by library staff to local readers for specific periods of time, based on their individual research needs or simple availability ("All group cards purchased from a neighboring university library are presently in use; would you like to reserve one, when it returns?" or "A group card is presently available; I will charge it out to you for two weeks"). When group cards are purchased and circulated among library readers, arrangements for centralized overdues and fine notices should be made with the host institution, and the local library must develop a mechanism to collect from its own readers. The appendix to this book includes information about such arrangements.

Evaluating Reciprocal Access Agreements

In evaluating its reciprocal access agreements, a library might do the following things:

1. Review partner libraries' circulation, reader registration, or other data that indicate the degree to which local readers used other collections.
2. Review similar locally collected data that indicate use of local collections by unaffiliated readers.
3. If the library pays fees for on-site access or borrowing, attempt to determine the cost per use of the remote collection or the cost per item borrowed. Compare these with the cost of borrowing items through interlibrary loan.
4. Consider the "added value" of providing readers accustomed to a smaller local collection with physical access to a larger, research-level collection. Some librarians observe that, while the cost of cards permitting "direct loans" from other collections is not inconsequential, its principal value rests in its ability to alleviate some of the frustrations serious researchers feel when they attempt to meet their scholarly needs through the much smaller local collection.

Notes

1. Information Systems Consultants, Inc., "Resource Sharing," 3.
2. Boucher, *Interlibrary Loan*, 4.
3. Patrick, *Guidelines*, 178.
4. Information Systems Consultants, Inc., "Resource Sharing," IV–13.

5. Boucher, *Interlibrary Loan*, 4.
6. Patrick, *Guidelines*, 179.
7. Information Systems Consultants, Inc., "Resource Sharing," IV–13.
8. Joan Neumann, "Enhanced METRO Cards to Provide Subject Referral," Letter to directors of METRO libraries, Feb. 13, 1991.
9. Patrick, *Guidelines*, 179.

CHAPTER 5

Interlending

Friends Share All Things
(Pythagoras, *Diogenes Laertes*,
Lives of Eminent Philosophers, Section 10)

I. ILL in the 1980s   79

II. ILL in the 1990s   80
   A. Complexity and Communications Barriers   81
   B. Psychological Barriers   82

III. Definition and Regulation of ILL: The National and Model Codes   83

IV. Beyond the Model Code: Other Types of ILL Agreements   86

V. When to Buy Instead of Borrow   88
   A. Monographs   89
   B. Periodicals   90

VI. Identifying "Best Partners"   90
   A. Reciprocal Lending   91
   B. Transmission of Requests   92
   C. Fill Rate   92
   D. Turnaround Time   93
   E. Delivery Mechanism   93
   F. Packaging   93
   G. Other Elements   94

VII. Automation for ILL Messaging and Location   94
   A. The Bibliographic Utilities   95
      1. OCLC (Online Computer Library Center)   96
      2. Research Libraries Information Network (RLIN)   97
      3. Western Library Network (WLN)   98
      4. Multiple Utility Access   98
   B. Electronic Mail Messaging for ILL   99
   C. The Reader-Initiated ILL Request   104
   D. Electronic Mail for Local Messaging   107

VIII. ILL Location Finders and Clearinghouses   110

IX. Statistical Analysis of the ILL Operation   110
   A. Borrowing   111
   B. Lending   115

C. Special Uses for ILL Data   117
      1. Copyright Compliance   117
      2. Collection Development   119
X. The Automation of ILL Statistics   121
   A. The Utilities' Statistical Packages   122
   B. PC-Based Statistical Packages   123
      1. Successful In-House Systems   124
      2. Commercial Software for ILL Management   126
XI. ILL Efficiency and Workflow: Is There Room for Improvement?   128
   A. Components of Interlibrary Loan   128
      1. The Borrowing Operation   129
         a) The Reader's Introduction to the ILL Process   129
         b) Verification   130
         c) Locating   131
         d) Requesting   133
         e) Other Factors   134
      2. The Lending Operation   134
         a) Confirmation   134
         b) Fulfillment   135
         c) Document Delivery   136
         d) Other Factors   137
XII. Cost Centers for ILL   137

XIII. ILL: What Does the Future Look Like?   138

Speaking at the First International Conference on Interlending and Document Supply in 1988, Maurice B. Line described the current state of interlibrary loan (ILL) and information delivery in this way:

> It is now almost universally recognised that interlending and document supply are an essential element in library services. Before World War 2 interlending was regarded as an optional extra, a grace and favour activity, to be indulged in sparingly; any research library considered it an admission of failure to have to obtain any item from elsewhere. Now every library, however large, accepts that it can not be self-sufficient, and some of the largest obtain the most from elsewhere.[1]

Can there be any question that interlibrary loan and document supply have become "universally recognised"? No librarian needs to be told that there is a rapidly expanding universe of information or that the funds for local purchase of this information are either static or diminishing. The recognition of the importance of ILL as a means of delivering any information, regardless of subject, date, format, or location, is a direct consequence of our own phenomenally successful efforts in providing access to bibliographic information. As one librarian stated:

> Though once seen primarily as repositories for the storage of collections, libraries are now viewed as places from which information is to be obtained. Emphasis on the need for access to and dissemination of information has discouraged developments in a number of areas. Interlibrary loan is an increasingly important component in the dissemination of information, and stems directly from access.[2]

Readers have access to virtually instantaneous bibliographic information through the use of printed and electronic indexes, table of contents services, as well as other libraries' online catalogs; and we, as the document deliverers, have an equally efficient verification and location capacity through bibliographic utilities and union catalogs. And yet, our capacity to control the elements that impede the delivery of the information held within that bibliographic gold mine remains frustratingly elusive. Therein lies the implicit irony and the explicit challenge for interlibrary loan in the 1990s; now that we have tantalized our readers with bibliographic possibilities, we are in the consequent position of wanting to "deliver the goods" with parallel efficiency.

ILL in the 1980s

Mary E. Jackson identifies the accomplishments of the 1980s that increased demand for ILL, improved its efficiency, encouraged the growth of alternative sources of supply for materials, and inspired imaginative resource sharing programs that capitalize on emerging technologies. Among the achievements cited are the following:

1. The introduction of electronic messaging systems (the bibliographic utilities) that streamlined verification and transmission of ILL requests;
2. The conversion of union lists into electronic formats;
3. An increase in the overall number of lenders, because of nationwide participation in the bibliographic utilities;
4. An increase in access to citation databases through dial-up access, CD-ROM files, and local tape loading of citation indexes;

5. The implementation of national, regional, state, and local ILL codes;
6. The standardization of ILL request formats;
7. An increase in the number of fee-based information services in libraries offering services to nonprimary clienteles;
8. The linking of local libraries' detailed serials holdings to bibliographic records, increasing ILL fill rates;
9. The production of both locally and commercially designed software that reduces labor-intensive ILL activities;
10. The introduction of electronic mail (e-mail) as a common means of communication between institutions;
11. The advent of telefacsimile (fax) as a proven method of expediting ILL requests and document delivery.[3]

Neither library-imposed restrictions nor the evolutionary developments within the field that we might have expected to slow the spiraling levels of interlibrary loan—copyright legislation, the introduction of stiff borrowing fees, and an increase in the number of commercial document suppliers and full-text databases—have had much impact on controlling demand.[4]

ILL in the 1990s

What can we hope for in the future? One consulting group envisions the "ultimate" library network of the 1990s to possess these features: all bibliographic resources are online, either as a single system or a network of systems with a "seamless" user interface. The system supports subject and key-word searching, as well as bibliographic and location verification, and there is complete interconnectivity with local circulation modules for the immediate confirmation of availability. To alleviate delays between document request and delivery, all libraries fax photocopies, and for those items not transmitted by telefacsimile, there is guaranteed overnight courier delivery.[5]

While great progress toward this dream has been made—much of the required technology already exists—the vision has yet to be fully achieved. Although we may recognize common and specific goals for ILL, agreeing upon implementation and governance is not quite so simple. We have yet to accomplish the "library without walls"; the "scholar's workstation" is still in technological flux; and the "virtual library" is as distant as the next visionary's reality. The universal availability of publications, a national periodicals center, a national coupon system, and federally funded programs encouraging national and international resource sharing seem particularly utopian in these days of dwindling government support. While we continue to work toward the future we desire, it is equally important to invest great energy in enhancing resource sharing within the context of the present technological, economic, and political environment.

In 1989 an ILL discussion group organized by OCLC defined the issues that will be of primary importance to interlibrary loan in the 1990s: funding; the disparity between bibliographic and physical access to information; agreement upon cost models; improvement of turnaround time; reimbursement of net lenders; efficient use of existing systems; the relationship between collection development and ILL; the possible demise of the *National Union Catalog*; staff training; standards for ILL data; and the potential negative effects of the rise of closed, local systems (there is some concern that migration to such systems will increase the costs of ILL nationally and decrease patron satisfaction locally).[6]

Other librarians have suggested that the interlending "barriers" we must examine and disassemble, if resource sharing is to succeed in the 1990s, fall into two distinct categories:

Complexity and Communications Barriers

In his analysis of ILL in the United States, Thomas J. Waldhart succinctly states, "To characterize the interlibrary loan system in the U.S. as complicated would be an understatement."[7] While citing Maurice B. Line's definition of ILL as "unplanned decentralization," Waldhart shrewdly observes that the national system is, in reality, an immensely complex layering of individual systems:

> At the local, state and regional levels, many interlibrary loan systems are carefully planned, structured, and coordinated. . . . Even at the national level, OCLC, RLIN, the Regional Medical Library Program, the national interlibrary loan code, and the policies and procedures which have been adopted by the library community provide some degree of structure, organization and control.[8]

It is the very complexity of available systems that may sometimes create a sense of chaos; the lack of interconnectivity, or common ILL language, as well as the sheer number of participants and the physical distances between them, impedes the efficiency of ILL on both national and local levels.

Dorothy W. Russell identifies significant barriers to service in Pennsylvania's Library Area Network (PALINET) that exemplify this lack of interconnectivity:

> Bibliographic networks: Libraries belong to different bibliographic networks that do not communicate with one another; hence, each must learn the protocols of a second system, rely upon referral centers, or resort to manual processing of ALA forms in order to use another system.
>
> Technology: Libraries operate on very different technologic levels, preventing the use of consistent forms for request and document transmission.
>
> Governance: Libraries are not controlled or governed by a single body that can provide standards to unify the diverse interests of network members.
>
> Delivery mechanisms: There is no single comprehensive delivery service for ILL.
>
> Funding: Each library has a different level of funding, inhibiting long-range technological planning as well as the development and implementation of broad standards for ILL activities, such as delivery mechanisms.[9]

Psychological Barriers

Librarians themselves may inhibit productive ILL relationships. Fear of the loss of autonomy, the clash of personalities between staff in different institutions, professional complacency or inertia, a lack of confidence in other libraries, the unwillingness to experiment, and assumptions about the uniqueness of local needs can impede effective interlending.[10] At the local level, there may be in-house power struggles that discourage a commonality of purpose. Noelene P. Martin reserves her toughest criticism for ILL practitioners themselves:

> In the enlightened 1980s the number of ILL participants "who do not know what it's all about" does not seem to diminish. Utilities and networks expend enormous effort in developing and publishing instructions. Much of the material either does not reach or is not read by the library workers responsible for implementation of the procedures.[11]

Although the semantics of the critics may differ, on national, regional, state, and local levels the barriers to the "ultimate" or "ideal" interlibrary loan system are repeatedly reiterated: funding, access, technology, and people. It is not the intent of this book to solve the woes of the national interlending system, but to offer suggestions about how we can work from the bottom up to improve ILL at the level of the local library. Quality creeps up; if we clean up our act at home, the effects will be manifest locally, regionally, and nationally. The suggestions offered in this manual may help to alleviate some of the barriers to service that have been discussed. For the next decade at least, we will be focusing our considerable cooperative and organizational skills on these practical ILL issues which we, both as a professional group and as individual participants, have the desire, skills, and means to control.

Definition and Regulation of ILL: The National and Model Codes

Interlibrary loan is defined by Virginia Boucher in the ILL librarian's bible, *Interlibrary Loan Practices Handbook*, as encompassing "both borrowing and lending, both sending of materials and providing of reproductions." Its purpose is "to borrow or obtain copies of materials not found in a local collection on behalf of that library's clientele, and to lend or provide copies of library materials requested by other libraries."[12]

Although eight years old and now out of print, Boucher's *Handbook* remains the most complete source of information on the day-to-day operations of an ILL unit. It outlines every step of the borrowing and lending process, includes extensive copyright information, reprints the "National" and "Model" ILL codes, lists possible sources of bibliographic and location information for hard-to-find materials, covers national cooperative library programs and international ILL, provides guidelines for managers, and incorporates a comprehensive bibliography of verification sources. It is recommended that every ILL unit, regardless of size or experience, have a copy on hand for immediate reference.

The dual ILL functions of borrowing and lending are formally governed by a hierarchy of codes with which participants are required to be familiar. By establishing regulations for the legal, ethical, and professional responsibilities of ILL librarians, many codes promote system self-sufficiency and an equitable distribution of traffic (attained by adhering to a recommended geographical hierarchy of lending partners). But do these codes accomplish all that they set out to do? And, are all their goals to be desired?

At the top and having the broadest scope (and the tightest restrictions) is the "National Interlibrary Loan Code, 1980" which contains general guidelines for borrowing and lending library materials.[13] It acknowledges that ILL is essential to the spirit of libraries of all types and sizes but, self-confessedly, it is "designed primarily to regulate lending relations between research libraries and between libraries operating outside networks and consortia."[14]

Thus, the "National" code addresses the concerns of the very large library, and the very small library that may wish to borrow from the largest collections. Small institutions are instructed to exhaust local, state, and regional resources first (although how one is to do this if the library functions outside of a network or consortium is not addressed), and to maintain "an appropriate balance between resource sharing and responsibility to its own clientele." According to the "National" code, the purpose of ILL is to "obtain, for *research* and *serious* study, library material not available through local, state, or regional libraries." (Emphasis added.) The intent is quite clear: research and serious study are the major rationale for interlending. The "National" code also delineates the responsibilities of both the borrowing and lending institutions.

The "Model Interlibrary Loan Code for Regional, State, Local, or Other Special Groups of Libraries" offers itself as a reasonable prototype for any library interested in formalizing agreements below the national level. It is designed as a framework for cooperation and consequently suggests a broader scope in its purpose than the "National" code. The "Model" code distinguishes itself from the "National" in that it asks each library to "interpret as generously as possible its own lending policy."[15]

Librarians understand the codes' enjoinders that every institution is responsible for meeting its readers' basic information needs, but neither the "National" nor the "Model" code addresses certain issues that pertain to the practical matter of running an ILL department. A case in point is the following rather dated and often ignored mandate:

> Material requested from another library . . . should generally be limited to those items that do not conform to the library's collection development policy or for which there is no recurrent demand.[16]

As early as 1974, Rolland E. Stevens remarked that restrictions on borrowing materials that one might logically find in one's own collection "are not always observed scrupulously, and they are generally ignored in intrastate and intraregional borrowing."[17] In fact, we borrow or ask for photocopies of that which is not on the shelf, whether or not we own the item or should own it. A book or journal volume may be unavailable because it is in use, lost, mutilated, or out of stock at the publisher. Thus, one important aspect of the codes is largely ignored because the rule is impractical and unenforceable.

Terry Mackey also takes exception to the restrictive nature of the codes. He makes an interesting case for a reexamination of the standard American Library Association (ALA) loan policy that refers to ILL as "an adjunct to, and not a substitute for collection development in individual libraries":

> For I submit that the research of the past two decades illustrates that interlibrary loan has matured beyond the point of being a mere adjunct and is an integral and vital portion of collection development in academic and public libraries.[18]

Of course, a balance needs to be struck in the issue of access-versus-ownership. As John M. Budd points out, it is the responsibility of each library in a resource sharing cooperative to discourage what he calls "resource rape."[19] No institution can be justified in plundering another library's collections; when a library cannot shoulder its share of the lending load, it should devise alternative approaches for compensating its partners.

Another somewhat dated concept reflected in the codes is that of a hierarchical structure for ILL. Along with increasing access to bibliographic data, the rise in membership in the bibliographic utilities provides equally impressive access to an enormous range of potential lenders. The question becomes, why limit or structure the lender group? In an effort to streamline interlending operations, some codes, including the 1987 "Pennsylvania Interlibrary Loan Code," have eliminated the stricture of hierarchy when known locations are available:

> The concept of efficiency is closely tied in with the ability to choose the most likely potential lender. No longer are libraries required to send requests to like-type libraries or regional centers when potential suppliers are easily identified. In part, the "Code" is a reflection of the significant impact that access to the holdings of the OCLC database has had on ILL.[20]

Ralph M. Sheffner's 1986 study of ILL in New York State also recommends eliminating the hierarchical approach in favor of the "point-to-point" transmission of requests. Similarly, the state of Wisconsin permits point-to-point borrowing when it can be established that the desired item is unavailable from the University of Wisconsin at Madison, but another institution can supply it. Certainly the emergence of union lists, new technologies, and the locally established resource sharing agreements of the past decade will influence the reappraisal of national regulations as well as local ILL agreements.

On a final note, it cannot be overemphasized that every institution, once it acknowledges its need to borrow, has also committed itself to providing services beyond its own readership. A commitment to resource sharing is an acknowledgment of bilateral responsibilities: if we borrow with an expectancy of economy and efficiency, then we must lend with the identical goals in mind.

Beyond the Model Code: Other Types of ILL Agreements

Before preparing an ILL agreement, it is important that each member of a cooperative system have its own in-house policies in place and in writing. Section IV (Interlibrary and other Delivery Services) of the "ACRL Guidelines for the Preparation of Policies on Library Access" suggests that the following subjects be covered in any resource sharing accord:

1. Availability of interlending, telefacsimile, document delivery, and other services;
2. Categories and formats of materials that can be lent or borrowed;
3. Patron categories and borrowing privileges for each service;
4. Special services available through resource sharing agreements;
5. ILL borrowing periods and turnaround time;
6. Charges associated with interlibrary loan and document delivery services;
7. ILL data to be collected for collection management staff (items requested; departmental use of service);
8. Policies and procedures for copyright compliance.[21]

With local objectives firmly established, negotiating agreements that do not conflict with the missions of the individual institutions will be far easier.

According to Fred M. Heath, local resource sharing agreements should, first and foremost, be "simple, unambiguous and flexible."[22] Any agreement that straitjackets the participants or that is difficult to interpret will probably be ignored (as is the case with certain elements of the "National" and "Model" codes). Broad-based issues that should be addressed include:

Member obligations: What utilities will be used? How will documents be transmitted? Are other special information services also to be provided? Will there be on-site access privileges for members?

Financial obligations: Is there an annual membership fee? How will it be determined (by number of students, library budget, collection size, net lending or borrowing status, or perhaps some combination of elements)? Will members agree to provide free service for all ILL activity, or will there be certain exceptions? Will net lenders be compensated?

Governance: Will there be an elected board? Will all members have equal voting power, or will net lenders have a "bigger" vote? Will the governing body have disciplinary responsibilities?

Collecting obligations: Will libraries agree to retain subscriptions to journals when they are the last member to subscribe? Will institutions agree to allocate funds to support collection development activities that benefit the membership as a whole?

Evaluation and contractual renegotiation: How will the success or failure of the agreement be determined? Who will revise it, if need be? Who will be responsible for purchasing special equipment or the evaluation of a courier service?

The beauty of local agreements for ILL and resource sharing within specific groups of libraries is in the potential for promoting liberality, as well as the opportunity to address site-specific issues. For example, the network may agree to fill subject requests. Perhaps libraries will agree to ignore time-consuming bibliographic verification (but never location verification if the information is readily available), or to lend noncirculating items, rare materials, or microforms. Lending bound journal volumes or even single issues may be considered a more efficient means of getting a group of articles to the borrower than photocopying.

Compensation for net lenders can also be addressed far more easily among a smaller group of partners. An interesting example is included in the by-laws of the Consortium of Educational Communications and Technology of the City University of New York, a university-wide film and media cooperative:

> Those colleges which have borrowed films in excess of those loaned will pay a fee over and above the dues fee. This fee will compute as follows: the number of borrowed films in excess of

those loaned will be $6.00 (20% of an average commercial rental fee of $30). Monies in amounts approximating the excess fees will revert to the individual colleges in the form of films purchased by the Consortium to be housed at those colleges.[23]

Thus, net lenders choose the items that will best enhance their local collection; in turn, this increases the consortium's pool of titles. All parties benefit, but net lenders benefit a bit more.

Local codes will not supersede statewide codes (once the library transmits a request to a lender outside the local network, regional or statewide codes may apply), but they will focus on the needs of smaller groups of libraries with similar goals, regardless of type or size. For example, Illinois not only has a statewide code, but at least one library network within the state, the Library Consortia System (LCS), has its own borrowing code developed to monitor its system-based reader-initiated electronic form of ILL. It specifically defines the procedures and protocols that the "application of this new technology requires."[24]

The variety, scope, and level of detail of statewide telefacsimile agreements provide a glimpse of the complexity in approaches to consortial agreements. Issues such as when to use "rush," how to transmit the request (versus deliver the document), turnaround time, and verification are addressed by each, according to its members' needs. North Carolina encourages the use of OCLC rather than fax for transmitting requests (probably in an effort to keep an unbroken workflow, as well as to eliminate the need for two separate statistical files). Kansas insists upon bibliographic verification by its members, while the Nassau County Library System requires a response time of *up to* thirty minutes![25] (If the library profession as a whole could not only require this Long Island standard but also police it, then we would not be discussing ILL as a service in need of repair.) Obviously, the rules and regulations that are incorporated in any local agreement will depend upon the human, fiscal, and technological resources available to the group as a whole. The principle of reciprocity and the restraints of common sense will determine its rigidity or flexibility.

When to Buy Instead of Borrow

Interlibrary loan staff are not only in the position to facilitate resource sharing agreements but are also perfectly situated to assist in developing local collections. Since the ILL staff will recommend titles for purchase (or perhaps purchase first, recommend later), the collection development officer may approve the purchase, and the acquisitions department may order the item, opening up communication lines between the three is the first step in successfully exploiting their mutual concerns. Another point also needs to be made early on: in some institutions complicated invoicing procedures, the absence of petty cash, or the want of a budget allocation for occasional purchases made by the ILL unit may make buying rather than borrowing difficult. In these instances, a simple adjustment in the ILL unit's funding may be the solution.

In deciding to purchase an item for the collection rather than to borrow it from another library, all aspects associated with acquiring a title—processing, shelving, preservation, etc.—should be considered. The decision to buy an item that one could borrow or "temporarily acquire" (as borrowing has come to be known) will be influenced by a number of factors.

Monographs

There are a variety of reasons for preferring to buy rather than to borrow, and current, easily obtainable titles are the best candidates:

1. The item is an obvious choice for inclusion in the collection. The definition of an "obvious" or logical choice will depend upon the staff's understanding of the library's collecting goals. If there is any doubt about the advisability of purchase, the staff member might borrow the item and send the information on to the collection development unit for consideration.
2. Buying is less expensive than borrowing. If we accept the common estimate of $16 for a completed ILL transaction, the outright purchase of a cheap edition, a trade paperback, or even a relatively inexpensive hardcover edition might be cost-effective.[26]
3. Speed is critical, and buying is faster than borrowing.

Again, the long-term costs associated with an acquisition must be weighed even though, once a title has been identified as being important enough to be part of the collection, those costs are not attributable to ILL. An alternative to including the purchased item in the collection and the accompanying costs is to contribute the item, once it is returned, to the annual library book sale or any local fund-raising effort.

The acquisitions unit may offer established methods of supply with built-in additional savings from heavily used vendors, or it may have deposit accounts with campus or local bookstores. Many bookstores give discounts for guaranteed annual purchase levels, and out-of-print booksellers can be invaluable if their inventories are easily accessed. The best sources of purchase for ILL are always those that can determine availability immediately. If a vendor's inventory is online through a telecommunications network, this has the potential for reducing turnaround time considerably.

When the speed with which a title is delivered is determined to be critical, the library might send a student to the college bookstore, ask the publisher to send an item by courier, or identify a source that will hand deliver free of charge. Rallying for online access to the campus bookstore's inventory is an excellent idea, and one that may encourage readers to go get the materials themselves, easing the lot of both ILL and the acquisitions unit.

Periodicals

If it is determined that purchasing an issue of a journal or placing a subscription for a title is advisable (for copyright compliance, for example, or for the enhancement of the collection), possible courses of action might include the following:

1. Initiate a subscription through the serials or collection development unit, but go ahead and borrow the requested item. Experience and common sense will determine whether the title will have a shelf life beyond a particular researcher's momentary need.
2. Order an entire issue from the Universal Serials and Book Exchange (USBE) for $7, or from a local magazine dealer, depending upon the local availability of such periodical vendors.

Identifying "Best Partners"

What elements constitute the ILL "best partner" relationship and how does the library identify its best *existing* partners, as well as its *potential* best partners? A best partner will be the most generous in its lending policies, fill every single request free of charge, and respond in a timely manner to both standard and "rush" requests. In turn, this partner will always verify the location and citation of the items it requests, return borrowed books on time, follow locally established guidelines for telefacsimile transmission, and return books in the same condition in which they were shipped. In a good partnership, costs and benefits are also equally distributed.

Extensive counsel on identifying productive consortial relationships is provided in an earlier chapter; however, not every member of a consortium will be an equally effective partner for ILL. Experience will tell the library more about its ILL relationships than a list of norms, but many organizations do not have any particular local objectives in mind when deciding from whom to borrow and to whom to lend. The following features are the most important qualities of an ILL relationship: while there may be few if any "perfect partners," the more of the following qualities another library exhibits, the more rewarding the partnership will be.

Reciprocal Lending

A partner does not assess fees for lending, photocopying, delivery, or any other aspect of the lending process.

This is the most straightforward means of determining potential best partners; unfortunately, as David Everett points out, "In the best of all possible scenarios, all ILL transactions would be free, but in the real world that is no longer a possibility and never will be again."[27] Many libraries will borrow from institutions that charge fees, however minimal, only as a last resort. Where reciprocal partners can provide excellent service as well as cost-free loans, this reluctance to pay charges for ILL is justified. However, avoiding fee-based loans or opting for those that appear to be more reasonably priced than others may not always be the best approach.

There may be hidden costs in overvaluing a "free" interlibrary loan; poor fill rates and lengthy turnaround time can make the transaction less efficient and therefore more costly than a fee-based loan. For example, libraries that make nominal charges for postage or photocopies may appear inexpensive in comparison to those that charge larger fees in order to recover actual costs, but the time the library spends writing out checks and processing multiple invoices for these "inexpensive" services may not justify their use. When a reciprocal partner cannot provide a loan, institutions that offer comprehensive, efficient service as well as simple methods of payment like coupons or quarterly invoicing may be worth pursuing.

Transmission of Requests

The way in which requests to borrow and other communications among lending partners are exchanged.

Best partners will be those that use the same mechanisms for transmitting requests. Whether a library uses ALA forms, a bibliographic utility, a local CD-ROM-based network, telefacsimile, or e-mail can determine how useful a partner it will be. Under special circumstances, best partners may agree to deviate from standard communication modes (for example, a library that only accepts requests through OCLC may receive "rush" requests through telefacsimile). Libraries that are flexible in handling requests, accepting of technology, and accommodating toward emergency requests are to be cultivated.

Although it may be considered a breach of ILL etiquette or policy to telephone requests, a library that will agree to accept them may prove to be very useful in a critical situation. While there are no hard and fast rules for transmitting requests, at least one study suggests that electronic systems are more efficient than telefacsimile for ILL messaging.[28] For more on this topic, refer to the chapter on delivery mechanisms.

Fill Rate

The percentage of borrowing requests a given partner routinely supplies.

For the borrowing library, the ability to verify holdings data through a utility as well as online access to circulation status will increase the probability of fulfillment. Libraries that are willing to specify why a request was not supplied (i.e., an incorrect citation was furnished), rather than simply passing the loan request on to the next institution in a string of potential lenders, generate information important in the evaluation of the local borrowing operation. Such information may indicate careless keying of request information or an inappropriate choice of bibliographic records.

When a lender charges a minimal fee for a loan but has a better fill rate, this may indicate a better partner relationship. Developing close ties with a few libraries that are able to fill the majority of one's requests (one study suggests two to three could be adequate) may be the most efficient approach.[29]

Turnaround Time

The length of time it takes a partner to respond to a request (confirmation time), combined with the amount of time required for the borrower to receive the item (delivery time).

Libraries should look for partners that have published or guaranteed confirmation times; in smaller operations, twenty-four hours may not be unreasonable. If a library requests that its OCLC symbol be listed twice in the lender string, this is an indication that it discourages requests and that confirmation time will almost surely be doubled over what the network requires. When a partner responds differently to various modes of request transmission (there is evidence that some do, jumping up each time the fax machine lights up, but batching utility requests for once-a-day processing), this may influence one's choice of potential lenders.[30]

Delivery Mechanism

The way in which a partner transmits the item or copy to the borrower.

Look for libraries that use agreed-upon technologies for the delivery of materials, or that have mechanisms such as courier service in place. The qualities that will be of ongoing concern are reliability, timeliness, and convenience. Libraries that will agree to special procedures, such as Federal Express for "rush" requests, can be valuable. Geographic location may influence one's choice of partners; however, although remote lenders can take a few extra days to deliver, they may have a better fill rate or be flexible in other areas: geographic proximity should be properly weighted when determining best partners. Knowing the library's own mail pickup schedule, as well as the efficiency of the partner's mail room, may be helpful in determining which library will be able to deliver the document the fastest.

Packaging

The type of wrapping and other security measures a partner takes when lending its materials or returning those borrowed from another institution.

Of course, loans should always be appropriately packaged. A partner's wrapping may seem to be of little consequence, but many libraries begin to bemoan the use of jiffy bags (whether padded or bubble-lined) the first time an item is returned either irreparably damaged or perhaps even missing from its container. Partners should agree upon the best and most practical packaging methods.

Other Elements

There are many other elements that can influence best-partner status: does a potential partner place restrictions on loans or photocopies by type of material, reader status, or the numbers of free photocopied pages? Will it fill subject- as well as item-specific requests? Does it consistently adhere to local agreements? Is it philosophically committed to making the system work?

One final note of caution: if the ILL unit is split between borrowing and lending, with dedicated staff assigned to each part of the operation, established methods of communication between the two are important. When partners receive preferred treatment from the lending group, but are not providing preferred service to the borrowing group, the situation should be acknowledged and adjusted. However, one needs to know before he or she can act. Statistics, memoranda, and the informal exchange of "insider information" will be important.

Automation for ILL Messaging and Location

Libraries use a variety of ILL messaging systems: the bibliographic utilities, national and local electronic mail systems, and centralized statewide polling networks. There are even "specialty" ILL messaging and supply services, like the medical community's DOCLINE, structured around a system of regional medical libraries and using the National Library of Medicine as the "source of last resort."[31] Most academic libraries have some sort of automation in place and use manual techniques only on the rare occasion when the potential lender does not have a compatible ILL system. Thus, the following discussion is a broad-based examination of the creative uses of technology that have enhanced ILL activities across the country.

The Bibliographic Utilities

In 1981, after comparing five online ILL systems, Danuta A. Nitecki described the "composite ideal online ILL system" as a "large, easily searched bibliographic database using complete MARC records for verification" and also possessing the following attributes:

1. Automatically links the bibliographic record and the ILL request form;
2. Displays holdings for each bibliographic record in an orderly grouping;
3. Requires minimal interaction with the system to process a request (automatically refers unfilled requests to other libraries and supplies shipping addresses; monitors delivery status; generates loan status reminders);
4. Provides linkages to online circulation data for requested items;
5. Enables regional networks to incorporate either centralized routing schemes (e.g., "send all requests direct to the state library for dispersal") or decentralized, point-to-point routing;
6. Encourages quick responses through financial incentives or monitoring member institutions to ensure quality service.[32]

A decade later, having seen many of these components become available, we have yet to realize the comprehensiveness of Nitecki's "ideal." We may not have on-the-spot circulation data or a reward system for efficiency (certainly, OCLC's meager credits for filling requests in no way compensate the lending library for its efforts) but we have gained immeasurably in other areas. No utility's ILL system is perfect, but most are efficient, cost-effective, and unquestionably the major factor in the huge increases in ILL over the past fifteen years.

While some small libraries may fear that participation in a utility will open the floodgates of ILL requests, this has not proven to be true. Yes, membership will demand the time and personnel to respond to new partners, but for many libraries that have joined, ILL activity has remained fairly constant; for others, borrowing has actually increased over lending.[33] As Dorothy W. Russell has suggested, "Small libraries are discovering that when they consider OCLC's overall benefits— cataloging, ILL, serials control—it is advantageous to join."[34] As OCLC began to offer

Group Access Capability (GAC) to noncataloging libraries and ILL also became available for nonparticipating WLN members, utility access for the small library became a reality.

By combining bibliographic data with local holdings (although stopping short of item-level circulation data), the bibliographic utilities all promote resource sharing among their members. Accordingly, a 1988 study of six utilities' ILL subsystems concluded that:

> Specific operational differences aside, these subsystems facilitate the identification of prospective lenders and preparation of loan requests. To expedite interlibrary loan transactions, requests are electronically routed to designated libraries which can accept, decline, or route them to other institutions. In most cases, messages can also be transmitted among a utility's participants.[35]

All the utilities provide ILL workforms, compile policy directories for ease in checking a potential partner's fees and restrictions, allow libraries to respond conditionally to requests or to pass them along to the next lender, compensate lenders financially, encourage use by nonmembers (either through subsidiary products or direct access), and provide detailed documentation and training. Unfortunately, each utility also offers different pricing structures and protocols. The following is a brief discussion of the bibliographic utilities' ILL systems and the features that a small- or medium-sized academic library may find useful.

OCLC (Online Computer Library Center)

In 1991, OCLC had over 1,300 academic and 91 research libraries as members, and a total number of 13,847 participating libraries. With over 300 million location listings, the online union catalog is the "largest single information resource for interlibrary loan activities" in the country.[36] The *de facto* national bibliographic utility is made up of regional networks of libraries, each with its own membership rules, pricing structures, special discounted services (such as access to DIALOG), and governing bodies. Each region is also responsible for providing documentation and training for its own members.

The ILL subsystem, introduced in 1979, enables would-be borrowing libraries to select an appropriate bibliographic record from the union catalog, display the coded names of holding libraries linked to the record, move the bibliographic information into an ILL request form, add a "string" of up to five potential lenders, and transmit the request to the first library in the list.

(The requester also has the ability to qualify its search for potential lenders by its own geographical region or state, which can be very handy if a library is interested in limiting its borrowing to local partners.) A potential lender then has four days to respond before the request is passed on to the next institution in the string.

A library tracks its daily ILL activity by examining an online "transaction log" that lists ILL requests sent to the library, as well as updates to its own outgoing requests. Groups of libraries can also develop union lists of journal collections and holdings; these can be very useful for ILL (although many libraries find searching the union list too time-consuming). The ILL subsystem currently supports 127 union list groups comprising over 8,931 libraries.[37]

Group Access Capability provides access to the OCLC ILL subsystem to nonmember libraries. A GAC group is made up of a group of non-OCLC member libraries and at least one full member. It can include a small group of local libraries, or it may be as large as the fourteen-hundred-member SOLINET Information Network, the largest GAC in the United States. To form the GAC, each library in the group contributes its cataloging records to a union list of machine-readable cataloging records. This union list is then loaded into OCLC. Each library has the capacity to search OCLC's full database for material, but can borrow only from the libraries that have contributed to its own union list. When a GAC library identifies a title in OCLC that none of the members owns, it can then turn to the GAC's full member to request location information or, in some instances, have the full member actually process the loan.

Research Libraries Information Network (RLIN)

The Research Libraries Information Network (RLIN) union catalog has more than thirty-five million items held in thirty-six major research institutions and sixty-five special libraries, plus over one hundred additional law, technical, and corporate libraries. The ILL subsystem supplies bibliographic records as copy for ILL requests and online statistics for borrowing and lending; additionally, there are simple per-search charges, a flat monthly charge for connection, and a one-time installation charge for the required dedicated line to the network. The top net lender is financially compensated in a substantial lump-sum at year's end, certainly an interesting method of encouraging efficient lending (as well as inspiring, perhaps, new heights of generosity). RLIN e-mail accounts allow ILL users to exchange messages through the BITNET network. By agreement, RLIN members do not charge each other ILL fees; on the other hand, borrowing by nonmembers may be very expensive indeed, although the uniqueness of RLIN resources makes the utility potentially valuable to the smaller academic library. Search-only access is available, and the Research Libraries Group (RLG), RLIN's parent, estimates that a library performing six hundred searches a year (fifty searches a month at about five minutes per search) will incur costs of around $1,000 ($480 for the searches and $530 for telecommunications). If the library has access to the Internet, the telecommunications charges will drop dramatically. RLIN also offers "blocks" of searches at a discount and accepts prepayment deposit accounts.

Western Library Network (WLN)

The WLN database currently has 502 contributing libraries, seven million bibliographic records, and fifteen million holdings statements. The network, which was originally formed to promote resource sharing in Washington state, now offers access to its ILL subsystem to any interested library. For a one-time charge of $150, any library can have dial-up access to WLN's ILL module. Such users (107 as of 1992) pay a connect-time charge ($60 per connect hour) for telecommunications, plus a fee ($1.495) for each ILL request.

Multiple Utility Access

For the small- to medium-sized library, the decision to provide access to more than one utility will depend upon the need to locate and verify materials not found in its primary database. For instance, institutions may be full members of OCLC but, because of a need for specialized materials, become search-only members of RLIN. With trained personnel, a quick pass through the Internet to access RLIN could save time and net results. The non-RLG library will then forward the actual request using an ALA form or e-mail. When fees must be determined ahead of time, the library can check the nationwide policies and cost directory, *Inter-Library Loan Policies Directory* (New York: Neal-Schuman, 1992).

When considering the possibility of multiple utility access, the library must weigh the pros and cons of becoming a full member or a search-only member of a second utility. If a significant portion of the library's ILL requests remain unfilled through its primary system, the library may consider the benefits of full membership in a second utility. If the cost of full membership is prohibitive, the library has the option of joining a referral network or a GAC whose central processing library has multiple full memberships. These factors also represent important considerations.

> Staff: Well-trained staff members are necessary for the efficient searching of a supplementary utility. Each utility has its own protocols, and mastering additional sets may demand more or different staffing. According to Ellen A. Parravano, dial access through a search-only account is convenient but can be "quite expensive" as charges accumulate by the number of minutes spent. In many cases, this extra expense will be alleviated through alternate telecommunications connections (the Internet, for example).[38]
>
> Workflow: The workflow of the ILL unit should be reevaluated. In many instances, the office's terminal or personal computer will be multifunctional, so that utility access will be limited by equipment availability. Perhaps the second database can be searched at the same time every day, or during non–prime time hours. ILL requests that cannot be filled by the primary utility can be batched for searching in the second utility on specific days and at scheduled hours.
>
> Statistics: Search-only access to an additional utility means that not only will a second form of request transmission be necessary, but a second group of statistics must also be maintained. Some statistical packages will accommodate downloading multiple utilities' records and manual keying of ALA requests for single-file maintenance.

Electronic Mail Messaging for ILL

> Electronic mail, or e-mail, allows its users to key and transmit messages to one another using telecommunications connections through a computer system.[39] Conceptually, e-mail functions very much like the U.S. mail; in the computer environment, the host machine acts as the post office. Individual users apply for and are assigned a personal address, sort of an electronic (rather than physical) mailbox located on the central computer, to which messages are sent, just as a letter would be. The sender keys a message at a local terminal or personal computer and transmits it to the host machine, where it is placed in the appropriate mailbox; the recipient then connects with the central computer from his or her own terminal or PC, checks his or her mailbox, and retrieves the message on the screen.

Interlibrary loan forms can be built into e-mail systems, so that ILL staff are automatically prompted to fill in each data element. When complete, the form is transmitted as an e-mail message to a potential lender's mailbox; some systems have the ability to transmit a message to a receiving fax machine as well. E-mail systems typically call for a local PC equipped with telecommunications software and a modem; a printer produces hard copies of ILL requests and other messages. Some e-mail systems are easier to learn than others, but all require training and practice for efficient use. The primary benefit of electronic mail is the substantial time saved in transmitting ILL requests and responses, although this benefit can easily be lost when partners do not regularly check their mailboxes.

Electronic mail is already available on many campus, state, and national networks, and the local computer center can help the library arrange for e-mail addresses and perhaps provide other support. In other cases, groups of libraries elect to design or implement a specific, dedicated e-mail system for use in interlending. Electronic mail has become an efficient way to communicate not just between resource sharing partners, but between the reader and the library as well. When considering an e-mail alternative for interlibrary loan, one should think about who will use the automated environment and for what purposes; the answers to these questions can help inform the library's thinking as it chooses a system:

1. How may users can the e-mail system accommodate?
2. Can the system automatically forward messages to other ILL partners?
3. Can it send messages to more than one mailbox at a time? Does it offer access to group mailboxes?
4. Does it permit batched downloading of messages to disk or printer, and batch uploading of messages created offline?
5. Will it allow messages to be entered online?
6. Does it provide ILL workforms?
7. Can it generate ILL statistical data?
8. Will local readers be allowed to send requests for loans to the ILL office's mailbox, or will the system be used only by resource sharing partners?

One example of a statewide e-mail network is KIC, the Kansas Information Circuit Interlibrary Loan Network. KIC participants enter ILL requests and responses into microcomputers offline. At predetermined times during the day, each library makes its microcomputer available to receive a "telephone call" from a central machine that retrieves the stored forms and sends them to prospective lenders' mailboxes. Thus, the library may use the microcomputer for other functions, such as word processing, during the time it is not "busy" transmitting requests to the central machine. The network software that provides the ILL workforms has separate screens for book, photocopy, and subject requests, as well as a form for short general messages. The Kansas State Library provides all the software, documentation, and training at no cost to participating institutions. According to Bruce Flanders, the greatest constant expense associated with any telecommunications network is telephone charges. Fortunately for Kansas's KIC participants, all charges are picked up by the state library.[40]

KIC has become a low-cost alternative to OCLC for ILL transactions in Kansas, offering most of the utility's features and speed, but its evolution was a bumpy one. Although all participants were involved in the design and implementation process, mistakes were made along the way. Inexpensive but incompatible terminals and inadequate modems were purchased. An inexperienced, mean-spirited programmer (who planted a "logic bomb" in the software, disrupting service) was hired. And, system administrators made a number of well-intended but unrealistic promises to participants. Having experienced long delays and demands for service from frustrated librarians eager to automate, Flanders offers the following practical advice:

1. Make automation decisions with broad-based input, and expect the system's design to evolve over the course of the project.
2. Make conservative hardware purchases. Hardware that meets "current industry standard" will be more expensive, but will usually be more reliable and better supported. Do not choose hardware before software, even if it seems like the economical thing to do at the time.
3. Use professional computer programmers. Large automation projects are complex and demand skilled systems analysts.
4. Do not project unrealistic goals. This will only cause anger and frustration among participants.
5. If no one on the project staff knows what to expect from a programmer in a given period (should it take three months? six months? a year?), hire a consultant who does.

6. For a large automation project, plan to use an administrator full-time for the first two months and to provide continued daily support thereafter.
7. Before distribution, have all locally developed software reviewed and debugged by a knowledgeable, independent programmer.[41]

Flanders reminds all librarians that the amount of time involved in creating an e-mail network is "horrendous," and that administrative chores (backup, answering emergency telephone calls) are virtually endless.[42]

The electronic mail system implemented at Eastern Oregon State College serves to "solidify the overall objectives of cooperation and resource-sharing" within a northwestern library network. The e-mail program, accessible to all network sites through a toll-free telephone number, includes participants' union list of serial holdings. Thus, members no longer have to search a catalog for verification and locations before using the mail system. The system has not only increased libraries' awareness of regional resources, but it spreads the workload more evenly among the members, since requests now go point-to-point, rather than being routed through the overtaxed ILL department of the designated "resource" library.[43]

An electronic bulletin board is a variation on electronic mail; instead of a means for one-to-one communication, it serves as a channel for either one-to-many or many-to-many messaging and enables a number of users to exchange ideas on a single subject.[44] For ILL messaging (which demands one-to-one communication), bulletin board software must also include an e-mail component. The difference between e-mail and bulletin boards for ILL is in the packaging: with a bulletin board system (BBS), the user logs on and is presented with a menu of topics as well as an e-mail function. Once he or she selects e-mail from the menu, the bulletin board functions just as any electronic mail system does.

David Belanger describes the positive experience of the Delaware County Library System's implementation of EL-MAIL and EL-MAIL 2, a full-scale, multiline bulletin board that services over thirty libraries and county administrative offices. For the convenience of novice bulletin board users, procedures for placing ILL requests through the bulletin board were based on existing paper transmission guidelines. From the main menu, users can choose to look at a variety of special bulletins, download files, or enter the e-mail system. There, users can type messages online, download messages to a disk or printer, forward messages to other libraries, and access group mailboxes to post the same message to a number of different institutions. The system also allows users to view the status of ILL messages they have sent.

Before sending an ILL request, the local library first checks a regional microfiche union catalog. The request is next created offline using PC-Loan software (which provides the ILL workform), and a connection is made to the EL-MAIL bulletin board using a standard telecommunications package. The ILL request is uploaded to the first of a string of potential lender mailboxes located in the main or central computer. The first lender reads his or her mail and responds through EL-MAIL about the material's availability. If the library cannot provide the requested item, the ILL request is then forwarded to the next potential lender's mailbox.

Although the cost to implement the service, including the price for the Chairman bulletin board software system, was not insignificant, the end results were worth it. A survey conducted to analyze turnaround time showed that the average time required to receive a book using the paper transmission system (a delivery truck) took 7.1 days, while with EL-MAIL messaging only 3.9 days were required. The bulletin board is also used to transmit general messages and memoranda between libraries.[45]

Another variation on this e-mail theme is the ILL messaging system developed by Auto-Graphics to interact with its CD-ROM public access catalog, IMPACT. A central file server manages the communications among all partners, each night dialing into every library's workstation (very much like the KIC system described above), gathering outgoing requests and delivering incoming ones; it can automatically forward unfilled requests to the next library in a string of potential lenders, collect interlending data, and generate a variety of local reports.[46] Similarly, Library Systems & Services markets LOANet, a CD-ROM-based ILL system designed to interface with MARC-based union catalogs. During the day, ILL staff search the shared catalog, identify potential lenders, and create loan requests. Overnight, the system polls all network members, gathers, sorts, and batches requests, and transmits them according to either a locally defined hierarchy or a library-supplied lender string. When a library cannot supply a loan, during the next polling session the system forwards the request to the next logical library. Both the Mississippi Library Commission and the Louisiana State Library use LOANet.[47]

The Reader-Initiated ILL Request

One of the latest trends in ILL, reader-initiated requests, is a direct result of the growth of shared or linked online public access catalogs (OPACs). A shared OPAC is an integrated union catalog containing the records of more than one library; examples include CUNY+, the integrated library system of the City University of New York, and the College Center for Library Automation (CCLA), the shared catalog of Florida's publicly funded community colleges. Separate OPACs may also be linked, using various types of software, so that readers in one institution can choose to search their local catalog as well as "menu" or "toggle" into the catalogs of other libraries. Readers in CCLA libraries can also search the separate catalog of Florida's publicly funded state university system (which runs on different software). Similarly, Indiana's SULAN (State University Library Automation Network) members can menu into each other's individual catalogs. (For more information on these projects, consult the appendix.)

A library may also offer access to other institutions' OPACs (as the University of Tennessee at Knoxville and Vanderbilt have done) by providing its readers with dedicated terminals, much in the same way it would offer access to an OCLC terminal. The major advantage of providing simple, multilibrary access through a single terminal (or two closely located terminals) is that it enables readers to access the collections of libraries other than their own (and perhaps even to ascertain the availability of wanted items), encouraging them to approach interlibrary loan with greater expectations and to take advantage of reciprocal borrowing privileges where these also exist.[48]

In traditional interlending, the reader completes an ILL form in the library, or perhaps sends an e-mail request to the ILL office. (For more on this, see "Electronic Mail for Local Messaging," below.) When shared or linked OPACs allow for reader-initiated ILL requests, the faculty member or student locates material in another library's catalog that he or she wishes to borrow, transfers catalog data to an on-screen ILL form, supplies certain reader information (in some systems, these data are supplied from the OPAC's patron file), and transmits the request, potentially (but not always) bypassing the local ILL office. Precisely *where* the request is sent for processing distinguishes the three general models of reader-initiated request systems:

1. Directly to the potential lender: The reader determines to which holding library to send the request, sidestepping

the local library's ILL unit altogether. Alternately, in very large systems the routing of the request may be automatically regulated, so that one library does not receive an unfair majority of the requests.
2. Indirectly to a centralized processing library: In this case, a single library or a separately established processing unit accepts all requests (rather like an e-mail file server) and chooses the library to which each will be sent.
3. Directly to the local library's ILL office: Following this model, all requests are sent to the home library's ILL unit for evaluation and routing (sometimes referred to as "mediation"). This system works much like reader-to-library e-mail messaging, except that the electronic request form can be sent to the lending library without rekeying of data.

An example of this third type of reader-initiated request system is the Consortium Loan System (CLS) developed by the George Washington University Library under a Title II-D grant and used by four of the members of the Washington Research Library Consortium (WRLC), a group of academic libraries in Washington, D.C., that share an integrated library system. Readers enter requests from a publicly located PC-based OPAC terminal; when the request is completed, it is downloaded to the machine's hard disk. Several times a day, ILL staff run a program that routes the request to the proper library within the network. The placement of the PC, advertising, and staff commitment to ILL seem to have a major impact on the success of reader-initiated requests when the service is limited by function-specific terminals.

Major systems vendors are also involved in the design of reader-initiated request "modules." One company, NOTIS, is testing its PACLink and PACLoan modules in several groups of academic libraries with individual NOTIS systems. Using PACLink, from a local OPAC terminal the reader menus into other libraries' catalogs and searches them just as he or she would the home catalog, following identical searching protocols. Locating an item to be borrowed or photocopied, PACLoan permits the reader to display a request form to which the system transfers both bibliographic and patron data. The reader may request that an item at another campus be sent to his or her office, or to the closest library, and local ILL staff have the option of reviewing or "mediating" requests before they are actually transmitted to potential lenders. PACLoan is designed to work in a shared or linked NOTIS catalog environment.[49]

The library at the University of Illinois at Urbana-Champaign (UIUC), a member of the ILLINET/LCS (Library Computer System), allows readers to borrow books directly from other libraries, using simple ILL commands and a PC. According to William G. Potter, the migration of reader-initiated requests from a standard LCS public terminal (whose use required an understanding of systemwide codes and a detailed command structure) to a simplified PC-based system caused the percentage of aggregate annual circulation represented by ILL borrowing to increase significantly.[50]

Using LCS, the reader circumvents the local ILL department altogether, accessing the online catalog which contains bibliographic records and detailed holdings for every title owned by the member libraries. When a search of the local collection fails to identify the wanted item, LCS asks the reader whether he or she wishes to see the holdings of other libraries. The reader can identify a specific geographical grouping of libraries to be searched; when none is specified, the system randomly examines the holdings of other libraries (an early example of automated load-leveling). When the needed item is found, it is automatically charged to the searcher, and a paging request or slip is generated at the lending library, notifying its staff to retrieve the book and forward it to the borrower's library through the Illinois Intersystems Library Delivery Service. When the book arrives (here, for the first time, the local ILL office becomes aware of this interlibrary borrowing activity), the patron is notified and picks it up at the local library.[51]

Linking disparate OPACs is chiefly inhibited by the lack of a common language; PACLink is successful, because the libraries it links are all NOTIS installations, but it is equally desirable to link NOTIS sites to Dynix locations, and Dynix catalogs to DRA systems—and what about linking OPACs to CD-ROM-based catalogs? In order to facilitate communications between systems, major OPAC vendors are actively researching the design of a common interface that will allow systems to talk to each other. It is generally accepted that the linkage should be based on the Open Systems Interconnection (OSI) Reference Model developed by the National Information Standards Organization (NISO).

Linkages based on these standards will be transparent to the users, thus requiring no special training for them to search systems other than their own. Obviously, the more systems that are linked, the easier it will be to access holdings and determine the availability of remotely held materials. When new linkages combine with other enhancements, like reader-initiated ILL requests, something almost Orwellian may occur, as the local ILL unit witnesses a marked decline in the borrowing aspect of its work, and a virtual explosion in the lending.

The decision to incorporate the reader directly into the ILL requesting process will not be made casually, as it has many potential repercussions. Some of the issues that should be addressed include the following:

1. Can the reader be successfully taught how to choose the "best" partner for any request? When the intermediary, the ILL unit, is removed, the reader may well request a title from a library already overburdened with requests, unless there is a built-in load-leveling mechanism or a centralized processing unit whose staff distributes the request to the appropriate institution.
2. The immediacy of reader-initiated ILL will undoubtedly increase ILL borrowing traffic; will libraries be prepared for the sudden onslaught?
3. How will the reader group authorized to place direct loans be defined? There must be an accountability mechanism in place, using social security numbers or passwords, that governs who has access to the system; this will be important for projecting the potential increase in activity.

As groups of libraries look to automate and share an integrated library system, they may wish to add requirements for an ILL module to those for the traditional catalog, circulation, serials control, and acquisitions subsystems. An excellent checklist that a library may want to incorporate into a Request for Proposal (RFP) has been developed by consultant Richard W. Boss. Virtually every aspect of the ILL operation is covered: direct linkage between ILL and circulation; internal and external e-mail capability; request routing protocols; record creation and generation techniques; automatic "alert" mechanisms for copyright compliance and overdues; and statistical and financial management functions.[50]

Electronic Mail for Local Messaging

Campuswide e-mail systems can be used to facilitate communication between the reader and the ILL unit; similarly, some OPACs offer messaging systems (the University of California's

MELVYL, for example) that are simply a variation on this theme. While not every reader will have an electronic mail account (or want one), many will. There is no requirement that each student or faculty member communicate with the library in the same way, and the library that offers a menu of approaches (e-mail, telephone, etc.) will earn readers' appreciation. By introducing electronic mail for ILL interchanges, the library will also strike a blow for campus computer literacy.

Using a local e-mail system, readers can log on to the campus computer, send requests to interlending staff, and receive messages from them in return. Once requests are received in ILL, they are printed out and processed just as if the reader had completed a form at some service point in the library. According to Amy Chang, Texas Tech's e-mail system for ILL communication between readers and the library "provides a convenient way for faculty and students to request articles and books through ILL for material not found in the library collection."[53] The menu-driven system allows the reader to log on to the campus network and request ILL forms to borrow books, articles, or dissertations, or to renew materials.[54]

The system is designed to be simple and self-instructing, since no librarian is at hand to help the remote reader. When a student or faculty member logs on to the ILL e-mail system, he or she is immediately asked, "Do you need instructions?" First-time users may call up a brief explanation of how the system works, or go directly to a patron-information form. After keying in the necessary data (name, department, etc.), the reader then requests the appropriate form (book, article, dissertation, renewal), completes it, and posts it to the ILL unit's e-mail mailbox. The staff checks the mailbox twice a day, printing out the requests on a laser printer. The e-mail system has distinct advantages over manual procedures for both the library and reader:

1. The library can send the same message to any number of recipients simultaneously ("The ILL office will be closed this coming Friday"; "The library is now absorbing all commercial document supply charges").
2. E-mail is a less costly method of notifying readers their materials have arrived than either the U.S. mail or the telephone.
3. Users have access to the e-mail system twenty-four hours a day from anywhere; they do not have to wait until the library opens, nor do they have to come to the library to submit ILL requests.

4. Readers can log on to the network and check the status of their own requests, and repetitive questions such as "How long will it take?" can be answered efficiently with "programmed" responses.[55]
5. The system can also be used for communication between libraries on a multilibrary campus; it can easily accommodate requests for items to be sent through campus mail or located and held for a reader.

Texas Tech is not the only campus where the library is using e-mail to good advantage to communicate with readers. Clemson's EDDIE (E-mail Document Delivery and Information Exchange) accomplishes much the same thing as the Texas system. Readers who are authorized to use the system (faculty, staff, remote student users) complete on-screen ILL request forms and dispatch them electronically to the library. Alternately, readers can place requests from public computer terminals located in the library.

At the University of California at Irvine (UCI) students and faculty have access to the Interlibrary Loan Electronic Mail Request Service. Searching MELVYL, the University of California's shared OPAC, the reader identifies an item he or she wants that is held by another UC library, requests an ILL form, and supplies certain personal information (address, telephone number) which is retained in memory and need not be rekeyed when subsequent ILL requests are made. The system transfers bibliographic data from the catalog to the request; for journal articles, the reader keys in citation-level information; the ILL office retrieves and processes the requests.[56]

The library may well work closely with the campus computer center if it introduces an ILL e-mail messaging system; the congenial relationships that develop can be an unexpected bonus. In reflecting on her library's e-mail implementation project, one librarian observed that "a final, extremely important benefit has been the increased respect engendered between library and computing center personnel as a result of working together."[57] Jan Keder of the Tutt Library, Colorado College concurs: "A very good working relationship between the campus computer center and the library *enables* the library to offer this service to the campus."[58] Later, when major projects like implementing an automated integrated library system or a local area network are initiated, these previously established relationships may prove instrumental in the project's success.

ILL Location Finders and Clearinghouses

When a library is unable to locate a potential lender, or has found a lender but does not have access to its ILL subsystem, clearinghouses or referral centers can act as ILL intermediaries. These agencies refer requests for loans to sources that can fill them; alternately, they may simply identify potential lenders and let the local library place the request directly.[59] In some instances, a library or libraries within a consortium may act as the network's clearinghouse or resource center. Requests from other members are sent first to the center, which either fills the loan from its collections or sends the request on to another appropriate library within the network. Libraries acting as resource centers under such agreements may be financially compensated by other network members; Wisconsin Library Services (WILS) follows this general model.

METRO supports an Interlibrary Loan Center as a "service of last resort." Its staff can search the holdings of bibliographic utilities (OCLC, RLIN, UTLAS) unavailable to the requesting library and provide location information. For unautomated libraries, the center provides verification and locations for point-to-point borrowing.

The New Jersey OCLC Access Center supplies non-OCLC libraries with access to the utility's database and ILL subsystem. Members make requests through toll-free telephone numbers; while they remain on the line, Access Center staff verify bibliographic and location information using OCLC and generate the ILL request. The lender ships the item directly to the borrowing library, which bears the cost of the transaction. When material is returned, each library notifies the center so that it can update its OCLC records.

The Access Center is supported by a combination of state and federal funds. In 1986, the center's first year of operation, it processed 11,249 requests; in 1990, it processed more than 60,000. To accommodate this enormous increase, new telephone lines, staff, and two answering machines were added. A limit of five requests per call was imposed, and the center began to accept fax requests (although not toll-free). The center's fill rate in 1990 was 94 percent; 76 percent of the items supplied came from New Jersey libraries.[60]

Statistical Analysis of the ILL Operation

The purpose for which the library wishes to use statistical data will determine the detail and complexity of its collection techniques. One study suggests that libraries compile statistics for many reasons: to assist in the evaluation of the ILL program, to identify potential service improvements, to strengthen collection development, to provide a picture of ILL activity locally, regionally, or statewide, and to supply concrete measures of the library's effectiveness as an information provider.[61]

Establishing the ways in which ILL statistics will be used—what data will be gathered to meet local goals, how it will be collected, and in what format—should be accomplished cooperatively between the ILL unit and other members of the library staff—the director, the head of public services, the collection development librarian, subject bibliographers, and others to whom reports will be distributed. The information's usefulness will depend on the recipient's perception of its value: raw, unevaluated data presented to an administrator as the justification for an increase in the ILL budget will be less persuasive than an analytical narrative supported by selected statistics. Similarly, reports should be carefully targeted at or tailored to their anticipated audience: a collection development officer may be much more interested in the number of articles requested from a given journal than in the number of unfilled requests received from a library located half a state away. Among the types of ILL data a library might choose to compile (and possible rationales for each) are these:

Borrowing

Reader's name: Who placed this request?

Who are the library's clients? Did a particular professor borrow a significant portion of the ILL unit's total volume? Are 20 percent of the readers responsible for 80 percent of the total transactions?

Reader's status: Is the reader a full-time faculty member, an adjunct, a graduate student, an undergraduate, a staff member, or a member of the "friends" of the library?

What population is ILL chiefly serving? What are the implications for better public relations with nonparticipating campus populations and other functional units within the library (for example, bibliographic instruction)?

Reader's department: With which (if any) academic department (physics, modern languages, Africana studies) is the reader affiliated?

Are readers in the sciences, social sciences, performing arts, or humanities consistently making the best use of ILL? What, if any, is the significance of these data for the allocation of the library materials budget?

Date of reader's request: On what date did the reader request this material?

This date can be profitably related to some of those listed below. For example, comparing the dates of the reader's and the library's requests may indicate how efficiently borrowing staff are processing incoming requests.

Date of the library's request: On what date did the library request this material from a potential lender or lenders?

When this date is compared to the date of delivery, the library learns something about the general efficiency of the supplier.

Method of request transmittal: How was the request transmitted to the lender (through a utility, electronic mail, or on an ALA form)?

When staff compare this information with the amount of time elapsed between the reader's request and the date of confirmation, the library can learn something about the most effective ways of transmitting requests.

Date of confirmation: On what date did the lender confirm it would supply the requested material?

When compared with the date of library's request, this will tell the borrowing library how responsive a given lender is.

Date the request was abandoned: On what date did the borrowing library cease to search for the material?

Some materials can never be secured; how long did it take the library to notify the reader that it could not obtain the requested item?

Reason request was abandoned: Why was the library unable to place the request?

Was the material classified as reference, rare, or otherwise noncirculating in all libraries that held it? This can suggest to the library that on-site access is a better option than interlending for certain requests.

Date of delivery: On what date did the requested material arrive in the borrowing library?

When compared with the date of confirmation, this will give some indication of the internal efficiencies of the lender's ILL unit, as well as the delivery mechanism that was chosen.

Date of notification: On what date was the reader notified the material had arrived?

When compared with the date of delivery, this will give the borrowing library an idea of its own internal efficiency: how long did it take staff, once the material was in hand, to notify the reader?

Date of delivery to reader: On what date did the reader receive the material?

In most ILL operations, readers call for their requests in the library; in such cases, a comparison of this date with the date of reader notification will give some indication of how urgently the reader needed the material. If notification is sent through campus mail, it may suggest to the library that hand delivery of the requested item to academic departments is a better option.

Due date: On what date is the material due back in the borrowing library?

This is necessary information if the library is to return the item to the lender in a timely fashion, and thus stay on good terms with its partner. A comparison of these data, actual return dates, and readers' names will indicate possible patterns of abuse.

Lender's due date: On what date is the material due back in the lending library?

How generous is the loan period? This information is also necessary for prompt returns.

Material type: What format (journal article, monograph, government publication, audiovisual item) is the requested material?

What percentage of borrowing traffic is filled by copies, what by originals? What are the implications of these data for delivery technologies, alternative supply sources, or purchase?

Journal titles: From what journals have articles been requested?

This information is necessary for copyright compliance and may have implications for the allocation of the library's materials budget.

Material imprint date: What is the publication date (year) of the material requested?

In the case of journal articles, this information is necessary for copyright compliance; for monographs and other materials, when compared with academic department, classification number, or other categories of data, it can indicate whether chemistry students or humanists want recent or older materials.

Classification number: What is the classification number of the requested material?

This gives a good indication of the subject areas of greatest interest to local readers and may have implications for the allocation of the materials budget.

Supplier: What library or vendor supplied the material? Was the material found in the home library, so that the loan was never placed?

To which partners does the library turn most frequently? If a library were to limit itself to two or three partners, what percentage of its requests could be filled within this group? In the case of material found in the home library, the library may learn something about reader's bibliographic literacy, the integrity of the local catalog, and the library's general "user friendliness."

Supplier location: Was the supplier in-state or out-of-state?

Should the local library concentrate on strengthening in-state partnerships if this is where the majority of borrowing is being done? Which materials are received more quickly, those from in-state or out-of-state suppliers? (Also compare this information with various dates above.)

Consortial relationships: What was the common consortial affiliation between the borrower and the lender?

Are some cooperative memberships more valuable than others? Should the library withdraw from less productive systems?

Cost and cost categories: What was the cost (if any) of the material, and into what categories (cost of the document itself; cost of photocopying; royalty fees; delivery costs) did it fall?

Which libraries are charging or not charging for materials lent or photocopied? Is the library paying for documents that it could have borrowed free of charge? Is the use of document suppliers more cost-effective than certain library partners?

Delivery mechanism: How was the document transmitted to the library?

When compared with the dates of confirmation and delivery, this will give some indication of the mechanism's efficiency. When these dates, delivery mechanism, and delivery costs are related, the library better understands which mechanisms are the most cost-effective.

Lending

Borrower's name: Which library placed this request?

Which requests are from local libraries? Did one library, or a small group of libraries, borrow a significant portion of the unit's total volume? When compared with "supplier" data, this information can help identify an imbalance of trade.

Date of request: On what date was the borrower's request received?

When this date is compared with those listed below, certain interesting information can be developed; for example, a comparison of the dates of request and confirmation may indicate how efficiently lending staff are processing incoming requests.

Method of request transmittal: How was the request transmitted to the local library (through a utility, electronic mail, or an ALA form)?

When compared with the time elapsed between the borrower's request and the date of confirmation, this can indicate which transmittal methods enable the best turnaround time.

Date of confirmation: On what date did the local library confirm it could supply this material?

When compared with the date of request, this will indicate the efficiency of the lending staff.

Date the request became a "no fill": On what date did the library either report it could not fill the request or (as some bibliographic utilities permit) allow the request to be automatically bumped to the next lender in a string?

When compared with the date of request, this information may suggest certain internal inefficiencies. Are difficult requests being neglected? When the ILL office is quite busy and knows it cannot process every incoming request, does it immediately pass the "overflow" along to other libraries, or instead let these requests languish until the utility bumps them to the next institution in the lending string?

Reason a request became a "no fill": For what reason (the library did not own the material; the item was noncirculating or charged out) was the library unable to fill the request?

When compared with the borrowing library's name, this information can indicate a failure to properly verify the local library's holdings. It may also indicate the need to update published lending policies or evaluate the integrity of the local catalog.

Date of shipment: On what date did the local library ship the requested material to the borrowing institution?

When compared with the dates of request and confirmation, this information can give the library some idea of its overall lending efficiency: was there a significant lag between confirmation and shipment?

Date of arrival: On what date did the material arrive in the borrowing library?

When compared with the date of shipment, this information will help determine the efficiency of the delivery mechanism.

Due date: On what date is the material due back in the home or lending library?

Monitoring this information will enable the ILL unit to exercise good stewardship over the library's collections.

Date of return: On what date was the material returned to the lending library?

When this date is compared with the due date, it will tell the lending library something about the dependability of its partner. Were there a number of renewals? This may suggest the need for a longer loan period.

Material type: What is the format (journal article, monograph, government publication, audiovisual) of the material that was supplied?

What percentage of lending traffic is filled by copies, what by originals? What are the implications for delivery technologies?

Material imprint date: What is the publication date (year) of the material lent?

What percentage of the lending traffic is for materials published within the past five years? the past ten years? This may suggest that older materials can safely be stored.[62]

Classification number: What is the classification number of the lent material?

This gives a good indication of the subject areas of greatest interest to borrowers and may suggest new and productive interlending partnerships. When considered in terms of on-the-shelf availability, such information may have implications for the allocation of the library's materials budget.

Consortial relationships: What was the common consortial relationship between the borrower and the lender?

If the library is supplying large numbers of loans to institutions with which it has no strong resource sharing ties, a reconsideration of local lending policies may be in order; the library may wish to consider withdrawing from less productive systems if there is no compensation for lending.

Cost and cost categories: What did the lending library charge (if anything) for lending, photocopying, or delivering the material?

These figures must be kept for accounting purposes. If fees are established to discourage lending, has this design succeeded?

Delivery mechanism: How was the document transmitted to the borrowing library?

When compared with the dates of shipment receipt, this information gives some indication of the efficiency of the delivery mechanism.

Special Uses for ILL Data

Interlibrary loan statistics are largely used to strengthen the operation, management, and evaluation of the ILL unit; they are particularly useful for evaluating staff productivity, costs, and ILL relationships. Two especially important and congenial uses of ILL statistics, copyright and collection development, are the focus of this section: how might a library best collect and maintain these data?

Copyright Compliance

No library can afford to be unfamiliar with copyright law, regulations concerning "fair use," and the guidelines for copyright compliance developed by the National Commission on Technological Uses of Copyrighted Works (CONTU). Some organizations provide special training for their librarians; the Network of Alabama Academic Libraries arranged for the University of Alabama School of Law to conduct a copyright workshop to ensure that ILL staff understood the law and could apply the CONTU guidelines correctly.[63] Although it is not our intent to examine each section of the applicable federal statutes (good sources of detailed copyright information are Boucher's *Interlibrary Loan Practices Handbook* and the Library of Congress's *Register of Copyrights*), a brief discussion is appropriate.

CONTU guidelines apply to reproductions (photocopies, facsimiles) of materials published within the last five years. The guidelines provide that, in any given year, a library may request (and receive) no more than five articles published within the last five years from the same journal title. They also require that a library maintain information on the number of these photocopy requests, by journal title. In addition, each year's data must be maintained for an additional three years. Thus, a library will maintain *one* active file for the current year's requests, plus *three* years' worth of dead files.

A library's commitment to copyright compliance is multifaceted, but on a practical level it means four steps for the ILL unit:

1. The borrowing library must indicate on all requests that it is in compliance with copyright law (for articles published more than five years ago) or CONTU's guidelines (for articles published within the past five years).
2. The lending library must not fill requests for photocopies or facsimiles unless an indication of copyright compliance appears on the borrower's request.
3. The lending library must stamp the photocopies it provides to partners with a standard copyright compliance notice.
4. The borrowing library must maintain records of the photocopied journal articles that it has received, following the guidelines suggested above.

Once the first and fourth objectives are accomplished, a library has taken the most important steps toward data collection. Although CONTU guidelines are not "law" and their violation may seem remote in some settings, the potential uses of these easily collected compliance data can justify the expenditure of time and energy for even the smallest operation.

Many libraries (including major research libraries that process tens of thousands of ILL transactions a year) maintain simple card files of journal titles for which they request articles; for each request which falls under the guidelines, a simple note on the card records the transaction. When the limit of five has been reached, the card is flagged. If readers place further requests for the title, the library has a variety of options; these include entering a subscription, ordering an article from a commercial document supplier like University Microfilms or Information on Demand, securing an offprint from the author, borrowing an issue or a bound volume, buying an issue from the USBE or a magazine vendor, writing to the copyright holder for permission, or providing the reader with on-site access to the material at another library.

Still another alternative is to join the Copyright Clearance Center (CCC), a centralized photocopy authorization service. For a $30 registration fee and an annual $75 membership fee, a library receives authorization to photocopy from over 1,500,000 journal titles for which it then pays the royalty fees established by the individual copyright holders directly to the CCC. Membership in CCC can streamline copyright compliance for the local library. Libraries that use its Transactional Reporting Service submit a monthly log of ILL borrowing activity; CCC then invoices the library for copyright fees.

Collection Development

Besides fulfilling its primary purpose of tracking copyright compliance, the information described above can also be used by the library's collection development officer. Heavy demand for a title may indicate that a local subscription should be considered. According to some ILL staff:

> An examination of titles borrowed five or more times should be undertaken to determine if subscriptions to those periodicals should be initiated. In addition to the operational impact that borrowing the same title five times may have on the ILL department, compliance with copyright law requires that special consideration be given to those titles.[64]

Of course, not all titles that are frequently requested are also appropriate to the collection; a flurry of requests may stem from a single professor's passing interest, or the short-term focus of a department's grant-funded research.

In these times of rising subscription costs and declining buying power, Jo Ann Lahmon underscores the importance of providing collection development specialists with information on readers' requests. She also offers helpful insights into the usefulness of ILL statistics by providing comments from collection development officers themselves: bibliographers want more detailed information about requests from journals, including volume numbers and dates; for book requests, they also need imprint dates. Reports arranged by call number are particularly useful, especially when each range begins on a new page.[65]

Brian W. Williams and Joan G. Hubbard describe the data fields that they have found useful in their dBASE III Plus program that collects information for selection officers:

1. Title of the requested periodical;
2. OCLC record number for the title;
3. Date the title was processed by the ILL unit;

4. Publication year of the request;
5. Status of the borrower;
6. Coded data for citation verification source;
7. Department of the borrower;
8. Code indicating whether the request is or is not regulated by copyright.

Using these data fields, Williams and Hubbard are able to generate what they believe to be the most useful report for collection development purposes: a list of periodicals requested by individuals affiliated with specific departments. The in-house program generates a list of alphabetically arranged journal titles and their OCLC numbers, along with a detailed analysis of the interrelationships among the department, borrower's status, and the year of publication of each title requested. The authors point out that this information can:

1. Imply interdisciplinary interest in a periodical (as Williams and Hubbard emphasize, "Being able to identify interdisciplinary need for journals is exceedingly important to collection management");
2. Indicate whether faculty or students are requesting the information;
3. Demonstrate whether there is a need to purchase back runs of a periodical, once a decision has been made to subscribe.[66]

The cost of ILL is another important reason for examining titles that are frequently requested. If a borrowing transaction costs the institution perhaps $8, subscribing to a journal that is frequently used may actually save money. Statistics gathered over a span of three or more years will be more helpful in determining whether the frequently requested title is more than an aberration. F. K. Rottman offers the following advice:

> Interlibrary loan personnel are in the unique position to become familiar with specific research projects of faculty and graduate students, and at the same time gain an overall understanding of general subject research requirements. Librarians may not be able to make title-by-title decisions on whether to buy or not to buy or to borrow, but specific titles which are valid repeat loan requests can and should be identified for potential purchase, and subject areas which are consistently supplemented by loans can be identified by ILL personnel for possible expanded acquisitions.[67]

The Automation of ILL Statistics

It would be all but impossible to collect, maintain, and interrelate even a small number of the data elements suggested above without the assistance of automation; just imagine typing up lists of every item Professor Jones borrowed and attempting to compare them with lists of what Dr. Brown requested. Time is money, and the ability to streamline an ILL operation through the use of automation makes it an invaluable tool. As Amy Chang points out:

> In most libraries, interlibrary loan is a unit that relies on a multitude of paper files. The complexity of records ... has grown tremendously in response to the necessity of maintaining the Interlibrary Loan Request File, Copyright Clearance File, Invoices File, Statistical Records File, Overdues File, etc. At the same time, the growth in the number of interlibrary loan requests [generates] more records and files. These labor-intensive tasks, however, can be streamlined and records can be organized and accessed more quickly by using microcomputers and appropriate software. The new technology will minimize operating costs such as space, time, and labor.[68]

According to Virginia A. Lingle and Dorothy L. Malcom, a library should ask the following administrative questions before embracing the automation of ILL statistics:

1. Does the volume of ILL activity justify the time and money necessary to utilize an automated system?
2. Are there staff members who are sufficiently computer literate to implement the software?
3. Does the library have the funds for both the necessary hardware and software?
4. Is there an institutional need for sophisticated report generation?

The library will also want to consider certain personnel and equipment issues. Who will be authorized to access the database? Who will input and maintain the data? Will the same person also be responsible for the maintenance of the software and hardware? Will the equipment (a PC, a printer) be used for functions other than ILL? What kind of backup will there be for the automated records—paper? Backup disks? Will archival records, other than those needed for copyright compliance, be necessary?[69] The answers to these questions will be quite different, depending on which of several approaches the library decides to take.

The Utilities' Statistical Packages

The statistics provided by most of the bibliographic utilities are excellent sources of comprehensively packaged, aggregate data. Although no library joins a utility for its statistics-gathering capability, the small ILL operation may find that these handy products are sufficiently comprehensive for its needs.

Each utility provides different data in various formats. For example, OCLC's printed reports (currently charged at $150 a year, plus $.15 a page) provide monthly and year-to-date data for both lending and borrowing. The reports include such data as total requests received and filled, total number of photocopies and loans, and total unfilled requests. Also included is a list of every institution borrowed from and lent to, arranged by state, with cumulative borrowing and lending data for each. OCLC also maintains monthly statistics online for easy perusal (as does RLIN), a handy feature that can be helpful in determining potential lenders on-the-spot.

RLIN's monthly statistics are quite similar to OCLC's; they include the total number of loans and copies requested and supplied, fill rates, and the dates of response and receipt of material. WLN users can either subscribe to or order online a variety of statistical reports. This "instant" ordering capability can have distinct advantages. For instance, the collection development officer may be interested in a report of borrowing activity arranged by call number. The ILL staff simply retrieves WLN's ILL statistics ordering screen and requests the appropriate document. Users also receive a "history" report on microfiche that profiles requests that have been completed or that are presently inactive for any reason.

The ILL reports provided by the utilities meet the needs of many libraries; however, there are also certain things they do not accomplish:

1. Copyright is not tracked: Libraries still need to maintain a copyright compliance file. WLN users can generate a report by journal title that will tell them whether five articles have been ordered from a journal within a single year, but there is no internal mechanism in WLN, or any utility, that will stop a sixth request.
2. Format is predetermined: What a report looks like and how it is arranged will influence its usefulness. One has only to look at a bulky OCLC report, with its page after

page of institutions borrowed from and lent to, to realize that the usefulness of the data may depend on the perseverance of the user.

3. Reports are system-based: Libraries cannot add requests that were generated by an ALA form or through another system. Hence, the library must maintain separate statistical data for each ILL system used. In some organizations, this may present no problem; in larger ILL units it can be a serious issue.
4. Data elements are predetermined: some of the elements included may be of little interest to the library; conversely, important elements may be missing.

PC-Based Statistical Packages

When a library decides to automate its ILL files (and has determined that utility-supplied statistics are insufficient), it has two choices: to purchase a specialized software package dedicated to ILL functions, or to design an in-house system with database management software. Either choice will demand appropriate technology including a personal computer, software, a printer, and perhaps a modem and telephone line to connect the PC with the library's bibliographic utility (the more data the system can extract from the utility and the less that must be keyed by staff, the better).

The choice of software may be based on the following criteria:

1. Ease of use: How sophisticated are the ILL staff members? Is the package user-friendly? Is documentation clearly written and indexed? Are there tutorials? How long will it take staff to learn the program? Does it have searching enhancements, such as key word, Boolean, and automatic truncation?
2. Equipment specifications: What equipment will the library need to access or buy? Will the unit need a new printer? Is a hard disk drive required?
3. Adaptability: Can the library modify the program? Will it integrate with the present ILL operation or cause more problems than it solves?
4. Report generation: Can the files be used with a word processing package? Can staff import ILL records from a utility? Can they sort records by a variety of fields? Is there a "counter" function in the program to produce numerical data?

5. Data security: Can data be secured through the use of passwords? Can backup copies be made? Does the software have safeguards to prevent accidental erasure?
6. Upgrades: Does the producer provide upgrades at discounted prices? Can older files be converted to the upgraded version?
7. User support: Is there a toll-free number? What are the hours of service? Is there a charge for this service?
8. Cost: How expensive is the package?
9. Comprehensiveness: Does it manage both borrowing and lending records? Does the library need a system that does both?[70]

A system's ability to generate reports may make it worth its weight in gold. If it allows the user to customize reports without having to rekey data, or if it reformats information in a word processing package, it can save even more time. Reports arranged by a number of different fields can eliminate cumbersome in-house information delivery mechanisms. In a manual system, ILL staff might suggest that the library's collection development officers review each and every ILL request, examine every borrowed title when it arrives, or peruse manually prepared summaries of titles requested. However, a software package that easily handles the majority of requests with little or no rekeying and that is capable of generating reports of sufficient clarity and depth can relieve the ILL staff of time-consuming processing that can delay delivery of the data to its consumer and siphon valuable time from the basic work of the unit.[71]

Successful In-House Systems

Locally produced records management systems require a great deal of planning, programming expertise, and a thorough understanding of the ILL operation. The advantages of "producing your own" include the ability to define the reports to be generated, decide how the indexes will be structured, and determine what repetitive manual tasks will be eliminated.

Creating an electronic database requires purchasing a software package, designing the database, collecting the data, keying the data, editing the database, and revising and updating the data as needed. If the library is considering using database management software, such as dBASE III, it will be wise to remember that this can also be "the most difficult to master, sometimes requiring weeks or longer to understand the fundamentals of the programming language, which is necessary to get the system to do what you want (or do anything at all, for that matter.)"[72] The beauty of a database management system is that it allows the user to compare common data elements from different files. Thus, the questions suggested above under "Analysis of the Interlibrary Loan Operation," all but impossible to address working from manual files, can be answered easily with the aid of automation.

There is a great deal of published information on the successful implementation of automated ILL application programs. The Briscoe Library of the University of Texas Health Science Center at San Antonio developed an ILL statistical system in which lending requests are downloaded from both OCLC and DOCLINE through a VAX 8700 minicomputer. The system, which is menu-driven for ease of use, produces monthly and annual reports, generates monthly invoices for borrowing libraries, tracks copyright compliance, and generates reports that assist in collection development.[73] Authors Elizabeth A. Comeaux and Susan Wilcox described the benefits of designing their own system:

1. The invoicing function provides an "elegant, readable, cumulated" invoice for each borrowing institution once a month; prior to automation, an invoice was either typed or handwritten and enclosed with each loan.
2. Since the data are maintained on the library's mainframe, the library can store as much cumulative information as it needs and wishes. Anyone with a password and access to an ethernet-capable terminal or a modem can access it.
3. Preparing for automation necessitated a complete analysis of every step of the ILL operation, including ILL policies, procedures, and scope; this self-study generates broad benefits in other areas.

The authors are very positive about the introduction of additional software enhancements. The potential for downloading reader-generated ILL requests directly into the program indicates that the system is flexible and has good capacity for growth.[74]

Mary Ochs and Bill Fenwick describe an ILL management program designed to work with RLIN records using a Macintosh microcomputer and 4th Dimension relational database software. The goal of the installation is the elimination of all paper files, a particularly noteworthy objective. The system maintains a database of both in-process and completed requests. Every step taken to obtain a document is included in the "history" field of the request record, offering not only an excellent means for evaluating the steps taken to fill the loan, but also a simple way to determine the best sources for certain types of materials.

The system alerts ILL staff members to requests approaching a reader's specified deadline and tracks copyright compliance. Reports that include numbers of requests by academic department, numbers of requests sent through a particular network or RLIN, alphabetical lists of requested journal titles by academic department, and turnaround time are also generated. Long-range goals include offering remote access to the system from personal workstations, which would permit reader-initiated requests and also allow students and faculty to track the status of their requests.[75]

Another example of a successful in-house system is Bradley University Library's ILL journal request file, which utilizes dBASE III. Not only copyright clearance reports but reports that list the number of times a title was borrowed, the year in which requests were made, the publication dates of requested journals, and the number of times articles from a given year were requested are also generated. A second report is indexed by academic department and reader's status within the university, providing the library director with "the information he or she needs to negotiate with the faculty on serial subscriptions."[76]

Commercial Software for ILL Management

Commercial packages for ILL management typically perform a specific group of functions, cannot be modified, are user-friendly, require little automation expertise, and are not terribly expensive, ranging from free to about $500. Some can accommodate records from different utilities or generate ALA forms, and some keep track of financial transactions or allow "special" files (not necessarily statistical) to be maintained. When a library decides its needs can be easily served by a commercial package, it will want to begin by researching the literature for comparative evaluations of available software. In many cases, the library can obtain demonstration disks and lists of active users from potential vendors. If a library in the vicinity uses the software, its ILL staff will be a useful source of information.

The software market is competitive and volatile, and any discussion of a particular product may be dated by the time it is published. As one author remarked, "keeping up with new software is like trying to hit a moving target: the field is always changing and updates are constant."[77] Thus, it is with some reservation that we discuss commercially produced software packages. The following were chosen for their apparent usefulness and staying-power.

Ann L. Kelsey and John M. Cohn (Sherman H. Masten Learning Resource Center, County College of Morris, Randolph, N.J.)

have assessed the advantages of FILLS—Fast Interlibrary Loan and Statistics—a software package designed for the IBM-PC or PC-XT and developed by the MacNeil Hospital in Berwyn, Illinois. "Through FILLS, the Masten County Resource Center obtains accurate data on return time, average cost, and total number of requests."[78] Each of these features has been useful in analyzing the type of material the library borrows, primary reader groups, and document delivery time. Nine different types of reports can be generated, and the program is menu-driven for ease of use. It generates both mailing labels and ALA ILL forms.

ILLRKS (Interlibrary Loan Record Keeping System) is used by the Colorado State University Libraries and has the distinct advantage of being able to merge downloaded RLIN and OCLC records with manually keyed e-mail records. The software produces a range of different reports, and the copyright file automatically blocks further transactions for the journal title when "fair use" is about to be exceeded. According to Julie E. Wessling, "ILLRKS is the best available package for managing borrowing files when a library sends requests on both OCLC and RLIN."[79] The author also offers helpful suggestions for the development of ILL software:

> The software should support local file management and the printing of ALA forms, transmission of E-mail requests, transfer of data from union databases such as OCLC, RLIN, or WLN and integration with local or regional databases. In addition, it should include the capability for optical scanning of incoming requests eliminating the need for paper files. Perhaps an even taller order is to make such a system affordable for even the smallest library. Future systems must be based on standards, including the NISO Interlibrary Loan Standard (ANSI Z39.63-198X), to ensure uniformity and compatibility. Above all, any effort to develop a workstation to handle ILL traffic should involve input from ILL librarians. The most successful software has been developed in close communication with ILL staff.[80]

Many libraries have found SAVEIT, the statistical software package produced by Interlibrary Software and Services, to be useful. SAVEIT converts OCLC ILL files into local database records, allowing the user to download records from OCLC for offline updating. The package maintains records of financial transactions, generates a multitude of statistical reports (including a profile of the library's ILL transaction with any single library or any group of libraries), integrates non-OCLC records into the database, prints ALA forms, and indexes on a number of fields for ease of searching. The software also supports a library policies file that allows the user to assemble important ILL agreements such as special consortial accords. An important feature of SAVEIT is utility support. For example, although OCLC has no stake in the success or failure of the software, the utility kept the SAVEIT software producers informed of all changes in its ILL subsystem during the conversion to PRISM (OCLC's enhanced online system) in 1992. Users received the PRISM-compatible SAVEIT software at reduced prices for easy migration to the new system.

One last note of advice: when moving to a new software environment, the library may wish to overlap its old and new systems (run them side by side) for a few months until all outstanding transactions in the old system have been cleared. This will also give staff members time to become familiar with the new software.

ILL Efficiency and Workflow: Is There Room for Improvement?

The bibliographic utilities and online citation databases were the first services to influence ILL volume dramatically, but once the automation floodgates were opened, traffic burgeoned. It is the combined elements of increased workloads and the changing electronic environment that have contributed to a reassessment in many libraries of interlibrary loan operations and their efficiency.[81]

How does the library decide whether the ILL unit can benefit from changes in workflow or other proposed improvements? Examining a list of the variable factors that can have a direct impact on ILL efficiency is a good starting point.

Components of Interlibrary Loan

ILL is much more than a simple process of borrowing and lending: it is a complex, detail-ridden, people-driven system that demands the expenditure of considerable amounts of time, energy, and money. For our purposes, the following procedural steps constitute an ILL transaction:

Borrowing	**Lending**
Bibliographic verification	Retrieval of request
Location verification	Availability verification
Transmission of request	Retrieval from shelf

Acknowledgment of receipt	Confirmation of availability
Notification of reader	Preparation for transmission
Processing of fees	Processing returns
Processing of returns	Processing of fees

To these two basic aspects of interlending can be added a third: the administrative work of maintaining statistics; processing recalls, renewals, and overdue notices; handling lost or damaged items; solving problems associated with the document received; and, of course, the ongoing training, supervision, and evaluation of the ILL staff.

Determining the efficiency of each component of ILL is a formidable task for many libraries. Information Systems Consultants Inc.'s (ISCI) study of resource sharing in Michigan suggests that the "best performance measure of interlibrary loan" is what they term "satisfaction time," defined as the time that elapses between the reader's placing a request and his or her receipt of the item. ISCI clusters the component steps of the ILL process into simple groups that can then be analyzed for possible streamlining: verification; locating; requesting; confirmation; fulfillment; and document delivery.[82] Here, we add our own suggestions for efficiencies that can help a library improve its overall "satisfaction time."

The Borrowing Operation

When examining the ILL borrowing operation, it is important to remember that there are what Richard M. Dougherty calls "inherent limits to a system's capacity."[83] To determine an acceptable level of performance is difficult. If one factor, such as limited access to a terminal, the lack of a fax machine, or the absence of student help, can be identified as the obvious barrier to an acceptable level of borrowing performance, then perhaps staff reorganization or terminal relocation may be in order. But, if the ILL unit has what appears to be adequate staff and equipment, then a closer examination of workflow is in order.

The Reader's Introduction to the ILL Process

If the reference staff is responsible for the initial distribution and acceptance of an ILL request form, is it adequately trained to be able to spot missing elements in the form, or even to suggest locally held materials that might better serve the reader? Do reference librarians inform the reader about potential costs, possible delivery mechanisms, and, if time is a factor, alternatives such as on-site access? One effective way to disseminate ILL information to the reader is to prepare an ILL fact sheet that can be distributed during freshman orientation or at the time of an initial borrowing request. The Association of Research Libraries' Spec Kit 127 *Interlibrary Loan in ARL Libraries* is an excellent source for sample "fact sheets."

If the library has campuswide e-mail, information about ILL can be posted on an electronic library bulletin board, along with other special services the library provides. And, if readers are lucky enough to have access to reader-initiated ILL requests through their OPACs or personal computers, the information fact sheet can be made available as a "read this first" document.

Verification: The time it takes the borrowing library to verify the bibliographic information submitted by the reader.

In most cases, thanks to the enormous databases of the bibliographic utilities and shared online or CD-ROM catalogs, for most libraries verification and location have become a single step. The availability of both the appropriate technologies and printed tools (is there anyone who has not been frustrated by a utility's downtime?) coupled with the experience of the person handling the requests will have the most impact on the speed and quality of these initial steps. At the very least, the ILL unit should have proximate access to major citation indexes and bibliographies, union catalogs, the library's catalog, and the fax machine. Ready access to ILL policy directories, commercial document suppliers' procedures and holdings lists, and even something so simple as supplies (ALA forms; pre-printed mailing labels; checks for prepayment requests) is also important.

When a request is verified, librarians assume this reduces the time necessary for the lending library to locate the needed item, thus reducing the borrower's wait.[84] But, is this true in all instances? One study reveals that the mean time to verify requests, even those that are complete and accurate, is 2.9 minutes per request.[85] If a library verifies twenty complete and accurate requests a day, close to five hours a week will be spent performing an unnecessary task that benefits neither the lending library nor the reader. Obviously, there will be requests that demand verification (those missing critical elements such as volume numbers, pages, or dates, for example), but a library may choose to deviate from standard ILL practice by experimenting with three time-saving strategies.

1. Agree with selected partners not to verify bibliographically complete citations. In this case, the borrowing library accepts the possible consequences (delays, dissatisfied readers, incorrect item supplied), and the lending library accepts no responsibility for verification of requests it cannot locate.
2. Alternately, agree that each library, when acting as lender, will go the extra mile and try to supply the item, even when the citation is found to contain incorrect elements. This approach will save a little less time than the first one, but it will still be more efficient than the traditional one in which the borrower verifies every citation. Assuming that readers at one library will prove about as accurate in their citations as those at another, the labor involved when the lender must occasionally verify a citation will be shared equally among partners.
3. Agree to institute reader-only verification. Many cooperatives are experimenting with reader-only verification. When libraries devote so many resources to bibliographic instruction and the concept of the self-sufficient reader, how do they reconcile this with ILL's position, "Readers can't get it right," that leads staff to verify every citation before attempting to fill a request? To some librarians, the need for a second verification by the ILL staff is deemed redundant.

   Since at least one study has shown that "requests for which the citation sources were not given were significantly more likely to have errors and/or omissions in them," to ensure a measure of quality control a library may require source data from the reader before accepting a reader-verified request.[86] In a shared or linked catalog environment, or one in which readers have access to utility terminals, it may be more difficult for the reader to get it wrong than to get it right, especially if printers are available. In this approach the lending library typically assumes no responsibility for verification: if the item cannot be located based on the citation supplied, the request is returned to the would-be borrower with a note that the citation is incorrect. With this system, readers quickly learn the consequences of carelessly transcribed citations and missing source data; perhaps this model could be labeled "ILL as BI."

Locating: The time it takes the borrowing library to locate a possible lender.

Locating potential lenders may be streamlined in the following ways:

1. Limit the number of partners. Relying on a small group of lenders for the majority of requests will alleviate time-consuming decisions and the requisite checking of many libraries' ILL policies.
2. Search union catalogs first. When detailed holdings and circulation data are available, searching the catalog will tell the library if an item is immediately available from a local supplier.

    This may appear to be almost gratuitous advice; unfortunately, it is not. Some ILL staff are very sensitive to the possibility they may overburden close colleagues by sending them too many requests: even though a geographically and politically "close" partner can supply an item, sometimes the local library will seek a loan at a distance from a "stranger" if staff sense they have recently requested too much from more immediate partners. This is a very damaging approach to ILL: it penalizes the local reader, who is certainly hoping to get the material he or she needs as quickly as possible. Just as important, it can disguise or even create inequities in resource sharing partnerships: when imbalances exist in a cooperative, the sooner they are identified and addressed, the healthier the cooperative will be.
3. Do not use lenders that request that their symbol be entered twice in the lender string. These libraries are letting the community know that confirmation will be delayed; they may also be not-so-subtly discouraging borrowers, and the aspects of their service that follow may be just as leisurely.
4. Check potential lenders' ILL policies. This may take extra time at the front end of the transaction, but in the long run it may save time if the lending library imposes fees that the borrowing library cannot pay, or indicates restrictions on the material type being requested.
5. Check online serials holdings. Once again, this may add time initially, but it can prevent the borrowing library's requesting materials the lending library says it does not own. Not only will this step expedite the request, but it will ease the potential lender's costly burden of handling a request it cannot fill and never claimed it could. When several libraries in a union list or catalog own a serial

title, but some are silent on the question of holdings, others supply only summary holdings, and still others give detailed holdings, it is clear which institutions will probably make the most efficient partners.
6. Keep a list of libraries that lend traditionally restricted materials or have special collections handy.

Requesting: The time it takes to prepare the request and to transmit it to the potential lender or lenders.

The medium for requesting an interlibrary loan will affect the time it takes for the request to get to the lending library. Certainly, a request sent through a utility will take far less time than sending an ALA form through the mail. Even when one batches and transmits requests on local e-mail systems or faxes requests after hours, this is still more efficient than paper transmission through the U.S. mail.

Many libraries do not like to receive ILL requests by telefacsimile unless the request is clearly "rush"; it can interrupt utility-centered ILL workflow and record keeping. The library that wishes to remain on good terms with important partners will discuss such matters with them. Some state guidelines demand that the library initiate requests through a utility rather than through telefacsimile, regardless of how fast the material is needed. Where such guidelines exist, if partners are not opposed, faxing a copy of the utility-generated ILL form alerts the lender of the request's "rush" status and may be the most efficient way to handle the transaction. These guidelines can also contribute to the efficiency of the request process:

1. Limit the number of transmission methods. Multiple transmission methods means maintaining multiple files and multiple statistics.
2. Use lender-specific bibliographic records for ILL requests. If the library has a shared catalog and locates a majority of its lenders in it, consider forwarding a copy of the bibliographic record as an ILL request. This supplies the lender with its own call number and location label (music; folio; juvenile).
3. Provide on-site access for readers. Agree among local libraries to allow reciprocal access and borrowing privileges. This will eliminate the ILL transaction altogether.

Other Factors

1. Fees. The library that recovers lenders' charges (fees for loans or photocopies) from its readers will find it more efficient to collect these when the material is picked up, rather than preparing and mailing invoices. An ILL checking account will facilitate prepayments and other lender fees.
2. Notifying readers. E-mail is a faster, cheaper approach to notifying readers they may pick up materials they requested than the U.S. or campus mails. Even readers who do not have e-mail accounts probably have home or office answering machines, making the telephone another good bet. While there are some disadvantages to having the lender deliver material directly to the local reader (rather than the ILL office), this certainly speeds the process.

The Lending Operation

Confirmation: The time it takes for a potential lender (or lenders) to determine whether it can or cannot provide the requested material.

On OCLC it takes an average of 1.6 requests to obtain confirmation of a fill. Thus, when the first lender in a string does not pass the loan on to the second before the system-imposed four-day response time expires, it may take over four days to obtain confirmation.[87] Lending libraries can speed the confirmation process by responding as quickly as possible to requests they will attempt to fill, and passing along to the next institution those they know they cannot.

The utilities' "automatic routing" capability (bumping a request to the next potential lender after a given period of silence has elapsed) can cause problems when the lending library is lax about confirming a fill online. In some instances, a lending library may successfully fill a request but neglect to update the online record promptly. In consequence, a second library receives and fills the request as well. It is critical that libraries confirm requests they intend to fill before these are bumped to other overburdened institutions.

These steps can also streamline the confirmation process:

1. Do not verify. Unless the library has a "no verification" agreement with partners, when a request does not indicate the borrower has verified the citation, pass it and

other questionable citations on to the next lender immediately.
2. Do not confirm. Instead, update utility requests on the date of shipment, not on the date of confirmation. (This means the library using a utility must ship before the system bumps the request to the next institution.)
3. Shorten the four- to five-day automatic routing system. Although there are complaints that the utilities already put too much corporate emphasis on the lending role of ILL (and do not supply enough rewards), a small group of ILL partners may agree among themselves to respond more quickly than the system actually demands.
4. Keep the library's ILL policies available and up-to-date. Make sure that lending restrictions are clearly indicated in online directories.
5. Automate the process. If an OCLC library processes more than twenty transactions a day, consider purchasing OCLC's Micro Enhancer software in order to batch process requests offline during nonpeak hours.
6. Make the collections accessible. If the library has multiple collections whose catalogs are not integrated, ensure that the several catalogs are available for immediate access by ILL staff.
7. Regulate workflow. Batch utility and fax requests and process them at the same time. Do not jump up every time the fax machine beeps, blinks, or rings.

Fulfillment: The time it takes the lending library to process the request, including retrieving it from the shelf and preparing it for shipment.

There are several ways in which the ILL unit may shorten its fulfillment time:

1. Consider lending bound journal volumes. If a library requests a lengthy article or multiple articles from the same volume, in cases where local access will not be seriously harmed, send the volume instead, packaging it well.
2. Train staff well. Make sure staff who retrieve items from the shelves know the collection thoroughly, where and what items are held in storage, and where different call number ranges are located.

3. Properly stock the ILL work space. Insufficient quantities of boxes and envelopes, inadequate working space, inaccessible photocopiers, and poor quality supplies (staplers, masking tape) will affect efficiency.
4. Know the campus mail room's schedule. Prepare loans for shipment before daily mail pickup. Prepare items for shipment first, and then update the ILL records. Shipping dates in ILL records should be quite accurate, or else data on document delivery efficiency are distorted.

Document Delivery: The time the requested material is in transit from lending library to borrowing library.

The most time-consuming element of ILL appears to be the transit time from lending library to borrowing library. A 1985 study of turnaround time for OCLC requests estimated that with a mean of 12.69 days elapsed time from the date of request to the date of receipt, request-to-delivery time had not radically changed since the days of manual verification and mailed requests. Five years later, another study estimated that turnaround time was running about six to ten days.[88] Although this is a slight improvement, it may well indicate that the elements that were once considered time-consuming and expensive, bibliographic and location verification (now veritable child's play), have not decreased turnaround time to any significant degree. These suggestions can help speed documents to their destinations:

1. Develop evaluative data for delivery mechanisms. It is important to maintain statistics on the actual dates of dispatch and delivery if delivery speed is to be fairly assessed. We may assume UPS to be faster than the U.S. mail, but in rural areas this may not be true. Personal experience (and the guidance in the chapter on delivery mechanisms) will determine what means are most appropriate.
2. Arrange for a cooperative courier service. Both the 1986 study of ILL in New York State and the 1991 study of resource sharing in Michigan recommend a statewide delivery service on par with Pennsylvania's Interlibrary Delivery Service (IDS), a cooperative association of multitype libraries that contracts with UPS to provide reliable document delivery service. The charging mechanism of the service "favors libraries with high volume," but the average cost in 1990 was about $1.75 per item, and the

average delivery time anywhere in the state was a consistent one to two days.[89] The Michigan consultants advised against purchasing vehicles and hiring drivers, and the linking of regional delivery services as being more expensive, more difficult to administer, and less timely than the blanket contract UPS service in Pennsylvania.[90] (For more information on IDS and regional delivery models, consult the chapter on document delivery.)

Other Factors

1. Fees. Agree among partners not to charge, since the processing of invoices is time-consuming and thus costly. Support efforts to institute utility-based automatic billing (remembering that this will make charging fees far easier, hence, more attractive).
2. Overdue notices. Charge out materials lent through ILL in the local circulation system, automatically generating overdue notices.

Cost Centers for ILL

The actual costs of ILL for a library will depend on the level of staff support, the complexity of the automated environment, the use of multiple document suppliers, and the efficiency level of both the borrowing and lending work environments. In chapter 8, "Making Decisions for Access," guidance is given on costing out access to remotely held materials through ILL and commercial document services. The cost centers for ILL, and a few examples for each, include:

1. Staff Costs: Salaries and fringe benefits. In libraries where staff work part-time in ILL and part-time in other units, it will be important to determine with some accuracy the percentage of his or her time each staff member spends on ILL activities.
2. Network and Communications Costs: Telephone (including local and long-distance costs); telefacsimile; electronic mail; dial-up and leased line telecommunications fees; basic network service fees; and terminal maintenance fees for network services.

3. Delivery Costs: All costs not charged to the requester, including insurance; postage; and courier and other commercial delivery fees. If a library maintains its own delivery van or participates in a cooperative delivery service, these costs are also included.
4. Photocopy Costs: A standard cost-per-page ($.07 is typical) multiplied by the total number of photocopied pages.
5. Supply Costs: Paper (telefacsimile; printer; photocopier); ink cartridges; special forms; mailing labels; special packaging materials.
6. Equipment and Software Costs: Terminals; computers; telefacsimile equipment; software packages; typewriters.
7. Rental, Maintenance, and Annual Software Licensing Costs.
8. Fees Assessed by Suppliers: Fees paid to other libraries or commercial document suppliers for the purchase of documents; on-site access fees; purchased coupons; supplier deposit accounts; consortial and membership fees for services used exclusively by ILL.[91]

Of course, the ILL unit should also tally any sources of income, such as fees paid by local readers or borrowing libraries; RLIN or OCLC network reimbursements; net lender reimbursements, and so forth, and consider these in balancing its economic picture.

ILL: What Does the Future Look Like?

Slightly dizzy from collecting statistics and analyzing automation options, the library may wish to relax for a moment and think about the future: what's on the horizon for interlibrary loan? If we return to the beginning of this chapter, we will find a discussion of various barriers to successful interlending. Prominent among these are technologic obstacles: specifically, most libraries use a single system (utility, e-mail, OPAC) for interlibrary loan; once the choice is made, they are all but locked into resource sharing with other institutions that have made the same decision, because disparate systems do not communicate with one another.

Recently, the Interlibrary Loan Protocol, a standard based on the OSI Reference Model, was accepted by the information community; as it is implemented by vendors and utilities, it will solve the problems associated with the present lack of interconnectivity, or common ILL language. The protocol is quite complex, defining twenty-one steps in an ILL request; its purpose is to standardize the content and structure of the request, enabling the exchange of ILL messages between institutions that use dissimilar computers, systems, and communication services. As with any new standard, some time will pass before widespread adoption occurs. According to Fay Turner of the National Library of Canada, some vendors are already building stand-alone ILL systems based on the standard; these can be customized and attached to libraries' OPACs. However, although OCLC and RLG were represented on the ISO committee that developed the standard, neither has begun the costly work of implementing it.[92] Nonetheless, perhaps the ILL Protocol is still the thing to keep an eye on: the fall of the barriers to effective ILL will not be quite so dramatic as that of the Berlin Wall, but it will come.

Notes

1. Maurice B. Line, "Interlending and Document Supply in a Changing World," in *Interlending and Document Supply: Proceedings of the First International Conference Held in London, November, 1988*, ed. Graham P. Cornish and Alison Gallico (Boston Spa, Eng.: IFLA Office for International Lending, 1989), 1.
2. Miller and Guyette, "Interlibrary Loan," 110.
3. Mary E. Jackson, "Trends in Resource Sharing," *Wilson Library Bulletin* 64 (Apr. 1990): 54–55, 128; Mary E. Jackson, "Trends in Resource Sharing," *Wilson Library Bulletin* 64 (June 1990): 99–100.
4. Thomas J. Waldhart, "The Growth of Interlibrary Loan among ARL University Libraries," *Journal of Academic Librarianship* 10 (Sept. 1984): 205.
5. Ralph M. Sheffner, and others, "Interlibrary Loan in New York State. Recommended Redesign. Results of a Study: Redesign of Interlibrary Loan in New York State," Beaverton, Ore.: Ringgold Management Systems, 1986. ED 274 351 (Jan. 1986), 110–11.
6. OCLC, "Interlibrary Loan," 3–9; Mary E. Jackson, "Library to Library," *Wilson Library Bulletin* 63 (Apr. 1989): 88–89.
7. Thomas J. Waldhart, "Patterns of Interlibrary Loan in the U.S.: A Review of Research," *Library and Information Science Research* 7 (July 1985): 209.
8. Ibid.
9. Dorothy W. Russell, "Interlibrary Loan in a Network Environment: The Good News and the Bad News," *Special Libraries* 73 (Jan. 1982): 22.
10. Sylvia G. Faibisoff, "A Study of Multitype Library Cooperatives: Including Developments in the Southwest Michigan Library Network, Michigan, California, and Texas, with References to New York State and Illinois," ED 257 458 (July 1984), 37–39.

11. Noelene P. Martin, "Information Transfer, Scholarly Communication, and Interlibrary Loan: Priorities, Conflicts, and Organizational Imperatives," in *Research Access through New Technology*, ed. Mary E. Jackson (New York: AMS Press, 1989), 7–11.
12. Boucher, *Interlibrary Loan*, 4.
13. Ibid., 139.
14. Ibid.
15. Ibid., 136–38.
16. Ibid., 137.
17. Rolland E. Stevens, "A Study of Interlibrary Loan," *College & Research Libraries* 35 (Sept. 1974): 338.
18. Terry Mackey, "Interlibrary Loan: An Acceptable Alternative to Purchase," *Wilson Library Bulletin* 63 (Jan. 1989): 56.
19. John M. Budd, "It's Not the Principle, It's the Money of the Thing," *Journal of Academic Librarianship* 15 (Sept. 1989): 219.
20. Mary E. Jackson, "Library to Library [Pennsylvania Interlibrary Loan Code]," *Wilson Library Bulletin* 63 (Dec. 1988): 85.
21. Association of College and Research Libraries, Library Access Task Force, "ACRL Guidelines for the Preparation of Policies on Library Access," *College & Research Libraries News* 51 (June 1990): 555–56.
22. Heath, "Library Cooperative Activity," 43.
23. City University of New York, Consortium of Educational Communications and Technology, "By-Laws," 7.
24. Karen L. Newsome, "Changing Strategies: Interlibrary Loan in the 1990s," *Illinois Libraries* 72 (Nov. 1990): 638.
25. Mary E. Jackson, "Library to Library [Telefacsimile Agreements]," *Wilson Library Bulletin* 63 (June 1989): 94-96, 141.
26. Budd, "It's Not the Principle," 219.
27. David Everett, "Interlibrary Loan Fees: A Different Perspective," *Journal of Academic Librarianship* 12 (Sept. 1986): 233.
28. Havelin Anand, "Interlibrary Loan and Document Delivery Using Telefacsimile Transmission: Part II. Telefacsimile Project," *Electronic Library* 5 (Apr. 1987): 107.
29. Information Systems Consultants, Inc., "Resource Sharing," IV–6.
30. Ibid., I–5.
31. Gale A. Dutcher, "DOCLINE: A National Automated Interlibrary Loan Request Routing and Referral System," *Information Technology and Libraries* 8 (Dec. 1989): 359–70.
32. Danuta A. Nitecki, "Online Interlibrary Loan Services: An Informal Comparison of Five Systems," *RQ* 21 (Fall 1981): 13.
33. Russell, "Interlibrary Loan," 24.
34. Ibid., 26.
35. William Saffady, "Six Bibliographic Utilities: A Survey of Cataloging Support and Other Services," *Library Technology Reports* 24 (Nov.-Dec. 1988): 742.
36. Ibid., 762.

37. OCLC, "A Summary of OCLC's Strategic Plan," 1991, 21.
38. Ellen A. Parravano, "Use and Management of Multiple Bibliographic Utilities in an Interlibrary Loan Referral Operation," in *Research Access through New Technology*, ed. Mary E. Jackson (New York: AMS Press, 1989), 30.
39. Joel M. Lee, "Telecommunications Applications," in *Information Technology: Design and Applications*, ed. Nancy D. Lane and Margaret E. Chisolm (Boston: G. K. Hall, 1991), 42–50.
40. Bruce Flanders, "Interlibrary Loan in Kansas: A Low Cost Alternative to OCLC," *Wilson Library Bulletin* 61 (Mar. 1987): 34.
41. Ibid., 31–34.
42. Ibid., 33.
43. Patricia J. Cutright and Terry Edvalson, "Online Reference and Document Delivery Service Library Network," ED 306 926 (Dec. 1988), 6.
44. Lee, "Telecommunications Applications," 56.
45. David Belanger, "Interlibrary Loan via Electronic Mail: Improving the Process," *Wilson Library Bulletin* 63 (Mar. 1989): 62–63.
46. "Auto-Graphics Introduces New Version of Electronic ILL Module," *Library Hi Tech News*, no. 90 (Mar. 1992): 7.
47. Glenda B. Holmes, and others, "Mississippi Interlibrary Loan: Protocol and Procedures Manual," Documentation, Nov. 1988.
48. Information Systems Consultants, Inc., "Resource Sharing," IV–4.
49. NOTIS Systems, Inc., "PACLink and Z39.50 Implementation"; NOTIS Systems, Inc., "PACLink ILL Patron Interface."
50. William G. Potter, "Creative Automation Boosts ILL Rates," *American Libraries* 17 (Apr. 1986): 244.
51. Ibid.
52. Richard W. Boss, "The Procurement of Library Automated Systems," *Library Technology Reports* 26 (Sept.-Oct. 1990): 719–25.
53. Amy Chang, "Developing an Electronic Information Service in an Academic Library," *College & Research Libraries News* 52 (Apr. 1991): 237.
54. Ibid., 237.
55. Amy Chang, "Computerizing Communication for Interlibrary Loan," *College & Research Libraries News* 50 (Dec. 1989): 993.
56. Sara Eichhorn, "The Making of MELDOC," *College & Research Libraries News* 51 (May 1990): 441–44.
57. Miriam Bonham, "Library Services through Electronic Mail," *College & Research Libraries News* 48 (Oct. 1987): 538.
58. Jan Keder, "Using the Campus Network for Interlibrary Loan and Book Orders," *Library Software Review* 8 (Sept.-Oct. 1989): 250.
59. Heartsill Young, ed., *The ALA Glossary of Library and Information Science* (Chicago: American Library Association, 1983), 118, 189.
60. Margie Epple and Carol Paszamant, "Providing a Statewide Citation/Location Service in New Jersey," *College & Research Libraries News* 50 (Dec. 1989): 998; Kathleen C. Mulroy and Mary Page,

"Who is NJQ and Why Do They Borrow So Much? A Library Network Success Story," *Journal of Interlibrary Loan & Information Supply* 2, no. 1 (1991): 9–24.

61. Prudence W. Dalrymple, and others, "Measuring Statewide Interlibrary Loan among Multitype Libraries: A Testing of Data Collection Approaches," *RQ* 30 (Summer 1991): 535.
62. A study of the external ILL requests received by Erasmus University during the 1988 academic year resulted in a reconsideration of the local access policies. "About 50% of the external requests were for photocopies of articles from periodicals published in 1987 and 1988. Ninety percent of the external requests were published in the previous twenty-year period indicating that, for space purposes, a stock of twenty years of back volumes could be acceptable." Cf. Ans Bleeker, and others, "Analysis of External and Internal Interlibrary Loan Requests: Aid in Collection Management," *Bulletin of the Medical Library Association* 78 (Oct. 1990): 352.
63. Medina, "Improving Document Delivery," 7–14.
64. Brian W. Williams and Joan G. Hubbard, "Collection Management Uses of an Interlibrary Loan Database," in *The Best for the Patron: Proceedings of the Research Forum, Academic Library Section, Mountain Plains Library Association*, ed. Randy J. Olsen and Blaine H. Hall (Emporia, Kans.: Emporia State University Press, 1990), 37.
65. Jo Ann Lahmon, "Using Interlibrary Loan Data in Collection Development," *OCLC Micro* 7 (Oct. 1991): 19, 21.
66. Williams and Hubbard, "Collection Management," 36, 34.
67. F. K. Rottman, "To Buy or to Borrow: Studies of the Impact of Interlibrary Loan on Collection Development in the Academic Library," *Journal of Interlibrary Loan & Information Supply* 1, no. 3 (1991): 26.
68. Amy Chang, "Interlibrary Loan Automation: An Implementation Guide," *Library Software Review* 8 (Mar.-Apr. 1989): 58.
69. Virginia A. Lingle and Dorothy L. Malcom, "Interlibrary Loan Management with Microcomputers: A Descriptive Comparison of Software," *Medical Reference Services Quarterly* 8 (Summer 1989): 44.
70. Ibid., 45–47.
71. Mary E. Jackson, "Library to Library," *Wilson Library Bulletin* 64 (Dec. 1989): 89.
72. Patrick R. Dewey, *101 Software Packages to Use in Your Library: Descriptions, Evaluations, and Practical Advice* (Chicago: American Library Association, 1987), 55–56.
73. Elizabeth A. Comeaux and Susan Wilcox, "Automating Interlibrary Loan Statistics," *Technical Services Quarterly* 8, no. 3 (1991): 35–57.
74. Ibid., 51–56.
75. Mary Ochs and Bill Fenwick, "Macintosh Management for Interlibrary Loan," *Library Software Review* 9 (Dec. 1990): 372–73.

76. Susan Eichelberger, "Using dBase III for Interlibrary Loan Journal Request File," *Library Software Review* 6 (July-Aug. 1987): 178–79.
77. Dewey, *101 Software Packages*, xiii.
78. Ann L. Kelsey and John M. Cohn, "The Impact of Automation on Interlibrary Loan: One College Library's Experience," *Journal of Academic Librarianship* 13 (July 1987): 164.
79. Julie E. Wessling, "Benefits from Automated ILL Borrowing Records: Use of ILLRKS in an Academic Library," *RQ* 29 (Winter 1989): 218, 210.
80. Ibid., 210.
81. Pat Weaver-Meyers, and others, *Interlibrary Loan in Academic and Research Libraries: Workload and Staffing*, ARL Occasional Pub. OP15 (Washington, D.C.: ARL, 1989), 1.
82. Information Systems Consultants, Inc., "Resource Sharing," 6.
83. Dougherty, "A Conceptual Framework," 288.
84. Jo Ann Bell and Susan Speer, "Bibliographic Verification for Interlibrary Loan: Is It Necessary?" *College & Research Libraries* 49 (Nov. 1988): 494.
85. Ibid., 499.
86. Ibid., 498.
87. Information Systems Consultants, Inc., "Resource Sharing," 8.
88. John M. Budd, "Interlibrary Loan Service: A Study of Turnaround Time," *RQ* 26 (Fall 1986): 79; Information Systems Consultants, Inc., "Resource Sharing," 4.
89. Information Systems Consultants, Inc., "Resource Sharing," IV–9.
90. Ibid.
91. Research Libraries Group, Inc., "Research Libraries Group Interlibrary Loan Cost Study," I–4—I–9.
92. Fay Turner, "The Interlibrary Loan Protocol: An OSI Solution to ILL Messaging," *Library Hi Tech* 8, no. 4 (1990): 73–82.

CHAPTER 6

Commercial Document Suppliers

For All We Take We Must Pay, But the Price Is Cruel High
(Kipling, *The Courting of Dinah Shadd*)

    I. Defining Commercial Document Supply Services   145
   II. The Rise of Document Suppliers   146
  III. Academic Libraries' Resistance to Commercial Services   149
  IV. Why Should Academic Libraries Use Document Suppliers?   153
   V. When to Use a Commercial Document Supply Service   154
  VI. ILL versus Commercial Services   155
 VII. Methods for Selecting Commercial Document Vendors   158
VIII. Types of Commercial Document Supply Services   159
      A. Collection-Based Services   160
         1. General-Interest Services   161
         2. Subject-Specific Services   165
         3. Material-Specific Services   167
      B. Cooperative Clearinghouses   168
      C. Universal or On-Demand Services   169
      D. Table of Contents Services (TOCs)   171
      E. Library Fee-Based Services   177
      F. Electronic Document Suppliers   178
      G. Full-Text Online Files   179
  IX. Choosing among Ordering Mechanisms: Some Guidelines   182
      A. Traditional Methods   182
      B. The Utilities   183
      C. Online Database Vendors   184
      D. Telefacsimile   185
   X. Document Delivery Methods   185
      A. The U.S. Mail and Courier Systems   185
      B. Telefacsimile   185
      C. Electronic Mail   186
  XI. Pricing Structures and Methods of Payment   187

A. Deposit Accounts   188
B. Invoicing   188
C. Other Methods of Payment   189

XII. Experimenting with Commercial Document Supply Services   189
  A. Before the Test Begins   189
  B. During the Experiment   191
  C. After the Experiment   191

XIII. Evaluating Commercial Document Supply Services   192
  A. Costs: How High Is Too High?   193
  B. Breadth of Coverage   194
  C. Depth of Coverage   194
  D. Ease of Ordering   195
  E. Service Response Time   195
  F. Fill Rate   195
  G. Accuracy and Document Quality   195
  H. Holdings Information   196
  I. Customer Service Support   196
  J. Other Factors   196

XIV. The Future   196

Whatever term one may choose to use—commercial document suppliers, information brokers, document delivery services, fee-based library services, or document clearinghouses—these vendors are in the business of delivering copies or facsimiles of printed information for a price. That price balanced by any subsequent benefits, including better fill rates, faster turnaround time, and improved public relations, makes commercial document services potentially attractive as alternatives to traditional ILL for document delivery.

Defining Commercial Document Supply Services

The 1991 *Information Industry Directory* lists 513 document supply services. Here, such businesses are defined as organizations that

> on a demand basis, locate, retrieve and deliver the full text of periodical articles, government documents, conference proceedings, patents, reports, and other materials requested by the

client. They include organizations providing services only from their own collections as well as organizations using publicly available sources.[1]

The variety of services is just short of mind-boggling: the ADONIS project, Chemical Abstracts Services Online (CAS), Brigham Young University's Computer Assisted Research Services, the Information Store, the Parapsychology Sources of Information Center, the Singapore Institute of Standards and Industrial Research, and the Tanzania National Documentation Centre are just a few of the vendors listed.

The *Directory* also includes 239 information-on-demand services, which it defines as

> organizations providing fee-based custom information services in client-specific areas using publicly available print and computerized information sources. Services usually include online searching; document delivery; literature compilations; library research; preparation of bibliographies; and the establishment of current awareness services.[2]

Thus, the distinction between document vendors and information-on-demand companies rests with the variety, scope, and consequent costs of the services available. Included in the second category are the Chase Manhattan Bank, N.A. Library, the National Legal Research Group, InfoQuest, BiblioData, and Facts Found Fast.

Other distinctive characteristics of commercial document services are identified by Douglas P. Hurd and Robert E. Molyneux:

> Non-library document services are generally operated for profit, do not support on-site borrowers, and are accessible in may ways, including online search services such as DIALORDER, bibliographic services such as OCLC and RLIN, electronic mail systems ... and by telephone, Telex, and mail. In addition, the cost for these services includes copyright compliance.[3]

This guide does not address full-text databases on locally mounted CD-ROMs, considering such systems to be the equivalent of paper-based journal subscriptions.

The Rise of Document Suppliers

What factors have contributed to the growth of the commercial document supply industry? For libraries, the sheer number and escalating costs of journal and document titles, the perceived inadequacies of interlibrary loan, and a growing realization of the true costs of interlending have had a major impact.[4] Technological advances, a drop in the cost of telecommunications, the use of telefacsimile for document transmission, and readers' new-found information awareness (the result of OPACs and electronic citation databases)—each has contributed in no small way. However, academic libraries should probably thank their colleagues, corporate and special librarians, for the large number of services available today.

Special and corporate libraries mushroomed in the late 1970s and 1980s, when businesses began to see distinct advantages to having libraries and qualified librarians as information collectors and deliverers. Not only was it prestigious to be able to include such services in a company's brochure, but in many instances the company with a library was perceived as having a certain "edge" over its competition. Without formal networks or interlibrary loan relationships to fall back on, the libraries found the direct purchase of documents to be an efficient means of providing access to information:

> Eventually libraries, especially small corporate libraries, began to use more commercial services as they often had such limited staffs that resource sharing with other libraries was a more time consuming option than the direct purchase of needed documents."[5]

It should prove interesting to see what happens to this "high-priced" industry in the recessionary 1990s, as commercial document services (including fee-based services in academic libraries) advertise themselves as "alternatives" to in-house corporate libraries.

As might be expected, the development of commercial services has mirrored the technological advances we have seen in ILL. For example, accessing University Microfilms International (UMI) through DIALOG for citation verification and DIALORDER for ordering is, in principle, no different from verifying and requesting an item through OCLC's ILL subsystem. As Connie Miller and Patricia Tegler observe:

> Commercial suppliers were a natural extension of the development of online bibliographic databases just as electronic ILL subsystems were a natural extension of the development of on-line cataloging systems. Each represented a step toward utilizing bibliographic finding tools as instruments of document supply. Each represented the technological improvement of one segment of the complex process of transferring a physical item

from one location to another and into the hands of an individual requestor, the segment that involves transmitting the request to the source of supply.6

Sue Kennedy defines a number of specific technological advances in the last decade that have transformed commercial document delivery in the United States:

1. The major commercial online search services—BRS, DIALOG, and SDC—all offer document ordering capabilities.
2. Commercial document suppliers promote telefacsimile transmission as a special delivery option.
3. Full-text databases online and on optical disk represent an alternative source of document supply not dependent on resource sharing.
4. There has been growth in the bibliographic utilities and increased acceptance of their associated ILL and document supply capabilities.7

In conjunction with technological innovation, information delivery has also experienced the purely evolutionary changes suggested by Richard W. Boss and Judy McQueen's 1983 study of document delivery: a gradual increase in the number and percentage of documents provided by commercial document suppliers, and a heightened awareness that the delivery of documents is the time-consuming element in the ILL system.8 Although times have changed since the early 1980s and new delivery options such as telefacsimile, text scanning, and electronic file transfer now exist, many libraries have not integrated the services or the technologies into their access units' day-to-day operation.

In another projection from the early 1980s, the Library of Congress Network Advisory Committee estimated that between 1981 and 1986 there would be gradual but nonrevolutionary changes in the document delivery process driven by one simple factor: technology. The committee concluded that:

1. The number of private sector document copy providers will not increase dramatically. Those that exist will be the ones that provide responsive and competitively priced services. As more and more libraries charge for document delivery and as these charges increase, the cost differential of acquiring a document from a public source versus the private sector will decrease appreciably.
2. The amount of for-free document delivery will diminish. Libraries or their readers will be paying more, not less, for document delivery.

3. There will be a gradual shift to telefacsimile for document delivery, but the percent of the total number of copies delivered will be low.
4. Only a few publishers will provide electronic delivery of full-text, since the revenue from document delivery cannot support the cost of full-text storage.[9]

The committee was incorrect in its estimate of the numbers of commercial services (in 1980, there were approximately 140; by 1987 there were 269; and by 1991 the number had doubled yet again), but otherwise it was accurate in its industrywide projections: for-free document delivery is rapidly becoming an anomaly rather than the norm.[10]

Academic Libraries' Resistance to Commercial Services

Librarians direct a number of criticisms at commercial document services; these are both practical and philosophical.

1. Turnaround time is not significantly faster than traditional ILL, unless the library is willing to pay an exorbitant delivery fee.
2. Fill rate and document quality are no better than those available through ILL.
3. The high cost is not accompanied by enhancements (turnaround time, fill rate, or document quality) that justify the use of commercial services.
4. Paying the profit-making sector for information, when the library is upheld as the information storehouse, runs counter to a lengthy tradition of access to "free" information held so dear by many librarians.

Every library will choose to use traditional ILL methods when a document can be obtained free of charge, expeditiously, and with little effort. But as Barbara Quint points out:

> In the search for "free" interlibrary loan, staff often overlook the internal costs. Since many ILL departments have not undertaken cost studies to determine their borrowing costs, it is easy to assert that it costs less to order from another library than from a document supplier. This may well be false economy.[11]

From the brokers' point of view the idea that information is in any way "free" is delusionary at best. It is important to keep in mind that document supply services and interlending may not be so very different from one another: indeed, many libraries charge for loans and photocopies.[12] Commercial services do not see themselves as undermining a library's information mission; in their own eyes, they are not "natural enemies" but supplements to the existing library system.[13] Perhaps we should ask ourselves whether another academic institution undercuts our access to information by charging us $15 for a loan. Do we undermine our own credibility as "free" information providers by charging $2 for a photocopy (just to keep frivolous requests at a minimum, of course)? Are we in competition with fee-based services, or are we the major consumers of their wares?

Many studies of commercial services have begun with the assumption that these concerns are thriving because they are all that they advertise; yet these examinations often conclude on a depressingly familiar note: in many cases, fee-based services are no better than they should be. Miller and Tegler's study of the use of commercial document supply services at the University of Illinois at Chicago began with high expectations:

> Since a systematic and relatively effective, even if unstructured and never centrally coordinated, interlibrary loan system has been functioning among United States libraries for nearly one hundred years, and since commercial document suppliers have sprung up only over the last two decades, we concluded that the latter's existence was directly related to the former's performance. It was assumed that commercial suppliers materialized to fill a service void, and that they proliferated because they could supply documents more quickly than libraries were supplying them to each other.[14]

The study tested the following hypotheses:

1. Commercial document supply services can provide better service than traditional ILL.
2. The documents will arrive more quickly and ordering will be easier and less time-consuming.
3. The higher charges will lead to faster turnaround time.
4. Local suppliers will have a better turnaround time than those located some distance from the requesting library.
5. Foreign language materials, materials published before 1970, and technical reports will arrive more slowly and cost more than other materials.
6. Cost, speed, and fill rate will vary according to subject matter.

To test these assumptions, the researchers ordered 165 documents from two different commercial suppliers that had already been successfully obtained through traditional ILL services. In order to gain experience with a variety of vendors, in each case the two were chosen from a pool of eleven that included five database-specific suppliers and six general suppliers.

> [The results] destroyed the notion that commercial document supply represents a solution to the problems hampering efficient interlibrary loan service. It also destroyed the tendency to view borrowing among libraries and borrowing commercially from nonlibrary suppliers as distinctly different processes.[15]

The commercial document suppliers were no faster (special services, such as overnight delivery, were not used) than the interlibrary loan process. The higher per-item cost did not visibly enhance the service. Locally based suppliers were just as slow as distant ones, and so-called hard-to-find items were not hard to find nor did they cost more. Finally, the cost, speed of supply, and fill rate did not vary significantly among subject areas (although engineering-related materials were somewhat more difficult to fill). Ordering through DIALOG proved to be a complex task requiring a highly skilled searcher with considerable experience. The authors concluded that the same inertia (and regressive reader expectations) that prevent a marked improvement in ILL infects commercial services as well.[16]

Conversely, other studies have concluded that commercial services are an economical and efficient source for needed documents. At the University of Texas at Austin (UT), overcoming "pride of ownership" was one of the first steps to be taken when the General Libraries considered purchasing articles rather than subscribing to the journals themselves. The science librarians at UT hypothesized that purchasing articles from commercial document suppliers might be more cost-effective than subscribing to infrequently used titles.[17] After a three-month pilot study in which selected commercial suppliers, including the National Technical Information Service (NTIS), Chemical Abstracts Services Online (CAS), and Global, were used to order articles from journals the library did not own, the researchers concluded that:

> If only 20 infrequently used journals with an average subscription price of $200 per year were cancelled, the resulting savings could be used to purchase 415 articles. Commercial document delivery would provide a method of cost containment and information on collection development. In addition, as a long-term strategy it would offer greater flexibility in space and facilities management.[18]

Other important results of the pilot project included improved public relations, better staff morale in the face of a serials cancellation project, an enhanced understanding of document delivery processes, and concrete data with which to make responsible collection development decisions. Kathleen Halsey's study of UMI's document supply service, which is discussed later in this chapter, concluded that commercial firms specializing in a particular subject, such as CAS, have a better potential for improving document delivery services.

The desire to get the document to the reader faster appears to be the main impetus for studying the viability of commercial document supply services. And yet Gary D. Wiggins's often-cited study comparing the document delivery mechanisms of academic libraries to those of corporate libraries concludes otherwise. Although both academic and corporate librarians were more concerned about speed than costs, only the corporate librarians seriously considered confirmation time, turnaround time, "rush" or call-in order capabilities, and deposit or charge accounts when considering the use of a commercial service.[19] The cost of the item was not the most important factor in either type of library (66 percent of the academic librarians surveyed passed along the charges to the reader while only 37 percent of the corporate libraries did). Thus, academic libraries may claim that turnaround time and cost are significant factors in the decision to utilize a particular ILL partner or commercial service, but evidence shows we continue to resist full-fledged use of commercial services, even when they have proven to be service enhancers.

Libraries may not use commercial services for other quite sensible reasons: the lack of funds to cover more than incremental ILL charges; the sheer number of potential commercial sources and the consequent problems of overlapping coverage; complex pricing schemes; and strikingly different indexing, searching, and ordering protocols. Just as with interlending partners, the universe of potential suppliers may appear boundless, but limiting the group to a select few that can do what the library wants, when it wants it, can streamline the decision-making process.

Commercial services are sometimes criticized for filling the easiest (and therefore the most profitable) orders and leaving the "tough nuts" for ILL units. And a few librarians have observed that commercial services are more *reliable* when filling "easy" requests rather than "difficult" requests.[20] Yet other librarians believe in the overall benefits of document vendors and especially in their positive impact on traditional ILL: the advent of commercial services has removed some of the burden of interlending from the library community, slowing the increase in the number of ILL requests received by libraries.[21]

Libraries that continue to feel justified in resisting the services offered by these commercial suppliers may be reassured by Miller and Tegler's ironic fantasy:

> The requests for widely and readily available materials presently clogging ILL channels could be sent instead to commercial suppliers, increasing demand to such an extent that these profit-oriented businesses would be forced to improve their mediocre performance.[22]

Yet, poor performance on the part of some commercial services has not stopped the growth of the industry. A more formal examination of the services and a more vocal library community are needed to determine their future place within the overall structure of document delivery in academic libraries.

Why Should Academic Libraries Use Document Suppliers?

David B. Allen and Johanna Alexander have identified a number of possible reasons for the regular use of commercial document services:

1. The use of such suppliers does not demand reciprocal responsibilities (as does ILL), other than payment.
2. Commercial suppliers usually take care of copyright compliance.
3. Such services have a single function—to supply documents—and usually do it efficiently.
4. For-profit services either have large noncirculating collections or access to a variety of collections along with published holdings data for easy identification of available materials.
5. Many services are available electronically through mechanisms (bibliographic utilities and database services) already functioning within the library.
6. All suppliers have reliable and flexible accounting and billing functions in place.
7. Access to full-text databases is growing by leaps and bounds and document supply services are generally attached to them.

8. The potentially higher costs of commercial services are offset by the potential for better service.
9. Discounts and group rates for library consortia are available from most services.
10. Most fee-based services offer a variety of delivery mechanisms, telefacsimile and e-mail the most effective among them.[23]

In addition, support of commercial services may enhance existing local library information services by validating serials expenditures and cancellations, allowing access to new materials the library may not be justified in ordering, and improving collection management by providing usage data.

When to Use a Commercial Document Supply Service

The first step the library should take is to examine its ILL patterns. If any of the following points hold true, a library may choose to consider commercial document services:

1. A "free" ILL partner, or a for-fee partner who charges less than the commercial service, cannot provide the material.
2. The request may have to be sent to ILL partners with which the library has no ties; hence, delivery may be unpredictable as well as untimely.
3. The staff time spent locating a free lender is more costly than quickly dispatching the order to a commercial service.
4. The request will cause the library to exceed copyright compliance guidelines.
5. The library has deliberately decided to cut back on ILL by buying more and depending less on lenders, thus freeing the library from reciprocal lending responsibilities.
6. A request has remained unfilled through ILL channels.
7. The library cannot verify the citation.
8. Requests in a particular subject area or for a certain material type have proven difficult to verify and locate through regular ILL routines.
9. The cost of a document from a vendor is appreciably more than ILL, but are there trade-offs, for example, faster service or more efficient delivery mechanisms.

ILL versus Commercial Services

By comparing the steps involved in traditional ILL, from verification to reader notification, with those of commercial document ordering, we can see that there are procedural improvements as well as drawbacks.

Verification: The process of verifying the bibliographic accuracy of a reader's citation.

The process of verifying a citation will not change appreciably when the library uses a document vendor. These points should be considered:

1. A vendor may charge an extra fee for filling an unverified request; however, many potential ILL partners will not even attempt to process one.
2. A vendor may charge an extra fee for filling requests with incorrect citations, whether through a reader's mistake in transcription error or a library error.
3. A vendor may not attempt to correct a mistaken citation (as an ILL partner might do); the order simply remains unfilled.

If the citation cannot be verified, let the service know at the time the order is placed; give the complete citation, and list the verification tools that were checked. This can save the service time in redundant searching.

Locating: The process of locating a potential supplier.

1. Many collection-based services have loaded their holdings into OCLC; others publish lists of their titles and coverage. Thus, the process of choosing an appropriate service has been greatly simplified.
2. If the library orders through a database (OCLC, for example) with document delivery capability, time will be saved in both verification and location.
3. If the library orders an online full-text printout, the entire ILL process of confirmation and document delivery will be eliminated.
4. Using an on-demand service as a "wild card" for difficult requests may be worth the extra expense when balanced against the staff time consumed locating an appropriate ILL partner.

5. Collection-based services may publish that they hold a particular issue of a journal but, just as with ILL partners, it can be missing from the collection, the service may not have permission to photocopy from it, or there may be copyright restrictions. The lack of issue-level holdings data continues to be a problem for both ILL and commercial services.
6. The problem of identifying sources that will supply "restricted" ILL materials, for example, microfilms and theses, can be eliminated using a commercial service that specializes in these materials.

Requesting: The process of preparing and transmitting the request.

1. If the library uses a utility to order, the process will be no different from placing an ILL request.
2. If the library uses a database vendor to order, considerable time may be saved in preparing the request if the citation has been identified online. It may be important to conserve connect time by using less expensive files with no delivery service to identify a citation, and the more expensive document delivery file to order.
3. If the library manually completes a service's order form, or an ALA ILL form, it should be prepared to fax the request, or send it by special courier, when time is a factor.
4. While many libraries will not take requests over the telephone, commercial services will; in some cases they will process this kind of request more quickly than an electronic one.
5. Some services will accept printouts, handwritten orders, or a photocopy of a bibliography as an order form.
6. For services that require system-based identification numbers (Biological Abstracts' document reference number, for example), the time spent searching and finding this code may well be worth the effort if surcharges are levied for requests missing the element.

Confirmation: The process of confirming availability.

1. Commercial services usually do not confirm, they ship. If the request cannot be filled, some services mail a statement of nonfulfillment, which can lead to lengthy delays.

2. Services that provide e-mail status reports may alleviate periods of uncertainty between document request and delivery.
3. Although ordering from a vendor through a utility may take the same amount of time as an ILL request, confirmation from a vendor (University Microfilms, Inc. (UMI), for example) will probably come within forty-eight hours rather than the four- to five-day "grace" period established by the utility for its member libraries.

Fulfillment: The process of preparing the request for shipment.

The process of photocopying, packaging, billing, and dispatching an item is the same for ILL and commercial services. But vendors, and especially collection-based services, may have streamlined the process to save time and money; undoubtedly, they will have more equipment and personnel than the small academic library.

Delivery: The process of transmitting the item from supplier to requesting library.

1. If the vendor uses the U. S. postal system for document delivery, there will be no time saved (and perhaps time lost) over traditional ILL.
2. As with ILL, if time is important, many vendors can fax the item or deliver it by courier. The sometimes high cost of fax transmission will have to be weighed against the advantages of same-day or overnight delivery, unless the library and vendor can communicate, for example, through the Internet.
3. Printing online from a full-text database is probably the most efficient means of document delivery, but the costs of connect time (waiting for a full-text article to print out online is rather like watching the proverbial pot; it seems to take forever) may be prohibitive.
4. In some cases, it is possible to have the vendor print the document offline and deliver it through o mail the next day; charges for this type of delivery are much more reasonable.
5. If the library does not have telefacsimile or electronic mail capability, the use of special couriers may be necessary to expedite "rush" requests. In some cases, the fee for overnight delivery can be less than the vendor's surcharge for faxed materials.

Reader notification: The process of notifying the reader he or she may pick up the document.

Unless the document is shipped directly to the reader, there will be little difference in time and effort between ILL and commercial services.

Administration: The process of monitoring usage, evaluating services, and determining future applications of commercial services.
1. Billing and accounting may prove to be more cumbersome than "free" ILLs unless the library has deposit accounts or efficient procedures for processing invoices.
2. If the library has many vendor requests in process, a tracking mechanism developed to alert the library to possible delays, non-fills, and items lost in the mail will be useful.
3. The maintenance of a separate and detailed set of performance statistics may be necessary.

Methods for Selecting Commercial Document Vendors

It has been suggested that "familiarity with commercial suppliers is an important factor in deciding when paying higher direct costs may be the best course among several options for obtaining a document."[24] Accordingly, librarians may decide to take such steps as these:
1. Talk to libraries that are using commercial document services on a regular basis about their experiences.
2. Go to workshops and conferences and talk with the vendors themselves.
3. Read journal advertisements and articles relating to particular services.
4. Read the documentation related to commercial vendors that accompanies a bibliographic utility's services.
5. Experiment with services that are easily accessed, then investigate alternative options. Smaller commercial services may offer special discounts or other features in order to increase their business.
6. Order and read the fine print of any service's brochures or written agreements.

In 1978, Georgia Finnigan and Sue Rugge of Information Unlimited developed a user's checklist for determining the best document supply services. Fifteen years later, with the exception of the introduction of unforeseen technological developments, their requirements have remained remarkably stable:

> Speed: Turnaround time should be less than a week. Materials from overseas should arrive within two weeks. A service should report immediately if there are to be delays.
>
> Low rates and charges per piece: Charges should be by the piece and the page, and not by the hour of vendor time. Some services charge by the staff-hour and the requester cannot know the charge until it is too late to stop a very expensive order. (Hourly rates may be very high. For instance, Purdue's fee-based library service charges $40 per hour to fill document requests from in-state clients and $80 per hour for out-of-state clients.[25])
>
> Forms: Suppliers should not require special forms or coupons that can be time-consuming to complete and burdensome to maintain.
>
> Verification: Users should not be required to verify a citation, although to do so can be helpful to the supplier. Fees for verification are acceptable if reasonable.
>
> "Rush" and telephone orders: Services should handle emergency requests routinely. Fees for special services (for example, courier service and overnight mail) are acceptable.
>
> Deposit/charge accounts: Demand for prepayment of orders is only acceptable if the supplier also offers deposit or charge accounts.[26]

Today academic libraries will also be looking for published holdings information from collection-based services, special pricing structures, the ability to negotiate discounts, electronic status reports, management reports, customer service support, and the seamless union of online catalogs and citation databases with a variety of ordering and delivery options— including the electronic delivery of information directly to the reader.

Types of Commercial Document Supply Services

Susan K. Martin observes that the present document supplier market is anything but simple to grasp. "Not all publishers are suppliers, not all suppliers are publishers, and the confusion expands to fill the available possibilities."[27] In every case, it is important to remember that commercial services are in business either to make money or (in the case of some services) to break even. There is a service for everyone; it is simply a matter of identifying those that are able to fill the local library's information needs with consistency and flexibility. If the library is dissatisfied with one service, there are countless others from which to choose:

> For the private sector, non-library suppliers, the document delivery business is highly competitive. Not only are these organizations competing with libraries and public sector services (e.g., the Government Printing Office, the National Technical Information Service, the Educational Research Information Center, and the U. S. Patent and Trademark Office), they compete with each other. To assure a market niche, some tailor their services to specific kinds of documents, e.g., government reports and patents, others back up specific bibliographic databases, while still others provide generalized document delivery services.[28]

This guide examines five types of commercial document services: private, nonlibrary suppliers that maintain collections of originals; private, nonlibrary suppliers that draw from the collections of others; cooperative clearinghouses; table of contents services; and fee-based library services. The following examination of commercial services should in no way be viewed as endorsing an individual company; rather the vendors described have been chosen simply for the variety of features they represent and, in some cases, for their uniqueness. The availability of published studies was also a selection factor. Prices (which can change) are included to give readers some basis for comparison.

Collection-Based Services

Collection-based services in the United States "typically leverage their document delivery service off of another primary product"; that is, the in-house collections from which documents are photocopied were originally designed to support other activities, such as abstracting and indexing services or microform republishing.[29] Value-added services, such as document delivery, were adopted as a profitable means of meeting subscribers' rising demand for information. Although the services are competitively priced, they are limited in the depth and breadth of their collections. There is also the problem of identifying the availability of the material (even when published holdings exist).[30] These services can be further distinguished by their collections: general-interest, subject-specific, and material-specific.

General-Interest Services

UMI Article Clearinghouse   The UMI Article Clearinghouse was developed by University Microfilms International to provide a centralized source of article photocopies in the United States. Most libraries are aware that UMI provides access to doctoral dissertations and masters' theses, as well as serials in microfilm. The Article Clearinghouse is a natural extension to these microfilming services; rather than supplying entire rolls of film or fiche, the service provides hard copy of articles from its stock. Since its introduction in 1983, UMI's collection has expanded to more than 12,500 titles, including journals, magazines, conference proceedings, newspapers, and government documents. Its subject coverage is broad, ranging from general interest publications to highly specialized scientific and technical titles. Publications are added to the clearinghouse based on customer demand and frequency of citation.

The clearinghouse was designed to meet three document supply imperatives: speed, broad coverage, and affordability. It has focused its marketing on communities that include libraries (particularly OCLC's GAC members), information brokers, and individual readers who can access UMI online using clearinghouse-designed software. The service advertises forty-eight-hour turnaround service for articles it supplies that were published within the last five years; it strives to ship pre-1987 materials within four business days.

All orders are shipped by first-class mail unless "rush" delivery is specified. "Rush" requests can be processed in three different ways: "rush" first-class promises twenty-four-hour processing with first-class mail delivery; "rush" overnight combines twenty-four-hour processing with shipment through an overnight courier; and "Artifax" offers same-day or overnight fax transmission. There are twelve different methods of accessing the service including DIALOG's DIALORDER, OCLC, BRS, and telex. The clearinghouse also accepts telephone requests, ALA forms, and UMI order forms.

Articles can be paid for in three different ways: prepayment (check or money order) by individuals and institutions, credit cards, or through a deposit account established either for single or multiple institutions. If a group or institution orders more than one thousand articles a year, there is an additional high-volume discount. Complete journal issues are available for $45 each; here the average turnaround time is about four weeks. For libraries concerned about copyright compliance, multiples of any photocopy may be ordered for an additional $2.25 each.

Kathleen F. Halsey conducted a study at the University of Wisconsin-Stevens Point (UW-SP) to determine whether the Article Clearinghouse could serve as an effective and efficient alternative to using UW-SP's traditional source, Wisconsin Interlibrary Services (WILS), for filling photocopy requests. One hundred twenty-four identical articles were ordered almost simultaneously from UMI and WILS; for thirty-seven consecutive working days, data were recorded to evaluate collection coverage, fill rates, turnaround time, document quality, and direct cost per article. The study considered the following questions in comparing UMI to traditional ILL as represented by WILS:

Did the Article Clearinghouse's collection of journals meet the library's needs?

Nearly 40 percent of the total number of requests the library received during the thirty-seven-day period were ineligible for inclusion in the study because the titles were not owned by UMI. Unavailable articles fell most often in the subject areas of medical science, psychology, education, chemistry, biology, and literature. Only twelve requests were considered ineligible because WILS libraries could not supply them.

Did UMI have an equal or better fill rate than WILS?

WILS was able to fill all 124 requests, UMI only 118. When the clearinghouse was unsuccessful, it was because the journal volume was not available; the year was not available; permission to reprint had not been granted; or UMI was unable to "locate" the article (although WILS obviously could).

Did UMI's turnaround time compare favorably to WILS's?

The mean number of days from request to delivery was 5.59 for Article Clearinghouse and 5.33 for WILS. For twelve of the articles, delivery through telefacsimile was requested. According to UMI's policy statement, any request sent before 1:30 P.M. (EST) will be delivered on the same day; all other requests are sent the next morning. Of the seven orders sent before 1:30, two arrived the same day, three the next day, and two on the third day. UMI charged an additional fee of $9 for each faxed article. Only four of the twelve requests for fax delivery sent through WILS were actually delivered by telefacsimile (in the other cases, the libraries holding the item had no fax machine); each of these arrived the day following the request.

Were the photocopies provided by each supplier of acceptable quality?

In every case WILS and UMI sent the right articles; however, in four instances each sent incomplete documents. For one of the articles, the Article Clearinghouse told the library to expect the missing pages by Federal Express on the following day. Instead, a complete copy of the item arrived four days later through first-class mail. There were legibility problems in seventeen of the Article Clearinghouse documents and thirty-one of those from WILS.[31]

Were UMI's charges competitive with WILS's?
The average direct invoiced charge for the WILS documents was $4.45, and $5.35 for the clearinghouse. Because of a billing mix-up (although a deposit account had been set up and the proper account number was listed on each request, UMI continued to bill the library under a previously established, less expensive multi-institutional account with WILS), the study's cost analysis of the commercial firm was made more difficult. If the library had been properly billed under the single institution account, the average cost per article would have been $8.42. With UMI there were also repeated instances of inconsistent billing, such as charges for unrequested multiple copies, failure to charge for telefacsimile transmission, and assessing "rush first-class" fees for faxing missing pages![32]

To summarize, the results of this study show that the Article Clearinghouse, when compared to WILS, performed less effectively in collection coverage and fill rate, provided copies of similar quality, equaled but did not better the turnaround time of the traditional source, and charged significantly more per article. Thus, the services of the commercial document supply firm provided no clear advantage.[33]

A second study of UMI's performance conducted by Information Systems Consultants, Inc. (ISCI) indicated that the commercial supplier could, for a higher price and with some unpredictability (the authors generously note that personnel changes at UMI could have been the cause of some of the "inconsistencies"), supply documents faster than their traditional ILL partners. UMI's limited holdings and the need to place a substantial deposit in order to obtain discounted prices were seen as possible disadvantages for some libraries.[34] A recent effort by UMI to strengthen its position in the article delivery market, a link with the H. W. Wilson's periodical indexes, which many libraries have already merged with their online catalogs, was announced in a 1992 press release. The link will allow authorized readers to identify journal articles through their OPACs and place a document order at the same time.[35] UMI has also become OCLC's first supplier for its document delivery service, ArticleFirst.

BLDSC   Probably the best-known general document supply service in the world, the British Library Document Supply Centre (BLDSC) satisfies the majority of the United Kingdom's library requests; in the past few years, its U.S. market has burgeoned, owing to its availability through such popular mechanisms as OCLC, RLIN, and CARL. The centre was initially created to serve the scientific, economic, and technological needs of the country; a descendent of the Lending Library for Science and Technology established in 1962, the BLDSC's collection has since expanded to include the social sciences and the humanities.

The British system is highly centralized; in most cases if an item cannot be supplied locally, e.g., by a county or metropolitan library system or campus library, the request is supplied by the centre and its system of backup libraries. The preferred method of payment is coupons purchased in blocks (U.S. requesters may establish deposit accounts) that are used not only for BLDSC requests but are also used to compensate regional lenders; for each photocopy or loan it makes at the centre's behest, the lender receives a BLDSC credit coupon to be used at its discretion. Thus, the centre becomes a "bank" and the coupons are the currency.[36] The cost of a document from the BLDSC is surprising low in the UK because the centre does not recover the full cost of its operations.[37]

The centre holds two hundred thousand journal titles, three million reports, five hundred thousand theses, three hundred thousand conference proceedings, and three million books. Orders to the United States are processed and dispatched by air within forty-eight hours of receipt (the centre will also ship a document by fax, courier, telex, or satellite). The cost of a document of ten pages or less is $9; if desired, a copyright compliance fee of $2.25 may be added to the total cost. The centre offers a variety of priority services, although the cost of a fax service, such as the Urgent Action Service ($54 for ten pages or less), may be prohibitively expensive. The BLDSC is available to U.S. libraries as a separate file in DIALOG, CARL Systems' UnCover and UnCover2, and through OCLC, now in the process of loading the centre's serials holdings into its online catalog.

While there is a strong belief within the UK in the BLDSC's efficiency and cost-effectiveness, COPEMAL (the Co-Operative Project East Midlands Academic Libraries) sought to examine the cost-effectiveness of using the centre: "Could the five major academic libraries of the East Midlands with their combined stock approaching 3 million volumes provide a cheaper or more cost effective service from their own resources rather than the BLDSC"?[38] In the academic year 1986–87 approximately seventy thousand ILLs were generated by the five libraries. Almost all were channeled to the BLDSC, achieving a 90 percent fill rate. At a cost of £2.725 per loan (less than $5 at 1992 exchange rates), plus local staff time, the cost of document supply for the five libraries was over £300,000.

A detailed analysis of ILL traffic was undertaken, which included the cooperative's ability to fill requests, the timeliness of document supply procedures, and costs associated with each operation. Results indicated that 26 percent of the loans sent to the BLDSC could have been filled by one or more of the five libraries. The study determined mean times of twenty-two minutes to process a monograph from loan to return-to-shelf, and twenty minutes to process a photocopy request. At a salary base of close to £5 per hour, it was found that the libraries would have lost almost £400 in processing the requests themselves. The mean response time for fills and non-fills proved to be about five days for both systems. The research demonstrated that in "strict cost terms alone, given ideal circumstances, a regional scheme based on the East Midlands academic libraries would not offer any significant saving."[39]

Results of studies such as these can inspire vaguely nostalgic feelings in the hearts of U.S. librarians. Our failure to organize a National Periodicals Center or a National Coupon System patterned after the hugely successful British one somehow smacks of a failure of will, or a paralyzing inability to place national over local interests. The American system is indeed complex and expensive; it is our job to find the simplest and least expensive means of maneuvering through it.

Subject-Specific Services

ISI's The Genuine Article For more than thirty years the Institute for Scientific Information (ISI) has been producing indexing/abstracting tools like Current Contents from its in-house collection for the scientific, academic, and business community. Its delivery service, The Genuine Article, supplies articles from over six thousand journals published during the current year and the past four calendar years. The service is promoted as a comprehensive, multidisciplinary source of full-text articles, but academic libraries may be more interested in its science-based research materials.

ISI receives several copies of each journal issue; when an order for a specific article is received, it is torn directly from the journal, ensuring visual clarity and completeness (clarity being of particular importance to the scientific community). Fifty percent of the articles shipped in 1990 were these tear sheets. When a tear sheet is not available, the article is photocopied. If the quality of the photocopy does not meet the reader's needs, the price of the document is refunded. Royalty fees assessed by publishers necessitate surcharges of varying amounts for photocopies and, in some cases, the tear sheets as well. Some journal articles cannot be photocopied; if a tear sheet is unavailable, the requester is notified that the article cannot be supplied.

Items can be ordered through the mail using almost any convenient device, including checked-off copies of bibliographies, computer printouts, or The Genuine Article's order cards. An ISI accession number (taken from its indexing/abstracting tools), the author, and the first page number of the article are the only items of information the service requires. A library can also order by telex; online through DIALOG, ORBIT, BRS, or OCLC; or by telefacsimile, telephone, or electronic mail. Orders are usually shipped within forty-eight hours. However, telephone orders are shipped within twenty-four hours. A thirty-minute fax service is available with a $10. 50 surcharge, levied on top of the $10.25 to $10.70 paid for each group of ten or fewer pages.

ISI offers a number of payment options, including annual contract accounts for libraries that can guarantee over twelve hundred requests a year; deposit accounts with monthly invoicing; and open accounts for sporadic ordering and item-level billing. Each plan has its own pricing schedule, but prepaid contract accounts receive the highest discounts. The service can issue statistical reports and provides customer service representatives. ISI's holdings have been loaded into OCLC and are identified by the holdings symbol TGA.

After three successive years of serials cancellations, the Iowa State University Libraries elected to use ISI to provide readers with rapid access to articles appearing in thirty-four canceled titles; even after paying ISI's charges, the libraries recovered much of the subscription costs of the canceled journals. The libraries subscribed to ISI's "ASCA" table of contents service. At a cost of $12 each, ISI provided copies of the tables of contents for each of the canceled titles. Copies were distributed weekly to branch libraries, where they were filed in a notebook and placed on the shelf where the journal was previously housed.

The second part of the project was designed to provide users with a prompt and dependable method of retrieving the articles from the table of contents lists. The libraries decided that using ILL would not be fast enough and that copyright compliance might become a problem. Thus, they decided to use ISI as a document supply service as well as a supplier of table of contents lists. When a reader wished to see an article, the request was telephoned in immediately. Turnaround time was one week or less, and the entire process was handled in the branch libraries, rather than through the centralized ILL office. Fees were not recovered from readers; instead, the costs were charged to the individual branch library's acquisitions budget. At the time of the project, ISI charged $8.95 per article of ten pages or less. The libraries found this method of "cost-effective" current awareness and quick document delivery "to compare favorably with interlibrary loan costs per article."[40]

Material-Specific Services

NTIS Most librarians are already familiar with material-specific sources such as UMI for theses and doctoral dissertations. The U.S. National Technical Information Service (NTIS) is the central source for the public dissemination of U.S. government-sponsored research, development, and engineering reports, as well as foreign technical reports and other types of analyses prepared by government agencies. In support of its mission NTIS maintains the NTIS Bibliographic Database, which contains abstracts of all the materials it supplies. Access is through BRS, DIALOG, and SDC, and all documents may be ordered from NTIS on fiche or in paper format.

A 1986–1987 study at the McKinney Engineering Library at the University of Texas at Austin sought to assess the use, cost, and effectiveness of the NTIS document supply program as compared to NTIS's Selected Research in Microfiche (SRIM) service, which automatically selects and distributes full-text reports from the nearly four hundred primary and secondary technological, sociological, scientific, engineering, and business-related subject categories determined by a customer. When the subscription to SRIM was canceled as part of a general serials cancellation project, the library decided to devise a means of providing documents to satisfy both readers' needs and the library's budgetary constraints. The library maintained subscriptions to full-text reports from two agencies and initiated a pilot project to provide on-demand document delivery of NTIS reports not available in the local collections. By comparing the two systems, the library could make informed decisions about whether to continue the document supply service, cancel the document supply service and campaign for the return of the SRIM service, or create a hybrid of both programs.

Reports were ordered online through direct dial-up to NTIS's QuikORDER service, a facility designed to minimize turnaround time and provide online verification of document availability and price. Documents were sent directly to the Engineering Library, which either notified the reader by telephone or sent the document directly to her or him. "When the dust settled," it was *felt* that the old SRIM program, with its unit cost one-fifth that of an individually ordered title, was more cost-effective, "in fact, a real deal."[41] But as it turned out, this was a false impression.

The NTIS document supply program proved to be a far more cost-effective approach than SRIM collection building. The item cost through the document supply service was six and a half times that of SRIM's, but the cost per use of SRIM documents was nearly five times that of those acquired individually through document delivery. Because of the sheer number of SRIM documents published in a year to which the library could *not* afford to subscribe, it was "very difficult and costly to anticipate such demand through collection building."[42] In other words, the staff could not focus its SRIM profile sharply enough to avoid receiving and paying for many low-use or unused documents. The library concluded that document supply should continue with careful monitoring of its future usage to determine whether subscriptions should be placed for any particular agency's publications. Of the major criteria for evaluating the program—cost, fill-rate, and turnaround time—the last named was found to be the chief weakness of the document supply service. The library determined that a reader-subsidized "rush" delivery mechanism might be the best solution to the rather slow delivery time.

Cooperative Clearinghouses

USBE If copyright compliance is in jeopardy, or a reader requests multiple articles from a single issue of a journal title, a library can choose to purchase an entire issue rather than paying for individual photocopies. One source for whole-issue purchasing is the Universal Serials and Book Exchange (USBE), a Cleveland-based clearinghouse for national and international serial publications of a scholarly or professional nature. It is a nonprofit corporation whose services are restricted to member libraries. USBE's stock consists of approximately five million back issues representing fifteen thousand serial titles, with emphasis on current materials in the areas of medicine, science, the social sciences, and the humanities. Members of USBE pay an annual fee ($150) and contribute their duplicate and surplus publications to the exchange. It is with these contributions that the USBE stocks its shelves; hence, the service has varying quantities of periodicals and cannot guarantee that a specific issue is in stock. Membership enables a library to order any back issue at a cost of $7, regardless of publication date, subject, or original subscription price (certainly a far cry from UMI's $45 fee). Entire journal volumes may also be ordered for $28, as well as sets and runs of periodicals (at $7 an issue). Users periodically receive the "Shelf List of Back Issues," a list of regularly stocked titles. USBE does not stock titles of local or regional interest, newsletters, or newspapers that are not recognized by the major indexing services. Also, USBE maintains only Roman alphabet publications. Members may order using traditional mechanisms such as telephone and the mail.[43]

Universal or On-Demand Services

A universal (on-demand; full-service) supplier usually does not maintain its own collection. According to Jeffrey Saldinger, a full-service supplier works as a "highly structured, centralized switching operation," referring each order it receives to the most effective of "several possible fulfillment sites, many of which are part of a dedicated, nationwide field network," the individuals and libraries that are the actual suppliers of the documents.[44] These on-demand suppliers will tailor their work to meet the requirements of any client. They generally do not require deposit accounts, and they will accept orders with special time requirements and receive requests in whatever form the client wishes.

> Full service document delivery is a labor-intensive, high overhead, service oriented field. Suppliers handle thousands of small-dollar-value transactions each month. They respond to a highly irregular and unpredictable incidence of single orders. They cater to the special accounting needs of large multi-site, often multinational corporations. They receive each day requests for special handling and follow-ups. They must assign experienced staff to research unique problems.[45]

These on-demand services include companies like Information on Demand, Find/SVP, Info-Mart, and the Information Store, each of which acquires copies of needed documents from established libraries. Although this group handles 70 percent of the requests processed by commercial document suppliers, academic libraries with fully developed ILL networks may find them less useful than do smaller corporate libraries that may lack this type of support.[46]

Why would an academic library choose to use an on-demand service that may be more expensive and less reliable than ILL? In most instances, the decision will be made on a case-by-case basis: can the citation be verified? Does the only other known ILL source charge more than the projected price of the on-demand service? Is the article unavailable through a collection-based service? Is it faster (thus, potentially less expensive) to immediately order a document online from Information on Demand (in BRS, for example) than to reprocess the request through a utility? The answers to these questions will help in decision making.

Information on Demand   Information on Demand (IOD) is a well-known universal supplier that fills requests for all material types and in all subject areas. It offers volume discounts and provides a 5 percent discount on all deposit accounts. The service will accept all types of orders: telephone, mail, telefacsimile, or electronic through database vendors and utilities; it also extends free electronic mail service. "Rush" orders are given priority for processing, but the method of delivery, specified by the client, is a separate matter. Priority shipping greatly increases a library's costs; for example, telefacsimile transmission is charged at $20 plus $.50 a page. Order status reports and "help" lines are available twenty-four hours a day and are free through Telnet.

Depending upon document availability, turnaround time can range from two to ten days; "rush" orders are processed in one to two working days. The price structure includes a base fee of $10 to $13, depending on the client's monthly order volume; a library must order one hundred items each month in order to maintain the $10 rate. For every item ordered, however, there are also applicable page fees, copyright fees, postal fees, service charges for unfilled orders, charges for ordering manually as opposed to electronically, and citation verification fees ($3 to $15).

Jean Currie's study of document suppliers at Cornell's Mann Library reaches familiar conclusions about the performance of a major player in the document supplier industry. Requests for 124 periodical articles were each sent to three different sources: another library, through RLIN or ALA form; a collection-based source such as ISI's The Genuine Article; and an on-demand source, Information on Demand. The study concluded that commercial requests were more expensive to fill, and that traditional ILL partners were just as fast (when using the same delivery mechanism) and had a better fill rate ("no-fills" from commercial sources were ascribed to "supply exhausted," "too old," or copyright problems). IOD proved to be "consistently" slow, the majority of requests requiring between twelve and thirty days (one request took 111 days) before they were filled. The average cost of $13.35 was $4 more than any of the collection-based services used. The study may have increased the library's flexibility in obtaining documents (particularly by using collection-based services), but it also strengthened the library's confidence in traditional ILL network efficiency.[47] (Conversely, a study done at the University of Nebraska-Omaha determined that using collection-based services, such as UMI and ISI, proved to be less useful [limited collections and slow turnaround time] than a universal supply service because the on-demand service "supplied a greater range of materials."[48])

Table of Contents Services (TOCs)

Table of contents services are among the latest products to appear on the information horizon. These services consist of three distinct features: journal citation indexes; electronic recreations of tables of contents pages for easy perusal of a journal issue's subject matter; and document ordering mechanisms. Typically, TOCs are created by scanning or keying journal issues' tables of contents into a database; descriptors and subject headings may be added.

Readers search these databases either by journal issue or the more traditional key word, author, title, and subject. When a table of contents is displayed, the reader may then choose to view information about a specific article. In many cases, the article will be locally available in the library's own collections. TOC vendors make the point that table of contents services reinforce readers' awareness of locally owned materials and increase their use, enhancing the cost-effectiveness of the library's subscriptions.[49] When the article is not available in the home library and the reader wishes to order it, he or she simply completes an on-screen order form supplying identification and method of payment (credit card, library account number). The document is then delivered (generally by telefacsimile) to the reader's library.

Journal publishers also find TOCs appealing. These systems supply them with managment data on document sales (who reads their publications?), and they represent an important new marketing tool—a way, without subscriptions, to sell their products. TOCs may also give new journal titles exposure long before their contents snake their way through complex indexing and abstracting systems.

Some wonder whether the table of contents portion of these services is a bit of a red herring. Will readers actually use TOCs to inform themselves about materials the local library does not own, or will faculty instead treat them largely as a convenient method of browsing the contents of the latest issue of their favorite journal that can (and will) be picked up at the local library on Monday morning? Rather than substitutes for at-the-shelf browsing, are TOCs the latest "information toy," designed by vendors to stimulate the imaginations or soothe the consciences of careworn and penurious librarians, general-service citation index systems with document ordering capability dressed up as something more? Time and experience will answer these questions; in the meantime, the prospect of merging TOCs and their document request capability with the local online catalog has enormous appeal to academic librarians for whom serial cancellations have become a dreaded annual rite. When OPAC and TOC screens and search commands are identical, this "one machine/many purposes" approach is even more appealing. These services are highly competitive, relatively inexpensive, and because of the guaranteed speed of delivery, may well be the ground-breakers for a truly efficient document supply system in the United States.

Providing readers direct access to a table of contents service linked to document delivery may appear to be the answer to the dreams of an overburdened ILL office. For example, for journal articles, the reader will bypass ILL altogether, only using the service for "difficult" requests where a librarian's verification or location-finding expertise is needed. But there are accompanying funding and procedural issues that also must be considered.

1. Who will pay? If the answer is "the library," will readers order items that the library owns or could get free of charge using ILL? Will orders be "screened" or reviewed before they are passed on to the vendor? If so, will the value of the service as an alternative to ILL be limited or even nullified?
2. If the reader orders documents using a personal charge card, who will handle problems as they arise? If the docu-

ment quality is poor, if there are missing pages or the document does not arrive on time, will the library act as intermediary between the reader and the service?
3. Will the library suggest that readers use ILL rather than a commercial service when the reader is unable to pay? What are the implications of such a policy for information "equity"?
4. Will the library find itself purchasing documents for which there is no need, as readers order willy-nilly?
5. Does the database/TOC contain a significant number of titles of local or regional interest? (If the service is produced by a university, are there a preponderance of titles in support of academic programs for which the local library is not collecting? For example, will a service aimed at researchers in the earth sciences be of equal interest to a campus focusing on the humanities?) If the service is being used as a substitute for serials the library has canceled, is it broad enough in coverage?
6. Are screens and search commands identical to, or different from, those in the OPAC? Does the library have the option to customize screen displays and protocols? If the reader has access to multiple databases from a single public access terminal, does software allow him or her to toggle back and forth between systems, rather than logging on and off?

CARL Systems' UnCover and UnCover2 CARL Systems, the for-profit arm of the Colorado Alliance of Research Libraries (CARL), markets a table of contents service, UnCover, linked with a document delivery service, UnCover2. UnCover is a multidisciplinary citation index (with over two million citations from more than 10,500 journal titles) created from journals supplied by CARL member libraries. As issues are received in each designated holding library, they are sent to UnCover's central office for TOC scanning and serials check-in. Within twenty-four hours the issue is returned to the holding library ready to be shelved. For an annual fee, non-CARL libraries are allowed Internet access to this locally produced database.

A reader or a member of the ILL staff can search the citation database or request the table of contents of a particular journal issue which the system "recreates" and displays on the screen. Once a needed document is identified, he or she requests and completes an on-screen order form. A reader may either charge the document fee to the library's account (if she or he is so authorized) or use a personal credit card. Documents are photocopied and faxed by an UnCover employee working in the library that owns the requested article. UnCover2 claims to fill 97 percent of its requests, the majority of articles delivered within twenty-four hours. The average cost, including a service fee and royalty payments, is $8.50.

One distinct advantage to UnCover2 is that the full cost of the document, broken out by component, is given online before the order is processed. There is a help number which readers can access from library, office, or home, as well as help screens, key word searching, and browsable indexes. If necessary, UnCover2 will forward requests for items to the BLDSC, which increases the turnaround time by about a day but adds nothing to the cost. UnCover also offers the BLDSC's serials holdings in a separate database from which readers are able to order faxed documents for $19.

CARL Systems offers three levels of service through the Internet, each with document ordering capability. For $900 a year, a library can buy twenty-four-hour password access to the full database; however, only one person may access the system at a time. Gateway Access costs $5,000 annually and readers are not required to use a password (libraries use "dedicated" terminals); however, Gateway users compete with other users for online access. Customized Gateway Access, which is designed for very large libraries or networks, costs $10,000 a year and gives the library two dedicated access channels, with more available for $2,500 each. Customized gateway customers are also allowed to design their own screens and menus. Libraries that wish to add their own serials holdings to the database may do so for $1 per title per year.

OCLC Dispatch Service   In 1992 OCLC introduced two new serials databases—ContentsFirst and ArticleFirst—to its FirstSearch subscribers. Primarily for researchers tracking specific disciplines, ContentsFirst contains each indexed journal's entire contents page including news stories, editorials, reviews, letters to the editor and, if available, abstracts. For readers interested in a broad range of articles about a particular subject or by a particular author, ArticleFirst contains the citations to the articles listed in the TOC database. Eleven thousand primarily English-language titles in all subject areas are indexed. Both databases include location symbols from the more than four thousand OCLC participating institutions that let the reader know immediately if the local library or another library owns the journal. Data provided by a variety of sources, including UMI, are upgraded daily; most issues are added to the databases within seventy-two hours of receipt.

FirstSearch subscribers have the choice of paying by the search, by an annual fixed fee that permits unlimited searching, or a combination of both. For example, a library may decide to pay for unlimited searching in ArticleFirst while purchasing a block of five hundred searches in ContentsFirst. With the introduction of the OCLC Dispatch Service in 1993, libraries can order articles online from the ArticleFirst database. UMI is the initial supplier, but OCLC will contract with other suppliers, allowing readers to compare costs and services. The price displayed on the online order form is comprehensive, including processing, delivery (fax, overnight mail, or regular mail), and copyright fees. The cost, averaging about $10.50 for UMI, will vary with the document and delivery method chosen. Payment can be made by personal credit card or institutional account.

The second phase of the service includes an optional link from FirstSearch to OCLC's ILL subsystem. Readers will be able to submit an ILL request (either from an OCLC terminal or an OPAC terminal, if the local library has interfaced its integrated library system with OCLC's services); ILL staff then review each request and process it as a traditional ILL or order it through a commercial document supplier. The size, scope, and accessibility of these OCLC services ensure them a strong position in the marketplace.[50]

Ei Page One The Ei Page One table of contents service is made up of a significant portion of the five thousand journals abstracted each year by Engineering Information, Inc. (Ei). The reader or librarian can also order any article included in the database, using Ei's Reference Desk software. He or she may opt to complete a free-text order form displayed on the screen, then transmit the order to Engineering Information (the software automatically dials Ei's Document Delivery Services and uploads the order file by modem). Alternatively, the user may print out the order file and fax, mail, or telephone it in.

A reader profile is maintained by the database, specifying shipping addresses and preferred delivery option. Documents can be mailed, faxed, or scanned; bit-mapped image files can be sent directly back to the user's computer through the workstation modem.[51] Page One is also offered in citation form on RLIN and incorporated into RLIN's CitaDel document supply program. The service supports RLG's Ariel scanning software, as well as Internet document delivery through e-mail. The cost of a single document is $9.50 when ordered through RLIN using Ariel. (For a full description of Ariel, see chapter 7, "Approaches to Document Delivery.")

CitaDel   CitaDel is the full-service citation and document supply service from the Research Libraries Group. Although strictly speaking, it is not a TOC service, it does provide for reader-initiated ordering. By connecting to RLIN through a dedicated RLIN line, the Internet, or SprintNet dial access, readers access popular commercial citation databases (the UMI/Data Courier, PAIS '80+, and Ei Page One "Premium" files) and scholarly citation databases (the "Special" files, which include Index to Foreign Legal Periodicals, ISIS History of Science Bibliography, History of Technology Bibliography, and Hispanic-American Periodicals Index), all through a single search interface. There are no tapes to load locally or CD-ROMs to maintain: the data do not reside locally. According to RLG's promotional literature, there are "no new staff to hire. No special training needed. No individual passwords or authorization cards. And no worries about multi-user access and slowed response time."[52]

Unlimited searching of the Premium files is available for a fixed annual fee, and there are no extra charges for "hits" or downloading. If accessed through a dedicated RLIN line or the Internet, there are no extra communications costs. A library may select all of the Premium files or only the ones for which it feels a need; the fixed-pricing structure is promoted as a means of controlling costs. Access to the "Special" files is charged by the search at the same price as regular RLIN searching ($.80 or less per search). Full-text copies of most articles cited in the CitaDel database are available for document supply; through a simple command, documents can be ordered by the reader or library staff to be delivered to the ILL department or directly to the reader. The cost of accessing the database depends upon two factors: the number of citation files the library wishes to make use of, and the number of "simultaneous users" accessing them. RLG estimates that the subscription price for a library with the potential for 1 to 10 simultaneous users will be $3,600 per year for access to Periodical Abstracts, 1986 forward. In stark contrast, libraries with more than 101 simultaneous users can expect to pay a subscription price of $18,750 for the same database.

Meckler's MC² In mid-1991, Meckler established MC², an Internet-based electronic publishing service comprising Meckler's publications catalog, conference program information, and a table of contents file for every issue of each of its journal publications (*Academic and Library Computing*, *Library Software Review*, *OCLC Micro*), beginning with January 1991. Any article, editorial, or column in the TOC file can be ordered online through the Internet and delivered by telefacsimile or mail within forty-eight hours. By using the MeckFAX order form in the MC² main menu, users order documents for $15 per item prepaid and specify the preferred method of delivery. Meckler plans to mount a similar database for chapter-level TOC access to its published books with the same on-demand ordering capability.

Library Fee-Based Services

As illustrated by the number of institutions listed in the 1990 *FISCAL Directory of Fee-Based Information Services in Libraries* (214 fee-based services from 145 academic libraries, 35 public and state libraries, and 34 special or corporate libraries) and the existence of an Association of College and Research Libraries (ACRL) discussion group for fee-based information service centers, a number of libraries do not find selling information objectionable.[53] Although some libraries are reluctant to charge fees for philosophical as well as practical reasons, others have chosen to set up fee-based services as separate entities from the ILL department: the pattern seems to be to continue to provide free, basic services to core users, as well as fee-based (enhanced or novel) services to new markets.[54] Many of the services are profit making, but in some instances the goal is simply to become self-supporting, while at the same time offering information services to the local community and beyond. In some settings, the library partially subsidizes these services from its own budget, rather than charging back costs or costs-plus to the reader.

Like commercial document suppliers, library-based services are characterized by different types of collections, ordering mechanisms, delivery options, fees, payment methods, and projected turnaround times. Some services are designed primarily to serve the local business community; some cater to other libraries; still others offer enhanced versions of free, basic services to local readers. For libraries that have few requests for specialized items or that are unable to obtain documents through traditional ILL services, local or regional library-based document services may be an appropriate, reasonably priced choice for document supply. Two important sources are recommended to libraries interested in learning more about these types of services: Helen Josephine's *Fee-Based Services in ARL Libraries*, SPEC Kit 157 (Washington, D.C.: Association of Research Libraries, 1989); and "The FISCAL Primer," a packet of useful information supplied by the ACRL Discussion Group.[55]

Engineering Societies Libraries   The Engineering Societies Libraries (ESL) operates a fee-based document delivery service. This member-supported organization's broad mission is to preserve engineering materials; hence, for those librarians concerned with the ethics of "buying" information, using the ESL document delivery service may be appealing. ESL provides photocopies within three days of receiving an order or, through its Quick Copy Service, on a same-day basis. ESL will photocopy entire books (something other services rarely do); it pays copyright and royalty fees through the Copyright Clearance Center. Libraries access ESL through DIALOG's DIALORDER/DIALMAIL, the Internet, CompuServe, and MCI Mail.

Colorado Technical Reference Center   Janet E. Holton, a corporate librarian, reports on the use of multiple document supply services including DOCLINE UMI and both full-text and order services from DIALOG. But for 70 to 80 percent of her library's requests, she uses the Colorado Technical Reference Center (CTRC), a not-for-profit, cost-recovery document service run under the auspices of the University of Colorado at Boulder's Norlin Library. If something requested through the CTRC is not available in the university's collections, it is located elsewhere and ordered for the requester. Holton's orders are usually batch-faxed to CTRC; in many instances, they are unverified.

The CTRC begins work on the request as soon as it is received. If the item is in the collection, turnaround time is twenty-four to forty-eight hours. Most documents are sent through the U.S. mail, but the center will fax "rush" requests. "The service is not inexpensive, but is competitively priced with other document delivery services of this type." The center publishes a base price list with a schedule of additional costs for enhanced services.[56]

Electronic Document Suppliers

Several references to DIALOG, BRS, and other online searching systems have been made in this chapter on commercial document services. Indeed, it is possible to order copies of documents whose citations are retrieved through online searches, but for a number of reasons this mechanism is not suggested for the interloan or access unit. Online database searching does not typically occur in the ILL office, but in another functional unit of the library. Further, ILL librarians are not database searchers, and they should not be asked to add these skills to their repertoire (unless for some reason the library decides to merge interlending and database searching into a single unit), so infrequently would they use them.

With the introduction of locally mounted citation indexes on CD-ROM and tape, online database searching has decreased significantly in most academic libraries, although it maintains a solid base in corporate and special libraries whose smaller staffs, larger electronic budgets, lack of solid ILL networking, and general sense of immediacy keep online searching flourishing. In online searching as performed in the academic library, unless a document identified by a search is quite inexpensive (an ERIC document, for example), or the reader has substantial grant support and time is a pressing concern, most institutions do not order documents online at the time the search is conducted.

Often the searcher has no way of knowing what items will be of interest to the reader who requested the search and which ones the local library will own or a reciprocal ILL partner can provide. The more typical practice is to conduct the search (with or without the reader present), print it out, and give it to the faculty member or student. He or she then identifies items of interest, locates and uses those the library owns, and heads for ILL with the rest. Again, unless unowned items are inexpensive, or money is no object yet time is a great one, it is unlikely the reader will return to the database searcher and ask her or him go back online and order wanted documents: the associated expenses, only one of which is the cost of the document itself, are simply too great, and there are more cost-effective methods of obtaining the material, whether commercially or through interlibrary loan. So, for all these reasons, this manual does not dwell on the document delivery mechanisms attached to online database searching systems.

Full-Text Online Files

Online full-text databases are beginning to gain some ground in academic libraries, although they are not yet widely used for document delivery because that critical mass that makes any given approach appealing by virtue of the percentage of need it can meet does not yet exist. Before the end of the century full-text seems certain to make major inroads in the academic setting, using the Internet as its vehicle; it has the potential to completely rearrange our existing set of access-related concerns, and its projected roles are discussed at length in the last chapter of this book. For these reasons, it deserves a look in its present state.

Full-text databases may contain the complete texts of periodical articles, newspaper articles, court decisions, and so forth. A full-text journal file can consist of either complete issues or selected articles. Some journals provide different coverage in different databases (DIALOG versus BRS, for example); in one system, coverage may be much more inclusive than in another.[57] Even "cover-to-cover" access (in which every article is included) will typically lack illustrations, letters to the editor, and, in some instances, tabular data. In some systems, each magazine exists in its own file (VuText, Mead, Reuters Textline); in others, it is simply part of a larger one.

Online full-text databases are the fastest growing segment of the textual database market. Of the total number of databases available in 1980, only 5 percent were full-text. By 1989 that number had climbed to 34 percent; almost seventeen hundred sources of full-text data were listed in the 1989 edition of *Fulltext Sources Online*.[58] The major U.S. vendors of full-text databases include BRS Information Technologies, DIALOG, Mead Central LEXIS and NEXIS, WESTLAW, STN International, Dow Jones News/Retrieval, DataTimes, NEWSNET, and VU/TEXT (full-text access to regional newspapers). As of August 1991, DIALOG provided access to 1,772 full-text sources through 161 full-text files.[59]

Full-text availability is centered on sci-tech journals, presumably because of the high cost of publication, the need for quick delivery, and the rapid obsolescence rate that acts to reduce the necessity of maintaining many years of material online.[60] One might also say that electronic full-text journals follow the money: customers in the fields of business, science, engineering, law, and medicine are more likely to be able to purchase electronic access and full-text. For one thing, they can often charge the costs to their clients; for another, there is frequently more funding available for scientific, engineering, and medical research, which will cover the costs.[61]

When considering access to online full-text databases or document supply capabilities, the library should weigh certain financial and political realities. Full-text access is not inexpensive, it may require the assistance of a skilled searcher, and most titles are based in the subject areas mentioned above. One author has suggested that faculty members in the humanities and arts may strongly object to the money spent on providing electronic access to materials in which they have no interest, especially if hard copy is being collected as well.[62] Time coverage, access methods (including links between citations and local holdings data), hardware (will full-text retrieval capacity be available on all machines on the campus network?), software protocols, print and downloading capabilities, and costs: all should be carefully examined. Ruth A. Pagell reminds us that the current state of full-text availability is seriously hampered by the limited range of subject areas, the small number of scholarly publications available, and the discrepancies between electronic full-text and hard copy.[63] In most cases online full-text journals have backfiles of fewer than five years.[64]

The Electronic Journal Retrieval Project (EJRP) at the University of Tennessee, Knoxville (UTK) was developed in an effort to provide readers with an up-to-date and comprehensive list of full-text journals online. Although the library found BiblioData's *Fulltext Sources Online* (the semi-annual publication that lists online, full-text journals, newspapers, newsletters, newswires, and the databases in which they can be found) useful, it felt the directory was not current or comprehensive enough for its needs. Using dBASE III, journals, host systems (DIALOG, BRS, NLM, STN, ORBIT), file names, time coverage, and library subscription information were entered into the locally developed Electronic Journal List (EJL) database and updated quarterly.

During a pilot project, readers completed request forms for articles that were later printed out and delivered to them the next day. Of ninety-one articles requested, eighty-three were retrieved; the eight that were not stemmed from reader citation errors or database gaps (most of these services do contain the disclaimer that they are not 100 percent complete). Business-related requests were the most popular, probably because so many of the databases are business oriented. For the sake of comparison, on occasion UTK ordered the same title from two different full-text sources. It preferred DIALOG because the Information Access Company's (IAC) files were not as complete in the BRS databases.

For libraries considering experimenting with full-text database services, the experiences of the UTK library may prove to be helpful. Knoxville's observations include the following:

1. DIALOG using delivery through DIALMAIL is more cost-effective if several articles can be ordered at the same time and next-day delivery through electronic mail is sufficient.

2. Costs can be reduced by performing searches in less costly databases, building and saving them, and then executing them for full-text document delivery in the desired database.
3. Preset function keys can further decrease connect times (and thus, costs).
4. If the reader's citation is not easily found, extensive online searches are typically costly and unproductive.[65]

The future of primary full-text online files will depend on how well their producers estimate the usefulness of the information to its targeted audience. John A. Hearty and Valerie K. Rohrbaugh suggest that the developers evaluate readers' needs and improve the way current information systems work. Because full-text services, as the new kids on the block, must overcome readers' existing information-gathering habits, they should not only publicize their services, but educate as well. Targeting ILL librarians (who are not normally trained to do database searching) for free professional development seminars could help both the vendor and the user. In the universe of ILL and document supply, familiarity does not breed contempt: on the contrary, vendors are more than willing to accommodate clients who are knowledgeable and communicate their needs.[66]

Choosing among Ordering Mechanisms: Some Guidelines

Traditional Methods

Telephone: Very few libraries will take telephone requests, but commercial document services often will, in some cases for an extra fee. The benefits of using the telephone are self-evident: there is the immediate satisfaction of knowing the request has been received and acknowledged. (However, this may not mean that the order is processed any more quickly.) There is also the hidden cost of communications (unless the vendor offers an 800 number), the possibility of incorrect transcription of the request, the frustration of busy signals, and the possibility of miscommunication between the library and the person taking the order at the other end.

U.S. mail: With the advent of electronic mechanisms for sending requests, the postal system is now used primarily for delivery of documents. When the mail is used to transmit requests to document services, there exists the added disadvantage of delayed confirmation time: if the request cannot be filled, it will be mailed back only to be retyped and resubmitted to an alternative source.

The Utilities

There are a number of advantages to using a utility to transmit document requests:

1. If the primary mechanism for ILL is the utility, ordering from the fee-based service will also be part of the access unit's familiar workflow.
2. As more and more services load holdings data into the utilities, the integration of commercial services and traditional interlending will be further streamlined; the procedural distinctions between an ILL request and a fee-based request will pleasantly blur.
3. The utilities' "guaranteed" turnaround times may cause commercial services to respond to requests in a timely manner.
4. The utility transmittal cost will be the same as that for an ILL transaction.
5. There will be no need for additional staff training.
6. The decision about which service to use will be simplified by the number available through the utility.

Resource centers and document suppliers that accept requests over the OCLC ILL subsystem include such familiar names as the BLDSC, the Center for Research Libraries, the Centre de Pret at the Bibliothèque Nationale, CAS, the Danish Loan Center, ERIC, ISI's The Genuine Article, NTIS, the Information Store, UMI, and Information on Demand. Thus, a library has a choice among the general-interest collection-based services, on-demand services, and special-interest services, yet the choice is also limited.

The enhancement of bibliographic utilities including online document delivery services, table of contents services, and access to international resources undoubtedly will affect the use of commercial services. For example, the British Library has become RLG's first overseas general member: RLG now has a European access point for RLIN borrowers and hopes that more European libraries will become members as the London hub reduces costs for foreign libraries entering data into RLIN. The British Library plans to use RLG's Ariel scanning software for transatlantic document delivery.[67]

Online Database Vendors

There are a number of advantages to ordering through these companies, including the speed with which the request is delivered and the elimination of location-finding and bibliographic verification; citation transcription errors are also eliminated. Most commercial document suppliers routinely accept orders online through DIALOG or BRS, as well as their own in-house systems.

The principal users of database vendors for document ordering are corporate libraries. Academic librarians have resisted incorporating database searching with the ILL operation, generally speaking, for good reasons. When these issues are considered, there is no reason to expect this behavioral pattern to change.

1. Academic libraries will probably utilize full-text databases only for very expensive newsletters and newspapers which they cannot afford or acquire in any other way. Common sense tells us that the coverage and real costs of full-text instantaneous document delivery currently prohibit its use as a dependable source.
2. Ordering documents online can be impractical: in the midst of a search, it may not be possible to determine whether the library actually owns the title, or has the ability to obtain it from a reliable ILL fax partner at no or low cost. The online meter is running, and the searcher cannot drop everything to evaluate other supply options.
3. The lack of two-way communication between requester and vendor can be problematic. Yes, messages are sent to the vendor instantaneously, but it must respond through traditional mechanisms, e.g., mail and telephone (unless the vendor has an e-mail messaging system).
4. There is no record-keeping system for requests made to vendors, like OCLC's ILL subsystem's transaction file, which could be very useful for heavy users of document delivery services.[68]
5. Forwarding mechanisms that would transmit requests automatically to other commercial document suppliers do not exist with individual suppliers as they do with utilities. In a utility, it is possible to incorporate commercial services within any lender string.

6. There is no standard infrastructure, linking capability, or common command language between online services. Unfortunately, this is the primary barrier to the interconnectivity of all electronic messaging systems. For the ILL librarian, it simply means one more system needs to be mastered to be used effectively.

Telefacsimile

Faxing an order to a commercial document supplier may not markedly improve delivery time if the service does not give faxed requests priority. When a library chooses to fax a request, the advantages of automatic citation transcription are lost. Libraries that do fax may want to consider batch-faxing requests to a single vendor; this approach may be less disruptive to the operation's workflow.

Document Delivery Methods

How to expeditiously transport a document from the source of supply to the requester at a reasonable cost has perplexed libraries for years; financially subsidized courier systems seem to have achieved the most satisfactory results. Commercial suppliers do not appear to offer a perfect solution to this long-standing, difficult transport problem, but there are many options among which to choose.[69]

The U.S. Mail and Courier Systems

The U.S. Postal Service can be the slowest vehicle for document delivery but special courier services such as United Parcel Service (UPS), Federal Express, or the Postal Service's own Express Mail will improve delivery times. The costs of such services may be prohibitive if the commercial document vendor tacks a $20 charge onto the cost of the document for what may be a day or two's decrease in delivery time. The library must measure its need for speed against the depth of its pockets.

Telefacsimile

Once the wave of the future, telefacsimile has now become the way of the world. Nonetheless, some commercial services still charge excessive amounts for a mechanism that has proven to save time and effort for the deliverer. As one author suggests, the cost of document delivery may be *the* inhibiting factor to timely delivery:

> It is significant that even though the users of commercial document services are relying extensively on electronic techniques for requesting materials and paying up to $14 per journal article, they are requesting overnight service only 7 to 12% of the time. It therefore appears likely that were one to offer rush service through telefacsimile at a yet higher fee in a library, demand would be low.[70]

One cannot overemphasize that, if a library wants a document fast, it should find a good fax (or scanning) partner (this applies to ILL and commercial vendors). Some services, like CARL UnCover2, fold the cost of telefacsimile into the document's price. In other cases, where separate and rather steep charges are assessed, libraries may wish to use telefacsimile for document delivery with discretion. If the library cannot justify the cost, perhaps the reader will bear it. (For more on charging the reader, see chapter 8.)

The library will also want to remember that, while telefacsimile may mean almost instantaneous document transmission, the supplier must first receive and process the request. If a service regularly processes a request upon receipt and sends the document on the same day through the U.S. mail, the receipt date may be equal to that for a faxed document from a service that processes the request two days after it receives it. In short, each vendor's habits should be examined. The library will need to look at the costs of premium services, whether the service is reliable and delivers on time, and whether higher costs for faster delivery mechanisms are reasonable or justifiable.

Electronic Mail

Although database vendors are not academic libraries' chief suppliers, some libraries may find their delivery mechanism to be particularly efficient. One institution orders documents through DIALOG, then has them sent directly to the library's own internal e-mail system through the Internet. According to Barbara Denton, "Internet delivery is a cost effective alternative to displaying and handling DIALOG output. We spend less time online, but our small savings in connect time is offset for the higher offline print charges.... Our real savings are in staff time, because fewer searcher-minutes are spent doing routine chores."[71]

Pricing Structures and Methods of Payment

The costs associated with fee-based services can be broken down into system ordering costs, suppliers' handling charges, and delivery costs. It is important not to forget the "access costs" also associated with some systems, such as CARL UnCover. The number of documents ordered from a service that charges a flat fee for access (a minimum of $900 for UnCover) may determine its long-term usefulness. For example, if a library orders ten documents from a service it pays $1,000 to access, each document costs $108.95; if it orders 100, the cost per item will drop considerably; only if it orders 1,000 or more items may the cost seem truly competitive with traditional ILL and other commercial services.

According to David B. Allen and Johanna Alexander, the library also pays for service, not just the document:

> Along with delivery charges you are paying for storage, personnel time, computer time, and the service itself. In conventional ILL many of these costs are hidden or not recognised because of reciprocal resource sharing agreements.[72]

Here it is worthwhile to note that, although the college or university may not explicitly bill the library for such hidden costs as space and electrical power, it almost certainly assigns them to the institution's overall cost of operating a library: these so-called invisible items are not free, nor is it efficient for librarians to think of them in that way when they make cost comparisons. The cost of each request for a commercially supplied document may also be affected by the subject of the material, the number of pages requested, the availability of discounts and deposit accounts, and communication links.

There are a variety of payment options available to both individual libraries and consortia; limiting the number of payment mechanisms that the library must accommodate is the key to efficiency. In some instances, a library's options are limited; deposit accounts are required or network agreements demand monthly invoicing. However, if at all possible an organization will want to avoid receiving a flurry of monthly invoices, individual item-level invoices, and usage statements from a group of different services. Pricing structures will also vary with each service, and a library may wish to consider which structure meets its local needs:

> Inclusive pricing: Inclusive pricing means that the library knows exactly how much it will be paying for a particular document before it is ordered. It may be a flat fee or a sum

total of all charges (the article, royalties). This particular pricing mechanism may be very important for libraries (or readers) who have a price "ceiling" above which they cannot pay.

Base pricing: Base pricing means that the total price will include incremental additions to a base price; these increments can include royalty fees, handling charges, delivery charges, photocopying fees, service charges for non-fills, charges for manual ordering, and charges for verification. All of these should be clearly outlined in the vendor's documentation.

Deposit Accounts

Deposit accounts with commercial vendors may be the simplest and most efficient means of paying for document supply services. A library places an agreed upon dollar amount (ranging from a few hundred dollars to many thousands) into an account from which monies are withdrawn after each transaction. Periodic statements are issued to let the library know how much money has been spent and how much is left. As funds are depleted, the library may be asked to replenish the account. The system is straightforward and effective, but each vendor has its own rules regulating deposit accounts. When considering this payment option, a library may want to ask the following questions:

1. Can amounts on deposit be carried over from year to year?
2. Must the library maintain a minimum amount of money (and how much) in its account, requiring deposits throughout the year?
3. Will the library receive a discount with a deposit account, or will services be enhanced in any other ways?
4. Will money be refunded if the library decides to cancel the account?
5. Does the supplier provide for group deposit accounts that give substantial discounts to all members, regardless of individual usage?

Invoicing

Many libraries may not wish to tie up funds in deposit accounts that may or may not be used. In this case, invoicing as a payment option may be the best solution. Some vendors will issue an invoice or bill to be paid upon receipt with each order processed, while others may agree to monthly statements cumulating the previous month's activities. The questions a library will want to ask include these:

1. How often will the library be invoiced? If the invoice is processed through the campus's accounting office, and payment is late, what are the penalties?
2. If the library is part of a group account, will invoices be sent to some central office or direct to the library? If they are sent to a central point, does the local library need to keep records to reconcile possible discrepancies?

Other Methods of Payment

Many libraries use commercial services so infrequently that deposit accounts or monthly invoices are unnecessary. In this case, prepayment may be an option. Most vendors accept credit cards, checks, and money orders. Checks may present difficulties, because the actual cost of the document may be difficult to determine in advance or necessitate a pre-order telephone call to the vendor. Although credit cards may eliminate the need for ascertaining the exact cost of a document beforehand, upon receipt of the bill a library may discover, to its dismay, that the total cost of the document is far more than was bargained for.

Experimenting with Commercial Document Supply Services

For libraries that are interested in exploring the world of commercial document services, experimentation can range from an all-out, highly structured, grant-funded, closely monitored test of selected vendors (like some of the studies described in this chapter), to a short-term, quick-and-dirty "quiz" of a single mainstream vendor to see whether unfilled ILLs can be supplied. Or, for the library interested in canceling high-priced journals, a year-long trial period of purchasing from a collection-based service may be in order. Whatever the depth of interest, the following suggestions may help a library before, during, and after the experiment.

Before the Test Begins:

1. Determine the scope of the test. It will be important to determine what the purpose of the experiment is. Is it to

help in the evaluation of ILL's effectiveness? Are the results intended to justify serial cancellations? Are commercial services to be used as substitutes for ILL or as complementary services? Is the intent to provide value-added service to readers, improve public relations within the academic community, or a combination of several of these possible purposes?
2. Determine funding options. Will the library apply for a grant or must the funds be taken from the acquisitions, serials, or some other part of the library budget? The amount of money a library has to spend and the way it spends it (deposit accounts, a checking account) will to a great extent determine the scope of the experiment.
3. Determine library needs, the vendors to be used, and how they will be assessed. Will several services be compared or is a particular vendor to be evaluated? If services are to be measured against each other, provide a prioritized list of qualities for which the library is looking. If fill rate is more important than speed, this needs to be incorporated into the evaluation.
4. Determine staff time, equipment, and documentation needs. Will staff members have to be trained in new searching or other techniques? Will the experiment require new or additional equipment, such as printers or terminals? Vendor documentation will need to ordered and mastered before the experiment begins.
5. Determine time parameters. Will the experiment be more valuable or revealing if it is long-term? Is a month of heavy usage a better gauge than a six-month pattern of intermittent usage?
6. Determine a targeted audience. Will the service be offered to the entire library community or to a select group? If the library is considering canceling subscriptions in a particular area, it may be expedient to offer commercial document delivery free to the faculty members who will be most affected. If the experiment is successful, faculty may then be less resistant to the loss of hard copy. Opening up the service to the entire library community (for one day or a week, for example) may negatively impact the results of the experiment if the library is inundated with frivolous requests.
7. Determine whether the service will be free to readers. On a short-term basis, this may be appropriate for any experiment, but if the library intends ultimately to charge for the service, initial "gifts" may distort potential usage

studies. However, if the library charges for the service and does not charge for ILL, the library community may perceive the service as discriminatory. (For an analysis of the issues related to charging readers' fees, see chapter 8.)

8. Determine whether the service will be advertised. Will advertising the service cause a flood of requests which the library has neither the funds nor the staff to process? (The answer is probably no; in most experiments, business for the new service has derived more from positive word-of-mouth than promotional materials.) If the library does not advertise, how will readers find out about the availability of document delivery services? Will announcements be sent to department heads? Or will staff simply inform the access unit's heaviest users and let the message spread?

9. Arrange for special instructions to appear online. If the library is offering an online TOC service, both online and printed instructions are desirable. If there are any restrictions, e.g., patron group or material type, these should be explained. (For example, the TOC's contents may be integrated with the library's online catalog, available to every reader to peruse, but the document ordering feature may be limited to faculty to whom passwords have been issued.) If the reader is to be charged, all fees must be clearly delineated so that there are no questions asked when the document is delivered. Special services and their accompanying charges (fax, online printouts) also need to be carefully explained.

During the Experiment:

1. Listen to readers' comments; if possible, keep a record of specific compliments, complaints, or suggestions brought to the library's attention.
2. Ensure that the experiment is being carried out according to its original design.
3. Monitor staff members to ensure appropriate, efficient, consistent usage of all services.

After the Experiment:

1. Ask staff members and readers what their perceptions of the experiment were. This can be accomplished informally or through a simple questionnaire sent directly to

the readers who actually used the service. Determining why a targeted audience member did not use the service may be important as well.
2. Evaluate statistical data. The library will look for overall performance factors identified at the time the experiment was designed, as well as direct costs, fill rate, and quality control. What the statistics "mean" will depend upon the original scope of the experiment. Did the experiment show that it would be less expensive to continue subscribing to a journal or journals? Or that, without charging the reader or increasing the library's budget, commercial services are not financially viable when compared to ILL?
3. Determine how the study will be reported to the library, college, or university administration. Determine who is responsible for reporting the results of the study and what form the report will take. A few significant statistics, combined with an overall evaluation and concrete recommendations for future use will be the most useful.

Evaluating Commercial Document Supply Services

If the library gets what it wants, when it wants it, and at a reasonable cost, then a given document service is the one the library will use. But if the library employs a variety of vendors, pinpointing the "best" service may be as difficult as identifying the "best" ILL partner. There are, however, consistent criteria upon which a document supplier of any kind can be evaluated. Documents should be available in a variety of formats, including hard copy, photocopy, reprint, microform, or electronic. The system should be easy to use and reliable. It should maintain status reports on all requests and possess simple billing procedures. The ability to preview materials (the inclusion of abstracts) is also very helpful.

As in interlibrary loan, statistics will be a valuable tool for evaluating commercial services. For institutions that use a single commercial service, statistical reports generated by the vendor may be an option. For those libraries that dabble in several services, a closer examination of performance may be in order. Collecting some or all of the following data may be important to the overall evaluation of vendor efficiency. (For a closer examination of statistics, the reader is directed to the chapter on interlibrary loan.)

1. Service name.
2. Ordering mechanism (telephone, utility, telefacsimile).
3. Cost of the ordering mechanism.
4. Base-rate cost of the item (exclusive of delivery mechanism, royalties, and any special fees).
5. Delivery mechanism (U.S. mail, telefacsimile, courier).
6. Cost of the delivery mechanism (if separate from the cost of the document).
7. Document type (thesis, government document, conference proceedings, journal article).
8. Year of publication.
9. Date of order and date of receipt.
10. Special fees (for pages over a certain number, for requests older than a certain publication year, for citation verification).
11. Alternative sources (an ILL partner).
12. Reasons for non-fills (material unavailable, no permission to reprint, citation error).
13. Reader information (status, department).
14. Document quality and completeness.

Costs: How High Is Too High?

Rightly or wrongly, the major stigma attached to commercial document suppliers is the perceived (or real) high cost of their services:

> The "bottom line" on document delivery will probably continue to be cost. If the price of fast transmission is higher than the benefits as perceived by librarians, much ILL traffic will continue to tolerate the lapsed time involved in slower methods.[73]

How much one is willing to pay for immediate access is dependent upon the "time value" of the information and the availability of alternative delivery systems.[74] It is easy enough to say that it costs only $8.50 to order a document from a TOC service, such as UnCover2, but the library will also pay at least $1,000 a year for simple access to the system. In this case, the library will need to ask whether its dollars could be better spent on traditional ILL or other library services.

One of the major problems in deciding whether a service is too expensive is that few libraries have determined the true costs of their interlibrary loan operation. At the very least, a library should calculate its unit cost for borrowing and compare that with the costs of using a commercial service. If the library decides deliberately to reduce lending, in consideration of its reduced borrowing, the associated savings should also be factored in. (For more on calculating the costs of interlending, see chapter 8.)

If the library decides to offer document supply services to its readers, the financial commitment in terms of staff time, equipment, subscription costs (to TOC services, for example), deposit accounts, and, perhaps, increased telecommunications costs should be assessed. Will the library need more or different terminals or more powerful PCs, better printers to accommodate better data transmission capabilities, customized software, new telephone lines or another telefacsimile machine, a scanning workstation, and special forms or handouts? As with ILL, the expense of using commercial services consists not only of the "known" costs of a piece of equipment, but the ongoing and sometimes "unknown" costs of actual usage. Budgeting for these services can become a maze of numbers and surprises unless the number of services utilized is sharply defined, sound accounting procedures are in place, and clearly stated guidelines are established for when, how, and by whom these services will be used.

Breadth of Coverage

The subject or material coverage the library seeks will depend upon its individual needs, its academic mission, and the research needs of the community it serves. If there is no specific subject area or material type the library has identified as a primary candidate for fee-based support, then evaluating one or two general collection-based or on-demand services may be the best approach. One factor to be considered is that broad-based vendors may be more expensive than smaller, more focused services. However, the library may wish to weigh the convenience associated with the use of a single vendor or a smaller number of services against the relative inconvenience of supporting multiple accounts.

Depth of Coverage

Once again, determining the needs of the library community will be an important issue. If the majority of requests is for current materials, the choice of vendors will be wide open. If older materials are needed, the choice of the right supplier will be very important, as will be tracking non-fills and surcharges often associated with providing older materials. Unfortunately, market demand often determines what vendors will stock or supply; a number of studies have shown that older materials are requested less frequently than newer ones, hence, vendors feel justified in ignoring items that few will seek. For libraries needing older materials, membership in the Center for Research Libraries or USBE may be in order.

Ease of Ordering

The most valuable services will be those easily incorporated into the daily routine of the access unit. When staff have the ability to order in a variety of ways and with little price differentiation among them, this suggests that the service is flexible and "client oriented." If access to a terminal that is not located within easy reach is necessary, or printers are unavailable, then the unit's workflow can be disrupted. If the commercial service has special requirements for ordering, such as including an index-related accession number, this too may have an impact on productivity.

Service Response Time

Is the commercial service's inventory centralized, or does it supply items on-demand from a wide range of collections and sources? This factor may affect turnaround time, depending on what the library is ordering and the service's local resources. Are confirmation and shipment guaranteed to occur within twenty-four to forty-eight hours? Are non-fill status reports issued in a timely manner? The answers to these questions will help the library assess a service's reliability and responsiveness.

Fill Rate

A commercial supplier's fill rate is a major factor in declaring it to be successful in meeting a library's needs for document delivery. No matter how inexpensive its prices, or how rapid its confirmation and delivery time, if a commercial service fails to fill a substantial percentage of requests, it ceases to be an attractive alternative to traditional methods of document supply.

Accuracy and Document Quality

Did the library receive what it asked for? Were there any missing or illegible pages? In the reader's mind, the quality of the product he or she receives relates not only to its availability and perceived informational value, but also to the physical quality of the document itself. If documents received on slippery telefacsimile paper are perceived as somehow less than adequate by the library's readers, perhaps the library may consider improving document quality by switching to a plain paper fax machine. The same principle applies to full-text printouts, when the printer ribbon has run out of ink, or the type font is difficult to read; these problems can be addressed in-house.

Holdings Information

That a collection-based supplier provide either online or published holdings information is crucial. In addition, these data must be reliable: if, after multiple orders, a service consistently reports non-fills for titles which are listed as available, the library should look elsewhere.

Customer Service Support

A commercial supplier should have knowledgeable and responsive service representatives to handle problems, complaints, and questions. At the very least, they should be available during regular working hours and preferably through an 800 number.

Other Factors

Does the service offer special promotional events that may give the library an occasional "bonus"? When it fails to deliver an item within its published parameters, does the library receive some sort of pricing consideration? Keeping an eye out for new services that might be willing to offer special discounts to new clients, or perhaps the free use of technologically advanced equipment for test purposes, can benefit smaller institutions.

The Future

As an information provider, the librarian is the human interface through which a reader's desire is communicated and realized; commercial document suppliers simply provide an alternative path to this realization. As with cooperative library agreements and interlibrary loan, commercial services are only as good as the people who make them run. As the Library of Congress Network Advisory Committee cogently stated:

The impetus to do something about document delivery comes from many sectors. Each has a vested interest. Library patrons and other end users want fast, low cost (or free) access to information. Net lenders want relief from an increasing drain on their resources. Net borrowers want not to become net lenders. Copyright owners want compensation for perceived financial losses. Commercial or private sector providers want a favorable balance between their expenses and revenues. Bibliographic utilities want to increase the use of their systems for request transmittal. Document delivery is. It will not go away.[75]

Thomas J. Michalak, long an academic library manager, believes document supply services will prompt librarians to examine both the real costs and the speed of ILL, as well as library/publisher tensions about copyright and fair use and the library's changing role from information storehouse to information conduit.[76] As librarians look at these important issues, at the same time continuing to cancel serial subscriptions and watching their book budgets decline, the role of commercial services as viable "partners" in the delivery process will undoubtedly grow.

Notes

1. Bradley J. Morgan, ed., *Information Industry Directory*, 11th ed. (Detroit: Gale Research, 1991), xvi.
2. Ibid.
3. Douglas P. Hurd and Robert E. Molyneux, "An Evaluation of Delivery Times and Costs of a Non-Library Document Delivery Service," in *Energies for Transition: Proceedings of the 4th National Conference of the Association of College and Research Libraries, Baltimore, Maryland, 1986*, ed. Danuta A. Nitecki (Chicago: ACRL, 1986), 182.
4. Sue Kennedy, "The Role of Commercial Document Delivery Services in Interlibrary Loan," in *Research Access through New Technology*, ed. Mary E. Jackson (New York: AMS Press, 1989), 72.
5. Ibid., 71.
6. Connie Miller and Patricia Tegler, "An Analysis of Interlibrary Loan and Commercial Document Supply Performance," *Library Quarterly* 58 (Oct. 1988): 362.
7. Kennedy, "The Role of Commercial Document Delivery," in *Research Access*, 77–78.
8. Richard W. Boss and Judy McQueen, "Document Delivery in the United States: A Report," ED 244 626 (Oct. 1983), 59.
9. Library of Congress, Network Development Office, "Document Delivery—Background Papers Commissioned by the National Advisory Committee," ED 221 214 (1982), 34–35.

10. Georgia Finnigan, "Review of Private Sector Involvement in Document Supply," in *Interlending and Document Supply: Proceedings of the First International Conference Held in London, November, 1988*, ed. Graham P. Cornish and Alison Gallico (Boston Spa, Eng.: IFLA Office for International Lending, 1989), 80.
11. Barbara Quint, "Connect Time: Where's Your Parachute?" *Wilson Library Bulletin* 66 (Apr. 1992): 85.
12. Kennedy, "The Role of Commercial Document Delivery," in *Research Access*, 71.
13. A. J. Wright, "No More Free Lunch: Commercial Fee-Based Information Services—Past, Present and Future," ED 221 163 (May 1982), 16.
14. Miller and Tegler, "An Analysis of Interlibrary Loan," 353.
15. Ibid., 361.
16. Ibid., 361, 363.
17. Susan B. Ardis and Karen S. Croneis, "Document Delivery, Cost Containment and Serial Ownership," *College & Research Libraries News* 48 (Nov. 1987): 624.
18. Ibid., 626–27.
19. Gary D. Wiggins, *Factors Which Influence the Choice of Document Delivery Mechanisms for Serials by Selected Scientific and Technical Special Librarians* (Ph.D. diss., Indiana Univ., 1985).
20. Kennedy, "The Role of Commercial Document Delivery," in *Research Access*, 77.
21. James L. Wood, "Private Sector, Non-Library Document Delivery Services," in *Prospects for Improving Document Delivery: Minutes of the 101st Meeting, October 13–14, Arlington, Virginia*, ed. Nicola Daval (Washington, D.C.: ARL, 1983), 93.
22. Miller and Tegler, "An Analysis of Interlibrary Loan," 364.
23. David B. Allen and Johanna Alexander, "A Document Delivery Alternative for the CSB Library: Using Commercial Suppliers to Supplement Conventional Interlibrary Loan," ED 275 330 (July 1986), 80–81.
24. Kennedy, "The Role of Commercial Document Delivery," in *Research Access*, 70.
25. Michael Rogers, "Library Searching Powers Attract Private Firms," *Library Journal* 117 (Apr. 1, 1992): 36.
26. Georgia Finnigan and Sue Rugge, "Document Delivery and the Experiences of Information Unlimited," *Online* 2 (Jan. 1978): 63.
27. S. Martin, "Delivery Systems," 167.
28. Wood, "Private Sector," 97.
29. Kennedy, "The Role of Commercial Document Delivery," in *Research Access*, 69.
30. Jay K. Lucker, "Document Delivery and Research Libraries," in *Prospects for Improving Document Delivery: Minutes of the 101st Meeting, October 13–14, Arlington, Virginia*, ed. Nicola Daval (Washington, D.C.: ARL, 1983), 85.

31. Kathleen F. Halsey, "An Evaluation of Document Delivery Service to Interlibrary Loan: A Commercial Firm and a Traditional Library Source" (Master's thesis, Cardinal Stritch College) ED 302 261 (Dec. 1988), 56.
32. Ibid., 56–63.
33. Ibid., 71.
34. Hurd and Molyneux, "An Evaluation of Delivery Times," 185.
35. H. W. Wilson Co., "Wilson and UMI Announce Product Link," Press release, Jan. 25, 1992.
36. Sharon Bonk, "Interlibrary Loan and Document Delivery in the United Kingdom," *RQ* 30 (Winter 1990): 231–32.
37. A. F. MacDougall, H. Wheelhouse, and J. M. Wilson, "Academic Library Cooperation and Document Supply: Possibilities and Considerations of Cost-Effectiveness," *Journal of Librarianship* 21 (July 1989): 188.
38. Ibid.
39. Ibid., 195.
40. Kathryn Kjaer, "Current Access to Scientific Journals: An Alternative Strategy," *Colorado Libraries* 16 (Mar. 1990): 21–22.
41. John Butler, "Collection Building vs. Document Delivery: An Evaluation of Methods to Provide NTIS Documents in an Academic Engineering Library," ED 286 510 (June 1987), 4.
42. Ibid., 7.
43. Universal Serials and Book Exchange, *Your Guide to USBE Services* (Cleveland: USBE, 1990).
44. Jeffrey Saldinger, "Full Service Document Delivery: Our Likely Future," *Wilson Library Bulletin* 58 (May 1984): 639.
45. Ibid., 640.
46. Wood, "Private Sector," 93.
47. Jean Currie, "Document Delivery: A Study of Different Sources," ED 262 786 (May 1985), 9–10.
48. Janice S. Boyer and John Reidelbach, "Document Delivery Pilot Project at UNO," *Nebraska Library Association Quarterly* 21 (Spring 1990): 7.
49. Fred M. Heath, "An Interview with Thomas J. Michalak," *Library Administration & Management* 6 (Spring 1992): 64.
50. "ContentsFirst, ArticleFirst Debut September 14," *OCLC Reference News*, no. 12 (Sept.-Oct. 1992): 1, 5; "Subscription Pricing for FirstSearch," *OCLC Reference News*, no. 13 (Nov.-Dec. 1992): 1–2; "Document Ordering Debuts on FirstSearch," *OCLC Newsletter*, no. 201 (Jan.-Feb. 1993): 28.
51. John J. Regazzi, "Designing the Ei Reference Desk," in *National Online Meeting: Proceedings, 1990*, ed. Martha E. Williams (Medford, N.J.: Learned Information, Inc., 1990), 346–47.
52. Research Libraries Group, Inc., "CitaDel," Folder, 1992.

53. Steve Coffman, ed., *The FISCAL Directory of Fee-Based Information Services in Libraries* (Norwalk, Calif.: FYI/County of Los Angeles Public Library, 1990).
54. Bryce Allen and Kathy Corley, "Information Brokers in Illinois Academic Libraries," *Illinois Libraries* 72 (Nov. 1990): 596–97.
55. Helen Josephine, *Fee-Based Services in ARL Libraries*, SPEC Kit 157 (Washington, D.C.: ARL, Office of Management Studies, 1989); "The FISCAL Primer" is a packet available from Gelman Library Information Center, George Washington University, Gelman Library, 2130 H. St. N.W., Room B07, Washington, D.C. 20052.
56. Janet E. Holton, "Document Delivery Services in a Special Library: How to Get What You Haven't Got!" *Colorado Libraries* 16 (Dec. 1990): 37.
57. *Directory of Online Databases*, vol. 10, no. 1 (New York: Cuadra/Elsevier, 1989).
58. Carol Tenopir and Jung Soon Ro, *Full Text Databases* (New York: Greenwood Press, 1990), 12.
59. DIALOG Information Services, Inc., "DIALOG Full-Text Sources, Alpha List," Documentation, Aug. 1991.
60. Lucker, "Document Delivery," 86.
61. Drew Racine, "Access to Full-Text Journal Articles: Some Practical Considerations," *Library Administration & Management* 6 (Spring 1992): 101.
62. Ibid., 102.
63. Ruth A. Pagell, "Primary FTDs for the End User: New Roles for the Information Professional," *Online Review* 13 (Apr. 1989): 153.
64. John A. Hearty and Valerie K. Rohrbaugh, "Current State of Full Text Primary Information Online, with Recommendations for the Future," *Online Review* 13 (Apr. 1989): 137–38.
65. David P. Gillikin, "Document Delivery from Full-Text Online Files: A Pilot Project," *Online* 14 (May 1990): 32.
66. Hearty and Rohrbaugh, "Current State of Full Text," 138.
67. "Late Bulletins," *Library Journal* 117 (Apr. 1, 1992): 15.
68. Gisela A. Roth, "Online Document Ordering Systems of Online Vendors," *Online Review* 6 (June 1982): 247.
69. Miller and Tegler, "An Analysis of Interlibrary Loan," 362.
70. Boss and McQueen, "Document Delivery," 62.
71. Barbara Denton, "E-mail Delivery of Search Results via the Internet," *Online* 16 (Mar. 1992): 50.
72. Allen and Alexander, "A Document Delivery Alternative," 48.
73. Boss and McQueen, "Document Delivery," 62.
74. Pagell, "Primary FTDs," 150.
75. Library of Congress, Network Development Office, "Document Delivery," 36.
76. Michalak, "Impact."

CHAPTER 7

Approaches to Document Delivery

Deliberate Speed, Majestic Instancy
(Thompson, *The Hound of Heaven*)

I. Defining Document Delivery 202

II. Document Delivery: The "New Frontier" for Access 202

III. The Need for Delivery Choices 203

IV. Speed: Is There a Need? 205

V. Delivery to the Library and Delivery to the Reader: They Aren't the Same Thing 207

VI. "No Frills" Delivery: The U.S. Mail 209

VII. Courier Services 211

VIII. Regional Delivery Services 212
   A. Cost Schemes and Centers 213
   B. Pennsylvania's Interlibrary Delivery Service (IDS) 213
   C. Other Regional Delivery Models 215
   D. Messenger Services 215
   E. Evaluation and Sources of Funding 216

IX. Telefacsimile Transmission 217
   A. The Uses of Telefacsimile 218
   B. Telefacsimile's Benefits 219
   C. The Feasibility Study: Is It Really Necessary? 219
   D. Telefacsimile Equipment 222
   E. Telefacsimile Cost Centers 227
   F. Copyright Implications for Telefacsimile 233
   G. Establishing a Fax Network 234
   H. The Internet: What Is It, What Does It Do, and How Do I Join It? 236
   I. Group IV Telefacsimile Equipment 238

X. Scanning for Document Delivery 239
   A. Scanning Explained: The Research Libraries Group's Ariel 239
   B. Scanning versus Fax: What's the Difference? 240

       C. North Carolina State University's Digitized Document Transmission Project (NCSU DDTP) 241
       D. Cost Centers for Scanning 242
       E. When Should a Library Implement Scanning? 242

  XI. Evaluating Approaches to Document Delivery 243

 XII. Experimenting with Document Delivery 244

Defining Document Delivery

In its 1983 report to the Council on Library Resources, Information Systems Consultants defined document delivery as "the transfer of a document or a surrogate from a supplier, whether a library or a document service, to a requesting library."[1] Several features of this definition make it quite serviceable today. It allows for both the physical movement of books, reels of microfilm, or videotapes, as well as electronic transfer (fax or scanning). It also separates a document's method of delivery from all other aspects of securing the information it contains, and includes both the delivery of interlibrary loans or purchased information.

Document Delivery: The "New Frontier" for Access

In earlier chapters, it has been mentioned more than once that the bibliographic utilities have largely solved the problem of efficiently locating wanted books and journal articles. However, as one librarian pointedly observes, "With ILL requests travelling at the speed of electrons, it is becoming more difficult to accept the delivery of requested items travelling at the pace of the U.S. mail."[2] Similarly, Sue O. Medina suggests that bibliographic access without physical access is an empty promise.[3]

In fact, many librarians believe that it is the delivery aspect of resource sharing that will govern our profession's success or failure in substituting access for assets for some portion of readers' information needs. Hewitt and Shipman also think that the poor performance of document delivery is the major factor working against the successful implementation of cooperative collection development programs.[4] For these reasons, today's "new frontier" in access seems to be the issue of achieving rapid delivery. If further proof of this statement's truth is wanted, we have only to examine why commercial document services continue to grow in number and market share; "speed of delivery" is certain to be the answer.

In a paper delivered before the first national conference of the Library and Information Technology Association (LITA), September 1983, Richard W. Boss and Judy McQueen made a number of valuable observations about the general state of document delivery in American libraries:

> The major barrier to effective and efficient interlibrary lending is the apparently simple process of physically moving the item to be loaned from one library to another.... The actual movement of materials takes longer today than it did before electronic technology began to be used in interlibrary lending.[5]

Unfortunately, these comments are still valid today. In 1990 librarians meeting in an interlibrary loan focus group sponsored by the Online Computer Library Center (OCLC) expressed similar concerns. Among the most pressing issues they identified were the disparity between bibliographic access and physical access.[6]

The Need for Delivery Choices

While the transmission of shorter documents by telefacsimile and scanning technologies has improved the general document delivery picture, most librarians agree that there is considerable room for still more progress: as we shall see, these innovations have had some impact, but they are far from pervasive and not without their complications. And, they are impractical for delivering books. As the librarians participating in the OCLC interlibrary discussion panel observed,

> New technologies and communications tools, which enhance librarians' ability to identify the existence of publications, promise wider, faster access to library material. However, fulfillment of that promise is still seriously limited by slow turnaround times and document delivery methods. Bibliographic access has improved markedly in recent years, leaving physical access as the next big obstacle to conquer.[7]

In his 1985 survey on document delivery, Gary D. Wiggins asked academic librarians to describe those factors most important to them in choosing a delivery mechanism. In descending order of importance, they listed (1) speed of supply; (2) rapid response from the supplier about availability; (3) availability of the supplier's list of serials; (4) cost; (5) availability of "rush" service; and (6) distance between the library and the supplier.[8] These priorities have the capacity to surprise, because librarians often act in ways that belie them: how often, for example, if we know we can get a document "for free" but slowly, do we opt instead to pay for it, so that we can obtain rapid delivery from a different source? And, as Richard W. Boss points out,

> The extent to which this concern [speed of delivery] is shared by the users who request the materials varies considerably and has not been the subject of detailed research. Anecdotal evidence suggests that many users are grateful to receive items through the interlibrary loan system, irrespective of the time taken to fill a request.[9]

To paraphrase Boss and McQueen, it is not the purpose of this book to argue that rapid delivery is essential for all interlibrary loans, but rather to examine the many ways in which books, journal articles, and other items can be delivered, and to compare the potential costs and benefits of each. Practically speaking, any plan to improve document delivery should incorporate several methods, depending on the size of the document, the distance between supplier and recipient, and the importance of speed.[10] Along these lines, Maurice B. Line points out that

> A clear distinction needs to be made here between "copiable" items such as most journal articles, and "noncopiable" items such as books.... Typically, over half of all requests are for journals, but that still leaves a very large quantity of book requests.[11]

Jay K. Lucker follows with his own observations:

> For materials of substantial length, basically monographs, it seems unlikely, given present technology, that there is an economical substitute for the original work.... The greatest potential for the application of technology to document delivery seems to be in the realm of shorter documents, especially periodical articles.[12]

Thus, we need delivery choices that allow for the various formats that must be transmitted, the distance a document must travel, and the recipient's sense of urgency. In some cases, there may be little debate about which delivery mechanism to choose: a given document having come to our attention in a certain way (through a table of contents service, for example), we may opt for a delivery mechanism linked to that "discovery" system (transfer to an electronic mailbox; telefacsimile transmission). In many cases, however, we may choose to separate the systems used for identification and delivery, or delivery choices will present themselves for other reasons. This chapter (which does not address the delivery of items from local collections but confines itself to the transfer of remotely held materials) is designed to identify the issues surrounding document delivery and to suggest the most promising delivery approaches, as well as the circumstances under which each might be used.

Speed: Is There a Need?

Boss and McQueen note above that no real research on the value readers attach to delivery speed has been conducted. British information specialist A. E. Cawkell speculates about the reasons for such negligence:

> The curious fact is that, to the best of my knowledge, no effort has been made to assess the value of "speed." What kind of publication, available from libraries, is wanted by what kind of people, and what would be the added value of receiving it in one hour or overnight? If no satisfactory work has been done on this subject the reason for its absence may be the same as the absence of satisfactory work on the value of information.... The value of intangibles is not easily assessed.[13]

Perhaps, he suggests, it has been difficult to find an entity or individual eager to fund the research necessary to assess the value-added aspect of speed in providing something (information) which itself is of undetermined worth. Possibly, he speculates, this is why telecommunication-based electronic document delivery systems are still in the experimental stages.[14]

In the absence of research on the importance of speed in document delivery, librarians have not been shy in expressing their personal opinions. Can we find a common view, or is the jury still out? In her 1984 article "Delivery Systems: Hurry Up and Wait," Susan K. Martin advances the idea that speed is not so important as some would have us believe:

> How quickly does anyone need the document? Does it matter that we hurry up and wait? I think not. Yes, the surgeon may need an article immediately, but the National Library of Medicine has established a functioning delivery system. The undergraduate always needs the document yesterday for the term paper due tomorrow. Most other scholars can wait.[15]

Martin goes on to modify her stance: when delivery speed is not economically harmful to the library (perhaps an example would be the virtually cost-free scanning of documents over the Internet), we can accept and appreciate speed. However, when higher costs are attached to speed (as they frequently are) we must be certain that we provide rapid delivery in those cases where it is actually required, rather than simply because the technology to supply it is easily available to us. In other words, we will probably not wish to deliver every periodical article requested of us by telefacsimile, just because we have a fax machine in the interlibrary loan office. Martin suggests that most institutions will provide at least two levels of delivery: "normal" and "rapid," the precise definitions of these terms being clearly understood among resource sharing partners.[16]

Many libraries do just as Martin suggests, some in a fashion more structured than others. At California State University at San Bernardino, for example, twenty-four- to forty-eight-hour delivery service is guaranteed for articles from journals the library has canceled, or those to which faculty have requested subscriptions, but whose acquisition has been prevented by budgetary restrictions. Delivery of all other requested articles is achieved by "normal" versus "rapid" mechanisms, and no attempt is made to obtain exceptional speed. In other libraries, staff in interlibrary loan may simply assess the reader's need for speedy delivery on a case-by-case basis, and request rapid or normal delivery technologies accordingly. On the receiving end of a request for a book or article, most libraries will opt for a less expensive (and often slower) delivery approach, unless the requester specifies the need for rapid transfer.

There are one or two more points to be made about the issue of speed. In an address before New York City librarians interested in document delivery, Thomas J. Michalak suggested that reliability (or, as he calls it, "predictability") is almost the equal partner of speed. At Carnegie Mellon, he reported, readers were happy to wait three to five days for items delivered through Pennsylvania's statewide delivery service, because the service was predictable: they knew it would work, and they knew how long it would take.[17] The suggestion that in many cases reliability or predictability may substitute nicely for speed is an important one for librarians striving to satisfy both readers' real and perceived needs, while also spending their access dollars as wisely as possible.

A related concept is the role of speed in building trust in access. Many librarians argue that, as we own less and access more, speed is the key to acceptance of the new access/ownership model; they say we will never be successful in persuading faculty and students that access can substitute for ownership in some portion of their information needs, unless the accessed material is provided almost as quickly as one could walk to the stacks and pull the desired item from the local library's shelves. If we assume that speed of delivery is greatest when the local library owns the wanted item, then we should acknowledge that significant growth in the number of documents obtained from remote sources (through interlibrary borrowing and commercial document services) in relation to locally obtained items (as measured by circulation figures or other indications of collection use) indicates a need for increased speed in the delivery of these remotely held items.

Delivery to the Library and Delivery to the Reader: They Aren't the Same Thing

It is critical that librarians not sit back and congratulate themselves once a requested item arrives: until the reader actually receives the material, the library's work is incomplete. In fact, the degree of confidence that faculty and students will have in the ability of resource sharing to meet a part of their research needs will depend on how much time elapses before they actually hold the requested item in their hands: they are not likely to be impressed if a book or photocopy arrives in the local library the next day, but they do not learn of its availability for another week.

Most libraries lend or provide copies of documents only to other libraries; however, many delivery technologies enable the transmission of items (chiefly, journal articles) directly to the reader, and some libraries and a number of commercial document services are capable of and willing to do this. What are the issues that will inform a library's decision about where a document should be delivered?

Certainly the reader receives a document most quickly when it comes directly from the supplier (nonprofit or commercial) to his or her mailbox, office, fax machine, or computer. A project suggested by the City University of New York's libraries to the Council on Library Resources proposes that commercial document suppliers will transmit items directly to a faculty member's workstation over the Internet or regular telephone lines. Receiving the document, the faculty member can then choose to read it online, store it on disk, or print it out.[18] Similarly, the Electronic

Document Delivery Service (EDDS) attached to the North Carolina State University Digitized Document Transmission Project (NCSU DDTP) enables interlibrary loan requests that are delivered by scanning technology to be sent directly by the supplying library to the workstations of researchers in the College of Forest Resources and the Department of Marine, Earth, and Atmospheric Sciences, completely bypassing the NCSU libraries.[19]

A library may wish to balance the kind of speed such delivery offers with some of the problems it can potentially present. If the wrong item is delivered, the reader will have to contact the library to straighten out the matter, since the library's routine procedure of matching the request with the material that has actually been sent will be omitted. There can also be the question of resolving claims of nonreceipt. However, when a partner (or commercial document service) willing to deliver directly to the reader has a good track record for supplying what was requested, and the reader who requests direct delivery is also reliable, the benefits of direct delivery will probably outweigh all other considerations.

Whether the interlibrary loan or access unit will provide a local, on-campus delivery service for those items lenders send directly to the library is a separate question, one on which much has been written. If it is the library's policy to deliver items available from local collections to certain groups of readers (faculty, for example), that same mechanism (campus mail or a library-run delivery service) could be used to deliver materials obtained from remote locations. In some cases, where materials have been lent with the stipulation that they be used within the library, local delivery service may be unsuitable.

In some institutions campus delivery services may be so slow that readers will much prefer to call at the library for their materials, or the campus mail service may be reluctant to deliver books because they are heavy. Here, one might consider having photocopies delivered, and asking that books be picked up. Libraries may decide against delivering materials for fear this will increase the incidence of loss (endangering borrowing relationships), or local policy may require readers to acknowledge receipt of material at the time it is placed in their hands, dictating a trip to the library.

When the reader is expected to come to the library to collect the material he or she has requested, libraries have a clear responsibility to notify students and faculty as quickly as possible that an item has arrived. Methods that are often used include post cards (sent by U.S. or campus mail), telephone calls (the popularity of answering machines increases the productivity of such calls), or electronic mail to notify readers that their requests have arrived and may be claimed. The objective, of course, is to get the material into the reader's hands as quickly as possible, once it reaches the library: clearly there is little purpose in having a document delivered by some rapid and perhaps costly system (telefacsimile; courier service) if days are to elapse before the reader learns the item has arrived and actually receives it. It is also worth noting that, while every library will wish to notify readers that requested items have arrived, when a student or faculty member has learned from experience that the library routinely achieves delivery within a given period of time, he or she is likely to respond positively to a suggestion to return in a day or two, because the document will have arrived by then.

Two articles that will be very useful to the library interested in starting a local delivery service are Marsha J. Stevenson's "Design Options for an On-Campus Document Delivery Program" and Evelyn Greenberg's "Book Express: Meaningful Access."[20] Finally, any library deciding to deliver to local offices should consider whether it will also pick up.

"No Frills" Delivery: The U.S. Mail

The book rate category of U.S. postage is probably the least expensive method of transmitting documents; it is also the slowest. As Maurice B. Line points out, "Over long distances, surface mail is unacceptable; it takes too long. In consequence, the book is away from the supplying library for a long period, a fact that may inhibit libraries from supplying many books at all."[21] Nonetheless, we know that, for the present and foreseeable future, physical delivery systems will be required for books, reels of microfilm, videotapes, and so forth: thus, we cannot afford to pass over a vendor as prominent as the U.S. Postal Service.

In a paper prepared for the 101st meeting of the Association of Research Libraries, Boss and McQueen make a number of interesting comparisons between postal rates and delivery speed:

> Of the various "overnight" delivery services, the Express Mail system operated by the U.S. Postal Service is the least expensive, offering "next day" delivery at [$13.95] for a two-pound package—the equivalent of an average size monograph.... Other postal service options are less expensive, but slower. A photocopy of an average 22-page journal article (6 ounces) may

be sent by First Class Mail for a cost of [$1.44] with an expected delivery schedule of three days over a distance such as that between Tucson, Arizona, and Eugene, Oregon. A two-pound Priority Mail package would cost [$2.90] over the same distance. The use of library rate is economically attractive—[$.65] for the first pound and [$.24] for every pound up to seven pounds—with a non-distance-dependent pricing schedule—but a disaster time wise, with postal officials quoting 10 to 12 days or more for a distance as short as 1000 miles and, because of the surface nature of the transaction, considerably longer for destinations not within the contiguous United States.[22]

There are other features of Express Mail and Priority Mail that should be considered. The library can deliver packages to designated Express Mail post offices; in some areas, libraries can arrange for regularly scheduled pickup by Postal Service staff of Express Mail and Priority Mail packages; the cost is $4.50 per pickup, no matter how many packages are collected. Alternatively, in some communities there are Express Mail collection boxes and mobile units, where library staff may deposit packages, and the Postal Service invites deposit accounts for convenience in paying. Any library unfamiliar with these services can call the local post office to request a free consumer's information kit about them and other postal services. The Postal Service reports its overnight reliability for Express Mail to be 97 percent, and improving.

Boss and McQueen point out that, even if cost were no object, Express Mail does not offer a perfect solution to document delivery, because the service is not offered to every destination.[23] Libraries will certainly use one or more U.S. Postal Service plans to ship a portion of the items they lend; in deciding when to use which service, it will be important to consider issues of distance and speed. Library rate, first class, and Express Mail are not affected by distance, and a Priority Mail package must weigh more than five pounds before the distance it is shipped begins to influence the cost of shipping. In a study conducted for Michigan's publicly assisted university libraries, Information Systems Consultants, Inc., notes another important issue relating to distance:

> While geography plays a factor in transit time, an even more important factor is the number of sorting facilities through which a shipment must pass. An item moving between two major cities on opposite coasts may go through one sorting center in each city. If the shipment goes from one small community to another, it may be sorted in the shipping community, in two intermediate centers, and again in the receiving community.

Each sort adds to the transit time. In the case of USPS library rate, it may be as much as a day in each center. For first class mail, the time is generally measured in hours.[24]

Courier Services

In the United States, even school children are aware that the Postal Service has its competitors, commonly called courier or commercial delivery services; among these services are United Parcel Service (UPS) and Federal Express, and for our purposes the latter will serve as a useful foil for the U.S. mail. That same two-pound package the Postal Service will deliver overnight for $13.95 (by 3:00 P.M. the next day, or by noon when traveling between major business markets) costs either $16.50 (Standard Overnight Service, which reaches its destination by 3:00 P.M. the following afternoon) or $24.25 (Priority Overnight Service, which will arrive by 10:30 the next morning). These delivery times are representative of what Federal Express calls "AA primary service areas"; for cities and towns designated for other classes of service, different times apply. While next-day is available to almost every city served, there are some differences, depending on whether one is shipping to Bogus Springs, Texas, or New York City.

A telephone call to a local Federal Express office or to FedEx's toll-free number (1-800-238-5355) will cause a copy of the latest issue of the *Federal Express Service Guide* to arrive the next day. This handy publication explains domestic and international rates, lists every city in the United States served by Federal Express and the level of service available to each, and describes special services, such as free pickup service, volume discounts, and FedEx Economy Two-Day Service ($14 for that same two-pound package, not a very favorable comparison to the Postal Service's Priority Mail at $2.90, which is delivered to locations within six hundred miles in two days, and those beyond six hundred miles in three days). Federal Express permits deliveries to be charged to a receiving institution's account, a very convenient service.

ISCI calls Federal Express "one of the most successful of the overnight services." Part of this company's achievement stems from its discovery that it is more effective to sort every package in a single national center, rather than in a number of regional centers. FedEx's center is located in Memphis, and whether a package is traveling from Miami to Seattle, or from San Francisco to

Los Angeles, it will be sorted once, in Tennessee.[25] Among members of RLG, Federal Express is the delivery mechanism of choice for books. Ten years ago, Barbara Brown reported that the typical RLG member's annual FedEx bill ranged from $1,760 to $7,500.[26] Although more recent comparative data are not available (the results of an RLG interlibrary loan cost study will generate this kind of information), Federal Express charges have nominally increased and interlending traffic has ballooned: we can see that choosing to ship a substantial portion of one's ILL business by courier is not an inexpensive proposition. Even the larger academic institution, which may well have a universitywide corporate account that results in a marked discount, will find its Federal Express bill significant.

Regional Delivery Services

By now it must be apparent that no one speaks of document delivery without consulting the writings of Richard W. Boss. He says:

> Where population densities, interlibrary loan transaction volumes, and appropriate sources of funding permit, the establishment of local or regional cooperative courier services dedicated to the movement of library materials provides an attractive document delivery mechanism.[27]

The variations on this theme are many: a number of states (Pennsylvania, Illinois, Connecticut, Washington) operate statewide surface delivery systems, but within others (New York, for example) a number of regional systems exist side by side; sometimes, as in the MINITEX Library Information Network, delivery systems cross state lines. Boss and McQueen note that few statewide systems can deliver materials for under $2.50 per item, and that the cost-per-item varies widely from system to system. Delivery time is typically three days or more, and when a system includes more than one route (making it necessary for various lines to intersect and exchange parcels), delivery time may exceed five days.[28]

In some cases these delivery programs are operated by a central agency, in others they are contracted out to existing commercial delivery or courier services. In her book *Guidelines for Library Cooperation: Development of Academic Library Consortia*, Ruth J. Patrick describes one consortium of academic libraries in which "the responsibility for providing transportation among the members [rotated], once every five weeks. The type of transportation was decided by each member and ranged from a student's car to a university-owned panel truck to a taxicab."[29] Sometimes a library's delivery system is associated with a primary resource sharing agreement; at other times the delivery mechanism results from membership in one consortium, and the interlending agreement from affiliation with still another.

Cost Schemes and Centers

In some cases (the New York Metropolitan Reference and Research Library Agency—METRO) the cost of a delivery service is included in a cooperative's membership fee. In other instances libraries are charged a flat annual fee for use of the delivery service, and in still others they pay according to the number of deliveries received. Whether the consortium buys vehicles and hires drivers or instead contracts with an existing courier service, the cost centers will be the same: overhead, such as vehicle depreciation, insurance, and driver benefits, as well as the direct costs of driver salaries, vehicle purchase, vehicle maintenance, and fuel.[30] Since these costs will vary widely, depending on locality, a group of libraries considering such a service will be wise to consider the local economy.

Pennsylvania's Interlibrary Delivery Service (IDS)

Pennsylvania's Interlibrary Delivery Service is a highly successful multitype library system that has undergone several identity changes before settling into its present sound and comfortable model; in 1990, it had 193 members. Each year Pennsylvania bids out this statewide document delivery service; at present, United Parcel Service (UPS) holds the contract, which is negotiated with the State Library. Each participating library anticipates the volume of parcels it will ship, and then pays a flat annual rate for use of the service, one which is not dependent on weight or distance. Some of Pennsylvania's experiences and techniques may be useful to other groups of libraries considering a delivery system, or making changes to an existing program.

In the early 1970s IDS used library-operated and leased vehicles, and an institution typically received three deliveries and returns per week; the state operated three separate and interconnected routes. In 1979 a financial crisis, sparked by rising gasoline prices, expenses for vehicle repairs, and the lack of uniformity and control of drivers' wages almost destroyed the service. A consultant recommended that the existing program be replaced by a contract with a professional parcel delivery firm, and that annual membership fees (at the time, a flat fee for each member library) instead be based on each institution's use of the service. In 1986 a major rate increase from Purolater, IDS's contractor, prompted another change, and UPS was selected; deliveries increased to five days a week. In 1990, a combination of State Library and LSCA funding supported 75 percent of the system's operating costs.

IDS members believe that part of the system's success stems from the requirement that the contractor pick up and deliver to each member library directly, even if a library is affiliated with a larger institution with other delivery points. IDS has contributed to the success of many resource sharing projects, including those among the Associated College Libraries of Central Pennsylvania (ACLCP) and the hundreds of libraries involved in the ACCESS PENNSYLVANIA CD-ROM union catalog project (also supported with state and LSCA funding).[31]

IDS's pricing scheme favors high-volume transporters; infrequent users can pay up to three times as much per item as frequent users do. In its 1991 study of resource sharing among Michigan's publicly assisted university libraries, ISCI reported IDS costs ranging from $650 per year for a library with fewer than five hundred transactions, to $1,950 for one with three to four thousand transactions. In a recent year, IDS moved more than 271,000 packages, at an average cost of $1.75 each (the per item cost was somewhat less, because a single package often contains several items). Perhaps the oddest aspect of the IDS system is that the shipping (rather than the receiving) library pays the costs. ISCI praised the Pennsylvania model, but recommended that Michigan, if it were to implement a similar system, instead levy charges on the receiving libraries. "This not only places the financial burden where it belongs," they wrote, "but also gives greater control over cost to the requesting institution."[32]

When one Pennsylvania library compared IDS delivery costs with those of U.S. mail and UPS, it estimated first-class postage was typically slightly more than twice the cost of an IDS-delivered package, while regular UPS charges were almost six times as high as the rate negotiated for the Pennsylvania blanket contract. IDS has a consistent one- to two-day delivery time throughout the state, making it superior to first-class mail, which Pennsylvania librarians report to take two to four days. Many Pennsylvania libraries now use telefacsimile transmission to send journal articles to one another, but IDS remains the backbone of intrastate document delivery. It is worth noting that UPS can be a cost-effective service, even on a considerably smaller scale. The Network of Alabama Academic Libraries (NAAL) also uses a blanket UPS contract to ship all interlibrary loans that are not transmitted by telefacsimile; the cost was reported at around $2.25 per package.[33]

Other Regional Delivery Models

Many other states and regions also operate cooperative delivery services. New York's METRO contracts with a local messenger service that guarantees delivery of packages on the next scheduled delivery day after pickup, regardless of a library's geographic location within the system. Unmetered access to the delivery service is included in the cost of belonging to METRO, whose graduated membership fee tops out at $2,000 annually for the largest university libraries belonging to the system (including those of Columbia and New York universities) and includes many benefits in addition to document delivery. Depending on their volume of interlending, members receive scheduled service two, three, or five days a week.[34]

The state systems in Connecticut, Maryland, and Illinois represent very different delivery models. Connecticut purchases its own vehicles and hires its own drivers, resulting in considerable overhead and a certain difficulty in adjusting to seasonal fluctuations in system use. In both Maryland and Illinois the state system is created by linking a number of independent regional delivery services. In Illinois, Intersystems Library Delivery Service (ILDS) links the local delivery services of the eighteen regional library systems, as well as the state's four Reference and Research (R&R) centers; such a model can slow delivery time, as packages sit at transfer points waiting to be loaded onto another region's van. There may also be difficulties in coordinating pickups and deliveries for separately administered services, and the delivery cost-per-package in such systems tends to be higher than in centrally operated services.[35]

Messenger Services

Some libraries or groups of libraries use messengers, traveling by foot, bicycle, public transportation, or private vehicle, to retrieve materials their readers want. Interesting examples, for which more detail is given in the appendix, are the CTW Library Consortium, whose members (Connecticut College, Trinity College, and Wesleyan University) jointly own a station wagon and employ a full-time driver to transport books from campus to campus, and Loyola Marymount University (Los Angeles), whose library also owns a car and employs a driver to courier materials borrowed from the nearby University of California at Los Angeles (UCLA) library.

When student runners are employed, such arrangements are sometimes referred to as "sneakernets." One of the most extensive of these is Polytechnic University's (PU, Brooklyn, N.Y.) InfoDash program in which students (called "dashers"), walking or taking the bus or subway, go to libraries throughout the metropolitan area, pull journal volumes off the shelves, and photocopy articles wanted by Polytechnic's readers. Since a given journal is likely to be owned by many libraries in the New York metropolitan area where Polytechnic is located, sources are chosen based on location (convenience to subway and bus routes) and ease of access (institutions in which bound journals are paged are avoided). Students are trained how to get into and out of libraries quickly and easily; they are taught to be unobtrusive. The budget for the service is about $70,000 per year, which includes money for bus and subway tokens, photocopying costs, and student salaries. The cost of obtaining some fifteen to eighteen thousand articles per year is about $3.75 to $4.75 per article and speed is excellent, making the service more than competitive with commercial document companies and other delivery mechanisms. More detail about this program appears in chapter 3.

The positives associated with messenger services are very clear: the library has a great deal of control over its document delivery service and can sometimes achieve very good per-item prices. The negatives are equally obvious: purchasing a vehicle is costly and fraught with ongoing costs (insurance, fuel, repair, eventual replacement, driver salaries and benefits) and their associated problems. Programs that employ student workers may suffer staffing shortages during holiday and examination periods, but they also have the benefit of flexibility (one need not pay a full-time employee in the summer months when demand is slight; wages are lower and benefits are not an issue).

Evaluation and Sources of Funding

Delivery systems that are centralized and contract with existing courier services often achieve lower per-package costs and greater speed than those that follow other models. In evaluating a delivery service, a library will certainly want to look closely at these factors, as well as issues like billing procedures (are they accurate and simple?), pickup and delivery schedules (are they frequent and reliable?), and the number of items lost in shipment (all couriers should keep such figures).

Many delivery systems receive state or LSCA funding; this sort of money is much easier to get when the delivery program includes multitype libraries. In its recommendations to Michigan's publicly assisted university libraries, ISCI suggested the Kellogg, Carnegie, Kresge, Mellon, and Pew foundations as likely sources of grant money to underwrite the first year of a regional or statewide delivery program. The idea here is to "buy down" the first year cost of the program until membership and volume have a chance to build, making costs easier to predict and control.[36]

Telefacsimile Transmission[37]

> Facsimile is a technology which has been looking for a library application for years. It has passed through the breathless-wonder, the grant-encouraged new toy, and the human problems phases, during which need and economic considerations received short shrift. These cycles are quite normal in IT [information technology]. Will the epitaph of library fax turn out to be "it was all possible, but they didn't really need it and they couldn't afford it"? Answers to questions such as "how quickly?" "at what price if any?" and "with what quality?" are needed.[38]

Resolving the questions A. E. Cawkell poses has not been easy for librarians. Ironically, just when we seem to have answered them, a new document delivery technology (scanning, examined in this chapter's next section) appears to be well on its way to supplanting fax transmission. However, many American libraries and library systems have invested in telefacsimile, and others will continue to do so. Furthermore, the questions librarians should ask themselves before implementing fax delivery are the same ones applicable to scanning technologies. Equipment costs have declined, and transmission through the Internet can eliminate concerns about enormous telephone bills. Perhaps more important, telefacsimile is an established library delivery technology in a way that scanning, as yet, is not: the library looking to achieve rapid delivery for a significant percentage of the journal articles it obtains from remote locations needs a sizable base of transmission partners, which telefacsimile can deliver.

Telefacsimile is likely to enjoy almost instant and strong reader support and acceptance (providing the copies are clean and clear) because of the excellent speed of delivery; recipients who have been given a choice generally prefer documents laser printed on plain (versus thermal) paper. Today it is possible for items to be faxed not only to libraries, but directly to readers' offices or homes: the fax machine seems to be replacing the telephone answering device or cellular phone as a late-twentieth-century status symbol; more and more members of the academic community have ready access to telefacsimile or equip their personal computers with send-and-receive fax modems. Libraries that use surface mail or courier services for nonurgent items and fax for rush materials have found it is important to explain their policies to readers in order to avoid frustration and confusion when not every request arrives instantaneously.

The Uses of Telefacsimile

Telefacsimile is only useful for the delivery of items it is feasible to photocopy; fax can be used to supplement but not replace the U.S. mail, UPS, and other delivery mechanisms. Some libraries (especially those that have not automated ILL request procedures) transmit interlibrary loan requests by telefacsimile, as well as the documents used to fill them; others find that this disrupts the office's workflow and prefer to receive all requests in a standard manner (through OCLC or a shared electronic mail system, for example). At least one library system reports using fax chiefly for requesting materials, and much less frequently for transmitting documents.[39] A certain loss of legibility does result when a library cannot fill a request and forwards (refaxes) it to another institution. In his article "Telefacsimile in Libraries: New Deal in the 1980s," Steven A. Brown reports that a National Agricultural Library study showed that the typical request was unreadable after the third transmission.[40]

Libraries that transmit documents by telefacsimile must examine the question of urgency and set goals for turnaround time. Will the library fax everything that's faxable, as do the members of the Network of Alabama Academic Libraries, or only rush materials (the City University of New York model)? Here, remember Susan K. Martin's caution that we not allow technology to dictate policy, but also consider whether multiple delivery options and complex conditions under which each should be used will aggravate the staff or consume too much time. Libraries will certainly wish to compare the costs and speed associated with telefacsimile with those of other delivery options (commercial courier service or U.S. mail, for example).

Telefacsimile's Benefits

The major advantage of telefacsimile is its usefulness in acquiring "time crucial" information for readers. A document can be sent across a city, a state, or from East Coast to West Coast, but fax networks have been especially successful where they reduce libraries' sense of geographic isolation by delivering documents swiftly.[41] Following a study of library telefacsimile projects, Richard W. Boss and Hal Espo agreed with this assessment:

> Attitudes about the future viability of digital telefacsimile as a document delivery medium appeared to correlate directly with the geographic isolation of the library. The Alaskan users believed that the technology would continue to be used because it had cut the minimum delivery time from seven to ten days down to one to three days. Users in Montana and Idaho also predicted continued use by at least some of the libraries.... The libraries that did most of their borrowing and lending within states with good courier services did not expect the telefacsimile equipment to be retained, even though technically it had been acceptable.[42]

The experience of the City University of New York libraries supports this conclusion: while each of the eighteen libraries in the system owns a fax machine, each is also a member of METRO and thus has access to its courier system; typically, only rush materials are faxed.

A second advantage to telefacsimile will probably be its low cost. Once the equipment is in place and paid for, the cost per transmission will be minimal both for local calls or if a library is faxing over the Internet rather than commercial telephone lines. Almost certainly it will cost less than Express Mail or courier service, unless a shared or subsidized delivery system like those in Pennsylvania and the New York metropolitan area have achieved very low costs. Susquehanna University (Pennsylvania) determined that faxing shorter documents was routinely cheaper than sending them through IDS, because telefacsimile eliminated the staff time required to package them for the delivery service.[43]

The Feasibility Study: Is It Really Necessary?

Only five years ago, every article on telefacsimile prescribed an assessment study prior to implementation. Today, as Steven A. Brown points out, "results of many studies are now being published in the literature, allowing libraries to survey applications and profit by the experience of others."[44] Still, telefacsimile is more practical in certain library environments than others, and an organization considering fax may wish to examine the following questions.

How great is the library's interlending volume?

It may not be worthwhile for the library with low ILL traffic to invest in telefacsimile, unless it has uses for the technology other than resource sharing; the occasional rush item can be handled through an alternative rapid but low-overhead system.

How many requests for periodical articles (versus books) does the library send and receive?

For the library that will not use telefacsimile for every journal article transmitted, an important variation on this question is, "What is the number of articles the library would consider urgent enough for the use of telefacsimile?" Information Systems Consultants, Inc. has developed guidelines to help a library determine whether its interlending volume is likely to make telefacsimile transmission economical:

> An acceptable cost appears likely to be achieved only under one of the following conditions: (1) very high transaction volumes among points in telefacsimile networks—volumes of at least 500 pages per month and preferably 1,000 pages per month at each site; (2) incorporation of the telefacsimile technology into the work patterns of the interlibrary loan staff rather than treating telefacsimile as an exception to regular routines. This involves not only batching the photocopying of such materials, but also lower-rate evening hour telecommunications rates using a staff member who is regularly scheduled to arrive before 8:00 a.m. or leave after 5:00 p.m.[45]

Volume, integration, and off-peak transmission time: these are key factors ISCI suggests for economy in telefacsimile.

How many interlending requests are sent outside the library's local area?

If a library's interlending is largely done locally or regionally, it may have less use for telefacsimile than a library whose primary partners are located at a greater distance.

Will the library use telefacsimile to receive material purchased from commercial document services?

Since the primary purpose of these services is speed, it makes sense to ensure swiftness at every step of the process by providing for fax transmission of wanted items.

Can the library presently respond to an interlibrary loan request within its network's specified time limit?

Telefacsimile will not significantly speed up an already slow interlending operation.

Do the library's chief access partners have telefacsimile capability?

The decision to acquire a telefacsimile machine assumes that there will be libraries with which an institution exchanges material that will also have fax capability, and that it will be possible to achieve acceptable standards for turnaround time with these libraries. Speed of transmission will not mean much if one's partners typically take several days to respond to a request. Patrick R. Dewey observes that, as more and more libraries acquire fax capability and the newness wears off, responsiveness often declines; what was once twenty-four-hour turnaround slips to a wait of two or more days. In place of a "we'll fax anything" policy and in response to the demands such a policy can often create, some libraries are now instituting procedures that discourage fax (imposing fees, faxing only under certain restricted conditions).

Are readers satisfied with the speed of current service?

The library that can routinely obtain a high percentage of the items it borrows within a period of time considered acceptable by its readers may not need telefacsimile. As Brown points out,

> When users can be satisfied with delivery by mail, telefacsimile is an unnecessary expense. When next-day delivery is adequate, there is the possibility of using courier delivery services. This may be a cost-effective alternative for libraries with only occasional need for rapid delivery.[46]

Do some readers ignore the interlibrary loan service, because of time delays?

The library that believes many readers avoid ILL because of their perception that resource sharing is unacceptably slow should certainly consider telefacsimile.

Will readers be satisfied with copy quality? Brown makes an interesting observation on this topic:

> Some recipients dislike the paper on which their facsimiles are printed. Thermal paper, used in many units, strikes some as unpleasant to the touch, discolors if exposed to intense sunlight or heat, darkens if colored with a highlighting marker, and may not be as permanent as regular photocopy paper. It should be noted, however, that copies made on thermal paper three years ago and stored in a filing cabinet are perfectly legible today.[47]

Telefacsimile Equipment

Every library considering fax should appreciate the degree to which this technology will increase the costs of the existing resource sharing operation; this means understanding the several cost centers associated with the technology, the first of which is the equipment itself.

Equipment Standards

The minimum standards for telefacsimile equipment include those established for CCITT Group III machines; in fact, it will be difficult to identify a machine that does *not* meet this standard, which has superseded those for Group I and Group II. Resolution should be 100 × 200 dpi (dots per inch), standard, and 200 × 200 dpi, fine. Dewey recommends that the library planning to send a fair amount of illustrated material consider a machine that will do halftones (shades of gray), rather than simple black and white. Here again there is variation: some equipment features thirty-two shades, others sixty-four shades.[48]

Equipment Options

A library considering fax should think carefully about how the machine will be used in order to make the best decisions about which of many features should be acquired. The considerations listed below apply to equipment used primarily for resource sharing; features such as "group dialing," for instance, are not included, as they have little relevance for interlending.

Paper The telefacsimile coordinator for one library system reports that few libraries purchasing new equipment opt for thermal paper machines: plain paper (which makes cleaner, clearer copies but may require toner) is today's more popular choice. Some plain-paper machines can accommodate different sheet sizes. Any type of paper may be used, and the paper need not be purchased from the machine's vendor; rather, it can be gotten as cheaply as possible.

Nonetheless, many machines are sold that use the more expensive thermal paper, generally purchased in rolls from the equipment vendor. Larger machines accommodate larger rolls of paper (up to 328 feet) and thus require less frequent paper replacement. As the paper nearest the end of the roll is used, the printed sheets sometimes curl (rather than lying flat) and bounce out of the paper tray, creating extra collating work. Some thermal machines will hold two or more different widths of paper.

While some readers object to the paper because of its unpleasant feel and smell, more than one library reports that some people are allergic to this paper or the associated fumes. In one institution where the fax machine and the database searching terminal shared a small and not very well ventilated space, the terminal was relocated because the thermal fax machine made the searching coordinator ill.

Memory and Memory Size A memory feature is useful for delayed transmissions, so that libraries can economize by sending long distance at night, when telephone rates are lowest. On the other hand, if a library's volume of long-distance transmissions is low, memory may be unnecessary; a machine that can hold thirty to fifty pages in a paper feed for delayed transmission may do just as well. Machines with memory are said to be "programmable" or able to "store and forward." This is a valuable feature, since it allows staff to scan hundreds of pages of text (depending on memory size) into the machine during daytime hours, and use programmable dialing to cause the machine to send the stored documents at night, when telephone rates are cheaper.[49] The equipment is also capable of faxing one document while another is being read into memory for subsequent transmission.

Timed or Delayed Transmission Whether or not it also has memory, a machine with this feature can transmit documents from a feeder at off-hours.

Time and Date This feature causes the date and time of transmission to be printed on each page of a document. The sender also receives a printout of a time and date transmission log.

Speed Dialing This quality allows frequently dialed numbers to be programmed into the machine, so that by touching one or two buttons, the fax operator can dial a multidigit telephone number. Human error in dialing is one of the major reasons speed dialing (also called autodial) is a cost-effective feature.

Autoredial A machine with this feature can retry a busy number at least twice before reporting it has not been able to transmit a document. In some cases, the library can set the redial time interval. As telefacsimile transmission has grown in popularity, this feature has become of greater interest.

Automatic Step-Down and Step-Up With this feature, a machine automatically adjusts itself to the baud rate (speed of transmission) available on the telecommunications line, adapting immediately to any line noise. It also enables a Group III machine to communicate with older, slower Group I or II equipment.

Error Correction Mode (ECM) This feature, standard on many machines, ensures correct transmission of documents by identifying errors caused by line noise and automatically resending data as need be.

Scanning Resolution Settings Many machines offer two or more scanning resolution settings (perhaps "regular" and "fine"). If the material being sent is very detailed (a photograph; scientific notations or formulae) or if the telephone line is poor, scanning the image at a higher resolution may be desirable; some machines will automatically adjust to finer scan levels if a telephone connection deteriorates. Higher resolution scanning contains more data and takes more time to complete.[50]

Automatic Document Feeder A document feeder will hold pages to be transmitted, and send them at a time programmed by the operator. This feature is essential for unattended (such as late-night) transmissions, unless a machine possesses memory into which documents can be read during the day for transmittal at night. There are limitations to the use of automatic document feeders, because unattended machines can jam and experience other problems.

Automatic Paper Cutter On machines that use rolls of thermal paper, this feature cuts the paper at the end of each transmitted page. Without an automatic paper cutter, the document will print on one continuous sheet of paper.

Choosing a Machine

Just as there is no single, perfect employee, there is no one fax machine ideal for every environment. Issues of ILL volume and compatibility with partners' equipment are important ones.

Equipment Capacity The size and capacity of the machine should be related to the volume of interlending traffic. While this suggestion is a generally sound one, it is not flawless:

A low number of transmissions, however, does not rule out the selection of a more advanced model. The higher-end models also come packed with many features. A library may buy a more powerful fax "just in case" its usage estimates are way off. If the budget can sustain the cost, such thinking is justified.[51]

Additionally, more expensive machines tend to come equipped with more features, some of which may save valuable staff time.

Stand-Alone Equipment or PC? An alternative to the stand-alone fax machine is the personal computer to which a fax board has been added, enabling the machine to be used both for PC-type tasks (word processing; spreadsheets) and to send and receive fax transmissions. This arrangement works very well for transmitting ASCII files produced by a word processor, for example, but it is not very useful for other types of document transmission; since it has no scanner, the data will have to be keyed into the computer a character at a time, and one cannot key in graphics. (A PC capable of receiving faxes can, however, receive a document transmitted by a fax machine.) While there are scanning devices that will copy a page to a file (the original material could be prepared using an application such as PC Paint), on the whole the combined PC/fax machine seems limited to rather specific applications.[52] Dewey observes other limitations to the PC/fax workstation:

> Several factors may make one rather buy a standalone machine. The convenience and simplicity of a standalone fax machine and the high cost of buying an entire microcomputer system are two good reasons. Microcomputers, especially when attached to a host of peripherals such as scanners, circuit boards, and coupled with complicated software, pose a significant period of learning for most people. . . . In contrast, the standalone fax machine requires little in the way of learning. It will send virtually any printed document that can be squeezed into its scanner accurately and instantly, and requires a modest investment. It also stands ready twenty-four hours a day to receive incoming transmissions.[53]

Memory, or Not? Larger libraries, and libraries that send requests to long-distance numbers, often find memory a useful feature. Smaller libraries, as suggested above, can rely on the delayed transmission feature. A library may wish to consider the following equipment scenarios:

1. Small library: at least five hundred requests received and sent annually. A basic autodial machine should enable the small library to respond to all requests; memory is unnecessary.
2. Medium-sized library: five hundred to five thousand requests received and sent annually. A machine permitting the library to delay and batch transmissions should be acquired. Libraries in the larger end of this group may find memory important in terms of efficient use of staff time.
3. Large library: over five thousand requests received and sent annually. Because of economies related to traffic volume, the large library should consider a plain paper machine with a flat copier bed, which does not require that the document be photocopied first. These machines generally have a laser printer, which makes cleaner, clearer copies. Large libraries also require the capability to send and receive at night. Depending on traffic, multiple machines may be necessary. Printed reports (the time a request was sent; the amount of transmission time required; error detection) are important, particularly for larger libraries.

Intra-Network Compatibility Within a network the use of compatible machines (in terms of generation and vendor) facilitates smooth transmission. "Group III units can communicate with each other regardless of brand, although slightly faster transmission or enhanced resolution often is possible between two machines from the same manufacturer."[54]

Identifying an Equipment Source Telefacsimile equipment is reviewed with less frequency today than in the past, but both library journals and magazines that cover office or computer equipment are good bets for current commentary. Patrick Dewey's book *FAX for Libraries* is one place to start; it contains a "Directory of Popular Fax Makes and Models" as well as an appendix, "Vendor Addresses for Fax Machines." There is also a good glossary.

While there are many different brands of fax machines, librarians who have examined the options have learned that, in a given price range, there are very few differences from product to product:

In reality all of the innards of the machines were produced by a very small group of manufacturers. A major discovery was that there was little difference in the features offered at comparable prices between one brand and another. Even the cost of machines from brand to brand remained within relatively close limits and seldom varied by more than $200.[55]

When librarians had to choose a machine for installation in Associated College Libraries of Central Pennsylvania (ACLCP) institutions, they first developed bid specifications for would-be suppliers; since Group III equipment remains the standard, their document can be useful to libraries or groups of libraries planning to implement telefacsimile transmission. The committee also arranged a workshop to which vendors came and demonstrated their wares, permitting librarians to observe and compare firsthand a number of previously identified features, as well as two important new ones not previously considered, the quality of the case or housing, and operating noise levels.[56] The workshop idea is a good one; as Patrick Dewey points out, "There is no shortage of salespeople willing to come to the library to demonstrate their product. . . . The on-site demonstration is useful because it allows the library staff to get together and ask questions as they see the product in action."[57]

Telefacsimile Cost Centers

Equipment: Purchase, Maintenance, and Leasing Costs

Today's fax machines are typically "compact, easy to use, and mechanically reliable."[58] They can cost from around $2,000 to more than $10,000, depending on the features that are sought. Something between $2,000 and $3,500 is probably typical for a machine that will meet a small- to medium-sized library's resource sharing demands.

A library may purchase a machine outright or lease one. In the first case, there is the price of the machine as well as the additional recurring cost of its maintenance agreement (typically, about 10 percent per annum of the machine's original purchase price). In contrast, when a library leases equipment, the leasing charge often includes maintenance; most leases require a minimum commitment of one year. Whether the library buys or leases, it will also incur a monthly charge for a dedicated telephone line.

The major advantage of leasing over purchasing is that the library can easily update and upgrade its equipment as needed (although some machines have optional additional memory that can be added as needed after purchase). On the other hand, new telefacsimile technology becomes available slowly; the latest equipment, Group IV, is very costly and requires a type of telecommunication line unavailable to most libraries.

Library consortia can often negotiate better prices through vendor contracts for group purchase than can individual libraries. As mentioned above, another advantage to such contracts is that each partner in the system then owns compatible equipment. There are other pricing strategies that have paid off in academic libraries. The Illinois State Library offers LSCA grants of one-half the purchase price (up to $800) for one or more fax machines in a library. In the City University of New York, in an effort to promote and speed resource sharing, the university's Office of Academic Affairs bought machines for each of the college and community college libraries. Several libraries have been successful when they asked the vendors of their photocopying services to provide them with gratis telefacsimile equipment. Others have gotten a fax machine as a "bonus" when they purchased a larger, more costly piece of equipment, such as a photocopier or microform reader/printer. Several libraries report that their "friends" groups have bought machines for them.

Communications Costs

> Telefacsimile is a turnkey technology—once connected it is ready for business. Libraries seem to have more problems with the installation of the dedicated telephone line than with the installation of the telefacsimile machine itself.[59]

There are many tales of fax machines sitting in boxes, gathering cobwebs, while the library waits for the telephone company's representative to arrive and install the necessary dedicated line. While it is technically possible for a library to disconnect a telephone and plug the fax machine into its jack when it wishes to transmit, unless the machine is constantly available (that is, attached to its own dedicated telephone line) other libraries may not be able to send documents without first telephoning and asking that the machine be connected. Thus, it is easy to see why many fax networks require that no human intervention be needed to make telephone connections between machines. A library should order the telephone line the moment it determines where the machine will be placed—there is no need to wait until the machine arrives.

In addition to the charge for installing the fax machine's dedicated telephone line, there are other associated communications costs. These include local transmissions (charged at the going rate for local telephone calls) and those for toll calls when documents are transmitted by long distance. (Some discussion of the relatively new and essentially cost-free procedure of faxing over the Internet appears below.) In cases where the college or university pays a single telephone bill that includes charges incurred by all campus units, telecommunications costs may be an "invisible" cost center.

Steven A. Brown points out one of the inherent inequities in document delivery by telefacsimile: the sender pays for the privilege of supplying the receiver with the document.

> One of the complications of telefacsimile is that the supplying library will be charged for the long-distance charges. Will these telephone costs be recovered, and, if so, how will charges be calculated when the precise cost may not be known until the telephone bill arrives? Can some sort of standard equitable charge for service be made? Can the library wait to take advantage of late-night telephone rates without counteracting too much of the speed benefit of using telefacsimile?[60]

We will reserve addressing the questions Brown asks about charging for fax transmissions for the coming chapter on making decisions for access.

Staffing Costs

Labor costs associated specifically with the use of telefacsimile are difficult to calculate because this work is generally integrated into regular operations. Further, telefacsimile does not eliminate the tedious work of photocopying journal articles and reviewing the copies for quality. One important cost-saving technique is to locate the machine in a place of convenient access: vendors and their brochures may create the impression that a fax machine requires little attention, but this can be most untrue:

> This impression rapidly dissipates in a high-volume operation where transmission problems can disrupt the workflow with surprising frequency.... Pages can jam, causing the telephone connection to be broken; or two pages can feed into the scanner at the same time, with only the page on top being scanned. Staff will need [to] be watchful for such developments, and it is probably best to have someone working in the area during transmission.[61]

Among the duties of the sending institution's staff are photocopying (unless a flat-bed machine is used); feeding pages into the fax machine; solving transmission problems and resending; adjusting the machine; handling telephone line problems; calling for repairs; and maintaining a file of original copies for a given period, in the event these must be resent. In a telefacsimile project between the libraries of the University of Tennessee at Knoxville and Vanderbilt University, in one out of every three documents at least one page had to be resent; other studies have produced similar estimates.[62] This is not an insignificant statistic, nor does it result in a trivial amount of work; the reasons for this rather startling figure are several: the receiving machine runs out of paper; the quality of the document received is poor; multiple pages are pulled through the machine at the same time, so that those on the bottom are not transmitted at all. Staff time can be saved when the telefacsimile machine is near both a photocopier and telephone. Staff at the receiving institution must keep the fax equipment ready to receive (that is, switched on and supplied with paper and toner), check incoming copy for clarity and completeness, and deliver documents to the readers who requested them.

Paper and Supplies

Since thermal paper is expensive, a library or library system may wish to identify a reasonably priced source and buy in bulk; care should be taken about the paper's expiration date, however. Plain paper machines can use any kind of paper of a size the paper tray or trays will accommodate; in some settings, where the college or university provides paper and other basic supplies to campus units free of charge (perhaps through a central "stores" service), paper for these machines can be an invisible item in the library's budget. Unlike thermal paper machines, plain paper equipment requires toner.

Miscellaneous Cost Issues

Some funds may be required for site preparation, including appropriate furniture for the telefacsimile equipment. Library photocopiers must be maintained in excellent condition in order to produce clear originals for faxing. When one accepts ILL requests (versus the documents that fill these requests) by telefacsimile, this may add to manual record keeping.

Requests that the library use its equipment and staff to send and receive documents unrelated to library business are almost certain to arise once the academic community learns about the availability of telefacsimile. A faculty member may ask the library to fax a scholarly paper to a distant colleague. The library should develop policies governing such requests, and perhaps appropriate fees. Such services may be a good source of additional revenue; one could advertise them and compete with local off-campus services.

Cost Per Transmitted Page

Cost estimates for telefacsimile are useful not so much because libraries wish to charge their interlending partners for telefacsimile transmission, but because we wish to compare telefacsimile costs with those for other delivery mechanisms. Typically, these costs are represented in terms of cost per transmitted page; however, libraries have calculated this figure in so many different ways that it is meaningless unless one knows what factors have been included in the determination. Among the candidates are the costs of purchasing or leasing the machine, a service contract, telephone line charges, long-distance charges, supplies, and labor. Thus, when we read that one fax project demonstrated the average transmission time per page to be ninety-three seconds at a cost of 10.5 cents we are unsure exactly what this means, much less whether it will hold true in our own environment.[63] Brown is right when he observes the enormous influence fixed costs can have on cost per page figures:

> Because fixed costs are constant, regardless of how much use is made of the machinery, these costs greatly increase the per page figure in a low-volume operation. The fewer pages sent during a month, the greater the share of the fixed cost burden each transmitted page must bear. Fixed costs include telephone line charges and telefacsimile machine costs.[64]

Indeed, depending on whether or not a library includes or excludes such fixed costs, one can see per-page estimates that differ not by a few pennies, but by a few dollars. If a library is determined to consider the cost and maintenance of equipment in calculating its telefacsimile delivery costs, it must first decide and declare the useful life of the machine (two years? three years?), as well as whether and how it will depreciate the equipment (will the depreciation be loaded up front or distributed in some other way?). Some fairly accurate projection of volume over the life of the machine must also be made, unless the library is willing to wait until the machine is declared "dead" before calculating the cost per page, not a particularly useful approach.

All the other cost factors mentioned above (supplies, staff time, telephone charges) are variable. If the library can decide to equate the staff time and supply costs associated with telefacsimile transmission with those required for other delivery mechanisms, estimating cost per page using telecommunications charges is a fairly straightforward proposition. Long-distance telephone charges can have the greatest impact on cost, unless most of the library's partners are in local call zones. Just as it is often difficult to estimate what one's home telephone bill will be, so can long-distance telefacsimile costs be tricky to predict and budget for; much depends on the length of time the line is in use, the time of day the transmission is made, and other factors with which we are familiar from our experiences with personal telephone charges.

During the University of Tennessee at Knoxville and Vanderbilt telefacsimile experiment, long-distance charges "substantially exceeded projections," causing the parties to investigate faxing over the Internet.[65] Of course, every page that must be retransmitted—because of broken connections, other telephone service problems, or mechanical difficulties with one of the telefacsimile units—means making an extra telephone call to complete the delivery, incurring a second premium charge for the first minute. A good cost-saving measure is a special long-distance arrangement, such as a WATS line. In an area where several telephone companies compete, the college or university may be able to negotiate a very favorable long-distance agreement. When transmissions are routinely sent in the early morning or in the evening, when rates are typically lower, savings can be obtained; batching documents destined for the same location also represents a savings, because it reduces the connect time and eliminates several first-minute premium charges. "Clean" (that is, static free) telephone lines also lower transmission costs, as does something as basic as a well-designed and simple cover sheet: the less text there is to be read by the machine's scanner, the quicker and cheaper the transmission.

Studies of the amount of time required to fax one page of a typical library document (a page from a journal, for example, which is denser with text than the typical interoffice memorandum) can vary but hover around forty-five to sixty seconds. Since most telephone companies charge a higher, flat fee for the first minute of a long-distance call, predicting the cost of transmitting a single page will be simple if not especially useful.[66] Boss and Espo point out, however, that cost data vary greatly among institutions. A library with access to an in-state WATS line could pay as little as $.14 per minute for documents transmitted in this way, whereas other institutions pay direct-dial long-distance costs at nearly twice that rate.[67] Still others do very little long-distance faxing, and in many libraries there is mixed use of long-distance and local service.

As a rule of thumb, the library that chooses not to include large fixed equipment costs in figuring cost per page, but rather confines itself simply to taking the fax machine's telephone bill (another good reason for a dedicated fax line) and dividing the number of pages faxed during the billing period into the amount of the bill, will find figuring cost per page a rather simple exercise. A review of the several studies of telefacsimile projects conducted among American libraries shows that, despite the many ways in which costs are calculated, the average cost per page is under $1 even when fixed costs are included, and substantially under $1 when they are not.[68] Keeping track of costs is equally easy and includes monitoring expendables (paper, toner) and the telephone bill, as well as keeping a log in which who uses the fax and for what purpose are recorded.

Copyright Implications for Telefacsimile

A telefacsimile machine is a photocopier that can transmit over telephone lines; the same sections of the copyright law that apply to photoduplication and interlending also apply to telefacsimile duplication. There is, however, one important wrinkle: most Group III telefacsimile equipment scans single sheets of paper, requiring that journal articles and excerpts from books be photocopied first, then fed through a paper feed. If, after an article is transmitted to a requesting library, the lender systematically destroys the photocopy of the article (perhaps retaining it only briefly, in the event retransmission of some or all of it is necessary), the library can assume that only one copy of the article has been made and supplied. Since many fax machines use thermal paper, which is deemed unpleasant to the senses of touch and smell by some readers and often produces copies not as crisp or clear as those printed on plain paper, some libraries routinely request that a follow-up photocopy of the article be sent by some conventional, nonelectronic delivery mechanism. Not only does this cancel any savings on postage or packaging time, but it means the borrowing library must also count the request for the particular article as two requests under the "rule of five" for fair use.[69]

It will also be important that library systems whose members engage in cooperative acquisitions programs ensure that the document delivery component of the program complies with copyright laws and guidelines. Because telefacsimile's electronic delivery enables libraries to cancel journal subscriptions and still have rapid access to materials located in another library's collections, full compliance with "fair use" will be very important.

Establishing a Fax Network

A number of library cooperatives have established telefacsimile networks. In some states and regions where effective ground-based delivery systems already exist, telefacsimile networks have been added to provide the type of "instant" delivery that is sometimes wanted. Libraries that link themselves for resource sharing through telefacsimile will want to publicize fax numbers by including them with the listings in some existing directory or by distributing a separate directory; they will also want to establish telefacsimile protocols.

These protocols are the "etiquette" or procedures for using telefacsimile in interlending. They typically include guidelines for sending requests (through one's bibliographic utility, electronic mail, or telefacsimile?), circumstances under which a receiving library will respond by fax, and response time. The Associated College Libraries of Central Pennsylvania (ACLCP) developed "Guidelines for Telefacsimile Use within Pennsylvania," which any library will find useful, as well as a related document, "Tips for Efficient Use of Telefacsimile Equipment" that includes suggestions such as "keep the machine turned on at all times" and "the borrowing library will notify the lending library immediately if transmission received is of poor quality and cannot be read."[70] Additionally, there are the "Guidelines and Procedures for Telefacsimile Transmission of Interlibrary Loan Requests," prepared by the Interlibrary Loan Committee of the Reference and Adult Services Division (RASD) of the American Library Association.[71]

There are numerous examples of library telefacsimile networks. One of the most intriguing is a pilot project underway at the National Library of Medicine (NLM) in which articles from the past three years of sixty-four newer journals available through DOCLINE have been scanned onto optical disks. This collection is called the Electronic Library; the project itself is called SAIL, System for Automated Interlibrary Loan. Since NLM serves as a "library of last resort," supplying materials when regional referral libraries cannot, the journal titles for this experiment were chosen because they were new and other institutions would be less likely to own them.

When a loan request is received, SAIL's routing mechanism automatically checks the Electronic Library. If the article is available, it is printed out and faxed to the requester, whenever the capacity to receive the document by telefacsimile exists. This is accomplished without human intervention, unless a platter must be changed because the desired article is not available on the disk that is currently mounted. The project is funded by NLM's Research and Development unit. During phase one SAIL filled a peak of about sixty ILL requests a day, and did so faster than NLM staff could do manually; however, the costs ($8 for a mailed document and $11 for a faxed one) were approximately the same as those for non–SAIL requests, because of the initial cost of equipment and staff time required to analyze ambiguous requests. The library continues to study the issues of copyright and document selection (when citations are unclear). Its aim is to use SAIL to fill requests from high-demand titles.

Many journal articles and independent reports describing the design and development of telefacsimile networks have been written. Interesting descriptions of individual projects include Margaret A. Wainer's "An Evaluation of the Facsimile Transmission Project among Multitype Libraries in West-Central Illinois"; Linda Brander's "Montana Faxnet Project"; Havelin Anand's "Interlibrary Loan and Document Delivery Using Telefacsimile Transmission," Parts I and II; and Charles Peguese's "Telefacsimile, The Pennsylvania Experience: A State Library's Perspective."[72]

The first of Anand's articles describes the preliminary study conducted by the National Library of Canada, the Nova Scotia Provincial Library, and the University of Alberta to assess the receptivity of the environment to fax and the likelihood of productivity; the second piece includes the worksheets used to collect data during the project in order to evaluate its success. Peguese's paper includes three useful appendices, "Specifications for Purchase of Telefacsimile Equipment," "Recommended Guidelines for Telefacsimile Use in Interlibrary Loan," and "Telefacsimile Project Questionnaire," which was used in evaluating the experiment.

Other good sources of information are Brown's "Telefacsimile in Libraries: New Deal in the 1980s" and Boss and Espo's "The Use of Telefacsimile in Libraries," each of which summarizes and synthesizes a number of different experiences in telefacsimile implementation.[73] Other pieces cited in this chapter are also useful, whether libraries intend to build fax into an existing consortium or create a new network whose primary purpose is resource sharing by telefacsimile transmission.

The Internet: What Is It, What Does It Do, and How Do I Join It?

While our principal interest in the Internet lies in its capacity for document delivery, a general explanation of this powerful resource is appropriate. As far-reaching and influential as it may be, at the same time the Internet can be difficult to grasp: it is not an organization and it has no address; many are mystified by how one goes about joining an entity so amorphous.[74] The Internet is a high-speed telecommunications network begun in the 1970s by the federal government that has evolved into a worldwide conglomeration of more than five thousand different networks and subnetworks in thirty-three countries. These networks are interconnected with five hundred thousand computers serving some three million persons.

The core of the Internet is the National Science Foundation Network (NSFnet); to this "backbone" are connected a number of regional midlevel networks that provide Internet access and communications to universities, government agencies, and other organizations in a specific geographical area. Once connected, whether by dumb terminals hard-wired to a larger computer connected to a midlevel network, or by a personal computer with a modem, readers can access resources located on host computers throughout the Internet. There are many reasons a library will wish to have access to the Internet, not all of them related to resource sharing and thus discussed here in any detail. Among these are exchanging electronic mail with other Internet users, participating in electronic interactive conferences on many different topics, transmitting documents (called file transfer, or FTP-ing) to other Internet users, and logging into an enormous number of remote databases located across town or across the world. These include library catalogs (as of March 1993, more than six hundred of them), as well as commercial databases (for whose use charges are levied) such as DIALOG and OCLC's EPIC. There are also a variety of full-text files available for searching, such as Dartmouth University's *The Shakespeare Plays*, *The Shakespeare Sonnets*, and *The Bible*. Other uses of the Internet, as well as projected future uses, are described in the last chapter of this book.

The Internet can be used in place of commercial telephone lines to transmit documents by telefacsimile, when both the sending and receiving libraries have an Internet connection for their fax equipment. The attraction, of course, is that libraries faxing over the Internet incur no long-distance telephone charges and thus save themselves significant amounts of money.

Academic Computing Services (ACS) of The Ohio State University has an ongoing research and development initiative in which it is exploring issues related to telefacsimile transmission over the Internet. The approach developed there (which is being emulated by other organizations) is to scan a document using a fax machine, transmit the image to an IBM-compatible personal computer equipped with fax and ethernet interface cards, and store the image as a file on the PC's disk. Next, file transfer protocol (FTP) software is used to transmit the file by an ethernet connection to a similarly equipped distant PC for storage on its disk. Finally, the image is transmitted by a fax interface card installed on the receiving machine to a nearby fax machine and printed out.

The procedure described above works, and libraries are using it. ACS is presently exploring several improvements to the protocol, including extending support to faster 386-based PCs, support for flexible delivery options using file transfer over local area networks (this would permit delivery directly to a reader's personal workstation), and support for laser printers (versus fax machines) as output devices.[75]

Thus, the ingredients for faxing over the Internet include Internet access, a fax machine, a PC equipped with fax and ethernet boards, and partners who are similarly equipped. Many colleges and universities across the nation are already connected to the Internet, although the connection may not yet have been extended to the library. A library interested in faxing through the Internet might want to take the following exploratory steps:

1. Contact the college or university systems office and determine whether the institution has Internet access.
2. If the answer is yes, inquire about whether access has been or can be extended to the library.
3. If the answer is yes again, ask for help in acquiring the equipment and software described above.

If the library's parent organization is not an Internet member, this is not an insurmountable obstacle; however, although using the Internet is largely "free" in that one incurs no long-distance telecommunications charges, Internet membership and connections (of which there are several choices) are not free or necessarily cheap, and a college or university may be reluctant to join unless it is persuaded that there are benefits that go beyond the library. Information and membership packets that describe Internet services and costs are available from the appropriate regional network; these include NORTHWESTNET, WESTNET, MIDNET, CICNET, NYSERNET, and several others. A telephone call to a neighboring institution already using the Internet can help identify the appropriate regional network.

As one might imagine, dozens of books, articles, and pamphlets have been written about the Internet and its many services. For those seeking a broader understanding of this powerful tool, recommended reading includes John S. Quarterman's book *The Matrix: Computer Networks and Conferencing Systems Worldwide* (information about current Internet networks and computer networking in general); Tracy L. LaQuey's *User's Directory of Computer Networks* (detailed lists of hosts, site contacts, administrative domains, and general information on over forty major networks); Brendan P. Kehoe's *Zen and the Art of the Internet* (a beginner's guide to using the Internet); Ed Krol's *The Whole Internet User's Guide and Catalog* (an Internet guide for the computer literate); and NYSERNET's "Beyond the Walls Instructional Workshop Package" (an instructional workshop package including all the materials needed to replicate the "Beyond the Walls" Internet workshop at one's own institution). A packet available free of charge from the University of California at Berkeley's Library Technology Watch Program is also a valuable tool for beginning Internet users.[76] There are also several Internet guides available through the Internet itself as electronic files; however, because their electronic addresses change so often, none is included here.

Group IV Telefacsimile Equipment

The next generation of fax equipment will be Group IV. These machines already exist, but common telephone lines cannot support them, so that their use is limited to environments in which digital high-speed data lines have been installed, eliminating "the economical universal access capability that makes telefacsimile valuable in library networking."[77] Thus, libraries will have to wait for Integrated Services Digital Network (ISDN) to become more widespread, or have dedicated lines installed. Even then, many more institutions will have to install these machines before they can be used extensively.[78]

What improvements do these machines promise? Group IV equipment is much faster than Group III machines, and it produces far better copies with resolutions of up to 400 x 400 dots per inch (dpi), versus Group III's 100 x 200 (standard) and 200 x 200 (fine). Operating at sixty-four thousand bits per second, it can send a business letter in three seconds or less. Although nearly ten times the cost of machinery that is presently available, Group IV's great speed lowers the unit cost of transmission over that of commercial telephone lines. In a few years' time, with a drop in equipment costs and the expansion of the ISDN, Group IV machines will make their way into libraries.[79]

Scanning for Document Delivery

A promising approach to electronic document delivery is scanning. The Research Libraries Group's (RLG) Ariel software and workstation is the most commonly used technology, and the members of RLG are not the only ones using it: non-RLG libraries and document delivery services like CARL UnCover2 are also installing Ariel. Meanwhile, North Carolina State University, with support from a Title II-D grant, is using another type of scanning equipment and software in a large resource sharing project with the National Agricultural Library (NAL) and more than a dozen other land grant universities across the country. What exactly is scanning technology, and how does it compare to telefacsimile transmission?

Scanning Explained: The Research Libraries Group's Ariel

Since Ariel has a much larger installed base than any other scanning technology, it makes sense to examine it. Ariel combines RLG application software with a personal computer, a document scanner, and a laser printer; together these can be understood to make up the Ariel workstation. It is a stand-alone system that works independently of the Research Libraries Information Network (RLIN).

The PC (an IBM PC AT or equivalent) is equipped with an 80 megabyte hard disk; a scanner that offers 300 × 300 dpi resolution as compared to fax's 100 × 200 (regular) or 200 × 200 (fine) is attached. The scanner accepts documents up to 8.5 × 14 inches in size that do not have to be photocopied first, unless they are very large and reduction is necessary. A laser printer equipped with an "Ariel accelerator card" is also connected to the PC; printing is accomplished on plain paper.

Ariel compresses scanned images, reducing disk storage requirements; the workstation's hard disk can store six hundred pages at any given time. When photographs are scanned, compression can be turned off, producing near-perfect copies of the original. When the Ariel workstation (which can scan and receive documents at the same time) is not transmitting, it can be used for word processing or other PC-based applications.

Scanning versus Fax: What's the Difference?

In her column for *Wilson Library Bulletin*, the University of Pennsylvania's interlibrary loan head, Mary E. Jackson, writes from her Ariel beta site experience:

> Ariel has eliminated the need to take journals to the photocopy room, to check for completeness and quality of copies, to find shipping labels and envelopes, and to mail articles. Even with a scan time of approximately 10 seconds per page, we believe that the overall process of supplying a journal article has been streamlined. Ariel was quickly integrated into our normal work flow. . . . We have rarely been asked to rescan pages.[80]

These comments explain a great deal about why librarians prefer scanning to faxing. Scanning technology is designed to be faster, more reliable, and less expensive to use than fax machines. Ariel transmits exclusively through the Internet, eliminating all long-distance telephone charges, although a version that will work with commercial telephone lines is planned. The equipment is flexible, rather than dedicated. Text, photographs, charts, formulae, tables, and any material that can be scanned result in print images of excellent quality.

RLG will send any library interested in Ariel an information packet that includes cost, equipment, and other data.[81] Scan/transmit/receive/print software (the only item purchased through RLG) costs around $500, although prices decline when multiple copies are purchased (if a library system buys twenty-five or more copies, for example, the price per copy drops to $200). The library is on its own to secure the necessary PC, scanner, and printer, although RLG provides complete specifications. With some luck in obtaining discounted prices, a complete Ariel workstation plus software could cost around $5,000.

North Carolina State University's Digitized Document Transmission Project (NCSU DDTP)

Ariel may rule the market at the moment, but it has at least one healthy and versatile competitor, North Carolina State University's Digitized Document Transmission Project (NCSU DDTP). DDTP is an outgrowth of a 1989 project between NCSU and the National Agricultural Library (NAL) in which a T-1 line connected a 386 PC at NAL to a Macintosh computer in North Carolina in order to transmit both ASCII and page image files of NAL documents wanted by NCSU readers. Subsequently, NCSU received both a Title II-D grant and an equipment grant from Apple Computer to expand the project to include fourteen land grant universities interested in resource sharing in the field of agriculture, representing most of the regional networks in the Internet.

NCSU organized a "competition" to choose the new participants. Its requirements included the purchase of the necessary hardware and a high-speed Internet connection located in the library. Each of the participating libraries uses a Macintosh to which a scanner and a printer have been attached; unlike the Ariel workstation and configuration, all of the equipment is off-the-shelf and none has been customized. Telecommunications are provided through the Internet. A document available free of charge from NCSU lists all necessary hardware and associated costs.[82]

DDTP participants send requests to each other through OCLC's interlibrary loan subsystem; a code indicating the document is to be digitized for transmission is added to the record whenever the article meets the project's criteria. The receiving institution photocopies the article, then scans it (participants have discovered that the quality of the document is better when scanning is done from a copy, rather than the original). The document is then compressed and transmitted. Participants report that the quality of the documents delivered by scanning is excellent; the resolution (like that achieved with Ariel) is 300 x 300 dpi.

At North Carolina State an important adjunct to the Digitized Document Transmission Project is the Electronic Document Delivery Service (EDDS), which allows readers to make requests for articles through electronic mail to DDTP project staff and later permits the delivery of the document directly to any network device, including the reader's computer. The digitized material (DDTP can also transmit digital sound and video) may be transmitted across like or different computer platforms (Macintosh to

DOS or UNIX, for example) and imported into any standard software package installed on the student or faculty member's workstation.[83] When a reader logs on to his or her electronic mail account and a document is waiting, the message "Your document is in" appears; the reader then performs a file transfer (FTP) operation and brings it into his or her machine. Initially EDDS was available only to researchers in the College of Forest Resources and the Department of Marine, Earth, and Atmospheric Sciences, but there are plans to extend the service.[84]

An expanded test of both DDTP and EDDS is presently underway at North Carolina State. Part of this effort is NAL's ongoing negotiations with academic publishers to provide copyright clearance for distribution of copyrighted research literature.[85] While the participants in DDTP strive for forty-eight-hour turnaround time and have waived all fees, the central purpose of the project is to gain experience and information about the value-added aspect of receiving a document in machine-readable (versus paper) format; the project's spring 1993 final report should provide information in this area.

Cost Centers for Scanning

The cost centers for scanning are all but identical to those for telefacsimile transmission. Rather than a single piece of equipment (the fax machine), the library needs appropriate software, a properly outfitted PC, a scanner, a laser printer, and associated maintenance agreements. There are no ongoing telecommunications costs, as both of the two major scanning technologies presently in use in libraries employ the Internet. Labor costs may be similar or, in the case of Ariel where photocopying is unnecessary, somewhat less than those associated with telefacsimile transmission.

When Should a Library Implement Scanning?

Many of the questions asked above in the section on telefacsimile transmission apply to scanning, particularly those on uses, needs, and feasibility. Just as with telefacsimile, issues related to the need for speed and the existence of a solid partner base will be significant. The nature of existing resource sharing agreements and the ILL unit's ability to process requests in a timely fashion is perhaps more significant with scanning technology than with telefacsimile, for some fairly obvious reasons.

RLG will supply information on institutions that have purchased Ariel to interested libraries, and non-RLG names do appear on the list. However, at this point the Research Libraries Group (where great emphasis is placed on rapid ILL turnaround time) represents the principal installed base for scanning technology. Additionally, many of these libraries charge non-RLG institutions for loans. A library considering Ariel (from an "installed base" perspective, the only practical scanning technology presently available) will do well to examine a list of prospective partners and the appeal of their collections, and to talk with these institutions about their willingness to engage in reciprocal resource sharing. No library will be wise to install Ariel without assurances that good partners will be available.

Several of the larger libraries in the City University of New York are planning to implement Ariel, and Philadelphia's Health Sciences Libraries Consortium is already using it in its HealthLink program. As the HealthLink promotional flyer advertises,

> Can you imagine a document delivery workstation that lets you scan in a document, and send it anywhere over an international telecommunications network, all while your laser printer is printing a document someone else is sending you? For less than the cost of a fax phone call?

It seems certain that more library cooperatives will move to implement scanning for resource sharing.

Evaluating Approaches to Document Delivery

Much of this ground has already been covered under the individual delivery mechanisms listed above. Most libraries will use more than one approach to document delivery; in choosing which ones to incorporate into an access program, these are the major factors libraries will consider and attempt to balance in the context of the local institutional setting:

1. Format of the original: It is impractical or impossible to send some formats (books, videotapes) using certain delivery mechanisms (telefacsimile, scanning).
2. Speed, and the need for speed: Some delivery mechanisms are much faster than others, and this speed often carries with it a price; how often and under what circumstances is speed important?

3. Cost: Costs associated with various methods of delivery vary widely and include different cost centers. Does the local library find it easier to budget for certain types of cost centers than for others? How much money can the library budget for document delivery, and how many documents must be delivered?
4. Ease of use: Will staff find an individual delivery system the library chooses easy to use, and the combination of systems uncomplicated?
5. Reliability: Is the system dependable?
6. Format of surrogates: When surrogates are provided, which of several possible formats (photoduplicated, faxed, scanned, or electronic copies) will best meet readers' needs? Humanists may find paper completely acceptable, while digitized documents may best suit some scientists.
7. Quality of surrogates: Are documents provided as copies clear, easy to read, and inoffensive to the senses?
8. Reader satisfaction: Are readers pleased with the service the system delivers?

Experimenting with Document Delivery

Although much has been published about each of these delivery options, a library may wish to experiment with a new delivery system in order to gather valuable information about costs, equipment features, and staffing issues that can enable it to make an effective and informed decision about the role the particular system can play in resource sharing. The library that opts to experiment may find these suggestions useful:

1. Pick an active part of the academic year, rather than a slow one. This ensures a fairer test.
2. Set a time frame for the experiment, and allow plenty of time to acquire necessary equipment, supplies, and so forth.
3. Select a logical partner or partners, libraries that have materials one wants, and who in turn will want materials from the local library. Interlibrary loan statistics may provide valuable indicators.
4. Over the course of the experiment, use project partners whenever possible, and give priority to one another's requests.

5. Establish parameters for turnaround time and develop other helpful protocols.
6. Maintain careful records of the library's experiences.
7. Analyze the results to determine whether or not to add the new approach to the library's array of delivery mechanisms.

Delivery technologies will continue to change. Five years ago a telefacsimile machine seemed an unimaginable luxury to many academic libraries; now this equipment is almost ubiquitous. Today, Ariel and other scanning technologies are the newest information transfer models in the market, but the library that implements any new technology and then rests contently will shortly find that it has been left behind.

Notes

1. Information Systems Consultants, Inc., *Document Delivery*, 1.
2. Russell, "Interlibrary Loan," 23.
3. Medina, "Improving Document Delivery," 7–14.
4. Hewitt and Shipman, "Cooperative Collection Development," 220.
5. Richard W. Boss and Judy McQueen, "Interlibrary Document Delivery: The Options," in *Crossroads: Proceedings of the First National Conference of the Library and Information Technology Association, September 17–21, 1983, Baltimore, Maryland*, ed. Michael Gorman, Library and Information Technology Series, no. 1 (Chicago: American Library Association, 1984), 137.
6. OCLC, "Interlibrary Loan," 4, 6.
7. Ibid., vii.
8. Wiggins, "Factors Which Influence," 165.
9. Boss and McQueen, "Interlibrary Document Delivery," in *Crossroads*, 137.
10. Ibid.; Richard W. Boss and Judy McQueen, "Interlibrary Document Delivery: The Options," in *Prospects for Improving Document Delivery: Minutes of the 101st Meeting, October 13–14, Arlington, Virginia*, ed. Nicola Daval (Washington, D.C.: ARL, 1983), 117.
11. Maurice B. Line, "Universal Availability of Publications in an Electronic Age," *IATUL Quarterly* 3 (Dec. 1989), 216.
12. Lucker, "Document Delivery," 84.
13. A. E. Cawkell, "Progress in Documentation: Electronic Document Delivery Systems," *Journal of Documentation* 47 (Mar. 1991), 42.
14. Ibid.
15. Martin, "Delivery Systems," 176.
16. Ibid.
17. Michalak, "Impact."

18. Marsha Ra, "A Centrally Supported Direct On-Line Document Delivery Service for the City University of New York: Planning Grant Request to the Council on Library Resources," Grant proposal, Aug. 28, 1991, 8.
19. North Carolina State University, The Libraries, "NCSU Digitized Document Transmission Project: Electronic Document Delivery Service: A Pilot Service," Press release, January 8, 1992, 2.
20. Marsha J. Stevenson, "Design Options for an On-Campus Document Delivery Program," *College & Research Libraries News* 51 (May 1990): 437–40; Evelyn Greenberg, "Book Express: Meaningful Access," *College & Research Libraries News* 48 (Oct. 1987):539–40.
21. Line, "Universal Availability of Publications," 216.
22. Boss and McQueen, "Interlibrary Document Delivery," in *Prospects for Improving Document Delivery*, 112–13.
23. Ibid., 112.
24. Information Systems Consultants, Inc., "Resource Sharing," 9.
25. Ibid., 9–10.
26. Barbara Brown, "Interlibrary Loan in the Research Libraries Group," in *Prospects for Improving Document Delivery: Minutes of the 101st Meeting, October 13–14, Arlington, Virginia*, ed. Nicola Daval (Washington, D.C.: ARL, 1983), 91.
27. Boss and McQueen, "Interlibrary Document Delivery," in *Prospects for Improving Document Delivery*, 113.
28. Ibid.
29. Patrick, *Guidelines*, 180.
30. Boss and McQueen, "Interlibrary Document Delivery," in *Prospects for Improving Document Delivery*, 113.
31. Much of this information about IDS comes from Peter Deekle, "Document Delivery Comes of Age in Pennsylvania," *Wilson Library Bulletin* 65 (Oct. 1990): 31–33.
32. Information Systems Consultants, Inc., "Resource Sharing," IV–9.
33. Ibid., IV–10.
34. New York Metropolitan Reference and Research Library Agency, *The METRO Handbook and Directory of Members, 1991–92* (New York: METRO, 1991), 15–17.
35. Information Systems Consultants, Inc., "Resource Sharing," IV–10—IV–11; Sloan, "Resource Sharing," 27–28.
36. Information Systems Consultants, Inc., "Resource Sharing," IV–10.
37. Much of this section is based on Barbra B. Higginbotham's article, "Telefacsimile: The Issues and the Answers," *Journal of Interlibrary Loan & Information Supply* 1, no. 1 (1990): 67–86.
38. Cawkell, "Progress in Documentation," 58.
39. Mark Wilson, "How to Set Up a Telefacsimile Network—The Pennsylvania Libraries' Experience," *Online* 12 (May 1988): 24.
40. Steven A. Brown, "Telefacsimile in Libraries: New Deal in the 1980s," *Library Trends* 37 (Winter 1989): 351.

41. Patrick R. Dewey, *FAX for Libraries* (Westport, Conn.: Meckler, 1990), 7.
42. Richard W. Boss and Hal Espo, "The Use of Telefacsimile in Libraries," *Library Hi Tech* 5 (Spring 1987): 36.
43. Wilson, "How to Set Up a Telefacsimile Network," 24.
44. Brown, "Telefacsimile," 344.
45. Information Systems Consultants, Inc., "Resource Sharing," IV-11—IV-12.
46. Brown, "Telefacsimile," 346.
47. Ibid., 351.
48. Dewey, *FAX for Libraries*, 4.
49. Brown, "Telefacsimile," 351.
50. Ibid., 347.
51. Dewey, *FAX for Libraries*, 22.
52. Wilson, "How to Set Up a Telefacsimile Network," 25.
53. Dewey, *FAX for Libraries*, 21.
54. Brown, "Telefacsimile," 343.
55. Wilson, "How to Set Up a Telefacsimile Network," 21–22.
56. Ibid., 22–24.
57. Dewey, *FAX for Libraries*, 24.
58. Information Systems Consultants, Inc., "Resource Sharing," IV–11.
59. Brown, "Telefacsimile," 350.
60. Ibid., 351–52.
61. Ibid., 348, 350.
62. Phillips, "IRIS," 15.
63. Dewey, *FAX for Libraries*, 12.
64. Brown, "Telefacsimile," 346.
65. Phillips, "IRIS," 13.
66. Wilson, "How to Set Up a Telefacsimile Network," 15.
67. Boss and Espo, "The Use of Telefacsimile," 36.
68. Brown, "Telefacsimile," 348.
69. Ibid.
70. Wilson, "How to Set Up a Telefacsimile Network," 19–21.
71. American Library Association, Reference and Adult Services Division, Interlibrary Loan Committee, "Guidelines and Procedures for Telefacsimile Transmission of Interlibrary Loan Requests," *RQ* 30 (Winter 1990): 266–67.
72. Margaret A. Wainer, "An Evaluation of the Facsimile Transmission Project among Multitype Libraries in West-Central Illinois (1983, 1984, 1985)," Unpublished report, Mar. 1986; Linda Brander, "Montana Faxnet Project," *Library Hi Tech* 5 (Summer 1987): 70–75; Havelin Anand, "Interlibrary Loan and Document Delivery Using Telefacsimile Transmission: Part I. Preliminary Study," *Electronic Library* 5 (Feb. 1987): 28–33; Havelin Anand, "Interlibrary Loan and Document Delivery Using Telefacsimile Transmission: Part II. Telefacsimile Project," *Electronic Library* 5 (Apr. 1987):

100–107; Charles Peguese, "Telefacsimile, The Pennsylvania Experience: A State Library's Perspective," in *Research Access through New Technology*, ed. Mary E. Jackson (New York: AMS Press, 1989), 82–102.

73. Brown, "Telefacsimile," 343–56; Boss and Espo, "The Use of Telefacsimile," 33–42.
74. Much of this general description of the Internet comes from James Dorsey, "What Federal Libraries Need to Know about Internet," *FEDLINK Technical Notes* 10 (Apr. 1992): 3, 5–6, 8.
75. "The Ohio State University Network Fax Project," Press release, July 1991.
76. John S. Quarterman, *The Matrix: Computer Networks and Conferencing Systems Worldwide* (Bedford, Mass.: Digital Press, 1990); Tracy L. LaQuey, *User's Directory of Computer Networks* (Bedford, Mass.: Digital Press, n.d.); Brendan P. Kehoe, *Zen and the Art of the Internet: A Beginner's Guide* (Englewood Cliffs, N.J.: Prentice Hall, 1992); Ed Krol, *The Whole Internet User's Guide and Catalog* (Sebastapol, Calif.: O'Reilly and Associates, 1992); NYSERNET, "Beyond the Walls Instructional Workshop Package," Packet; "Library Technology Watch Program, Packet.
77. Brown, "Telefacsimile," 353–54.
78. Line, "Universal Availability of Publications," 217.
79. Cawkell, "Progress in Documentation," 53, 59.
80. Mary E. Jackson, "Library to Library [Ariel]," *Wilson Library Bulletin* 65 (Apr. 1991): 86.
81. Write to the Research Libraries Group, Inc., 1200 Villa St., Mountain View, CA 94041-1100, or send electronic mail to bl.mxr@rlg.bitnet; request information on the full Ariel workstation.
82. North Carolina State University, The Libraries, "NCSU Digitized Document Transmission Project: Improving Access to Agricultural Libraries," Press release, Oct. 11, 1991, 3.
83. Tracy M. Casorso, "Research Materials: Now Only Keystrokes Away," *College & Research Libraries News* 53 (Feb. 1992): 128.
84. North Carolina State University, The Libraries, "NCSU Digitized Document Transmission Project," 2.
85. Tracy M. Casorso, "The North Carolina State University Libraries and the National Agricultural Library Joint Project on Transmission of Digitized Text: Improving Access to Agricultural Information," *Reference Services Review* 19 (Spring 1991): 21–22.

CHAPTER 8

Making Decisions for Access

A Mighty Maze! But Not without a Plan
(Pope, *An Essay on Man*, Epistle I)

I. Delimiting the Access Program   250

II. Access: What Does It Really Cost?   252

III. Cost Models for Interlending: A Review   254

IV. The Cost-Benefit Approach to Interlibrary Loan   255

V. The Research Libraries Group ILL Cost Model   257

VI. Deciding When to Choose Which Option   259

VII. Adjusting Lending as Borrowing Declines   261

VIII. Linking Access to Local Information Values: The California State University at San Bernardino Experience   262

IX. Cost Recovery: To Charge or Not to Charge?   264
- A. Charging the Library's Own Readers: What's Right about It?   265
- B. Why We May Not Want to Charge Our Faculty and Students   266
- C. If You Charge, What Are the Options?   267
- D. Assessing Fees against Other Libraries: Yes or No?   268
- E. Why It's Good to Charge Your Friends   269
- F. On the Other Hand . . .   270
- G. Developing the Access Budget   270
- H. Where Do I Get That Kind of Money?   271

X. Evaluating the Access Program   275
- A. Assessing the Borrowing Operation   275
- B. Assessing the Lending Operation   281
- C. Assessing Staffing Levels   282

XI. Communication with Readers   283

XII. Staffing the Access Unit   283

XIII. Public Relations and Promotion for Access   285

XIV. Placing the Access Unit in the Organization   287

Thus far, the individual elements that make up an academic library's access program have been discussed and analyzed; among these are consortial relationships, reciprocal access, interlending, commercial document services, and document delivery mechanisms. Now it is time to consider the access program as a whole, and to establish guidelines within which some important decisions about delimiting, costing, shaping, funding, evaluating, and administering the service can be made.

Delimiting the Access Program

1. Defining the Service Group

Some libraries provide interlibrary loan and commercial document services for all categories of readers, including undergraduates, graduate students, full- and part-time faculty, staff, administrators, and even other unaffiliated or semi-affiliated groups (retirees, alumni, or perhaps students from local high schools). However, because providing access to remotely held materials is a costly business, more and more institutions are looking closely at the groups to which such services are extended, examining the ability of local collections to meet the needs of various patron types, and considering the information options available to readers who may be excluded. Many libraries have concluded that information delivery from remote sources will be one of the most jealously guarded services they offer.

It is a given that faculty will have access to interlibrary loan and other document delivery options; in fact, some libraries limit such services to faculty, relying upon local collections to meet the needs of students and other groups of readers. While limiting the size of the service group is one way to control costs, a number of libraries oppose interlibrary loan and similar services for undergraduates for philosophical reasons. As one librarian wrote, "Most academic libraries express a strong commitment to bibliographic instruction and feel that the availability of a delivery system would discourage the development of library use skills."[1]

When local collections are fairly strong, this can be justified; after all, faculty are presumably engaged in active research and need access to a wider range of materials than do students. Good arguments can be made, however, for extending such services to graduate students, whose information needs may be quite similar to those of faculty and who often act as faculty research assistants. Of course, each library is free to make an exception to any policy on a case-by-case basis; this ensures that the undergraduate working on a special senior project, for example, can receive permission to use interlibrary loan.

2. Limiting Subject Areas

Some institutions supply only materials directly related to the reader's academic interests, excluding recreational and other interests. If the library also imposes limits based on reader status (faculty, or faculty and graduate students only, for example), subject limitation will probably be unnecessary; however, when a broader patron base is served (undergraduates, high school students, retirees), this technique can make a significant difference; furthermore, it is consistent with existing ILL codes.

3. Limiting the Number of Requests

Some libraries limit the number of requests that readers, or certain categories of readers, may place at any given time, or during some specific period of time (a month; per annum). An arrangement of this sort may be helpful in controlling use of the service by groups of readers whose information needs should be satisfied largely by local collections (undergraduates; members of the local community), but it will certainly not be productive with faculty or graduate students. Additionally, it requires yet another form of record keeping.

4. Combating System Abuses

Readers who misuse interlibrary loan do so in two ways: they request materials but never pick them up, or they do not return items that have been borrowed for them. No library can afford to obtain documents that readers do not claim and use, nor can an institution risk its credibility with lenders by securing loans for readers who keep them far beyond the due date. However, unless a library experiences widespread problems in these areas, it is probably best to deal individually with the occasional offender, however blatant the crime. A conversation with someone's department chair or dean may be much more effective than a blanket policy. In worst-case situations, the library can suspend the borrower's ILL privileges for some period of time, or levy fines as a deterrent. Some institutions charge a nominal fee when a request is placed and refund it when the item is claimed; others resort to this tactic only with readers who have proven their ability to misuse the service.

The library should also consider the needs of the "remote" reader: what sort of policy will it adopt for faculty who are off campus for the summer, or away for a year on sabbatical? It is likely that their information needs have not been placed on hold; indeed, they may have escalated. Will the library obtain materials for the off-campus faculty member and arrange for their delivery? The ability to communicate over great distances through electronic mail at virtually no cost, combined with the availability of commercial document services, makes serving the remote reader a fairly simple proposition.

Access: What Does It Really Cost?

Some college and university administrators (and some library managers) have latched onto "access" as a palliative for reduced acquisitions budgets and buying power, without analyzing the price of access. As Donald B. Simpson suggests, "When you add the average cost of acquiring, processing, storing, and weeding a science journal . . . to its average purchase price . . . the $20 [spent to get something on ILL] looks cost-beneficial."[2] However, cooperation has its own very concrete costs, and we should spend our access dollars as carefully as we do those for collections.[3] In an article for the *Journal of Library Administration* Sheila T. Dowd writes:

> If we are to continue to serve as our society's information centers, we can not just go along with the budget formulae of earlier years. We must assess realistically the costs of modern services, the possible trade-offs, and the ultimate needs.[4]

Yet, many librarians will say that interlibrary loan is free when they rely upon reciprocal borrowing agreements, and that commercial document services cost money, because one must pay for the articles and their delivery. They might find the conclusions of Information Systems Consultants, Inc. (ISCI) quite startling: "Were it to be assumed that the true cost of ILL to both borrower and lender is over $16 per request, the annual cost of the ILL activity in the United States is more than $500 million."[5]

Other librarians still do not fully appreciate the bearing that "balance of trade" has on the cost of running an access unit. Never one to mince words, Herbert S. White has a very contemporary comment on this topic:

> We don't really know what interlibrary loan costs, primarily because we don't want to know.... Even classically socialist countries such as China, Yugoslavia, and the Soviet Union are discovering that [the profit motive] provides a more tangible incentive for performance than ideology.... Treat the determination of costs honestly, in terms that meet the accounting criteria of the supplier whose perception is ultimately all that matters.[6]

Nonetheless, as stark economic factors force librarians to reevaluate how much they buy and how much they borrow, they are becoming more realistic about the real costs of interlending. When OCLC sponsored an interlibrary loan focus group made up of eight library administrators from all parts of the country, among the issues identified was the lack of general agreement on costs and cost models. "Although many different library cost models exist, there is apparently a need for some consensus on what, if any, existing model would be useful in ILL."[7]

It is far from easy to figure out how much interlending and the provision of related document delivery services costs. While calculating the cost per loan or purchase would be fairly simple if we considered only direct costs such as the necessary supplies (shipping envelopes, labels), delivery (postage, courier service, telecommunications), and fees levied by suppliers, such costs do not tell the whole story. What about staff time, by far the largest cost associated with running an access operation? And, since we must give in order to receive, the costs of both borrowing and lending must be identified and the measure of the two fairly taken.

Before going further, we will do well to consider Maurice B. Line's sage counsel: "No costing exercise can be carried out satisfactorily unless its purposes are clearly defined."[8] Do we want to determine the average cost of a transaction? Comparative costs between or among materials in various disciplines? Between the use of various supplier types? The answers to such questions will make a great difference in how we go about collecting data. In truth, we will probably want to determine different costs with different purposes in mind.

For example, a college library might wish to know the gross cost of securing a remotely held item for a local reader, whether that item was borrowed or purchased; here, its costs in making loans will be taken into account, since lending is a condition of borrowing. Alternately, a library might want to isolate the cost of obtaining a loan from another library, from that of purchasing an article from a commercial document service, while also separating the costs of borrowing from those of lending; this could be especially useful for the institution that has decided to borrow less and buy more (through commercial services or libraries that charge for loans), and consequently to cap its lending operation.

Line suggests other uses for reliable cost data, which can help librarians determine the comparative costs of using different requesting methods (bibliographic utility; electronic mail) and delivery approaches (telefacsimile; courier). Many institutions will also be interested in measuring the efficiency of their own access operation, but in order to accomplish this, a standard cost model upon which librarians can agree will be necessary.[9] Such a model would have many benefits, including one cited by Paul M. Gherman and Lynn S. Cochrane:

> A recent proposal for library networking in Virginia includes funding to pay interlibrary loan "netlenders." Having fully documented cost data for interlibrary loans should be of great benefit in establishing a funding rate for netlenders. If each of them had similar data available, a comparison could be made, and funding could be set at the level of the most efficient netlender. The other libraries might then examine their operations to see if the same efficiencies could be attained.[10]

Similarly, the library that charges some or all comers when making loans will find such data valuable;[11] its clients may also feel somewhat more satisfied when they sign their checks, knowing that the fee they are paying is based on something more than caprice.

Cost Models for Interlending: A Review

In the late 1970s librarians (or the consultants they employed) began to show an interest in interlibrary loan cost data. Between 1977 and 1985 several studies were conducted, but most of the figures they generated are no longer very meaningful. For one thing, the value of money has changed considerably since 1977 (and even since 1985), so that cost data from eight to fifteen years ago mean very little today. Additionally, the mechanics of interlending have altered greatly in recent years; cost information that predates the use of the bibliographic utilities' ILL modules, telefacsimile transmission, and other technologies that have increased the speed of interlending has little if any modern relevance.

Nonetheless, since librarians continue to toss off the names of these earlier studies when discussing ILL costs, we too should be familiar with them, and a simple chart will do the job. Between 1977 and 1985, King Research, Inc. conducted three such studies, and Jo Ellen Herstand one:

		BORROW	LEND	TOTAL
King	(1985)	$ 4.25	$6.93	$11.18
Herstand	(1981)	$10.69	$6.23	$16.92
King	(1981)	$11.60	$8.40	$20.00
King	(1977)	$10.02	$7.27	$17.29[12]

These figures are unadjusted for inflation and yield an average total cost (for what it is worth) of $16. Sue Kennedy suggests that the advent of the utilities' ILL systems may explain 1985's lower figure;[13] perhaps borrowing is now cheaper than lending because OCLC, RLIN, and their kin have made it easier to identify locations and place requests.

Having reviewed "more than 30 interlibrary loan cost studies," ISCI comments that "the cost of ILL appears to vary widely depending on the size and type of library and methods of cost accounting used." After inflating the various costs by 5 percent per annum since the date of the study, the consulting firm concludes that studies suggesting costs below $10 for borrowing and $6 for lending have not included all indirect costs.[14]

The Cost-Benefit Approach to Interlibrary Loan

A study of any operation's costs must first choose what kinds of data will be included; it follows that, in order for different studies to be comparable, they must incorporate the same types of costs. As Line cautions, it is important to differentiate among direct costs and indirect costs, fixed costs and operating costs, hidden costs and visible costs, and any cost study must make clear what sorts of costs have been taken into consideration.[15]

The ILL cost studies cited above, as well as the Research Libraries Group's cost model, typically include what we could call transaction or service costs (what are the inclusive direct and indirect costs required to make this loan?). However, Charles B. Lowry, director of the library at the University of Texas at Austin, suggested an interesting and novel approach to costing interlending, one which goes beyond the activity of determining the transaction costs associated with interlibrary loan to calculate the extent to which a loan reduces the value of a library's investment in its own collections:

> Cost benefit would work something like this: a library borrowing on ILL pays to the lending institution a cost based on the high fixed cost experienced by the lending institution for maintaining materials in its collection and recovering them for lending purposes.... The actual unit cost for ILL activities must be established in order to judge the cost-benefit.[16]

Lowry goes on to cite a Virginia Tech in-house study, "Cost Data for the Virginia Tech Library," that established the total cost of buying and shelving books at $106 each, and the total cost for serial volumes at $181. He points out that such per-item investments represent a finite number of uses: each time a library lends a volume to someone other than a local user, its investment is diminished.

If we assume a book in an ordinary publisher's binding can withstand twenty-five circulations, Virginia Tech dissipates $4.24 each time it lends a monograph to another institution. Similarly, if a "class A" serial binding can weather fifty circulations and we equate a photocopied article with a circulation, the loss each time an article is provided on interlibrary loan is $3.62. Conversely, Lowry concludes, the borrowing library saves an equal amount. Any library can multiply the number of books and articles it provides through interlending during any given year by its unit costs for purchase and shelving, and determine the aggregate loss on its capital investment in collections.

> Using the unit cost method, a formula could be developed that factors in the lending libraries [sic] staff expenditures, periodical expenditures, and monograph expenditures over a five-year period.... By gathering these statistics annually, libraries would provide the basis for establishing the unit cost for lending both photocopy and book stock. This unit cost would be an added value to the interlibrary loan transaction, which would be paid directly to the lending institution by the borrowing institution.[17]

To avoid the "billing nightmare" such a system could generate, Lowry suggests that the accounting capability of the OCLC ILL module be expanded to include collecting and disbursing ILL fees, reconciling monthly the differences between each library's lending and borrowing costs. Such a system could allow for the continuation of reciprocal borrowing agreements, and it would save many institutions a great deal of money in local accounting costs (processing a state of Texas interlibrary loan payment voucher, says Lowry, costs more than $40 in paperwork, perhaps to pay the lending library as little as a dollar). Were the cost-benefit approach to establishing and recovering interlending costs implemented, Lowry believes that "Interlibrary Loan would cease to be Interlibrary Sacrifice."[18]

The Research Libraries Group ILL Cost Model

The newest (and, from the standpoints of simplicity and inclusiveness, the most appealing) approach to calculating interlending costs has been developed by the Research Libraries Group (RLG). The approach was adapted from the methodology published by Stephen P. Dickson and Virginia Boucher in *Research Access through New Technology*[19] and was piloted and refined by five institutions (Michigan, University of California at Berkeley, Stanford, Penn, the State University of New York at Albany, and the New-York Historical Society). In the spring of 1992 some seventy members of the Association of Research Libraries (ARL) applied the RLG Interlibrary Loan Cost Study and forwarded the completed worksheets to RLG for analysis. In a letter to ARL directors, Joan Chambers described the cost study's intent:

> The two goals of the project are (1) to collect benchmark data on costs of this key component of resource sharing programs, and (2) to provide participating libraries with a management tool for assessing the economies of document delivery. . . . All responding libraries will receive a confidential analysis of the ILL costs incurred in their individual institution, including a unit borrowing and lending cost for ILL transactions. . . . The aggregate data will provide benchmarks for assessing the cost implications of resource sharing, including a cost comparison of ILL lending and borrowing with alternative methods of obtaining information and other forms of document delivery.[20]

Thus, the data provided to each participant include information on the range of costs the seventy libraries achieved in the several activities surveyed, as well as where the individual library's costs fall, high or low, in relation to those of its peers. "Group" cost data were broken down by type and size of institution for greater relevance in comparing an individual library's costs to those achieved by others.

The introductory material provided with the cost study work forms (available free of charge from RLG)[21] describes a number of purposes a library might have in completing the study:

> Libraries experiencing increased demand for information services without increased resources, may use unit cost information to: 1. Decide whether to borrow an item through ILL rather than acquire it for the collection, 2. Decide when to use a commercial document delivery service in lieu of traditional ILL procedures, 3. Study the impact of serial cancellations.[22]

To this list, one could add a fourth broad purpose: to identify operational areas in which efficiencies seem warranted. Costs related to selection, acquisition, cataloging, and shelving (Lowry's "unit costs," as described above), considered "necessary preconditions for an ILL service ... are viewed as indirect costs and are not included in th[e] study."[23]

The RLG Cost Study is thorough, simple to apply, and not onerously time-consuming (ARL libraries were given one month to return the necessary worksheets). It requires libraries to collect cost information in several different areas: staffing, network and communications, delivery, photocopying, supplies, equipment and software, rental and maintenance, direct and indirect charges for borrowing from other suppliers, and cost recovery from both borrowing and lending activities. Librarians are given guidance in how to factor in subsidized services for which the library may not budget (state or regional delivery services, for example) and fully or partially cost-recovered services, such as loans, photocopies, and faxes. Participants are instructed to use the most recent year's cost figures and statistics, whether these be fiscal, calendar, or academic year. There are also provisions for projecting costs when certain figures are unavailable, or for breaking out the interlibrary loan unit's share of those costs when the only information available is for the library as a whole: the study aims at identifying all relevant costs, not just those budgeted for by the ILL unit.

RLG hoped to analyze cost study data for other libraries after the ARL project was completed; the organization spent some time considering what a suitable fee for this service might be. Although staffing and other constraints now rule this out, any library or group of libraries interested in conducting a self-study can obtain the necessary instructions, logs, and workforms from RLG. Data collection and analysis are not difficult, and the result will be solid information the library can use for decision-making purposes. Inconspicuous costs (staff time for interlibrary borrowing) will take their places alongside obvious ones (charges from commercial document services), enabling a library to determine which of several approaches to obtaining remotely held materials is more cost-effective. Libraries that have typically opted for the "free" fill over the "for-fee" one may change their minds.[24]

Deciding When to Choose Which Option

When the access program consists of several options for obtaining remotely held materials (on-site access, interlibrary loan, purchase from a commercial service), how should staff decide among them? It comes as no surprise that the primary factors to be considered are speed and cost.

The library that actually analyzes its ILL costs, perhaps following the RLG ILL cost study, may decide to make an overarching decision that it will tend toward either borrowing or purchasing, because the results of the study have shown one to be more cost-effective than the other. A more general approach will be to find out how quickly the reader needs the material, and to choose accordingly among the various approaches. Ideally, the method that is fastest and least costly will be chosen, with speed placed ahead of cost as the reader's needs dictate. If a faculty member who is just beginning a new research project submits a fistful of requests, the library may get her started by obtaining two or three quickly, through telefacsimile partners or commercial document services, and placing the others using "nonrush" methods (interlibrary loans delivered through a regional ground-based service, for example). If a graduate student needs quantities of material held by a library a few miles away, on-site access could be the best approach. On the other hand, if the college or university president needs an article for a presentation the next day to the board of trustees, no delivery approach can be either too fast or too costly.

Sue Kennedy points out that "familiarity with commercial suppliers is an important factor in deciding when paying higher direct costs may be the best course among several options for obtaining a document"; the library may have determined it is desirable to buy a document rather than borrow it, but it is still important to get the best price for the same service, when several companies compete.[25] Here, academic libraries can learn from special libraries, who may purchase as much as two-thirds of their information from fee-based services.

Many libraries will have policies that tell them very specifically where to go for what. Some allow a request's subject matter to determine how it will be obtained. A health sciences library, for example, may obtain most medical requests in one way (through DOCLINE, a nationwide, computerized medical interlibrary system), while nonmedical requests may travel more traditional ILL paths. Libraries that consistently value speed may get what they can from partners who share a rapid delivery technology (telefacsimile, scanning, or perhaps even a surface service), and rely upon commercial document services for all else. These guidelines may be useful in deciding among several interlending and document delivery options:

1. For what sorts of things can the library most easily budget?

This will be the most basic question. Whether the answer to this question is "staff" or "equipment" can make a big difference in the access options a library will favor. The library that finds it fairly easy to hire may prefer traditional interlibrary loan and delivery methods. On the other hand, when staffing is the most difficult item in the library budget, greater reliance on commercial document supply services and the electronic transfer of information can have more appeal.

There is a reason why special libraries have long relied on for-profit document supply services rather than interlibrary loan: not only has speed traditionally been important in these settings, but the staff has generally been small—too small for the labor-intensive activities of interlending. When a library purchases much of what its readers need, it not only frees itself from borrowing but also eases the burden of lending to others from its own collections.[26]

2. What are the access policies of neighboring libraries of interest to local readers?

If one has reciprocal access or borrowing agreements with libraries within easy traveling distance and the reader has the time (or needs access to large amounts of material), on-site access will be a good choice. "Easy traveling distance" will have different meanings in different settings: in Idaho a sixty-mile drive may be reasonable, while in New York City a trip from Brooklyn to the Bronx could seem absurd.

3. How fast or consistently will the supplier deliver the material?

This is an experiential factor: the library will know how long it takes a given library or document supplier to deliver (as well as what delivery mechanisms are available), and whether its service is reliable.

4. What are the direct costs associated with this approach?

Will the library that owns this material supply it free of charge? Is one commercial service less expensive than another? Will a commercial service charge less for the document than a library with which one has no reciprocal borrowing agreement?

5. What kind of processing activity does this method entail?

A library may often opt for the simplest of several approaches to obtaining a document. When a library can avoid "citation verification, ALA forms, ILL protocols, and all the other baggage that tend to inhibit commerce between libraries" by choosing a commercial document supply service, it may do so.[27]

6. What is the library's position as a net borrower?

Another way of phrasing this question is, how large a net borrower will the library permit itself to be? Some argue that it is the net borrowers of this world who are responsible for many libraries' retreat into smaller, more productive resource sharing arrangements and the use of various techniques to discourage outsiders. For a variety of reasons, at a certain point a library may feel ethically obligated to buy, rather than continue to borrow.

Adjusting Lending as Borrowing Declines

It is a simple economic fact that the library that borrows less is entitled to lend less (this is a different question, however, from whether it chooses to do so). Those who have argued that the use of commercial document supply services is less costly than processing interlibrary loans have factored into their calculations the obligation to lend (and the associated costs) that borrowing carries with it. If a library begins to purchase approximately one-third of the items it formerly obtained through ILL and yet does nothing similarly to reduce its levels of lending, the use of commercial services may not prove especially cost-beneficial.

This having been said, exactly how does a library go about adjusting or reducing its lending? There are two effective approaches that work best in combination.

1. Require all borrowers except those who are primary resource sharing partners to enter the library's location symbol twice in a bibliographic utility's ILL system. This will give the lending library twice as much time to fill the loan and discourage borrowers that need material promptly and can identify some other source.
2. Impose fees on all but primary partners. These charges should be competitive with those of commercial document services or else they may unwittingly invite borrowing. Fees will discourage most libraries and obtain payment from those that are not deterred. A library charging a fee can specify the amount through OCLC's ILL system and require that would-be borrowers indicate a willingness to pay. Such libraries generally forward immediately all requests they receive that do not meet this criterion.

Linking Access to Local Information Values: The California State University at San Bernardino Experience

The California State University at San Bernardino library owns six hundred thousand volumes and twenty-one hundred journal subscriptions; it primarily serves undergraduate readers. In 1988–89 serials expenditures represented 46 percent of the library's total materials budget. In 1991–92, $60,000 worth of subscriptions were cut; without those cancellations, the percentage of the resources pie allocated to serials would have been 87 percent. Facing the same frightening economic realities confronting academic libraries everywhere, San Bernardino made some difficult but courageous collecting decisions and linked the outcomes with document delivery.

Over a period of many years, teaching (versus library) faculty had developed a periodical subscription list; in many cases, faculty desires and student needs were rather isolated. Finally, finances forced a decision to reassess the titles to which the library subscribed. The library, its director and staff contended, was not a research library, but primarily existed to serve an undergraduate population. The new periodical list would reflect high-use titles that met their needs.

San Bernardino immediately proceeded to design journal use studies; during the first two quarters the studies were conducted, they identified $75,000 worth of titles that were not used at all. At the same time, reference librarians were asked to develop an "ideal" journal collection for San Bernardino; one important criterion was whether the title is included in the Wilson indexes, since the library is a NOTIS site planning to bring up these indexes in conjunction with its online public access catalog.

The faculty library committee proposed a final list, based on use studies and the reference librarians' recommendations, to the faculty as a whole; in May 1992 this list was accepted. In a letter to the university librarian, the head of collection development described the process leading up to the presentation of the new subscription list:

> We are going to department heads and outside of science have met with little resistance. There seems to be little or no hard feelings about the library. The general attitude seems to be that the library should get more financial support. Of course, no one wants to reduce their budget so the library can have more money![28]

The library's journal subscriptions expired on December 31, 1992, and on January 1, 1993, a new core collection of periodicals was in place. But what about access to those costly canceled titles, the ones with so much faculty support? This is where San Bernardino's new three-tier approach to periodicals and their access comes in.

Tier one represents the new "core" collection of journal subscriptions; these are the high-use titles to which the library continues to subscribe and readers have immediate access. Tier two titles are those to which the library once subscribed but which it has now canceled, as well as requested subscriptions that the library cannot afford. Faculty and students are able to see the "universe" of articles of potential interest through the Wilson indexes installed as part of the library's online catalog, or by searching the CARL UnCover database.

The library guarantees twenty-four- to forty-eight-hour turnaround time for tier two journals through interlibrary loan. San Bernardino has reciprocal agreements with several academic libraries in the area whose holdings it can readily view, and each gives the others' requests a higher priority for ILL turnaround. Telefacsimile speeds delivery, and when a special partner cannot supply a wanted item, San Bernardino goes immediately to a commercial document vendor. The library estimates filling twelve hundred requests in this way in 1993 and at $10 per item has set aside $12,000 to pay for them. Tier three titles are those to which the library has never subscribed and in which faculty have not expressed a specific interest; for these titles, regular ILL channels are used. The San Bernardino experience can be a useful and sensible model for any library; it combines logic, speed, and cost-effectiveness.

Cost Recovery: To Charge or Not to Charge?

Like Herbert S. White, Barbara Quint is usually good for something controversial. Writing about what she calls the old "Fee v. Free" polemic ("If we can't all be informed, none of us should be informed"), she demonstrates little patience with information's radical fringe:

> Unfortunately, this line of thought has a tradition among members of the library profession. One can find it impeding the course of progress throughout the few decades of the Information Age.... It offers the weak the excuse of simulated strength. But, most significantly, it diminishes service to our users.... We are not social philosophers or political activists working for a new social order, at least not during our day jobs. We are librarians. We have a unique professional ethic. We inform. Our mission is to serve the minds of our clients, to provide the information and knowledge they want and need as effectively as our professional judgment and resources can achieve.[29]

While Quint must not be understood as arguing for fees, she certainly contests the idea that no service should be offered unless it is free to all. Indeed, in the present environment in which state agencies that once paid much of the resource sharing bill (often with federal funding) are now woefully short of funds, many libraries face a difficult decision: "In the tradition of open or 'free' access for the user to library resources, shall libraries increasingly absorb transaction costs and in the process forgo capital collections, or shall such costs be transferred to the user?"[30] Perhaps as we consider the pros and cons of charging (either our own readers or other libraries), we can decide that the issue is not quite so black and white as this.

The first issue of *Collection Building* in 1986 is devoted to the question of fees. It begins with the National Commission on Libraries and Information Science's (NCLIS) now classic position paper, "The Role of Fees in Supporting Library and Information Services in Public and Academic Libraries," and includes a series of responses from academic and public librarians, library educators, publishers, and consultants. The NCLIS piece describes existing library fee structures; mechanisms and rationales for setting fees; arguments for and against charging; the types of services for which libraries assess fees; and the suggested effects of fee-based services. There is also a substantial bibliography by Marsha S. Clark.[31] In a way, the issue is dated, focusing as it does on charging for database searching, but it is still valuable for its philosophical content and some amount of practical advice on charging fees for access.

Charging the Library's Own Readers: What's Right about It?

There are several arguments for charging readers for obtaining remotely held materials. Some institutions' motivations are purely practical: they feel they cannot fund the service unless they charge for certain aspects of it, probably by passing on any direct costs they incur (fees other libraries charge for making loans or photocopies, the cost of articles purchased from commercial document services). Fees are simply a way to fund a service the library believes will be valuable to some readers, but which it otherwise could not afford.

Other libraries are more philosophical; they levy charges for services they label "enhanced" or "value-added" (commercial document services, for example) but do not charge for basic (and typically slower) services. Some institutions shore up this position by suggesting that these "enhanced" services (which are presumably needed by a minority of the readership) must not be offered at the expense of the library's primary clientele and mission. The University of California at Berkeley's BAKER program is a good example of a fee-based service available under alternate circumstances free of charge. BAKER derives its name from two clever connections, the first to Sherlock Holmes's Baker Street and the detective work that location evokes, and the second to the service's telephone number, XXB-AKER; this alone will attract fun-loving scholars to the program.

By visiting the library, any Berkeley reader can withdraw materials or place an interlibrary loan request at no charge; BAKER is there for those who prefer to work from home or office. At $3 per request plus $.10 a page for photocopies, BAKER staff will secure and deliver any locally or remotely held materials a reader wants. Faculty and students visit the BAKER office and open a deposit account. They can then place requests for books and journal articles through the online catalog, telephone, electronic mail, campus mail, the postal service, or telefacsimile. When readers open accounts, they specify whether or not they want requests for items unavailable at Berkeley forwarded automatically to the ILL unit. When items arrive, they are delivered to readers' campus addresses.

Some libraries charge for services because they contend that doing so increases the value in the eyes of the reader (also known as, "If it's free it must not be worth much"). Fees also prevent misuse of interlending by discouraging faculty and students from asking for more information than they really need; they force readers (in the view of some librarians) to ascertain somehow in advance whether or not an item the local library does not own is necessary to their research. In short, fees prevent trivial use of the system.

Why We May Not Want to Charge Our Faculty and Students

As one librarian puts it, why are we frantically building all these bibliographic databases to let readers know what exists elsewhere if we're just going to turn around and discourage the use of anything that isn't locally held? Herbert S. White puts it a little differently:

> Charging our clients for interlibrary borrowing is the greatest injustice of all. We have already penalized them by not having the foresight to buy the item, and now we want to penalize them again, to charge them for the honor of waiting.[32]

It will be difficult if not impossible for a library to convince readers that it feels a genuine responsibility to provide them with needed materials in a timely fashion, whether it owns them or not, if it charges fees for acquiring some or all remotely held items. As a small group of City University of New York chief librarians grappling with serial cancellations asked themselves, how are we going to justify charging readers today for an article in a journal to which we subscribed as recently as yesterday? It is one thing, they concluded, to charge a reader when the local collection meets a substantial portion of his or her research needs, but as the percentage of "met need" drops, one can hardly justify fees. As Carolyn Dusenbury and William Post point out, "It may not be a viable service posture for a journal to be 'free' if it is in a subscription to the paper copy while charging the user of other delivery systems the fee for those systems." And, when no abstract is available for local consultation, how does one justify charging readers for information whose content's value they have had no opportunity to assess? Indeed, some libraries that previously recovered the fees charged by document suppliers from readers are now lifting those charges.[33]

Fees also have the potential to create unequal access to scholarly information, because researchers will have differing abilities to pay. Consider the pocketbooks of the scholarship student, the instructor in the English department, and the professor in the physics research center: if fees are charged, it is easy to guess who is likely to have a grant and the ability to pay his or her way, and who will be left with traditional (i.e., slow) access to remotely held materials through interlibrary loan. Will the library risk supporting one type of scholarship over another by charging fees? One can scarcely argue that expansive access services are "extending" the library if large numbers of readers have no access because of the imposition of fees. And, what cost do we impose on users if we deny them access to options other than interlibrary loan?[34]

More practically speaking, there is a great deal of record keeping associated with collecting fees. As one librarian reports, "A significant problem is that the cost of the service is substantially increased by the expense of collecting money. Administrative overhead looms as a larger factor, and impacts the amount of money needed to make the service break even."[35] When a library charges, important factors include the costs of making an invoice, depositing a check, and so forth.

If You Charge, What Are the Options?

Like most things in life, fees are not necessarily black or white, assessed or not assessed: a library may charge fees under some circumstances but not others, to some groups but not others, in full or partially subsidized. The library that seeks to recover all costs, both direct and indirect, from any or all reader groups will find that this will act as a serious control on requests, screening out not only casual ones but many serious ones as well. Partial cost recovery, on the other hand, can provide control while not discouraging as many genuine requests. These are some of the models a library can consider:

1. Pass on to readers any fees levied by document suppliers (libraries or commercial services); provide everything else free of charge.
2. Charge a flat fee for every request filled, whether through interlibrary loan or commercial document services and regardless of whether the library incurs any direct costs.

3. Each semester (quarter; year) provide every reader up to a given number of items free of charge, whether the library has to pay for them of not; thereafter, charge a fee for every item.
4. Provide items free of charge (whether the library pays or not) to readers in certain patron categories (faculty; students); fully recover costs from other readers (staff; local high school students).
5. Levy only special "add on" charges for services like placing requests by telephone, citation verification, rush delivery, delivery to home or office, and so forth.

Libraries that do charge fees must consider whether to accept as payment cash, personal checks, charge cards, and departmental charge accounts.

Assessing Fees against Other Libraries: Yes or No?

The issue of "universal access" (a grand way of libraries saying "we won't charge each other") has gone the way of most other "universal" concepts. As federal and state funding have disappeared, libraries all over the country have begun to charge one another various fees for loans and photocopies. As the librarians participating in the OCLC-sponsored ILL focus group put it,

> From a practical standpoint, libraries do not always have the resources to make information universally accessible. Thus, libraries end up defining their "primary clientele" and serving them. According to one participant, "the debate of [universal access] is swinging toward nonuniversal access.[36]

Unless a library is a public institution mandated not to charge others, it is realistic that it will probably charge some institutions and not charge others. Imposing fees is often a way of "load leveling," that is, a library does not charge its primary partners who in turn provide much of what it needs, but does charge others. In the past, we might have felt guilty about a policy so blatantly self-serving; however, times have changed. As the OCLC panelists reluctantly observed, "Some kind of compensation mechanism has to come into place sooner or later."[37] Perhaps the obligation is to lend as much as one borrows, and no one in today's environment could argue for substantially more than that.

Why It's Good to Charge Your Friends

The additional workload in interlibrary loan has forced libraries to increase staff and find some way to pay them; often fees have been the "way."

> The tradition of "free" interlibrary loan (ILL) was based on the moral obligation that librarians felt to share their resources with other libraries. Free ILL was feasible as long as it was voluntary and as long as the volume of requests was limited—largely by the inefficiencies of the traditional manual location, request, and delivery systems. But the rationale for free interlibrary loan no longer holds in the new, high volume, and more demanding resource sharing environment. . . . Libraries with close network, political, or regional affiliations may choose to continue to give free reciprocal ILL services where it is mutually beneficial while taking full account of the costs.[38]

Thus spake Richard De Gennaro, some thirteen years ago. In this article written for *Library Journal* he suggests that OCLC's ILL subsystem be modified in order to serve as a clearinghouse for the type of interlending payments he suggests. There was no reason then that this could not be done, and there is no reason today: OCLC bills libraries for its own services, why not use this same accounting capability to collect and disburse ILL fees? De Gennaro continues with specific reasons for assessing ILL fees:

> Interlibrary loan is becoming too important to be continued as a free service and . . . it is time to put a realistic price on it and establish it on a more rational and businesslike basis. . . . ILL fees will be necessary and beneficial because they will compensate the lending libraries for the cost of providing the service, they will ration demand, and they will serve as a measure of value for the service.[39]

Remembering De Gennaro's large, private university bias, it is easy to see that the issues that began to affect the Penns, Harvards, Michigans, and Berkeleys more than a dozen years ago have at last descended on smaller institutions. Twelve years later another librarian writing for *Library Journal* echoes De Gennaro: "Charging fees is an effective method of controlling demand from nonaffiliated users and ensuring that the library is adequately compensated when it provides research or other services to those outside its organization."[40] Maybe the OCLC ILL subsystem will be adapted yet to manage such charges.

On the Other Hand . . .

Some librarians remain strongly opposed to charging other institutions for interlibrary loans. "The costs of preparing an invoice and cutting a check are often higher than the amount of compensation sought," notes one consulting group.[41] (Indeed, in recognition of such costs, some libraries that charge other institutions significantly reduce the fee when payment is enclosed with an ALA form, eliminating the need to invoice.)

A librarian from the Pacific Northwest regrets interinstitutional fees for other reasons as well:

> A giant step backwards in the mutual sharing of information and resources has taken place through the imposition of fees for interlibrary loan services. While these services cost money to provide, users and institutions formerly were not charged. . . . Interlibrary loan departments have been burdened with billing and accounting. Libraries are spending a not inconsiderable amount of time keeping track of how much who owes whom. It may be argued that many of us are spending a lot of time just shuffling dollars around, not gaining anything financially in the process, but losing worker time that would otherwise have been spent processing requests.[42]

Thus, it can be costly to charge our fellows, in the sense that accounting costs money and also drains resources away from the real work of the access unit. For these reasons, some libraries will elect not to charge others when they lend.

Developing the Access Budget

Thomas J. Michalak notes that, despite all the breast beating of the 1980s, colleges and universities still found ways to fund the automation of their catalogs and related activities (circulation, serials control, acquisitions).[43] Thus, there is good reason to suspect we will also identify paths for funding access to materials the local library does not own. Perhaps the first question is, how do we determine what the access budget should be? Will it be possible to determine an "appropriate" sum to spend on access? Can we build a rationale for access as a flat percentage of the library's budget, or perhaps the materials budget, just as such formulas have been developed for preservation and other programs?

It is unlikely that any standard formula can be successfully applied to funding for access. First, a library must determine what it wants to buy with the access budget—articles from commercial document services? Equipment, like a scanning workstation or a telefacsimile machine? Will there be other costs as well, such as software and supplies? A library should also weigh whether its choices may call for some adjustment in staffing: will a new group of partners necessitate hiring? Or, will heavier reliance on commercial document services cause the library to take steps to decrease lending? Perhaps the additional staffing required by increased borrowing can be provided by reassigning lending staff to borrowing duties if the library makes fewer loans to other institutions.

A library might begin by setting aside whatever sum it can for access. Or, it can identify the methods it plans to use most frequently, and multiply the average cost of an item acquired in these ways by the number of items it expects to receive; it is easy to identify the fees commercial document vendors charge, and several of the access programs described in the appendix suggest unit costs. Once a library decides what elements its access program will contain—perhaps by following the guidelines that appear under "Deciding When to Choose Which Option," above—designing an access budget should not be difficult.

Where Do I Get That Kind of Money?

Once the access budget is in place, the library can see whether additional funds will be needed and consider different approaches to obtaining them. These are some of the approaches academic libraries have used:

1. Charging local readers for full or partial cost-recovery

The pros and cons of this funding approach have been discussed at length, above. Though many libraries may find it unappealing, it is still a viable source of program funding. There may even be some fairly painless and indirect ways of "charging" local readers. If, for example, campus policy dictates that a percentage of every sponsored research grant comes to the library, this money could easily become the access budget, subsidizing materials for a great number of readers.

2. Charging other libraries for full or partial cost-recovery

This approach has also been fully debated earlier in this chapter. If we are honest, it probably holds little promise for funding access programs. At best, charging those who are not our principal partners will fund access only indirectly, insofar as it discourages other borrowers, acts as a cap on lending, and financially underwrites those loans the library does indeed make to its nonprimary partners.

3. State- or consortium-reimbursed lending

Some states and consortia reimburse libraries that lend to other libraries, either for every loan or for net lending. (And, different library systems have very different definitions of net lenders: "those who loan more than they borrow, those who loan twice as much as they borrow, and those who loan in vast quantities, say more than 2000 items a year.")[44] The Network of Alabama Academic Libraries, in order strongly to encourage resource sharing, reimburses both borrowers and lenders. The bottom line is: can a library expect to fund its access program through such reimbursements? The answer, it seems, is "probably not." As with the previously considered technique, charging other libraries for loans, it is likely that reimbursements for net lending will do little more than balance the books.

4. Direct subsidy by the college or university administration

Some librarians have successfully justified increases in their budgets when they have significantly expanded access to information; such a service *should* have a price tag within the institution, they have argued. In some settings the college or university administration has generated funding to support remote access for students by initiating or increasing a campus library fee.

Special campus funding sometimes comes with certain strings attached: for instance, some administrations have stipulated that documents be obtained for faculty only, and that requests be limited to materials needed for research.[45] Such conditions should not seem especially oppressive when, by accepting them, the library gains funding to improve information access for an important segment of the campus community and, by extension, the opportunity to demonstrate that other groups of readers (students) can benefit from the same services.

5. Taking money from other library programs

Many academic libraries have bitten the bullet and redirected existing library funds to pay for an expanded access program. Polytechnic University (Brooklyn, N.Y.) implemented the InfoDash program by reallocating funds from its little-used but expensive government publications program. Fairly recently libraries all over the country elected to carve money for CD-ROMs from their general resources budgets; now, we may elect to tap money earmarked for collections in order to fund access to materials we do not own.

Some librarians refer to interlibrary borrowing and the use of commercial document services as "temporary acquisition," strengthening the link between funds for collections and funds for access: "Librarians need to recognize that the costs of resource sharing constitute the same kind of expenditures as those made for library acquisitions."[46] This does not mean, however, that we should be naive about the potential campus reaction to such decisions:

> If the library decides to fund this program out of its regular budget, it must have a strong philosophical commitment to the service, and must be prepared to defend the merit of its argument.... There will surely be critics on the faculty who believe that the money could be better used elsewhere, such as in the acquisitions budget. There will just as surely be library staff who would prefer to see those financial resources diverted elsewhere.[47]

Perhaps librarians can use California State University at Chico's experience and philosophy to reassure both themselves and the faculty about the "rightness" of using the materials budget to fund access:

> Is Chico uncomfortable with the idea of paying for a service with materials funds? Not at all.... Chico feels rather strongly that this is inevitable. As all collections are diminished by increases in inflation, more and more journals, steady state or diminishing budgets, and the evolution of new electronic delivery systems—this agreement is a harbinger of the future.[48]

6. Cost-savings from subscription cancellations

This funding approach is similar to yet different from the one that precedes it; because of its popularity, it deserves its own evaluation. Many libraries have funded expanded access programs by dropping costly, little-used journals. Metz and Gherman provide them with considerable support and comfort:

> As serials inflation forces individual libraries to look hard at their subscription lists, a new emphasis on relative costs and benefits is dawning. Libraries can no longer accept blindly the bias of faculty, which is to vote yes or no on titles without respect to their costs, but are learning that a few respectable, but

seriously overpriced, journals can be cut to save many less expensive titles.... Publishers should be aware that librarians will not find it so difficult to cut significant journals once they have done it the first time.[49]

Similarly Harold Billings, librarian at the University of Texas at Austin, suggests "redistributing some of the massive sums that are consumed by serial costs, to help leverage alternative means of information access."[50] Bernard H. Holicky describes what actually happened in a small academic library (156,000 volumes) when such a plan was implemented and the library absorbed all costs associated with rapid delivery of remotely held materials:

> It was discovered that it was cheaper to give "free" service than to try to absorb the never-ending annual subscription price increases. The actual cost of the "free" service has now stabilized at $7,000 annually. Periodical prices on the other hand, were increasing by $10,000 each year.... With or without faculty support, librarians of smaller academic libraries must have the gumption to cancel seldom-used journals, reallocate poorly spent periodical funds, substitute online searching for expensive print indexing and abstracting services, and emphasize resource sharing.[51]

At Chico, where for a set annual fee the library "subscribes" to a given number of articles from nearby Berkeley's journal collection (details of this arrangement appear in the appendix), the library added up the subscription costs of journals it requested more than once from Berkeley and found that it had, as it were, saved tens of thousands of dollars through this arrangement. "Chico might seriously consider a policy that when we have to cut subscriptions, a percentage of the savings will be invested in document delivery services to mitigate the effects of the cancellations."[52]

Some beleaguered academic librarians for whom serial cancellations have become an annual rite may find it hard to see how they can create access budgets when they are dropping titles because they cannot pay for them: where is the "extra money" in such an operation? Can the library justify canceling even more subscriptions than those needed simply to balance the materials budget in order to fund access? If one compiles serials use data, then compares the prices of little-used but costly subscriptions to the cost of obtaining articles from the same journals through remote sources, perhaps the answer is yes, and there is a good case to be made to the campus administration for what might otherwise seem "gratuitous" cancellations.

Evaluating the Access Program

Suggestions for evaluating the various elements in the access program (interlending, document delivery) appear throughout this volume, as those elements are presented. Now, however, it is time to assess the effectiveness of the access program as a whole. Maurice B. Line's article "Measuring the Performance of Document Supply Systems" is a key piece, recommended reading for every access manager. Here, he outlines the objectives in measuring the performance of an access program:

> To assess how well a system ... is doing; to identify areas of weakness where improvement may be needed; to aid planners in deciding between possible alternative systems to assist a user (primarily a library) in deciding which of one or more alternative available systems it should use for all requests or for particular types of requests; to enable a library to decide which method of requesting or supply to use; to enable a supplier to measure its effectiveness and efficiency.[53]

Methods for assessing performance should be practical; ideally, the evidence to be considered will be collected routinely, if not automatically, as part of the access program's normal operations. When it is unrealistic to gather information about every request that is processed, libraries may instead sample, perhaps during two or three different times of the year, to account for changes in workload and other seasonal factors.

How will we know if the access program is a success? The RLG Interlibrary Loan Cost Study will tell us whether our access costs are in line with those of other libraries. The guidelines that follow will help in assessing borrowing, lending, and the adequacy of staffing levels.

Assessing the Borrowing Operation

These evaluative factors may be helpful in assessing borrowing services:

1. Location finders: Do the library's principal location finders (its bibliographic utility, a shared CD-ROM catalog) include the holdings of its primary resource sharing partners?
2. Number of requests submitted: While it is difficult to suggest what volume of requests represents success, if a library publicizes and invests in access, it should see a

corresponding increase in traffic. The library may also want to evaluate the number of requests submitted by different reader groups; for example, if the service is primarily aimed at faculty but undergraduates submit the most requests, this is an indication that some adjustment in program content or promotion is probably in order.

A related service measure is F. W. Lancaster's observation that "it would also be valuable to know something about the hidden mass of the iceberg: the number of ILL requests that are not made." Do readers fail to use the service because they are not aware of it, because they think it is too slow, or for other reasons? According to Lancaster, "Library performance should be evaluated in terms of user needs (latent demand) as well as actual demands made."[54] As much as we may agree with him, for the present perhaps we must content ourselves with suitably funding and promoting the access service.

3. Growth in service: This factor is closely related to "number of requests submitted," above. A steep growth or decline in demand will tell the library something; it is important, however, to think carefully about what that something is. Often extraneous occurrences (the introduction of a new academic program or the dismantling of an existing one) may be the explanation, rather than greater or lesser reader expectations for the service.[55] On the other hand, if the library's ratio of "accessed" to circulated items grows, this can probably be safely taken as a broad if somewhat imperfect indication of the service's success.

4. Fill rate: Maurice B. Line suggests that fill rate (the number or percentage of our readers' requests for remotely held materials we are able to satisfy) "is an essential but rather crude indicator of performance":

> A high figure suggests that the system is working well and a low one suggests that there are deficiencies. An overall fill rate, which is most commonly used, is much less useful than one broken down by form (monographs, serials, etc.), subject, or date, since only by detailed analyses can one discover how well (e.g.) pre-1900 monographs are supplied compared with those published after 1900, or how well agriculture is served compared with medicine.[56]

The small- to medium-sized academic library may not care so much as the larger one about the very fine points

Line proposes to measure, and it will perhaps decide that overall fill rate is a sufficient measure. A study of interlending workload and staffing in seventy-six ARL institutions established benchmarks for fill rates and output that other academic libraries can use as measures of their own effectiveness:

> Median fillrates and outputs give libraries a basic checkpoint against which they can measure their own efficiency and effectiveness. When comparing efficiency and effectiveness measures, libraries need to keep in mind how their goals might differ from the group studied [seventy-six ARL libraries]. . . . The process of examination may reveal strengths or weaknesses in your operations and the results may serve as a viable argument in a justification for increased staffing or other desired changes.[57]

Interlibrary Loan in Academic and Research Libraries: Workload and Staffing, published as ARL Occasional Paper 15, includes instructions and workforms any library can use to replicate the study and compare its own fill rate and output to those of the seventy-six ARL libraries. This is a very useful adjunct to the Research Libraries Group's Interlibrary Loan Cost Study.

5. Speed of delivery: Richard M. Dougherty has an interesting outlook on the role of speed in readers' overall acceptance of the access/ownership model for academic librarianship:

> It is probable that the attitudes of some users toward interdependence have changed; it is probably also true that others remain staunchly opposed to the proposition that access to collections should be dependent on delivery. For this latter group, the memory of four- to six-week interlibrary loan delivery performance may never fade away.[58]

Information Systems Consultants, Inc. (ISCI) believes that delivery speed may be the most important single measurement of interlending success:

> The best measure of performance of interlibrary loan is "satisfaction time," the elapsed time from the placing of the request by the patron to the time the material is made available to that patron. The dozen most frequently cited satisfaction time studies that have been

done suggest that, at best, the average time from request to receipt of materials varies from just over 10 days to nearly 16 days. It is not uncommon for requests to be subject to satisfaction delays of up to a month. Certainly satisfaction time is shorter within consortia, and longer when the material is being supplied by libraries which are not regular suppliers to the requesting institution.[59]

While we can easily accept "satisfaction time" as a prime measure of the access unit's success, we will probably not be persuaded that ten to sixteen days represents satisfactory satisfaction time. The point is, the library must decide how fast is fast enough, and then measure speed of delivery accordingly. As Line suggests, "a slow service cannot satisfactorily supplement access to local holdings, and it certainly cannot serve as a substitute for local access. . . . A service that is slow lacks credibility and deters demand."[60]

According to Line, we cannot adequately evaluate what he calls "speed of supply" (ISCI's "satisfaction time") unless we break down the borrowing process into its various components. After all, he argues, if the purpose of evaluation is to see where improvements can be made, it is important to examine closely, rather than broadly. Some parts of the borrowing process the local library will be able to control, others it will not; but, even where no power to influence exists, there is often the ability to choose among alternatives.[61] For libraries wishing to follow Line's advice, the chapter on interlending breaks down the borrowing operation into its several components.

Libraries may also wish to evaluate different "types" of speed: was speed of delivery satisfactory for materials requested both "rush" and "nonrush"? Quite possibly a system will succeed well in one area, but not in another. Reliability or consistency (the ability of the access unit to obtain an item within a predictable time frame, but not necessarily "rush") could also be measured.

There are other aspects of delivery speed that are, at the same time, both very desirable and almost impossible to measure:

> It would be valuable to go beyond response time to determine what proportion of all items had arrived in time to be useful to the individuals requesting them. Some

indication of this could be derived, perhaps, by counting ILL requests that are canceled by their initiators, as well as cases where items are borrowed but not collected by the requesters. It would be more useful, however, to undertake a survey to determine the actual impact of ILL delays on library users; that is, to determine, for a sample of requests, whether delays in delivery reduced the value of the material to the requester.[62]

For the moment, perhaps we will have to leave the design of such a study to the library futurists and content ourselves with measures that are now within our grasp.

6. Document quality: Not all documents are created equal, and some documents are more equal than others. Photocopies can be clean or covered with lines and splotches. Faxes received over plain paper machines will be more pleasant to the senses than those printed on thermal paper. Scanned documents (where plain paper and higher resolution converge) are likely to meet with even more satisfaction.

7. Flexibility and ease of use: These factors should be considered from the perspectives of both the reader and the library. As Line suggests, "a 'good' but difficult system may attract less demand than a 'poor' but easy one."[63] That is, when readers find impediments (poor physical location; brusque staff; complex forms that must be completed) to the use of a highly efficient system, they simply may not use it. From the library's viewpoint, the system should provide enough alternative sources of supply and delivery to meet readers' needs, stopping short of a bewildering array of choices requiring complex decision making. These supply and delivery sources should also be easy to monitor and measure.

8. Reader satisfaction: Perhaps there should be no separate evaluative factor for reader satisfaction; in fact, if we add up all the preceding factors, will the sum not be "reader satisfaction"? If there is a high level of system usage, and we can locate and deliver wanted items with sufficient speed, readers should be satisfied; however, reader satisfaction should not be viewed simply in terms of the happiness of those using the system; as Lancaster suggests above, what of the readers who never take advantage of the access program? Certainly, they cannot be said to be "satisfied." According to Line (very much in accord with Lancaster on this issue),

What is needed therefore is some measure of potential demand; the proportion that actual demand constitutes of potential demand can then be calculated. Unfortunately, potential demand is extremely hard to measure. It can be measured directly only by surveying users, to ascertain how far their needs are translated into requests.[64]

One modest and rather unscientific approach might be to measure the percentage of a given reader population availing itself of the system, and then compare the results with the experiences of similar institutions; for example, if 50 percent of the faculty at a peer college or university use ILL services, while only 10 percent of local faculty do so, this could be taken as some indication of reader satisfaction. Similarly, comparisons of local ILL/circulation ratios with those at other institutions can be helpful in gauging reader satisfaction.

There are other measurements that could also be excellent gauges of reader satisfaction: how much time did the access service save the reader? What was the ultimate usefulness of the material to him or her? (A related issue is the ultimate usefulness of the material to the institution—did a faculty member get a large grant, thanks to the information?) Unfortunately, measuring such factors is far beyond the means of most libraries. A final test for reader satisfaction is the question of whether the access service has positively affected the campus's perception of the general effectiveness and friendliness of the library. The program is probably succeeding if the perceived answer is "yes."

9. Balance and fairness: These are criteria that consider suppliers' perspectives. Are borrowing requests fairly distributed among appropriate resource sharing partners? Are borrowed materials returned promptly and in good condition? Is there any significant loss rate for borrowed materials?

10. Costs: Costs are not properly a measure of performance, yet to exclude them from any discussion of program effectiveness is impractical. The total cost of the access program must be considered an important evaluative factor:

> Ultimately all systems have to operate within constraints of cost (and staff time, which is money); if one system can provide as good a fill rate, speed of supply etc. for a given number of requests as another at lower cost it is clearly a superior system.[65]

Assessing the Lending Operation

Many of the factors suggested above for evaluating a library's borrowing service also apply to lending; thus, this section can be brief. Often libraries find that their lending operation is more efficient than their borrowing—that "partner satisfaction" is greater than "reader satisfaction." Probably because of network turnaround time requirements, many institutions slight borrowing (which benefits their own readers) in favor of lending.[66] This could be called the "solid citizen" approach to resource sharing, and it is one libraries should be wary of: if some edge must be given to either local or partner needs, local should be given priority. We should care less about our "image" on the utility's ILL system, and more about satisfying our own readers.

The library evaluating its lending operation may wish to consider these factors:

1. Number of requests received: While a library will probably not establish policies intended to generate quantities of requests to borrow from its collections, when an institution receives either an especially large or small number this may be an indication that there is an imbalance between lending and borrowing, and some review of the situation is probably in order.
2. Growth in service: Again, this is a phenomenon to be avoided, rather than sought. A steady growth in the number of requests received may indicate that the library is lending on terms that are too liberal.
3. Fill rate: Whatever its fill rate, a library should examine the reasons why it was unable to supply certain items; this information can be extremely valuable in other areas of the library's operation. For example, the library that consistently reports "no fills" because items are owned but not on the shelf may wish to examine the reliability of its circulation or catalog systems.

    On the other hand, if negative responses occur because the library cannot manage to search for items within the utility's established time frame so that many requests are "bumped" to the next location symbol, it may be that the lending operation is understaffed. If the library is also a net borrower, it should certainly look to increase staff in the lending operation; if it is not, it should consider some method of discouraging more requests than it can manage to process.

4. Speed of delivery: To use ISCI's terminology, what is the "satisfaction time" for filling the requests of other libraries? And, how does that time compare to network or consortial guidelines?
5. Flexible delivery systems: Can the library deliver documents in almost any format and by almost any method the borrowing institution specifies?
6. Document quality: Are surrogates (photocopies, faxes) clean and easily read?
7. Partner satisfaction: When the first several factors are combined, are the library's primary partners generally satisfied with the service they receive?
8. Safety of materials: Does the access unit ensure the safe return of lent materials? This factor can be improved when the library packages books that it lends in certain ways and insists on the same type of packaging when books are returned. Often library consortia (such as RLG) specify the type of boxing and packing required for interlending.
9. Costs: The RLG Interlibrary Loan Cost Study will help the library identify its lending costs and assess how these costs compare to those of other libraries of similar size.

Assessing Staffing Levels

Here, we return to the 1989 ARL study of interlending workload and staffing that established benchmarks for fill rates and output useful to other academic libraries in assessing their own effectiveness:

> The labor-intensive nature of libraries makes analysis of efficiency an important part of operations.... This study looks at efficiency and effectiveness in ILL with the intent of establishing some guidelines for lending and borrowing activity in academic and research libraries.[67]

The study (forms and instructions are included in ARL Occasional Paper 15) concludes that median fill rates and outputs are valid bases for measuring the efficiency and effectiveness of the ILL unit and suggesting when staffing levels should be adjusted. It assesses libraries in terms of both their effectiveness (requests filled divided by requests processed) and efficiency (requests processed divided by FTE staff), and establishes 61 percent as a minimally successful fill rate in lending, and 84 percent as a base effective fill rate in borrowing.

The study demonstrates that lending operations judged to be both effective and efficient have a greater ratio of librarians and students to paraprofessionals; it also makes allowances for differences in local emphases and internal office procedures, such as whether staff do their own wrapping and photocopying. The authors caution that, since fill rate (effectiveness) and output (efficiency) do not correlate, turnaround time (delivery speed) or some other performance measure should also be reviewed if a library contemplates increasing staffing in the access unit.[68]

Communication with Readers

The access unit will probably communicate with local readers in several ways; one of these (electronic mail for local messaging) has been covered in the chapter on interlibrary loan. The more flexibility the library can offer students and faculty, the easier and more appealing they will find it to use the access unit's services. Certainly the telephone is a useful option; few homes and offices are unequipped with answering devices, and a message left on a machine will typically reach a reader more quickly than one sent by campus or U.S. mail; staff time and postage are also potential savings, as a telephone call replaces the completion of a postcard. Some access units have their own answering devices and offer readers the ability to leave ILL requests on them. While staff may have difficulties interpreting such messages, especially when foreign language data are involved, this approach is certainly considerate of the reader's time.

Of the various notification options, e-mail will probably be the least expensive, with telephone calls (depending on whether the library pays its own telephone bill and its telecommunication vendor's charging scheme) and postcards sent by campus mail coming in second. The library that pays its own postage bill may wish to avoid sending cards through the U.S. mail. Additionally, a card mailed to someone's home may reach the reader who does not come to campus every day more quickly than a card sent through campus mail.

Staffing the Access Unit

A well-trained staff of sufficient number is the key to a successful ILL operation. The ILL supervisor, generally a professional librarian, should be a skilled manager. As Noelene P. Martin points out, interlending is presently confronting the same staffing needs that arose in technical services when these functions were first automated:

> Despite managerial expectation that ILL can be clericalized, it is becoming clear that more and more sophistication and training is needed to determine priorities, unravel bibliographic snarls, and choose between mechanisms, in order to respond to user needs.[69]

The depth of expertise needed in the access unit will necessarily depend on the type of searching the operation supports. For example, access to multiple utilities and password-only access to OPACs on the Internet all incur costs: if the staff has not mastered the necessary skills, the library may be spending less on staff costs, but more than making up for it in telecommunications and other expenses.

As a rule, it is important to assign a task to the lowest-level staff member who can do the job competently. For clerical processes, the *Interlibrary Loan Practices Handbook* can be used as a preliminary checklist of typical supporting staff duties. ALA's "Interlibrary Loan Training and Continuing Education Model Statement of Objectives" is a comprehensive list of training objectives, from familiarity with ILL codes to maintenance of the fax machine; every library interested in better-trained and more effective staff should examine it.[70]

Virginia Boucher's article "The Interlibrary Loan Librarian" provides a useful description of the qualities an interlending professional should have.[71] If the library intends to rely upon access to meet any significant portion of its readers' needs, the head of the access or interlibrary loan unit must be a solid manager, well versed in technology and unafraid of it, mentally agile, and almost intuitively capable of choosing well from a maelstrom of access options.

Perhaps the traditional interlibrary loan librarian, the one we mentioned a few chapters earlier who has had such success in training his or her readers to wait ("Oh, that will take at least two weeks, probably more") should cast about for something new to do, stepping aside so that someone energetic, flexible, and perhaps a little crafty can assume responsibility for this enormously important library unit. Joe A. Hewitt's observation that faculty hostility to resource sharing is often "abetted and magnified by the attitudes of librarians" will give us all something to think about seriously.[72]

Both lending and borrowing can be hindered by staff's resistance to change and their clinging to outmoded procedures.[73] Thus, it is important that staff members are properly trained and feel completely comfortable with new technology. Library managers must consider what new skills and competencies are necessary to run an effective access unit. If the attitudes are right but the competencies are wrong, this is easier to fix than the opposite circumstance: there are many opportunities for staff development that are relevant to contemporary interlending. Vendor-organized workshops and on-site training are often a part of the service associated with new equipment, and the library should avail itself of such programs. Local consortia, state referral centers, and the utilities all offer useful workshops; at the very least, every supervisory staff member should be encouraged to participate.

Staff resistance to change may also stem from a lack of communication between library administrators and the ILL unit. Is the professional staff routinely consulted about new technology or new consortial arrangements the library is considering? In some instances, the ILL librarian is the last to know about new cooperative agreements and the first to have to cope with new technologies and the consequent upsurge of ILL requests from both local patrons and ILL partners. As Noelene P. Martin observes:

> Decisions as to network participation or discontinuance . . . are seldom evaluated for their effects on interlibrary loan. . . . The result is that the interlibrary loan departments are faced with a range of technological and cooperative improvements to which they have had little input and with which they have only limited abilities to find ways of coping.[74]

As libraries buy less and borrow more, the importance of the access or ILL unit increases: only when its staff are well trained, technologically confident, and involved in designing the unit's services and objectives will access succeed.

Public Relations and Promotion for Access

In some libraries, the access unit has been the equivalent of the Victorian "family secret." Hidden away in basement corners, crowded into windowless rooms that are little more than ambitious closets, located at the ends of corridors where no one ever goes, interlibrary loan sits, existing more to fill an empty space on the library organization chart than to serve any significant purpose. Even so, the unit probably has its devotees—the truly dependent who will wait any length of time, so critical is their need.

Interlibrary loan has to come out of those cellars and corners, to bright, inviting, easily identified and well-located prime library space: this is an important step in telling the academic community that what this unit does is important (after all, where are reference desks and circulation desks located?) and getting readers in the door. If business is going to be reshaped—if everyone is going to use the access unit, in the same way everyone uses reference services—the library must make a very visible statement about its new commitment.

What of all the readers who don't bother with the library, because they perceive its collections to be too limited for their purposes? And those who come to the library, but leave if the material they want is not in the collection and on the shelf? Susan K. Martin suggests that most people either find what they need immediately when they go to the library, or they leave and forget about that particular information need.[75] Perhaps even more difficult to convert will be those who used ILL once, probably several years before, had a negative experience, and have never gone back. Perhaps the book never came, or perhaps it came a month after their research project was completed: whatever the precise details, they remain convinced that ILL is not for them.

The library will have a job ahead of it, persuading both types of disaffected readers that it can get them anything they need. However, there are some simple ways to get readers' attention; once that happens, as has been suggested throughout this book, positive word-of-mouth begins to take over, and business builds. A few years ago Columbia University's main library developed a plan to improve reader satisfaction with the availability of locally owned materials. Reshelving of returns was accelerated, and a scheme by which the entire collection could be shelf-read annually was implemented. Finally, signs reading, "If you did not find the material for which you were looking, please ask at the circulation desk," were placed in the stacks, on alternating range ends. The program was highly successful, and the results of the signs were startling, as readers did as they were bidden in significant numbers.

In the Columbia University program, searches were placed on missing materials. However, the library that wishes to increase its readers' access to remotely held materials can place similar signs near the catalog, and perhaps in the stacks as well. Once the reader successfully uses the access unit's services the first time, he or she will be back and will also tell a friend. The access unit may also wish to have a broadside or brochure, distilled from its access policy, to distribute to interested readers.

Among the purposes of the brochure will be to describe the access services, their purpose, who can use each approach, and what delivery mechanisms are available. One academic library that offers full-text periodical articles on CD-ROM recently discovered that students were routinely reading the articles, then requesting those that were relevant through interlibrary loan, rather than paying the $.30 a page the library charged for printing. Thus, if the library will not borrow materials readily available in-house, its access policy and brochure should say so.

Some libraries have had success with other types of signs and flyers. When the catalog of another institution with which the library has a good resource sharing agreement is available for searching by local readers, it should be prominently placed and labeled. If new services are introduced (a new commercial document vendor, for example) a separate flyer, or an article or advertisement in the student newspaper may be useful.

Placing the Access Unit in the Organization

Ron Henshaw notes that "the boundaries between interlibrary loan and other library functions, such as circulation, database search services, acquisitions, and, most importantly, collection development, are becoming increasingly blurred," and most librarians will agree with him.[76] There are many models (each with its own logic) for where ILL can best function in the library's organizational structure.

1. Database search services

It is unlikely that anyone will attempt a persuasive argument for merging interlending and database searching, yet there is a relationship that should be recognized and cultivated. The advent of CD-ROMs, local and wide area networks, and tape-mounted citation databases has caused the decline of online database searching in many libraries; it is no longer the boom operation of the seventies and early eighties. In the sense that it identifies items (often journal articles) on a given subject that the local library may or may not own, database searching is little different from any similar readers' service that generates grist for the access unit's mill. Perhaps it is database searching's ability not only to identify documents but also to purchase them (through commercial document services, linked to DIALOG, BRS, and similar services) that makes it seem similar to interlibrary loan, in a way that catalog and CD-ROM searching do not. Nonetheless, unless the identified documents are very inexpensive (ERIC documents, perhaps), database searching staff seldom routinely purchase items that result from searches. As noted in the chapter on commercial document services, the more likely academic library scenario is that the search is printed out and supplied to the reader, who identifies relevant items, makes use of those available locally, and goes to the access unit for the rest. Thus, the similarities between database searching and interlending are not so great as might seem at first glance.

2. Information services

This is probably the traditional ILL reporting model, and there is not much that can be said against it: access to remotely held materials is, indeed, an "information" or "public" or "readers'" service, depending on the local taxonomy, and thus the manager of the larger unit can be expected to have some sympathy with the objectives of the smaller one.

3. Circulation

Circulation (sometimes called, either alone or in combination with other units, "access services," generally to differentiate it from "information" or "readers'" services) has much in common with the interlibrary loan operation. Indeed, both units lend materials, and the library's circulation system is often used to charge out items lent by the access unit to other institutions. The similarity of mission (one unit provides access to internal collections, the other to external) makes a good case for the combination of the two.

4. Acquisitions

If acquisitions may be understood as separate from selection or collection development—the process of identifying the best vendors and delivery mechanisms for materials bibliographers have chosen for the collections—in terms of function, one can say it has a great deal in common with interlending and the use of commercial document vendors. And, as noted in the chapter on interlibrary loan, interlibrary loan staff may sometimes elect to buy rather than borrow, enlarging the relationship with acquisitions. Nonetheless, acquisitions is not a "public" or "readers'" service, and this is an important factor in the access unit's reporting relationship.

5. Collection development

Many librarians see interlending and the use of commercial document delivery services as "temporary" (versus "permanent") acquisition. As noted earlier in the chapter on interlibrary loan, collection development officers are often vitally interested in data collected by the access unit about which titles are borrowed and from what journals articles are most frequently requested. As we become more and more dependent on access (versus ownership), and because the access budget may well be carved from the materials budget, there is some argument for the merging or parallel reporting of the two functional areas, so that their common yet different purposes can be balanced in the way most advantageous to the organization's larger mission.

Notes

1. Stevenson, "Design Options," 437.
2. Simpson, "Library Consortia," 93.
3. Dowd, "Library Cooperation," 66.
4. Ibid., 80.
5. Information Systems Consultants, Inc., "Resource Sharing," 4.
6. White, "Interlibrary Loan," 53.
7. OCLC, "Interlibrary Loan," 4–5.
8. Maurice B. Line, "Measuring the Performance of Document Supply Systems," *Interlending and Document Supply* 16 (July 1988): 86.
9. Ibid., 85.
10. Paul M. Gherman and Lynn S. Cochrane, "Developing and Using Unit Costs: The Virginia Tech Experience," *Library Administration and Management* 3 (Spring 1989): 95.
11. Line, "Measuring," 85.
12. Sue Kennedy, "The Role of Commercial Document Delivery Services in Interlibrary Loan," *Interlending and Document Supply* 15 (July 1987): 71.
13. Ibid.
14. Information Systems Consultants, Inc., "Resource Sharing," 4.
15. Line, "Measuring," 85.
16. Lowry, "Resource Sharing," 15.
17. Ibid., 16.
18. Ibid.
19. Stephen P. Dickson and Virginia Boucher, "A Methodology for Determining Costs of Interlibrary Lending," in *Research Access through New Technology*, ed. Mary E. Jackson (New York: AMS Press, 1989), 137–59.
20. Joan Chambers, "Surveys on Interlibrary Loan," Letter to directors of ARL libraries, Feb. 20, 1992.

21. Research Libraries Group, Inc., "Research Libraries Group Interlibrary Loan Cost Study."
22. Ibid., 1.
23. Ibid.
24. Line, "Measuring," 85.
25. Kennedy, "The Role of Commercial Document Delivery," *Interlending and Document Supply*, 70.
26. Holton, "Document Delivery Services," 36–37.
27. Steve Coffman and Helen Josephine, "Doing It for Money," *Library Journal* 116 (Oct. 15, 1991): 34.
28. Marty Bloomberg, "Serial Costs," Letter to William Aguilar, Feb. 11, 1992.
29. Barbara Quint, "Connect Time: Wars, Roses, and Standards," *Wilson Library Bulletin* 65 (Feb. 1991), 108–109.
30. Billings, "The Bionic Library," 41.
31. National Commission on Libraries and Information Science, "The Role of Fees in Supporting Library and Information Services in Public and Academic Libraries," *Collection Building* 8, no. 1 (1986): 3–17; Marsha S. Clark, "Fees for Library and Information Services in Libraries: A Bibliography," *Collection Building* 8, no. 1 (1986): 57–61.
32. White, "Interlibrary Loan," 54.
33. Dusenbury and Post, "Subscribing," 13; Holicky, "Collection Development vs. Resource Sharing," 147.
34. Kennedy, "The Role of Commercial Document Delivery," *Interlending and Document Supply*, 70.
35. Stevenson, "Design Options," 440.
36. OCLC, "Interlibrary Loan," 5.
37. Ibid., 3.
38. Richard De Gennaro, "Resource Sharing in a Network Environment," *Library Journal* 105 (Feb. 1, 1980): 353–54.
39. Ibid., 354.
40. Coffman and Josephine, "Doing It for Money," 34.
41. Information Systems Consultants, Inc., "Resource Sharing," 10.
42. Burroughs, "Who Can Stop the Lemmings?," 5.
43. Michalak, "Impact."
44. Burroughs, "Who Can Stop the Lemmings?," 6.
45. Stevenson, "Design Options," 440.
46. OCLC, "Interlibrary Loan," vi.
47. Stevenson, "Design Options," 440.
48. Dusenbury and Post, "Subscribing," 12–13.
49. Metz and Gherman, "Serials Pricing," 318–19.
50. Billings, "The Bionic Library," 41.
51. Holicky, "Collection Development," 147.
52. Dusenbury and Post, "Subscribing," 13.
53. Line, "Measuring," 81.

54. F. W. Lancaster, *The Measurement and Evaluation of Library Services* (Washington, D.C.: Information Resources Press, 1977), 235.
55. Line, "Measuring," 84.
56. Ibid., 82.
57. Weaver-Meyers, and others, *Interlibrary Loan*, 13.
58. Dougherty, "A Conceptual Framework," 288.
59. Information Systems Consultants, Inc., "Resource Sharing," 4–5.
60. Line, "Measuring," 83.
61. Ibid.
62. Lancaster, *Measurement*, 235.
63. Line, "Measuring," 84.
64. Ibid.
65. Ibid.
66. Weaver-Meyers, and others, *Interlibrary Loan*, 14.
67. Ibid., 13.
68. Ibid., 14, 13.
69. Martin, "Information Transfer," 6.
70. American Library Association, Reference and Adult Services Division, Interlibrary Loan Committee, Subcommittee on Continuing Education and Training, Barbara Beaton, chair, "Interlibrary Loan Training and Continuing Education Model Statement of Objectives," *RQ* 31 (Winter 1991): 177–84.
71. Virginia Boucher, "The Interlibrary Loan Librarian," *Interlending and Document Supply* 17 (Jan. 1989): 11–15.
72. Hewitt, "Interlibrary Cooperation," 100.
73. Weaver-Meyers, and others, *Interlibrary Loan*, 11.
74. Martin, "Information Transfer," 6.
75. Martin, "Technology and Cooperation," 43.
76. Ron Henshaw, "Library to Library," *Wilson Library Bulletin* 60 (Sept. 1985): 55.

CHAPTER 9

Shaping Our Future

Such Stuff as Dreams Are Made On
(Shakespeare, *The Tempest*, IV, i)

I. A Time of Change 293

II. New Measures for Success 294

III. The New Academic Library Model 295

IV. Trends in Access and Resource Sharing 297
   A. Improved Document Delivery Mechanisms 297
   B. The Reader-Initiated Document Delivery Request 297
   C. Merging Files of Books, Journals, and Articles 298
   D. Access to Other Libraries' Catalogs 299
   E. The Influence of the Internet 299
   F. The National Research and Education Network 300

V. New Information Delivery Models 301

VI. The Universal Workstation 302

VII. Electronic Document Delivery 303

VIII. Electronic Publishing: Which Materials and When? 304

IX. The Electronic Book 305

X. The Electronic Journal 306

XI. The Appeal of the E-Journal 308
   A. Speed of Publication 308
   B. Speed of Access and Delivery 309
   C. Flexibility 309
   D. Cost-Effectiveness 309

XII. The E-Journal: Unanswered Questions 310
   A. How Will the E-Journal Be Used? 310
   B. Distribution, or How Will the E-Journal Be Accessed? 311
   C. Scholars as Publishers 311
   D. The Role of the Intermediary 312
   E. The Coalition for Networked Information Models 313
   F. Some Examples of Contemporary E-Journals 313
   G. How Will the E-Journal Be Priced? 315
   H. Protecting the Contents of the E-Journal 316

I. Access versus Ownership: Can Libraries Afford the Trade-Offs? 316
  J. The Validity of the E-Journal 317
  K. Textual and Content Limitations 318
XIII. The Role of the Library and Librarians 318
  A. Who Will Pay? 319
  B. The Librarian as Information Specialist 320
  C. The Librarian as Navigator along the Information Highway 322
  D. The Librarian as Selector, Organizer, and Preserver 324
XIV. Electric Dreams 324
XV. The Information Concerns of the Twenty-First Century 325

For some time now, many of us have felt that the worlds of librarianship and technology which we inhabit are whirling through space more and more rapidly. The first chapter of this book suggested "choice" as today's access theme; in terms of getting materials for readers that they want but that the local library does not own, academic librarians have many more alternatives than were available even five years ago. But what should we expect in the next five years, and on into the early part of the new century? We will be wise to plan now for a time and a theme of "change."

There is something rather tedious about a library futurist; the genuine prophets and their imitators have predicted for too long what has yet to come to pass. The paperless society? Undesirable, and unlikely. The printed book's death knell? Not in our lifetime, and probably not ever. Yet something new *is* coming.

A Time of Change

In a 1992 issue of *Lingua Franca*, Erik Davis asks whether librarians dream of electric books. "Libraries are beginning to dematerialize into ghostly data-nodes," he continues, "characterized less by the breadth of their collections than by the depth of their access."[1] Whatever our response to this "Star Trek" imagery, we have probably begun to agree with Davis's assessment that access will continue to make gains over assets, as a measure of the academic library's effectiveness, and new technologies will ease the transition.

A number of librarians have begun to interest themselves in how new electronic mechanisms for information delivery will alter our present set of access and collecting concerns. The Research Libraries Group (RLG) assembled groups of library directors and their provosts to explore their visions of the future of academic libraries. In the summary of these workshops, Richard M. Dougherty and Carol Hughes report:

> The period of forthcoming change could be characterized as the transition from the physical library to the logical library. . . . There is no consensus as to what the future holds for research libraries. There is general agreement that technology will play a profound role, but the specifics remain much less clear.[2]

This idea that the emphasis in academic libraries is shifting from one of collection building to one of access is consistent with Joan Blair's suggestion:

> For the library of the twenty-first century, the stand-alone collection is a starting point rather than a self-contained environment. A library's immediate collection will serve as a core resource, with circles of additional available information grouped around it.[3]

The future as foretold above has already begun: we are collecting less and accessing more and, whatever we may call it, the joint ownership/access model seems to have gained a strong foothold in the American academic library. Dougherty and Hughes ponder whether, in the future, a library's success will be gauged in qualitative rather than quantitative terms; "how much library is enough?" they ask.[4] Perhaps "as much as we have" will be the necessary economic answer, with access to remote materials taking up the slack. If so, what new goals and measures will replace the ancestral one of collection building?

New Measures for Success

Harsh economic reality has sobered academic librarians, helping them to overcome "pride of ownership," and to suggest other measures for institutional self-esteem. As Herbert S. White counsels, "We must recognize that we are in the business of supplying materials and answers, not of building monuments."[5] Not long ago Barbara Quint posed a number of interesting questions in her column for the *Wilson Library Bulletin*:

What is the Library? Books? Magazines? Microfiche readers? Computer terminals? "Yes," most people would answer. The Library is a palace of print, an edifice filled with prepackaged, preferably printed information through which individuals can prowl—with or without assistance—looking for some item to amuse, inform, or enlighten them. Or is it? Is the general public right? Or is the Library where librarians work? Is the Library the set of tools that the librarian uses to perform library services?[6]

Before resource sharing and the use of commercial document services can become standard information approaches in academic libraries, librarians must answer "yes" to Quint's final question; we will have to articulate and accept new standards for greatness or effectiveness that can be applied to the institutions we serve, measures that can stand honorably alongside the traditional ones of collection size and circulation. Only then will we emphasize access as (for so many hundreds of years) we have venerated ownership. And, only after we can convince ourselves, will we convince our faculty, students, and administrators.

The New Academic Library Model

How well has the academic library model favored by many faculty and librarians ("buy as many subscriptions as you possibly can") served us? It is not working today, and it has not worked for some time. Even when libraries pump every available dollar into periodicals, they cannot achieve or even approach the more comprehensive collecting levels of the past. Faculty dissatisfaction with the library remains keen, and librarians are equally frustrated, feeling that their most strenuous efforts to please are still not enough.

At the same time, in attempting to satisfy faculty by pursuing this unfulfilling and unobtainable model, some librarians have nearly bankrupted undergraduate research on their campuses by seriously slighting monographic purchases. The academic library model that places serial subscriptions above all else is one in which everyone loses—faculty, librarians, and students alike. A new model, however, may be emerging, one that gives all three groups what they really want, as opposed to what they say they want.

If undergraduates want books, tempered with a moderate number of instantly available journals, faculty want the ability to browse and exploit the entire world of serial literature, as well as ready access to monographs, and librarians want to provide rapid access to whatever their readers desire and need, a new ownership/access model must begin to be the norm in all academic libraries. Librarians will start by getting spending for journals and books back into proportion in their collections (some range between 60/40 percent and 70/30 percent, serials/monographs, will be typical), while also factoring in a new information cost, that for access to the unowned. In an effort to increase the effectiveness of local collections, use studies of various types (rather than faculty and librarian opinion) will govern how collecting budgets are spent.

Access dollars will be spent on efficiently securing copies of that which is not owned (temporary ownership), as well as indexing and abstracting services that are integrated with the library catalog. Such systems make readers aware of a broad range of journal literature, both locally and remotely held, rather than leaving them to identify wanted articles through the vagaries of chance or some dusty bibliography. Unable to justify charging today for that to which they subscribed yesterday, libraries will absorb the costs of document delivery.

The character of resource sharing agreements will also change. The practice of viewing equally (for purposes of seeking an interlibrary loan) every library participating in the same automated ILL system will cease. Hugh C. Atkinson's support for broad-based sharing, his idea that every library, large or small, has something to lend and that, in a large cooperative environment everything equals out, may have been adequate to some libraries' needs as recently as the mid-1980s, but it will not serve us well in the nineties.[7] We have seen evidence of this in the many enterprising arrangements mentioned earlier in this book: libraries are already seeking to develop smaller, more generous, and productive interlending arrangements.

A recent conversation with the director of a large, urban multitype library association bears this out: as libraries lend and borrow more, they return to the practice of sharing chiefly with "friends," since they find they cannot share with everyone. These friends, however, will be defined as the handful of other institutions—perhaps as few as one, two, or three other libraries—whose collections analysis has shown can meet a large percentage of their readers' needs for unowned books and journals. Can interlibrary loan remain "free," at least in terms of direct charges made by one library to another? Yes, but only in an environment of genuine reciprocity, such as these more closely tailored arrangements are likely to create.

Trends in Access and Resource Sharing

Interlending and document delivery are reshaping themselves everywhere, and in different ways. The pervasiveness of automation (OCLC's GAC program, which opens up its ILL subsystem to smaller libraries that are not users of its cataloging services; regional CD-ROM catalogs that interface with electronic mail interlending systems) anticipates the demise of clearinghouses, those centers that locate materials for unautomated libraries. Increasingly point-to-point interlending is the approach of choice.

Improved Document Delivery Mechanisms

Concern about the marked contrast between ease of access to bibliographic data and the delivery speed of the materials themselves is escalating; having largely solved the first problem, it is natural librarians will now concentrate on the second. Librarians who met at OCLC headquarters to discuss their concerns about interlibrary loan expressed the hope that "new technologies, such as electronic document delivery and optical scanning, would help resolve this disparity in the future."[8] Scanning projects like those using RLG's Ariel software and North Carolina State University's DDTP indicate that such hopes are not ill-founded.

The Reader-Initiated Document Delivery Request

The reader-initiated interlibrary loan or document delivery request is also the way of the future. Several libraries are already either using this approach or experimenting in this area, including those belonging to the Washington Research Library Consortium, ILLINET members, and libraries testing NOTIS's PACLoan software. Much remains to be done, since the most effective systems will allow disparate hardware and software to communicate and permit the reader to place requests for both books and journal articles directly from the online catalog, pulling bibliographic data into the interlending request and thus avoiding the errors and time-consuming work associated with rekeying.

It will only be possible for readers to draw article-level information into the interlending request if the library has also associated journal indexing and abstracting systems with the online catalog. Some libraries, as described in earlier chapters, have already begun to do this, giving readers a choice of the online catalog or an array of periodical indexes from the same terminal. The next step will be reader-initiated interlending or document delivery requests, when the desired article is not locally owned.

Merging Files of Books, Journals, and Articles

Once we accept the desirability of providing access to article-level information from the online catalog, it is a quick step to considering the benefits of merging bibliographic records for books and journals with those for individual articles in a single file—an author search under "Dougherty, Richard M." would retrieve not only books by Dougherty, but articles he has written as well. Certainly the ability to merge such files is coming, and the benefits are clear.

A system that labels locally owned articles will be of considerable use in increasing the utilization of local collections, something greatly to be desired as part of the new ownership/access model for the academic library, and especially helpful to undergraduates. There are undoubtedly riches in our local collections that go undiscovered and unused; Paul E. Peters, referring to the underutilization of modern academic libraries' materials, expresses doubt that the blame lies with "the declining quality of the literature record," but rather with a lack of adequate access.[9]

David Cohen speculates about the impact the ability to fully exploit local collections could have on interlibrary loan: all readers would certainly be better satisfied by locally held materials, and libraries would obtain more use and better value from their journal collections.[10] Merged catalogs or indexes of books, journal titles, and articles would also promote access to unowned materials, simply by removing one more barrier (log out of the catalog and into the periodical indexes) between the reader and the material itself.

The implementation of such merged indexes may shift both the interlending and purchase of materials toward monographs; this could happen in several ways. By making locally owned journal literature more accessible, libraries may increase its use and offset readers' needs for remotely held serials; this could free dollars for monographic purchases. In a catalog where the article-level citations are also linked to document delivery systems, libraries could decide to obtain the majority of unowned articles their readers want directly from these commercial services, relying on interlending arrangements chiefly for monographs.

Access to Other Libraries' Catalogs

Access to the catalogs of other libraries has also had considerable impact on resource sharing. Sometimes this access takes the form of shared catalogs (CD-ROM or online). This type of access is likely to have the greatest impact on interlending, either because the catalog itself has an associated interlending module, or because the libraries whose holdings are represented have an established resource sharing agreement that promotes relying first on sister collections. However, access to the Internet, the "network of networks," has already had some impact on resource sharing; as the Internet is succeeded by the National Research and Education Network (NREN), this impact will surely increase.

The Influence of the Internet

The Internet, described more fully in chapter 7, connects a number of physical networks located across the United States and in other countries. A few libraries have begun to use its capability to deliver information electronically through scanning and telefacsimile; this type of use will certainly grow. The Internet also enables researchers who can access it to utilize free of charge many of the resources mounted on local member networks, wherever the researchers themselves may be located. The cost is negligible (typically the cost to the home institution of a local telephone call) and access is almost instantaneous. Thus, someone at the University of California, Berkeley, can log on to the catalog of the City University of New York and search it as if he or she were a local reader. As they explore the variety of resources available through the Internet, many faculty who are active computer users are discovering catalogs, full-text resources, and other bibliographic databases with no assistance from librarians.

Some time will pass before the potential indicated by the Internet is fulfilled, and many changes will occur. As Sue O. Medina observes, access to bibliographic information is an empty promise without interlending agreements and mechanisms that make the delivery of wanted items a reality.[11] The Internet is not a universal interlibrary loan system; furthermore, search access to its resources is a very different matter from exploiting its information transfer capability.

In a paper published in the *Annual Review of Information Science and Technology*, Clifford A. Lynch and Cecilia Preston cite some of the other yet-to-be-resolved issues associated with the use of the Internet for resource sharing. While the cost of accessing the Internet is small in terms of telecommunications charges, because there is no common search language for all available resources, the searcher must learn different or unique protocols for every database, text file, or catalog. Additionally, there is no easy method of locally consolidating records and information from different resources for analysis and storage.[12]

Perhaps the greatest potential impact of Internet access on resource sharing is its consciousness-raising quality, much like that demonstrated by the bibliographic utilities over a decade ago:

> User demand quickly extends to document delivery, which places great strain on libraries and interlibrary loan systems, and to the availability of source material in electronic (ASCII text or page image) form—an overwhelming challenge involving negotiations with thousands of publishers, enormous potential retrospective conversion projects, and tangled copyright questions.[13]

Lynch and Preston indicate that the Internet, beyond whetting academic appetites for more information, also piques desires for electronic delivery of the identified items, in ways the bibliographic networks never did. Electronic delivery through the Internet carries with it a unique set of difficult, intricate, and yet-to-be-resolved copyright and licensing issues. The authors also suggest that in the future some of the costs associated with locally mounting commercial databases (such as tables of contents systems linked to local journal holdings) may be eliminated, as such systems are instead mounted on the Internet or its projected successor, NREN.[14]

The National Research and Education Network

On December 9, 1991, President George Bush signed into law the High-Performance Computing and Communications Act, legislation which authorizes $153 million to establish the National Research and Education Network, a high-speed computer network that will link government, industry, and education. NREN proposes to include every public, school, and college library in the country and will probably replace the Internet. It will run at faster speeds, provide more reliable communications lines, and take advantage of newer technological improvements in communications.[15]

While both the Internet and NREN were conceived as mechanisms that could bring advanced computing and computing capacity to researchers throughout the country, they also provide for the transmission of much data of interest to librarians and the readers they serve.[16] The Commission for Networked Information (CNI), a joint effort of EDUCOM, CAUSE, and the Association of Research Libraries (ARL), is presently working to find solutions to some of the problems cited by Lynch and Preston that have direct bearing on the use of NREN for resource sharing and document delivery. Among these policy issues are intellectual property rights, standards, licensing, service arrangements, charging algorithms, and cost-recovery fees. CNI is also attempting to identify those information resources that should be available through NREN.[17]

New Information Delivery Models

What does the promise of growing amounts of electronically accessible information, much of it available through a national high-speed computer network, mean for the modern mainstay of information delivery models, the printed book or journal, and thus for our existing set of resource sharing and document delivery concerns? Robin Downes, the University of Houston's librarian, has something to say on this topic:

> It is certain that even an ideal combination of technology and network composition will not stand up to the pricing trend we have seen. The traditional system of scholarly communication is out of control. The diversion of funds from library service units and processing operations to the journals budget will be profoundly destructive to current levels of service.[18]

Will there be a transition to new methods of scholarly communication that supplant the printed book and journal? What will they be, and how will they be priced? Will these new methods or models be shaped by emerging technologies and readers' needs or, as Harold Billings suggests, by economic forces beyond the control of librarians and researchers?[19] Paul E. Peters considers some of the forces that might drive such changes:

> The transition from card ... catalogs to online ones may have something to tell us about the transition that we may or may not now be making from paper form publications to electronic ones. In my experience, card catalogs collapsed and became unworkable under the pressure of the information explosion. I propose that something quite similar is happening now with printed primary research materials—the existing system is collapsing and becoming unworkable. No matter how difficult it is for us to

imagine, the transition from an exclusively print to a progressively more electronic information distribution and access system may well be something about which we have very little choice.[20]

Those using the academic library's present to extrapolate its future make different predictions about how changes in the publishing industry may affect document delivery and access concerns.

The Universal Workstation

In each of the workshops conducted by the Research Libraries Group for library directors and their provosts, the vision of the wired campus and the scholarly workstation that provides "seamless" or "transparent" access to a variety of information resources emerged.[21] Erik Davis draws a colorful picture of this sort of research environment:

> For the individual user, the library environment—once a broad, softly lit room strewn with bookshelves, ladders, and even couches—has been telescoped down to a single chair before a single screen. Inside that small plastic frame, however, lurks an immense field of data that is expanding like never before.[22]

Other academic library specialists, including Carolyn Arms, Susan K. Martin, and Harold Billings, describe their personal conceptions of the universal workstation. Ten years ago Martin wrote: "We need a black box which will allow us to access all these various systems with one terminal." She visualized a powerful microcomputer offering sophisticated telecommunications capabilities and the ability to use a standardized searching language; an accounting system would keep track of the use and costs of the many different commercial systems that would be available.[23] Similarly and much more recently Billings predicted that, because of the wealth of information resources that will one day be available through workstations, "the library will soon never sleep, and electronic information will always be, so to speak, 'on the shelf.' "[24]

Mark Kibbey and Nancy H. Evans explain why the electronic library, available through the universal or scholar's workstation, will succeed as a new information delivery model:

> Costs of computer storage are declining. Many campuses have the infrastructure of personal computers and computer-literate users that is necessary to make an electronic library widely useful. But, none of these factors are more important than advances in data communications and networking.[25]

Not all the standards necessary for the creation of a genuine universal workstation exist at present. There is certainly no common search or command language, and the amount of information presently available electronically, while impressive in quantity and growing rapidly, is by no means sufficiently complete to supplant or substitute for print collections in any meaningful sense. As Kibbey and Evans point out, some of the electronic workstation's essential features are not yet even in development.[26] But, as Caroline Arms points out, wherever the information accessed by the anticipated universal workstation resides (on the desktop, or at the library, campus, or national levels),

> There is no doubt that the computing environment of the future will consist of workstations on individual desks, linked to a campus network that provides resources to meet most of the general computing and information needs of the scholar. The campus network will also be the gateway to more specialized resources around the country and even across the world.[27]

The benefits of the universal workstation—this shift from paper to pixels—are as yet more visionary than they are understood in terms of their real costs and budgetary implications.[28]

Electronic Document Delivery

> Inseparable from the concept of the universal workstation is electronic delivery of wanted items. An article in the *Chronicle of Higher Education* speaks of "a kind of Holy Grail among information vendors for the last decade: direct electronic transmission of documents."[29] What more precise visions of this Grail exist? There is general agreement that librarians, faculty, and students want to be able to see complete documents through the universal workstation in order to assess their quality or appropriateness. Minimally, there is a desire to see abstracts that include the conclusions reached by the author. Readers then want to verify any associated prices, and choose among a variety of delivery mechanisms, including telefacsimile transmission or delivery to an electronic mailbox.[30]

Electronic Publishing: Which Materials and When?[31]

Jay K. Lucker was right ten years ago when he surmised that "the speed with which disciplines adopt electronic publishing will be in direct proportion to the ratio of the importance of journals to monographs." The sciences will be first in line, followed by the social sciences; the humanities will be last, because of the low ratio of journals to books and generally lower subscription rates.[32] In 1991, library directors and provosts of research institutions agreed with Lucker's ideas: "The global publishing community is not prepared to move into a totally electronic environment, and certain disciplines will not shift to electronic texts as quickly as others."[33]

Similarly, Dusenbury and Post believe that "the movement toward true electronic scholarly communication . . . is inexorable, although all fields of study may not advance at the same rate."[34] Roy Adams, author of *Communication and Delivery Systems for Librarians*, offers his variation on this same theme; "high-value" material like financial market information migrated to electronic form in the 1980s, and much more will follow in the 1990s:

> Heavily used material will continue to be made available in print, but with electronic editions. Materials produced in medium volume, particularly those in science and technology, will increasingly become available only in electronic form, but distributed by conventional agencies. Low volume materials, especially in the non-academic sphere, will disappear from the large organized distribution systems and appear again in paper copy but largely produced using desk top publishing techniques. Other low volume communications journals will gradually become confined to electronic forms circulated among peer groups on new, high-speed networks.[35]

There seems to be some consensus that a core of print journals will continue to exist; these will be the most popular titles, the ones that will continue to make money through subscriptions for the paper formats that give their publishers better copyright protection. It seems likely that prices for such titles will continue to escalate. For those periodicals that publishers wish to bring forth electronically, what barriers must yet be overcome?

In an article for *Publishers Weekly*, Robert Weber cites a hurdle familiar to anyone experienced in academic libraries. Five years ago, a librarian was delighted to receive a personal computer with 256K of memory and double-floppy drives. Today we cannot please even the most junior staff member with this sort of machine; unless a PC has at least a 20-megabyte hard drive, a modem, and a color monitor, we can scarcely find a taker. Unfortunately, even this equipment may not be equal to that high-power, high-definition machinery needed to manipulate text and images that will be necessary to support and take advantage of electronic publishing. Weber points to millions of machines that may have to be replaced or augmented by equipment and software with advanced capabilities.[36] However, perhaps it is not unreasonable to comfort ourselves by looking around our libraries and observing how many of those double-floppy machines are still around; the answer is probably "not very many." Maybe by the time the digital libraries are here, our equipment will be ready for them.

Maurice B. Line suggests another obstacle in the route to the electronic library: for the present, very little text is held in electronic formats. "Admittedly, much of it goes through such a form on its way to computer typesetting, but these texts are unsuitable for retrieval or transmission, because they use character, rather than digital, encoding and are full of computer typesetting instructions." Line goes on to explain that it is costly to convert these word processing documents into forms appropriate for electronic publishing and retrieval.[37]

This parallels one scientific and technical publisher's caution that there is a big difference between an electronic typesetting file and a usable database; the transformation of the former into the latter represents not only a considerable expense, but will require a major retooling for publishers. While acknowledging that such investments must be made, she also makes a useful analogy to card and online catalogs: the records contained in both have electronic origins, yet we know that creating the automated catalog required much more than taking a single simple step beyond its manual precursor.

The Electronic Book

The Internet is already host to several hundred full-text books. Among the better-known conversion projects are the Dartmouth Dante Project (a database of six centuries of commentary on the *Divine Comedy*) and the University of Illinois's Project Gutenberg whose goal is to convert ten thousand of the world's most-read books to electronic format by the year 2000. One researcher refers to the electronic book as a " 'textual chainsaw,' hacking pathways through the brush of scholarly research in a matter of minutes."[38]

How will electronic books be used? In many cases, scholars may use the electronic journal much as they use print serials: compared to books, even a lengthy journal article is short. It can be read online, or (because it is relatively brief) downloaded or printed out with a small expenditure of time. If we educate readers properly about electronic books, however, it is likely they will be used very differently from their print equivalents: even the least sophisticated undergraduate is unlikely to sit at a workstation and print out a copy of War and Peace, rather than borrowing one from the library or purchasing an inexpensive paperback edition. As British librarian A. E. Cawkell observes:

> It seems to me that aesthetic considerations outweigh experiments. The promise of an array of books on a shelf followed by the satisfaction of selecting and reading one has no parallel with text displayed on a CRT. ... In due course, perhaps a screen-reader will be regarded as "progressive," a book-reader as "fossilised," but let Huxley have the last word on the subject.[39]

Cawkell refers to Huxley's admonition (which plays on the words of Alexander Pope), "The proper study of mankind is books." One must agree that, for reading convenience and pleasure, the printed book will probably continue to be unbeatable.

The Center for Electronic Texts in the Humanities (Rutgers University) has interested itself in how readers may wish to use monographs in electronic formats. Certainly computational linguistics and literature scholars are very interested in the ability to study words, their occurrences, and patterns that electronic texts offer. The center maintains a catalog of electronic monographs on the Research Libraries Information Network (RLIN); while it does not own every title listed, it can provide information on how to acquire these texts.

The Electronic Journal[40]

Fewer than a hundred electronic or "e-journals" and newsletters now exist; fewer than a dozen are scholarly refereed or edited publications.[41] For the present, print journals more than dominate the market; a few of these have parallel electronic versions, chiefly on CD-ROM. Line speculates that, if journals were available inexpensively on compact disc, libraries could achieve a much greater degree of local self-sufficiency, interlending would drop dramatically, and almost everyone would be satisfied: publishers, libraries, and readers. However, he perceives at least two serious economic barriers to this scenario.

If the journals did not sell well, they would be too costly for general purchase; even if libraries bought them in large quantities, it is unlikely that publishers would forgo any of the profits they are currently earning from paper-based subscriptions, raising questions about whether the CD-ROMs could really be "reasonably" priced from librarians' standpoints. Also, those libraries that have not already done so would be forced to invest considerable amounts of money in CD-ROM technologies, including networks permitting multiple users.[42] A number of factors may continue to keep the course toward electronic publishing careful and slow. There is considerable uncertainty about what to charge for electronic journals, accompanied by fears that uncontrollable copying will cause profit losses. A general lack of user-friendliness and problems distributing nontext also inhibit the growth of the e-journal.[43]

Nonetheless, over the next two to three years, many publishers will take the plunge into electronic publishing, pulled along by the declining purchasing power of libraries and seeking to meet their needs in more cost-efficient ways. Full-text electronic journals will be available either free or for-fee through national networks, or on tape, for mounting locally or regionally. Ann Okerson predicts that by 1995 heavy journal cancellations will have significantly strengthened the market share of commercial document delivery services. Midway through the last decade of the century, she puts the number of juried electronic journals at one hundred, ten times the number published today but a small number still, compared to the universe of serial literature.[44]

By the year 2000 Okerson sees the market for "e-journals" and print journals split fifty-fifty; she feels it likely that publishers lacking electronic delivery capability will be forced from the marketplace. The subscription model will continue to lose ground, while the purchase of single articles and the licensing of journals in full-text will grow.[45] Indeed, at a time when more and more journals are published electronically and readers have had almost ten years of "training" in thinking of articles as independent pieces of information rather than individual segments of some other published whole, there is every reason to anticipate the decline of the subscription with its concept of regularly issued thematic clusters of articles called "journals."

Paul Metz and Paul M. Gherman make their own predictions about the future of electronic journal publishing, and they are a bit more conservative than Okerson:

> It is too soon to say whether this decade will also bring structural changes in scholarly and scientific communication, electronic alternatives to the printed journal, or both.... While the e-journal has arrived, and while new journals can be expected to appear at an increasing pace, it does not follow that electronic journals will supplant or supersede existing print journals.... The electronic journal may become part of the problem rather than part of the solution.[46]

Metz and Gherman go on to suggest that the dual publication of every journal, first electronically then subsequently in print (the "archival and canonical version"), could create new and unheard of economic problems for libraries, pressured by faculty to subscribe to the initial electronic edition, yet requiring the ensuing paper edition for preservation purposes as well as access by nonspecialists and the readers of the future.[47]

Some futurists have suggested that the electronic journal will revolutionize the entire process of scholarly communication. In the present academic cycle, scholars conduct research, supported by the universities that employ them or perhaps the federal government; they then give their findings to commercially published journals, so that their institutions can buy them back at enormous additional costs. Some believe that this process is nearing the end of its life, that before long academic libraries will no longer "repurchase institutional research results," as Okerson terms it, as today's expensive juried periodical is replaced by a global and highly interactive process in which papers are floated on electronic networks, critiqued by other scholars using "the net," revised accordingly, and perhaps only in some perfected form committed to paper or electronic permanency.[48]

The Appeal of the E-Journal

Speed of Publication

It is chiefly speed of publication that makes the electronic journal appealing to its readers. An article appearing in a print journal within six months of its completion is considered "fast-track"; as papers queue for peer review and editing, publishing delays mount until an article takes as long or longer than a book to reach its public. For these reasons, more rapid electronic publishing may have appeal for researchers hungry for the latest ideas.[49]

Speed of Access and Delivery

Electronic publications will always be "on the shelf," available when the reader wants them; they will never be stolen or mutilated. They will also be available without the necessity of a trip to the library if the reader has the proper equipment in his or her home or office. There will be many delivery options: on-the-spot downloading; overnight delivery to an e-mail account; or, telefacsimile.

Flexibility

In the electronic environment journal articles and perhaps even book chapters have been "unbundled" from the parent publication and are available individually, leaving the reader free to capture as much or as little information as he or she wishes. There will also be enormous flexibility in the ways faculty and students can work with the material they retrieve.

The question is, will electronic versions of print titles be used in the same ways as their paper parents? Or will readers wish to take advantage of the new digital format to manipulate and analyze (as well as read) the electronic journal, perhaps to merge downloaded and local information? Probably the answer is, "some of both."

One publisher points out that scholars can do far more interesting things with electronic formats than with paper, but will every reader need or want this capability? Clearly the answer is "no," and Tracy Casorso, project manager of North Carolina State University's Digitized Document Transmission Project, suggests that an important role for librarians will be determining which of several potential formats will best meet the reader's needs, and delivering the document in that format. The days of "one format fits all" are ending.

Cost-Effectiveness

When a journal is completely electronic, its publisher can save the costs of printing and mailing, presumably passing these savings along to libraries, stemming the tide of journal cancellations, and thereby putting money back into publishers' pockets. Of course, librarians perceive other cost-effective aspects of the e-journal, which will require far less space to house and eliminate many other costs associated with the print journal, including those for processing and shelving.

The E-Journal: Unanswered Questions

At least two barriers electronic publications must overcome have already been mentioned, a large installed base of equipment unsuitable for taking full advantage of electronic formats, and the costliness of converting word processing documents into forms appropriate for electronic publishing and retrieval. There are also many questions about electronic journals that need to be explored before these new formats can make significant inroads in academic libraries.

How Will the E-Journal Be Used?

One publisher already experimenting with electronic journals acknowledges that the push for this format is coming from libraries (hoping for economic relief), not from the researchers who read the journals, and that very little is known about how the e-journal will be used. Maurice B. Line underscores certain characteristics of the e-journal its readers may find irritating:

> Reading on screen is unsatisfactory even when a specific article is wanted. If one wants to browse through a whole current issue to find what is of interest, and to scan a particular article which looks likely to be of interest, there is really no substitute for the printed version. I simply do not see CD-ROM's, or for that matter any online system serving as a substitute for printed journals for current browsing purposes. If this is so, it means that libraries would have to buy current issues in conventional form and CD-ROM's; the current issues could be thrown away after two years or so, and binding and storage costs could thus be saved, but nevertheless the additional cost would be very high.[50]

What Line really questions is how the reader and the e-journal will interact. It is interesting that his view of the potential "chicken and egg"-ness of print and electronic versions of the same publication mirrors that of Metz and Gherman, who foresee the e-journal coming first, later to be replaced by the "archival and canonical" print version: indeed, there is little agreement about how the electronic journal will be used.

Once the electronic journal makes serious gains in academic libraries, will there still be some demand for print? If so, at what point in the journal's life? Will readers want to use electronic articles as they use print today, that is, as whole, discrete information packages, or will they also or instead want the ability to manipulate them, to break them up into smaller parts, to rearrange them, to merge them with other data? These are questions yet to be answered.

Perhaps a more preliminary question is, how will the reader (or, for that matter, the librarian) identify the e-journal to begin with? This is, as Charles W. Bailey says, "a daunting task."[51] By and large, these journals are not indexed in conventional sources. There is a directory of electronic journals published by the Association of Research Libraries and available either in print or through the Internet; it is quite helpful, but its use presumes a basic knowledge that electronic journals exist.[52]

Distribution, or How Will the E-Journal Be Accessed?

If librarians must still face the costs of print subscriptions, while (as Line speculates) adding those for electronic access, it is hard to imagine how the market for scholarly journals can do anything but collapse: we must assume that the developing models, when mature, will be more cost-effective than existing ones, both for publishers and libraries. However, there are other issues pertaining to the distribution and publication of electronic journals. Will electronic journals be accessed online and "metered" by their publishers? Mounted on networks like the Internet and offered free of charge? Or sold in tape or CD-ROM format, to be mounted locally or shared regionally by a group of libraries? Right now, each of these approaches is being tested by one publisher or another.

Scholars as Publishers

Paul E. Peters, Ann Okerson, James C. Thompson, and others have raised the possibility that, whatever the distribution format, scholars may (as Peters says) "take back the rights" or assume control of publishing their own research, cutting out that powerful middleman, the commercial publisher.[53] Thompson charges:

> The idea of the academy retaking control of the bulk of scholarly publishing is being forced into consideration by the practices of the commercial publishers themselves. Their bills simply cannot be paid indefinitely, and something must give.[54]

Presumably, the lower costs associated with electronic publishing could enable this enormous change.

Metz and Gherman suggest that each university (or at least each major university) can publish its faculty's research in its own e-journals, and make these periodicals available free to other institutions in return for free access to their journals— a sort of "interlibrary loan" of electronic serials. Smaller colleges and universities, since the research giants would perceive their responsibility to share resources because of the value the total system offers, would be granted access to everyone's journals, free of charge.[55] This is an interesting idea, but considering the relative lack of open-handedness with which many large libraries treat smaller ones for purposes of interlending, this assumption about the exchange of e-journals seems questionable.

Robin Downes also encourages the university to publish that whose production it has supported; "an expansion of journal publishing as an academic cottage industry—where it has coexisted with commercial publishing for many years—might modify the pricing trends which are damaging the journal as a method of scholarly communication."[56] Okerson, however, sees no evidence of much activity along such lines:

> A vision of university-based electronic networked publishing is expressed by many librarians and other members of the university community in conversations about academe's regaining control and distribution of its own intellectual output. . . . In spite of good rhetoric, there are no vital signs of university electronic journal publishing activity.[57]

The Role of the Intermediary

Many publishers will continue to assign rights to the contents of their journals to commercial document delivery services in return for handsome royalty fees which they, not these intermediaries, set. It is also possible that more commercial publishers will enter the document delivery business themselves, selling articles directly to libraries and readers rather than relying on middlemen. Unable to answer the key question of what will happen to their revenues once journals are largely sold "by the piece" rather than by subscription (in this new environment some material probably will not sell at all), they may wish to control the distribution system more closely.[58]

The Coalition for Networked Information Models

In the spring of 1991 the Coalition for Networked Information (CNI) sponsored a two-day workshop in Monterey, California, on new models for information delivery. The attendees developed four models for publishing or disseminating electronic information which seemed feasible to them, identifying for each its relative advantages and disadvantages in relationship to printed scholarly communication. The participants' underlying thinking was that, through the distribution of their work to other interested parties, a useful evaluation of the economic, technical, and service implications of electronic publishing could occur.[59]

The proposed models include those for regional or large-area site licenses; the sale of individual articles; discipline-specific databases; and the "augmented print model," in which print would precede, but eventually be superseded by, electronic publication, eliminating or alleviating some of academic libraries' preservation and space concerns.[60] If we examine a few of the electronic journals already being published, some experimentation with each of these models is already evident.

Some Examples of Contemporary E-Journals

We can obtain clues about the future distribution and publication of the e-journal by examining a handful of titles published today. The *Journal of the International Academy of Hospitality Research* (*JIAHR*) debuted on November 26, 1990; it is a product of the Scholarly Communications Project (SCP) of Virginia Tech. For $30 a year, anyone with Internet access can subscribe to this "electronic only" journal. The print version costs the SCP over $5,000 an issue for printing and distribution; the same costs for the electronic journal are reported to be "nearly nothing." "The significance of this enormous advantage," the publisher writes, "cannot be overstated."[61]

The belief that scholars and institutions who purchase a subscription will take the publication more seriously because they have paid for it prompted the Academy of Hospitality Research to offer the journal for a price, rather than gratis. The academy also wanted to place an electronic journal before the library community in the same way a printed journal is presented—through subscription. There was a third reason as well to charge for access to *JIAHR*: some members of the academy disagreed with the popular argument that everything available through BITNET and the Internet should be without cost. They feared that a policy of this sort would eventually exclude a certain amount of valuable scholarly material, and perhaps even promote the distribution of less valuable information. "Income from the sale of subscriptions—amounting to less than $1,500 in the first year—will never be more than a very small fraction of the University's and the Academy's investment of time and resources into the journal," the editor writes. In this case, profit is not the publisher's objective.[62]

The *Online Journal of Current Clinical Trials*, a joint venture of OCLC and the American Association for the Advancement of Science (AAAS), can be accessed through OCLC at a cost of $95 per year; this includes a microfiche backfile. Subscribers have several options for obtaining copies of desired articles, including printing them out locally, or having them downloaded or faxed for an additional cost. Unlike *JIAHR*, *Current Clinical Trials* has full graphics capability. The publishers do not require institutions to purchase multiple passwords or subscriptions.

OCLC reports that this journal will be indexed in Biosis, and that the National Library of Medicine has been approached about including it in Medline. The publishers feel that the added value of multiple-point access that electronic formats bring will (when coupled with a reasonable subscription price) encourage readers to experiment with e-journals, despite the absence as yet of common search protocols.

It is interesting that the publishers of both the *Journal of the International Academy of Hospitality Research* and the *Online Journal of Current Clinical Trials* attempt to do something more than promote and sell their own publications; each has also taken certain steps aimed at establishing the e-journal in the minds of scholars and librarians as a worthwhile method of information delivery to which one subscribes (much as we do to print periodicals) for a fee. It is likely that publishers understand that only a general acceptance of the electronic journal can lead to the development of the critical mass of such publications necessary for real profitability, and that the creation of comforting equivalencies between familiar print journals and new electronic ones will contribute to this acceptance.

Elsevier, a large publisher of scientific materials, has introduced TULIP (The University Licensing Program), a project that makes the full text of forty-two journals available to sixteen different universities as a long-term experiment in determining how journals might be used on a university's electronic network.[63] This licensing approach is quite different from the one taken by the two publishers mentioned above. The purpose of the three-year Elsevier project is to give the publisher and librarians hard information about how e-journals and their print equivalents will be used when both are available to the reader: how will network access change the ways in which readers work with journals? Elsevier hopes that the project can also generate information that will suggest appropriate pricing structures.

How Will the E-Journal Be Priced?

Neither publishers nor librarians as yet understand how electronic serials should be priced, or what payment schemes will best serve the marketplace.[64] It seems certain that publishers will develop pricing models that sustain existing profits, but pricing mechanisms are still very much an area for experimentation. Ann Okerson suggests that initially, when parallel systems for the publication of print and electronic journals are maintained, information prices will be higher than ever, but what will happen after the dust settles is anyone's guess:

> After research and development costs are stabilized and the print and electronic markets settle, who knows what pricing structure will prevail? ... It is conceivable that, like older movies rented for a dollar at a video outlet, older science works will become cheap, and new works, very much in demand, will be expensive.[65]

Some have argued that electronic publishing will cost substantially less—perhaps more than 50 percent less—than producing print journals; ideally, publishers will be able to maintain existing profit margins, while lowering subscription prices and alleviating some of the present and terrible burden felt by academic libraries. But some publishers maintain that there will be little savings in switching to electronic delivery models, because the managerial and editorial costs associated with any format constitute as much as 60 percent of total publication costs. Metz and Gherman believe that production costs make no difference whatsoever and are irrelevant in pricing journals: prices charged for journal subscriptions typically reflect the "value" of the journal (as measured by citation counts and numbers of holdings libraries), rather than the cost of producing it.[66] Thus, prices and pricing structures remain areas for concern, discussion, and experimentation.

There are also certain hidden or indirect costs associated with the electronic journal, similar to those identified with the implementation of CD-ROMs. Depending on the size of the library's reader population and the amount of hardware, software, and telecommunications capability the organization already possesses, the introduction of the e-journal can be a costly proposition. In many cases, faster, more powerful hardware may be needed, including printers that can handle bit-mapped page images. Some colleges and universities still are not connected to the Internet or to BITNET; on other campuses, such connections may exist but may not yet have been extended to the library. These are matters for serious and specific exploration.

Protecting the Contents of the E-Journal

There are still major questions about how to safeguard the contents of the e-journal from "unauthorized modification as well as from misuse and misappropriation."[67] That very flexibility cited above as a source of appeal for the electronic journal becomes a source of concern when authors and publishers think of the researcher downloading material, then rearranging it, perhaps even incorporating it with local data so that its origins and identity are lost or masked. Some have even suggested that the lack of a mechanism to prevent the duplication and redistribution of electronic text may cause publishers of strong money-making journals to think twice about developing electronic versions, comparing their concerns to "the fear and suspicion that the entertainment industry has had of dual VCRs or digital audio tape, both of which have faced legal and economic roadblocks despite their technological feasibility."[68]

As protection against unauthorized copying Okerson foresees that, rather than subscribing to journals, in the electronic environment libraries will instead license them. "Licenses," she writes, "are intended to compensate the publisher for the potentially broad and possibly undisciplined electronic copying of scholarly materials which could violate the 'fair use' provisions of the Copyright Act."[69]

Access versus Ownership: Can Libraries Afford the Trade-Offs?

In an article in *Information Technology and Libraries*, Charles W. Bailey raises a question that troubles many librarians, but one we seem almost hesitant to discuss, perhaps because it suggests such bald-faced lack of trust in the publishing industry, an important partner in information delivery:

> Commercial firms own the information in these full-text serials, and, one way or another, we rent it. Is access versus ownership a problem? ... How much will it cost? How will it increase or decrease the cost of accessing serials information? How rapidly will these costs rise over time? How easily can we obtain the print equivalents of these electronic serials if the vendor discontinues the electronic version or we can no longer afford it? How sure are we that information that is solely in electronic form will be preserved? ... We will have rapid access to selected serials information using powerful searching techniques, but we will have paid for this improved access by sacrificing ownership.[70]

Bailey's suggestion that we may be entering an information monopoly is a disturbing one, and an even more troubling question could be added to his list. Suppose publishers decide there is little profit but considerable expense associated with retaining older issues of their journals, and routinely dispose of backfiles? This is not a concern that can be easily dismissed or rationalized when information becomes the sole property of the profit-making sector. Bailey recognizes that even the computer centers presently archiving electronic journals produced by the academic community have made no special commitment to continue to do this indefinitely.[71]

The Validity of the E-Journal

The e-journal will be legitimized only when those who presently publish in respected print journals consent to contribute their research to electronic periodicals as well. Will researchers want to publish their results in journals that are infrequently refereed, read by small numbers of people, and rarely indexed in standard sources? Or will electronic journals struggle with the taint of the vanity press? What weight will tenure committees give to papers that appear in such journals?

Metz and Gherman believe that, for the e-journal to gain a real foothold in the scholarly market, faculty must experience a major shift in values and "accept this new medium as a valid means of being vested in the academy."[72] We know that scholars value greatly the refereeing and editing processes associated with the modern scholarly journal; perhaps if the means of publishing e-journals is also placed in their hands as Peters and others suggest (rather than being centered in the commercial sector), this new format will make greater gains more quickly as an accepted publishing vehicle.

Textual and Content Limitations

At present, many electronic journals are distributed as ASCII text files, which severely limits the kind of information they may contain. For example, color, foreign characters, illustrations, and mathematical notations are impossible with this kind of file structure.[73] Lon Savage, writing about the *Journal of the International Academy of Hospitality Research*, notes the problems created by a lack of graphics capability:

> The inability to use graphics, although initially considered only a minor handicap, is now considered of much importance. The publisher and editors have placed increased emphasis on finding a way to use graphics in the journal, perhaps by sending it out in both ASCII and PostScript formats.[74]

The use of PostScript would permit graphics display.

The Role of the Library and Librarians

Karen A. Schmidt points out that changes in publishing and formats will have a strong effect on the academic library, whose policies and services are largely governed by the types of publications and information resources available at any given time:

> Beyond this, the *raison d'être* of the library is brought into question by such a drastic change in the nature of publishing. Those foreseeing the demise of the book predict a similar fate for the library, with the gamut of observations running from a drastically different library to the actual end of libraries. . . . A seasoned view of the economics of publishing and the mission of the research library suggests a mixture of the new (electronically transmitted and produced items) and the old (the book and the journal).[75]

This same idea—that access is only one part of an ownership/access model, that ownership will continue to be important and print materials necessary for many years to come, and the task of organizing and preserving local resources will not disappear—received strong support in the workshops for library directors and their provosts sponsored by the Research Libraries Group.[76] This view is at the same time both comforting (in the sense that it offers the hope of continuity) and discomfiting (in that it leaves us with everything we are doing now, plus a great deal more).

It seems certain that libraries will cease to grow at the rates of the past; perhaps they will even shrink. The principal service emphasis may well be helping the reader structure research questions and locate materials, wherever and in whatever formats they may exist. We will probably purchase on-demand a great deal of what people want (whatever the format or delivery mechanism), and buy less material in anticipation of some unknown scholar's needs. In this respect, academic libraries of the future may become much more like the special or corporate libraries of the present.

We can say with equal certainty that information storage will continue to increase in capacity and decrease in cost, and that more and more material will be made available electronically, potentially for access directly by the user from his or her own "scholar's workstation" (for the moment, a powerful microcomputer with a modem). Will this new electronic storage and distribution system make the traditional, location-specific library redundant, and as well as its denizen, the librarian? To paraphrase Mark Twain, "The reports of our death are greatly exaggerated."

Who Will Pay?

Much that is electronic (library catalogs available through the Internet, many networked journals) will continue to be available to researchers free of charge, but other resources (commercially published electronic journals, indexing and abstracting databases) will cost money. Who will pay, and what impact will the answer to that question have on the role of librarians and libraries as we move from the collection-based model toward the ownership/access pattern?

Writing about the "pay-for-use paradigm" Harold Billings commented:

> Information access by transaction is a market virtually waiting to explode—a consumer-driven market that can better feed authors and publishers, as well as allow libraries to reduce some of the huge costs of journal subscriptions and monographic acquisitions and the unseen overheads that support paper-based library collections.[77]

It is unlikely that colleges and universities will turn away from funding the sort of information presently available in print, just because it becomes electronic and it is possible for readers to "pay per view." Access to electronic information must be arranged and funded by some campus entity, and the library will probably retain that role. It also seems certain that many researchers (certainly students and those faculty not lavishly endowed with grants) will continue to turn to libraries, so long as we provide for free that for which, accessed independently, they themselves will have to pay. This does not say that one would have to visit the library to access this information; with the proper arrangements and instruction the appropriately equipped reader could review and select electronic materials from home or office.

Some libraries may find it necessary to address issues of control: today a library buys a subscription for a fixed, known cost; the information it contains is then available to any number of people, and cost-per-use decreases as the number of uses increases. But how will the expenses associated with the purchase of information change when scholars pick and choose, and libraries pay by the item? We all know of readers who abuse existing interlending services by rather casually requesting large numbers of loans: what economic havoc could these people create as they "purchase" articles with an equal lack of discrimination? If we have good assessment mechanisms in place, allowing the reader to view a document, its conclusions, or perhaps an abstract before he or she selects it, we should be able to assume that readers will no more binge on information purchased item-by-item than they did on print materials.

The Librarian as Information Specialist

The thought that libraries may survive in an electronic age because they will continue to hold the information purse strings will provide most librarians with only cold comfort: surely the next century will support some role for us other than plugging the reader into the computer and paying the ensuing bills. Some librarians fear predictions that, as information is placed closer and closer to the reader and the need to enter the library building is all but eliminated, their services will no longer be required—perhaps some Darwinian principle dictating the demise of the library profession has prompted so many library schools to close:

> With user terminals capable of undertaking the technical requirements to receive such document delivery, service agencies will be geared to deliver directly to the individual. The organizations which today almost exclusively serve libraries and which are themselves library-based will switch marketing to

the user who, as an individual, is probably easy to handle under the new technology, and at the same time will find it more difficult to form a pressure group.[78]

But perhaps there will still be a strong purpose for librarians, although a changed one. Susan K. Martin sums up the pessimist's rationale, then responds to it:

> People will be able to use information services directly, without the mediation of the library. Many will say that this event will signal the end of the library, and that as more information seekers establish accounts with online services, libraries will become museums of the past. I don't believe that libraries will disappear. If information systems are truly becoming increasingly complex, people will need information professionals to sort through all the available services, costs, and capabilities.[79]

Many people (not all of them librarians) agree that, if anything, the role of the librarian will not only be changed, but also strengthened. Erik Davis's view of the coming library bears this out:

> It's information technology that's dissolving our picture of the leatherbound, wood-desked university library into a shimmery haze of pixeled surfaces.... More and more technological bombshells are scudding our way every day.[80]

Davis goes on to suggest that librarians will be researchers' only salvation in the coming information glut. Information literacy, he says, is "not just technical training but tactics for maneuvering through swamps of source material, and tools to evaluate the data dredged up."[81] Presumably, it is not the technical training necessary to crack the many new information codes that will emerge (that being simple enough for many computer-expert researchers to teach themselves), but rather the ability to separate the wheat from the chaff that librarians will contribute to this effort.

New resources will spring up with great frequency. One British librarian suggests that librarians will become indispensable counselors in the coming electronic information environment:

> The range of facilities available through the new technologies will be such, that attempting to keep up with developments in those services used regularly will tax even the most persistent and attentive user.... Advice on the most suitable sources to access will become a growth industry.[82]

In the near future, he continues, it is "the ability of the librarian to identify and access materials through networks for delivery directly to the user" that will define the role of our profession as "the librarian becomes a true advisor rather than a custodian."[83]

For the future-present, researchers and librarians also need the patience and energy to master different search protocols for almost every electronic resource, although programs like the Sonoma Internet Library Access Software (which acts as a search gateway to hundreds of library catalogs available on the Internet) will someday lead to the common command language futurists have predicted for almost as long as they have the paperless society.[84] Roy Adams in his book *Communication and Delivery Systems for Librarians* suggests that one day intelligent front ends to databases will guide readers.[85] In the meanwhile, it seems a safe bet that not all academic library users will wish to scale this electronic tower of Babel alone; many will want a librarian close at hand to guide and help translate.

The Librarian as Navigator along the Information Highway

Little has been said as yet about the enormous amount of electronic hand-holding that will be required of academic librarians in the near future. While some faculty and students are computer literate (or at least "computer eager"), many are not. A healthy combination of salesmanship, instruction, and careful decision making is vital if we are to make electronic journals, books, and other resources part of the academic library user's experience.

The central question is, how will we teach readers to access electronic publications? When journals exist only online (or the reader wishes to use them in that format), who in the library will help interested faculty and students work with such materials? Where in the library will the tools of access (workstations and their peripherals) best be placed—will there be dedicated workstations in the periodicals reading room, or will readers be expected to work from any station of the library's or institution's network?

How will library staff handle readers who want articles from e-journals, but do not themselves want to access the journals (the faculty member who does not know what e-mail is, for example)? Will libraries expect every reader wanting access to e-journals to apply for an electronic mail account and learn to navigate the appropriate access channels? As Charles W. Bailey points out, "Users may not understand the mechanics of network e-mail and file transfers, the operation of useful mainframe software, or downloading procedures."[86] Will we require that every public services librarian be proficient in these tasks, or will we elect to have systems staff download issues of the e-journals to which we subscribe to local area networks or microcomputers for simplified access by librarians and readers alike?

Will we add records and holdings for e-journals to our online catalogs and bibliographic utilities? What sorts of information will we insert in these records to be certain the reader understands that the journal or book is electronic, rather than print? Will the catalog records contain instructions on where such resources reside and how to access them? A MARBI discussion paper, "Providing Access to Online Information Resources," provides a framework for the discussion of some of these questions; among the information types included are electronic bulletin boards, mailing list servers, computer discussion groups and forums, data archives, full-text databases, and numeric databases. Among other things, this discussion paper suggests the development of new MARC fields for location and access information.[87]

There are already tales (which are not apocryphal) of librarians subscribing to e-journals without realizing they were electronic, and without having access to BITNET or the Internet. One publisher reported problems with librarians "losing" issues of e-journals, generally through equipment failure or procedural error.[88] Certainly there will be much that is new for librarians to learn, including the intricacies of communications software, electronic mail, file transfer protocols, and several different networks (BITNET, the Internet).

The Virginia Tech Library has developed a task force to determine how best to integrate the electronic journal into the library's existing procedures and service programs. These are some of the questions that are being examined:

> How will bibliographers determine which [electronic journals] the library should subscribe to? Will it list them in its OPAC? How will the patron locate them? Should the library include the e-journal's Internet address in the OPAC? How do patrons receive or claim an e-journal? Should the library create a full text file of these journals on its computer or simply allow its patrons to access the host computer files over the Internet if it exists?[89]

In fact, libraries may take multiple approaches to the electronic journal—through local area networks, the campus mainframe, microcomputers (on hard disks or floppy disks), and even printouts. Whatever the access strategy, librarians have a major role to play in educating readers about electronic information resources and introducing the concept of their value; unlike costly CD-ROMs, this new information resource is available largely free of charge if we will only dedicate the necessary staff time and equipment to making it available on our campuses.

The Librarian as Selector, Organizer, and Preserver

Karen A. Schmidt believes that new formats will change the roles of those who organize library materials as well as those who help readers locate, evaluate, and interpret them:

> If historical precedent serves any predictive function, there is reason to suspect that these new forms of publication will necessitate a new menu of procedures and substructures within the research library. . . . Current operations generally found in research libraries in the United States point out the problems associated with handling the new forms of publications using currently established procedures for acquiring and disseminating research information.[90]

One can fairly substitute "academic" for "research" library and see that the roles of collection development officers and catalogers will also undergo change. Perhaps some tasks will even disappear, freeing staff time for other assignments. In their article "How Scholarly Communication Should Work in the 21st Century," Sharon J. Rogers and Charlene S. Hurt suggest that the many hours print publications have required library staff to spend processing, shelving, and reshelving materials will be redirected to developing expert journal indexes and assisting readers to locate the information they need.[91]

As more information is accessed electronically, librarians will have important new preservation tasks before them. How will electronic journals be archived? After a time, will publishers create backfiles in print, microform, or optical disk? Or will the work of archiving be left largely to librarians? Librarians will have the weighty and dual responsibilities of ensuring that publishers do not simply forsake electronic information as it becomes less current and therefore possibly less profitable, and that the formats in which it is archived are sound and enduring. Already some publishers of e-journals do not maintain backfiles on the network; instead interested readers must request them from the journal's editor.

Electric Dreams

In his article "CYBERLIBRARIES," Erik Davis asks the question, "Do librarians dream of electric books?" An honest answer would probably be "no." But if not electric books, then what *does* fill the fantasies and hopes of librarians? If we are frank, we will probably admit that it will be some time before the longing for large, relatively self-sufficient collections fades completely: it is one thing to accept the inevitable (increased reliance on access), but quite another to forget the dream of something else.

But perhaps if we probe our own psyches a little more deeply we will see there are other things that also have great importance for us, things that are nearer to our grasp than the enormous collections we attempted to build in the past, collections we might now term monuments to misplaced confidence in that impossible goal, self-sufficiency. As librarians, we want to make our readers aware of the vast amounts of information available to them, wherever it may be housed, and in whatever format. We want to make it possible for them to evaluate this information, even when it is remotely held, and to obtain for them that which is relevant to their research quickly and at no cost to the reader.

We want to find ways to use whatever dollars are available to us to serve readers more directly; if we can choose information resources that require less space, processing, and handling by library staff, we will have more money for information services. We want to feel confident that decisions about the retention and preservation of information resources, whatever their formats, still rest with us as librarians.

In the present, most of these goals are attainable. We can reallocate our acquisitions budget, so that some part of it supports indexing and abstracting services that inform our readers what is "out there" that isn't "in here," while also funding effective resource sharing and document delivery programs. We can cooperate with our closest interlending partners to ensure that last copies of important journals are not canceled. Through use studies, we can identify those areas in which we are best advised to collect, thereby maximizing our acquisitions dollars. But, as more and more information becomes electronic, will we draw nearer to our dreams or further distance ourselves from them?

The Information Concerns of the Twenty-First Century

As information delivery models change, so will our present set of information concerns. Suppose Ann Okerson is correct, and that by the year 2000 half of all journals are electronic, with evidence that those publishers lacking electronic capability are being forced from the marketplace? (If this scenario is not in place by

2000, it surely will be shortly thereafter.) It is likely that one or more of the new pricing structures for journal literature suggested above will prevail, and that libraries will be buying more serial literature directly from publishers (perhaps article by article), and lending and borrowing much less from each other.

For access to those publications still existing only in print, commercial document delivery services (having profitably linked themselves to computerized table of contents or indexing services integrated with online catalogs) will have increased their share of the journal literature market, reducing interlending among libraries even further.

In this coming age, most resource sharing will occur with monographic material, which will still be wanted in the traditional codex format unless the intent is some sort of textual analysis. As libraries increase their spending for access (versus assets), they will begin to spend far more carefully, selecting each title with some specific use in mind; today's "special library model" in which much information is purchased for readers on-demand will make inroads in academic libraries.

However, unless we take action now, at some point within the next ten years we may begin to realize that, as Charles W. Bailey suggests, we have sacrificed something precious while making the transition from ownership to an access/ownership model: at some point, the backfiles of the bulk of scholarly journal literature will exist solely in the hands and computers of the profit-making sector. We will become seriously concerned about pricing, preservation, and retention issues, knowing well that monopolies raise prices, that newer materials sell more briskly than older ones, and that, while the cost of computer storage has decreased, it is not free and the amount of materials to be archived will only grow. Thus, while today's anxieties center around declining collecting budgets and the difficulties associated with effective access, tomorrow's worries will be even more basic: not only will the local library be unable to buy and preserve all that for which it perceives a need, but publishers may have become the sole owners of much contemporary journal literature, which they may or may not archive and properly preserve.

At a time when information delivery models are changing so quickly and so radically, among the most important qualities librarians can have will be vigilance and thoughtfulness. Caroline Arms counsels, "As the existing technologies develop and as new ones appear librarians will continue to face tough decisions concerning how to harness the new potential in a way that will serve their clients best."[92] *Access versus Assets* can prepare librarians to meet their responsibilities for the near future. However, as the ways in which information is distributed continue to change, so will our present set of access concerns shift dramatically. If we are to serve the readers of today, and ensure information access for the faculty and students of tomorrow, we must create time now to think and plan for the future.

Notes

1. Erik Davis, "CYBERLIBRARIES: Do Librarians Dream of Electric Books?" *Lingua Franca* 2 (Feb.-Mar. 1992): 47.
2. Dougherty and Hughes, *Preferred Futures*, 6.
3. Blair, "Information Revolution," 73.
4. Dougherty and Hughes, *Preferred Futures*, 12.
5. Ardis and Croneis, "Document Delivery," 624; White, "Interlibrary Loan," 54.
6. Quint, "Connect Time: Wars, Roses, and Standards," 108.
7. Atkinson, "Atkinson on Networks," 432–39.
8. OCLC, "Interlibrary Loan," 4.
9. Peters, "Networked Information Resources," 36.
10. David Cohen, "A National Networked Solution to Improving Access to Journal Articles," *Journal of Academic Librarianship* 15 (May 1989): 79.
11. Medina, "Improving," 7.
12. Lynch and Preston, "Internet Access," 282.
13. Ibid., 284.
14. Ibid., 283.
15. Sharon C. McKay, "The Internet: Its Origins, Uses, and Future," *At Your Service*, no. 20 (Mar. 1992): 11.
16. National Research and Education Network, "Fact Sheet," Broadside, Apr. 1991.
17. Lynch and Preston, "Internet Access," 297.
18. Downes, "Resource Sharing," 119.
19. Billings, "The Bionic Library," 40.
20. Peters, "Networked Information Resources," 37.
21. Dougherty and Hughes, *Preferred Futures*, 11.
22. Davis, "CYBERLIBRARIES," 47.
23. Martin, "Delivery Systems," 169–70.
24. Billings, "The Bionic Library," 38.
25. Mark Kibbey and Nancy H. Evans, "The Network Is the Library," *EDUCOM Review* 24 (Fall 1989): 15.
26. Ibid., 16.
27. Caroline Arms, ed., *Campus Strategies for Libraries and Electronic Information*, EDUCOM Strategies Series on Information Technology (Bedford, Mass.: Digital Press, 1990), 34.
28. Lynch and Preston, "Internet Access," 266.

29. David Wilson, "Researchers Get Direct Access to Huge Data Base," *Chronicle of Higher Education* (Oct. 9, 1991), A24.
30. Roy Adams, *Communication and Delivery Systems for Librarians* (Brookfield, Vt.: Gower, 1990), 220.
31. A good overview appears in Clifford A. Lynch's "The Development of Electronic Publishing and Digital Library Collections on the NREN," *Electronic Networking* 1 (Winter 1991): 6–21.
32. Association of Research Libraries, *Prospects for Improving Document Delivery: Minutes of the 101st Meeting, October 13–14, Arlington, Virginia*, ed. Nicola Daval (Washington, D.C.: ARL, 1983), 26.
33. Dougherty and Hughes, *Preferred Futures*, 15.
34. Dusenbury and Post, "Subscribing," 11.
35. Adams, *Communication*, 221, 220.
36. Robert Weber, "The Clouded Future of Electronic Publishing," *Publishers Weekly* 237 (June 29, 1990): 78.
37. Line, "Universal Availability," 217.
38. Davis, "CYBERLIBRARIES," 50.
39. Cawkell, "Progress in Documentation," 57.
40. *Public-Access Computer Systems Review*, ISSN 1048-6542, v. 2, no. 1 (1991) contains a "Special Section on Network-Based Electronic Journals," eight articles about the e-journal, present and future.
41. Ann Okerson, "The Electronic Journal: What, Whence, and When," *Public-Access Computer Systems Review* 2, no. 1 (1991): 19.
42. Line, "Universal Availability," 218–19.
43. Okerson, "Electronic Journal," 12.
44. Ibid., 20.
45. Ibid., 21.
46. Metz and Gherman, "Serials Pricing," 315, 320, 321.
47. Ibid., 322.
48. Okerson, "Electronic Journal," 9–10.
49. Ibid., 7.
50. Line, "Universal Availability," 219.
51. Charles W. Bailey, "Network-Based Electronic Serials," *Information Technology and Libraries* 11 (Mar. 1992): 33.
52. Association of Research Libraries, *The Directory of Electronic Journals, Newsletters and Academic Discussion Lists*, 2nd ed. (Washington, D.C.: ARL, Office of Scientific and Academic Publishing, 1992).
53. Peters, "Networked Information Resources," 37.
54. James C. Thompson, "Journal Costs: Perception and Reality in the Dialogue," *College & Research Libraries* 49 (Nov. 1988): 481–82.
55. Metz and Gherman, "Serials Pricing," 323.
56. Downes, "Resource Sharing," 122.
57. Okerson, "Electronic Journal," 16.
58. Adams, *Communication*, 221.

59. Czeslaw Jan Grycz, "Models for Networked Scholarly Information," Unpublished material, Mar. 18, 1991.
60. Nos. 1–2 (1992) of *Serials Review* is devoted to the reactions of a number of librarians to these "CNI" information delivery models.
61. Lon Savage, "The Journal of the International Academy of Hospitality Research," *Public-Access Computer Systems Review* 2, no. 1 (1991): 64.
62. Ibid., 58–59.
63. Blair, "Library," 96.
64. Peters, "Networked Information Resources," 38.
65. Okerson, "Electronic Journal," 13.
66. Metz and Gherman, "Serials Pricing," 322.
67. Peters, "Networked Information Resources," 38.
68. Metz and Gherman, "Serials Pricing," 321.
69. Okerson, "Electronic Journal," 13.
70. Bailey, "Network-Based Electronic Serials," 29.
71. Ibid., 33.
72. Metz and Gherman, "Serials Pricing," 325.
73. Bailey, "Network-Based Electronic Serials," 32.
74. Savage, "Journal," 65.
75. Karen A. Schmidt, "Electronic Publishing and the Library," in *Crossroads: Proceedings of the First National Conference of the Library and Information Technology Association, September 17–21, 1983, Baltimore, Maryland*, ed. Michael Gorman, Library and Information Technology Series, no. 1 (Chicago: American Library Association, 1984), 182–83.
76. Dougherty and Hughes, *Preferred Futures*, 15.
77. Billings, "The Bionic Library," 41.
78. Adams, *Communication*, 220.
79. Martin, "Delivery Systems," 177.
80. Davis, "CYBERLIBRARIES," 47.
81. Ibid.
82. Adams, *Communication*, 199.
83. Ibid., 223.
84. Blair, "Library," 73–74.
85. Adams, *Communication*, 199.
86. Bailey, "Network-Based Electronic Serials," 32.
87. American Library Association, MARBI, "Providing Access to Online Information Resources: Discussion Paper No. 54," Unpublished paper, Nov. 22, 1991, 2–3.
88. Savage, "Journal," 63.
89. Metz and Gherman, "Serials Pricing," 326.
90. Schmidt, "Electronic Publishing," 183.
91. Rogers and Hurt, "How Scholarly Communication Should Work," 8.
92. Arms, *Campus Strategies*, 34.

APPENDIX

Case Studies in Resource Sharing

While writing this book, the authors talked with academic librarians throughout the United States and Canada about interlending and the use of new delivery technologies; many interesting and effective examples of resource sharing were identified, and much of what we learned has been incorporated into *Access versus Assets*. However, some cooperative arrangements seemed particularly appealing, perhaps because of their simplicity, creativity, or potential as models for other institutions developing similar activities. From these we have created an appendix of miniature case studies, organized into a few subjective but sensible categories, based on each one's most salient feature—the characteristic that has proved most important in the cooperative's success. This inventory is by no means exhaustive, nor do the authors maintain that the examples are necessarily the best of their type; they do, however, represent activities worthy of further study. A handful of cooperative arrangements involving large research libraries have also been included where these provide models that may be useful to smaller institutions.

Not every arrangement is examined in equal detail, nor are identical elements included in each précis: these examples are the results of conversations, not a formal survey instrument. Where there is a natural fit in more than one category, this is mentioned in the introductions to other sections where the program might have been described. We hope these miniature case studies will spur the imaginations of other libraries that are seeking to design new cooperative arrangements or strengthen existing ones.

Shared Catalogs

Many groups of libraries have enhanced resource sharing by implementing a shared catalog. The cooperatives described in this section represent college libraries, medium-sized academic libraries, and combinations of both research and smaller institutions. Some of the systems are very large, with dozens of participants, while others have a half-dozen or fewer libraries; in most cases, members also belong to larger, "umbrella" networks, such as OCLC or the Research Libraries Group. In some of the cooperatives, members enjoy geographic proximity, but in other cases they are far apart. Whatever their differences, however, the similarity of a shared catalog has caused each of these networks to succeed. The large number of examples in this section is a good indication of the value of a common catalog to resource sharing. A description of Center for Research Libraries' "User Membership" (a suitable category for smaller institutions) is also included.

College Center for Library Automation (CCLA) (Florida)

In her Spring 1992 article in *Library Administration & Management* Joan Blair writes that Florida's Center for Library Automation (CCLA) "is pioneering an integrated library automation system that is already setting standards for state community college systems around the country."[1] In the 1991–92 academic year this ambitious project developed an online catalog and cataloging support for the state's twenty-eight public community colleges. In 1992–93 a circulation module will be added; later, when CCLA is fully implemented, a student at any participating institution will have the ability to peruse the collections of more than sixty public college and university libraries in the state (exceeding five million volumes), place an ILL request, and receive the material within a few days.

Several of the community colleges have multiple campuses and libraries; when a student searches the CCLA shared catalog he or she first retrieves records for materials shelved in the library where the search originates. With a single keystroke, the records for every library affiliated with the college appear. If an additional key is pressed, materials owned by every community college in the state become available. When the student needs still more information, he or she can "toggle" into the state university's catalog (which runs on different software from the CCLA system), or retrieve an online encyclopedia. Presently, keystroke response time is eight seconds. Dr. Richard Madaus, director of the center, reports that task forces are designing resource sharing agreements that will complement the system's abilities.

CTW Library Consortium (Connecticut)

Connecticut College, Trinity College, and Wesleyan University make up the CTW Library Consortium, located in Hartford, Connecticut; they share an integrated library system and aspire to appear and act as one library to readers affiliated with the three institutions. The campuses are twenty to sixty miles apart, so that the consortium operates a daily delivery service, Monday through Friday, among the three institutions, using a station wagon and a full-time driver.

A reader at any CTW library submits requests for materials from the other two collections at the local circulation desk; this serves to emphasize the "oneness" of the system. Turnaround time is typically forty-eight to seventy-two hours, and circulation staff forward requests through electronic mail or telefacsimile (viewed as somewhat more efficient, as it does not require rekeying the request data). The three institutions process a total of about ten thousand CTW loans each year.

NOVANET (Nova Scotia)

NOVANET is a consortium of eight smaller academic libraries, six of them located in Halifax (Dalhousie, Saint Mary's, Mount Saint Vincent, the Technical University of Nova Scotia, the Nova Scotia College of Art and Design, and the University of Kings College) and one in Sydney (the University College of Cape Breton). These institutions share an online catalog and integrated circulation system; the system is funded by the members based on four equally weighted factors: annual circulation, institutional budget, collection size, and student enrollment.

Reciprocal borrowing is an important part of the NOVANET program, and the shared catalog makes it easy for readers from one institution to ascertain what another owns and whether it is available to be charged out before making a trip. In 1991 an average of 17.4 percent of each library's direct loans were to readers affiliated with other NOVANET institutions.

NORWELD (Northwest Library District), Nola Regional Library System, and the Toledo-Lucas Public Library (Ohio)[2]

Often small academic libraries can benefit significantly from participating in multitype systems. The NORWELD, Nola, and Toledo-Lucas library systems include approximately seventy institutions, some of them small colleges. Initially, resource sharing efforts centered around a microfiche union catalog (very few of the institutions belong to a bibliographic utility); then participants switched to a CD-ROM catalog containing 950,000 monographic records and holdings for 4,000 serial titles. Requests to borrow are faxed to potential lenders, although the three systems are considering a switch to an electronic mail system. Journal articles are faxed within twenty-four hours ("rush" titles within six hours), and other materials are shipped via the U.S. mail.

The CD-ROM catalog offers both keyword and boolean searching, as well as "scoping" levels that correspond to the ILL code the participating libraries follow. For instance, NORWELD members first search the collections of the local library, followed by county libraries, Nola libraries, and, as a last resort, Toledo-Lucas, the largest library in the cooperative. Among the academic participants are the University of Findlay (Findlay, Ohio; 117,000 volumes and 750 journal subscriptions), Defiance College (Defiance, Ohio; 95,000 volumes and 480 journal subscriptions), and Northwest Technical College (Archbold, Ohio; 14,400 volumes and 200 journal subscriptions). The CD-ROM catalog is updated annually.

Libraries of the City University of New York (CUNY)

The libraries of the City University of New York (nineteen institutions, roughly split between four-year colleges and community colleges) are scattered throughout the five boroughs of New York City. Each of the larger institutions enrolls upwards of ten thousand full-time students and supports masters and Ph.D. programs; each individual library collection exceeds a million volumes. In 1988 CUNY libraries began to implement a shared integrated library system. Today, the holdings of each of the nineteen institutions are represented in the database, and most libraries are using the circulation, serials control, and acquisitions features of the system. In 1992 periodical indexes were integrated with the online catalog.

In 1990 pressures for enhanced resource sharing led the university to purchase a telefacsimile machine for every library in the system, speeding interlending. That same year, CUNY also began to underwrite the use of several commercial document supply services, and this support has since been institutionalized; librarians on all campuses order documents from a number of vendors, and the university's office of cooperative library services (rather than the local library) pays the bills. In 1993

CUNY will add a table of contents service to the integrated library system.

The university's libraries have an ILL code and turn to each other before they turn to others for interlending. Nonetheless, the size and mission of the various colleges differ greatly, and these differences are often reflected in the priorities of their libraries. In the fall of 1991, somewhat discouraged by CUNY's modest success in resource sharing, the chief librarians of the four largest senior colleges (Baruch, Brooklyn, City, and Queens colleges) suggested to their interlending and systems staffs that the four institutions form a "miniature consortium" within the larger group: each would agree to respond to the others' requests within twenty-four hours, give priority to these requests over all others, and use telefacsimile where it was requested (the libraries receive daily service from an effective regional delivery system). Requests are transmitted through the OCLC ILL subsystem. While figures indicating what percentage of its total fills each institution obtained from within the group are not yet available, the interlibrary loan and systems staffs (who designed and who run the project) are pleased with the results. They feel the program shows that libraries with similar goals, leadership committed to resource sharing, and complementary collections can succeed in interlending.

SULAN (State University Library Automation Network) (Indiana)

Indiana's State University Library Automation Network (SULAN) began in 1987. Throughout the state, colleges and universities were installing automated library systems; the desirability to communicate with each other and potentially to share bibliographic information led seven state-assisted institutions, Notre Dame at Evansville, and six private colleges to choose to implement the same software, not as a single, shared catalog, but as fourteen separate installations of the same integrated library system. Six of these institutions (Indiana State University, Indiana University, Notre Dame, Purdue, the University of Evansville, and Vincennes University) have now established a communications link that allows readers at one to search the collections of the others, menuing in through the local catalog terminal or workstation.

In the 1992–93 academic year two SULAN libraries, Indiana University and Indiana State University, began to test a new aspect of this communications link, the reader-generated interlibrary loan request. Since the system requires a patron ID before it permits readers to place requests to borrow, campuses can limit this new feature by reader group (faculty only, for example) if they wish. When the software is fully functional, authorized faculty and students at any institution will be able to identify journal articles or books in other participants' catalogs, transfer citations into an on-screen interlibrary loan request form, and forward that request to the holding library; the system will also retrieve readers' names, local addresses, telefacsimile numbers, and other relevant information from a patron file and associate them with the ILL request. When a reader has a fax number, an article can be faxed directly to him or her by the lending library.

If the library has incorporated periodical indexes into its online catalog, the system will also transfer article citations into the ILL record, just as it does bibliographic records. ILL staff have the option of reviewing reader-generated requests before allowing them to go on to other libraries; this feature is called "mediating." The ILL unit may decide to allow requests destined for certain libraries to be transmitted to them, unmediated, but review requests to be sent to other institutions. In all cases, the system verifies that the item is not locally held before transmitting a request to borrow. Eventually, all SULAN libraries will have access to this ILL software; they are presently developing access policies that will complement this resource sharing capability.

Washington Research Library Consortium (WRLC) (Washington, D.C.)

The eight members and three additional participants in WRLC support an integrated library system (ALADIN, which also includes access to periodical indexes), daily delivery service, and on-site borrowing privileges for faculty and students. Four members use a reader-initiated interlibrary loan request system developed by the George Washington University Library. The consortium is funded through an annual membership fee based on factors that include collection size and funding levels; WRLC also has a six-million-dollar grant from the Department of Education to build a remote storage facility. The member institutions vary in size and mission, and only one (Georgetown University) belongs to the Association of Research Libraries.

There are several interesting features to WRLC's interlending policies. The burden of verification is placed on the reader; the local interlibrary loan unit verifies the reader's eligibility for ILL and little else. Borrowing libraries are explicitly permitted to request from partners items they own but that are unavailable, either because they are lost, charged out, or for any other reason.

The elapsed time between a borrowing library's receipt of a reader's request and the material's availability for patron pickup is set at an ambitious three days: one business day for the borrowing library to place the reader's request, a second for the request to be received and the material shipped by the lender, and a third for the borrowing library to receive the item and notify the reader. There are no data on the network's actual average turnaround time.

Triangle Research Libraries Network (TRLN) (North Carolina)

Duke University (Durham), the University of North Carolina at Chapel Hill (UNC/CH), and North Carolina State University at Raleigh (NCSU) are the members of the Triangle Research Libraries Network (TRLN). For decades these libraries have had a cooperative collection development program for both monographs and serials. TRLN also sponsors a van service (funded by UNC/CH) that delivers materials among the three institutions, speeding interlending; it makes one daily circle through the Research Triangle.

Since 1985 a shared catalog has been in place; a circulation system was recently added. In 1993–94 the libraries of TRLN plan to replace the present locally developed catalog with a purchased system. Reciprocal on-site borrowing for faculty and students is part of the TRLN program, and a reader from any site can apply for a borrower's card at the circulation desk of the home library, allowing him or her to borrow from the other institutions. When this program was first discussed some four years ago, there was concern that Duke, with eleven thousand students, could be overwhelmed by the readers from the two larger institutions; however, this did not happen. Because parking is problematic, readers use a bus route called the Blue Line (part of the Chapel Hill bus system) that runs between Durham and Chapel Hill; it stops at Duke every ninety minutes throughout the day.

Each library gives priority to the others' ILL requests, which are transmitted through OCLC's ILL subsystem. Telefacsimile is used to deliver journal articles; Duke has implemented Ariel and hopes its TRLN partners will do the same. Duke reports filling between 20 and 25 percent of its ILL requests at the other two TRLN libraries. In the past, Duke's goals included twenty-four-hour turnaround, but the library now has a large number of serial volumes in off-site storage: recalling them takes a day, so that a one-day response is no longer always possible.

ILLINET Online (Illinois)

ILLINET Online is a large database that supports resource sharing within the state of Illinois; however, not every participating institution enjoys the same level of access to the system. Some forty libraries, including those of each state-supported university, nineteen privately supported academic institutions, and four community colleges, can actually use ILLINET Online for local operations and interlending. However, ILLINET Online also contains the catalog records (supplied through OCLC) of another eight hundred Illinois libraries; twenty-six hundred more libraries can dial into ILLINET Online. Each of these libraries has been assigned a borrower identification number and can request materials from the forty larger libraries using the system at its "highest" level (at this level, ILLINET Online functions as an online catalog and circulation system and is also called the Library Computer System, or LCS). Several LIBRAS member libraries (see College and University Libraries, below) use LCS.

One of the most interesting features of LCS is the ability it gives readers at the large University of Illinois at Urbana-Champaign (UIUC) campus to place their own interlibrary loan requests from LCS terminals. A reader-generated request bypasses the local ILL office and goes directly to the potential lender. (The reader has literally identified the item and charged it to him or herself. As a result of the transaction, a paging slip prints out at the lending institution, which retrieves the book and sends it to UIUC through the statewide delivery system.) Readers can also process their own ILL renewals from LCS terminals, or by calling the UIUC library's Telephone Center, a unit that will search ILLINET Online and renew items for readers by telephone.[3]

The ILL office at Urbana likes the system because of its paper- and labor-saving aspects: library staff are unaware that a request to borrow has even been placed until the material arrives.[4] Lending libraries are pleased by the fact that they do not have to open envelopes, print out lengthy utility-generated lists of ILL requests, search local lists or catalogs to verify call numbers, or notify the requesting library that items are charged out and therefore unavailable. And, LCS automatically generates its own overdue and recall notices, further reducing the work of the lending library.[5]

OhioLINK

OhioLINK, a consortium of fifteen public and two private universities, along with the State of Ohio Library, is a new project that will supply a shared catalog, circulation, serials control, and acquisitions to its participants.

> Ohio's public universities make a $20 million investment annually in library materials. If the state can increase circulation and access to those materials, it will, in effect, be getting a higher return on its investment. Better use of available resources will also help the OhioLINK participants target their periodical purchases more precisely.[6]

Faculty and students will be able to access the system from terminals, PCs with modems, and through the Internet, and all OhioLINK libraries will appear to readers as if they are a single collection. By 1994 a database of twenty million items that can accommodate twenty-five hundred concurrent users is planned. Once the initial group of libraries is up and running, other institutions will be welcomed into the network.

Center for Research Libraries (CRL) (Illinois)

The Center for Research Libraries is a membership organization "whose mission is to make available to the scholarly community research materials that are rarely held in North American libraries."[7] A very interesting feature of CLR membership is that tapes of the center's complete holdings are available for loading into affiliates' online catalogs, making center membership seem very much like participating in a shared catalog. Membership can help smaller academic libraries "compensate" faculty for a paucity of on-site research materials, and can even be influential when institutions attempt to persuade faculty accustomed to easy access to the collections of large research libraries to join their staffs. One librarian recently confided that his university was considering joining CRL because a well-known scholar whom it was courting maintained he would not come unless the library belonged to the Center for Research Libraries, on whose materials his current research was largely dependent.

The center offers three membership categories; since many CRL members are large research institutions, most small- and medium-sized libraries think of affiliation as beyond their more modest means. Indeed, the costs of Voting and Associate memberships are rather steep; one's annual fee is determined each year using a formula based on membership category and a five-year average of acquisitions and binding expenditures. However, User membership (designed for libraries with fewer than 250,000 volumes or those that spend less than $300,000 annually on acquisitions and binding) is quite reasonable: in 1991–92 the mean User member fee was $896. A one-time new member fee is also assessed; in that same fiscal year, it was $403. There are several optional programs within CLR for which members pay small additional fees. Whereas Voting and Associate participants pay nothing for interlibrary loans from the center (in consideration of their substantial membership fees), User members pay a modest $8 per fill, and deposit accounts are welcomed. Among the materials which CRL collects are foreign dissertations, large microform sets, and domestic and foreign newspapers. The center receives ILL requests through RLIN, OCLC, telephone, the postal service, or telefacsimile; fax delivery of articles is routine and without additional charge. The center will supply literature about its collections, membership categories, and costs to any interested institution.[8]

Electronic Document Transmission

The libraries engaged in the cooperative agreements described in this section are hundreds of miles apart. Yet, thanks to electronic document transmission technologies each is satisfying a great many of the other's resource sharing needs. These arrangements demonstrate that libraries with similar collecting emphases and the wish to cooperate need not be deterred by distance. Other resource sharing programs that hinge on successful electronic document transmission appear below (California State University (CSU) at Chico, with the University of California (UC) at Berkeley; and James Madison University, with the University of Virginia (UVA) and Virginia Polytechnic Institute (Virginia Tech) ("Subscribing" to Other Collections); Network of Alabama Academic Libraries (College and University Libraries); and MINITEX (Multitype Library Systems)).

North Carolina State University Digitized Document Transmission Project (NCSU DDTP)

With the help of a Title II-D grant and an equipment grant from Apple Computer, North Carolina State University has expanded a joint project with the National Agricultural Library to include fourteen land grant universities interested in resource sharing in the field of agriculture; these institutions represent most of the regional networks in the Internet, the project's telecommunications system.

Requests for loans are sent through OCLC's interlibrary loan subsystem. For transmitting documents, each of the participants uses a Macintosh-based workstation to which a scanner and a printer have been attached. At North Carolina State an important adjunct to the Digitized Document Transmission Project is the Electronic Document Delivery Service (EDDS), which allows readers to use electronic mail to request articles from interlibrary loan and later permits the delivery of the document directly to the reader's computer. The participants in DDTP strive for forty-eight-hour turnaround time and have waived all ILL fees. More information on NCSU DDTP appears in chapter 7.

The Universities of New Brunswick (UNB) and Alberta (UA) (Canada)

The University of New Brunswick (Fredericton; ten thousand students) has established a document delivery relationship with the larger University of Alberta (UA) library in Edmonton. The University of New Brunswick (UNB) supplies the salary of a library assistant in Alberta's library who handles its requests; it also pays photocopying and courier fees, and processes free of charge whatever ILL requests it receives from UA.

Staff in the UNB library check Alberta's catalog (using the Internet) to be certain it owns an item that is wanted. The request is then faxed to UA, also through the Internet. At the University of Alberta, UNB's staff member processes requests each morning; articles are copied and books signed out by early afternoon. Everything is shipped by courier at 3:00 P.M. and arrives in the UNB mail room by the same hour, the next day. By 4:30 P.M. that same day, packages are opened and materials are delivered to the appropriate branch library, to be picked up by the reader. UNB calls this relationship with Alberta Quick Loan; it has publicized the program to readers, who are enthusiastic. New Brunswick believes that Alberta will be able to fill 50 to 65 percent of its total ILL volume, an excellent figure. Before embarking on the project, UNB compared its serials cancellation list with Alberta's holdings; the number of hits suggested that much of what New Brunswick would request Alberta could supply. The program is so new that a per-item cost has not yet been developed, but UNB feels confident it will be less than that charged by commercial suppliers.

In the near future UNB hopes to search Alberta's catalog through the Internet, find a record for a desired item, copy it to an electronic "clipboard" to which the requester's name and address are added, then return it electronically to Alberta, through the Internet. In this way, the request Alberta receives will consist of its own record with its own call number, facilitating retrieval. Both UNB and UA are installing Ariel, which will greatly reduce courier costs. UNB is interested in identifying more Ariel partners, but recognizes that it must also be able to search partners' online catalogs if these relationships are to be efficient.

When asked what might motivate Alberta to show such generosity toward UNB, New Brunswick pointed out that its director came from the University of Alberta, which has already established a similar program with the University of Regina (described in The Miniature Consortium, below). Further, libraries in Canada are seen as a public resource, paid for from the public purse, that should be made available as broadly as possible.

The Miniature Consortium

Today, many institutions are seeking closer, smaller resource sharing arrangements. These libraries still belong to large systems like OCLC, RLG, and the state networks, but at the same time they have developed partnerships with a small number of institutions whose collections can meet a large percentage of their borrowing needs, and enhanced these arrangements by according special privileges (including speed of delivery) to one another. The arrangements listed in the section that follows this one, "Subscribing" to Other Collections, are also good examples of "miniature" cooperatives, as are the CTW Library Consortium, NOVANET, NORWELD, and the Triangle Research Libraries Network (Shared Catalogs, above); the University of Alberta and its partner the University of New Brunswick (Electronic Document Transmission, above); and Bentley College, Massachusetts Institute of Technology, and Brandeis University (Reciprocal Reading and Borrowing, below). It is clear that the smaller, highly productive library cooperative is one of the strongest trends in contemporary resource sharing.

Keene State College (KSC) and the University of New Hampshire (UNH) at Manchester

In the spring of 1992 Keene State College (KSC; 230,000 volumes) began a new resource sharing relationship with the University of New Hampshire at Manchester (UNH; 950,000 volumes). Keene now funds two student assistants in the UNH library for a total of fourteen hours per week; these students process KSC's faxed ILL requests and send the items out through a van system that delivers twice weekly. If the timing is right, Keene receives a fill from UNH within two to three days of placing the request, versus more than a week under the old system.

At Keene State, ILL staff have a paper list of UNH's serial holdings, as well as access to OCLC (New Hampshire libraries do not participate in OCLC's New England Union List of Serials). Manchester will supply books as well as journal articles. Keene State's rationale for this new spin on an old partnership is interesting: New Hampshire's ILL protocol, which requires going first to the university system, was overloading UNH, which has many of the titles Keene's readers requested. The new program, where Keene provides some monetary support for the services it receives, is designed to give balance to the system, while also expediting Keene's requests.

In the past, KSC sent 15 percent of its ILL requests to Manchester, or nearly twice as many as it sent to its next-highest in-state lender, Dartmouth College. More requests could have been sent to UNH (whose OCLC lender string Keene rotated, at Manchester's request); now that the "guilt" factor has been removed, it probably will be. Because the program is so new, no per-item cost has been determined.

The University of Michigan (UM) and Michigan State University (MSU)

Though only seventy-five miles apart, the University of Michigan and Michigan State University never considered each other viable interlending partners because they participated in different bibliographic utilities and could not see each other's holdings; once both libraries had access to OCLC, they could look at each other's collections quite differently. Starting in 1986, the University of Michigan began to pay a student worker at Michigan State to retrieve materials it wished to borrow through interlibrary loan. A check of UM's old ILL requests against MSU's holdings determined that 20 to 30 percent of them could have been filled from Michigan State's collections. In March of 1991, the program became two-way; today, each school employs a student worker devoted solely to filling the other's requests, approximately fifteen hours a week; the libraries use the OCLC ILL subsystem to exchange requests. Each library pays its own student workers because, six months into the new arrangement, the "balance of trade" seemed quite even. Wayne State University has shown an interest in joining the arrangement; the University of Michigan believes this could enable it to fill another 10 to 20 percent of its requests through this "miniature consortium."

If MSU's main library owns the requested title, UM receives twenty-four-hour turnaround for a faxed journal article; when the material is located in a branch, filling the request takes a little longer. UPS is used to deliver books; if they are sent out before 2:00 P.M., they are received the next day. The delivery mechanisms are not particular to the special arrangement between the two libraries, but derive from the universities' representation on the Committee for Institutional Cooperation (CIC). When MSU cannot satisfy a request, UM sends it to another CIC institution then, when necessary, to another RLG member. The two universities also offer a reciprocal borrowing program for faculty (the laws of the state of Michigan provide for free access to the these libraries by any member of the public).

The University of Tennessee at Knoxville (UTK) and Vanderbilt University (VU)[9]

In 1988 the University of Tennessee at Knoxville (UTK) and Vanderbilt University (VU) received a Title II-D grant to expand an existing resource sharing program between the two libraries. Difficulties in determining serial holdings and whether books that were wanted were on the shelf complicated interlending, and typical turnaround time was two to three weeks. The project, called IRIS, focused specifically on improving access to science materials. UTK and Vanderbilt do not have a shared catalog, but each established access to the other's collections through PCs with modems and placed these near the local online catalog, along with a stack of ILL request forms. Fax machines were installed.

Each library agreed to request from the other anything it could supply. Requests and articles were faxed, and everything else was shipped first class or via courier. Turnaround time ranged from a day for items delivered by telefacsimile to four days for books, a great improvement over previous satisfaction time; fill rates remained at 85 percent throughout the project. Among the surprises Vanderbilt and UTK experienced were long-distance telephone expenses, which "substantially exceeded projections"; plans were made to substitute the Internet for commercial telephone service. Ink cartridges were another unexpectedly steep cost, proving shorter-lived (about three weeks) and more expensive ($80 to $85) than anticipated. UTK and Vanderbilt continue to fine-tune their resource sharing project.

The Universities of Regina (UR) and Alberta (UA) (Canada)

This arrangement is very similar to that between Alberta and the University of New Brunswick, described in Electronic Document Transmission, above; it differs in that a commercial courier service is used for document delivery. In 1988 the library of the University of Regina introduced an experimental document delivery service using telefacsimile and courier links with the University of Alberta, which has the largest collection in western Canada and the third largest in all of Canada.[10] In the interlibrary loan office at Regina (staffed until 9:00 P.M. each evening) as requests are received, staff use a variety of tools to determine whether Alberta can fill them. Readers' handwritten forms are faxed overnight to UA, where the next morning a clerk goes to various campus libraries, retrieving books and photocopying articles. In mid-afternoon these are picked up by a courier service, and packages are received by Regina the next morning. Regina funds the salary and benefits of the full-time clerk located at Alberta, the courier service, photocopy costs at $.15 per page, and the costs of faxing their requests. Additionally, UR bought its partner a PC and a modem (used to receive the faxed ILL requests) and a backpack for the staff member who messengers requested materials.

Regina sends 60 percent of its ILL requests to Alberta; the "no fill" rate is a relatively low 10 percent, which means that Alberta can fill half of Regina's total ILL volume; the overwhelming majority of the requests are for journal articles. The dedicated staff member at Alberta can handle about forty requests a day, depending on the amount of photocopying required. On some days Regina sends as many as seventy requests, and Alberta contributes the additional staff time to process them. (During slower periods, when Regina's dedicated employee is not busy with UR requests, he or she does work for Alberta.)

At Regina, the project has proven so popular that the ILL unit's workload grew by 85 percent; undergraduate borrowing particularly increased. Regina's ILL office now has four full-time employees and a student. After six months of service, factoring in all cost centers, Regina estimates that each request costs between $9 and $11. A handsome report, "Stand and Deliver: An Assessment of the FAX Link, University of Alberta/University of Regina, September 1988-February 1989: Report to the University Librarian," rationalizes the project and describes its structure and costs in some detail.[11] Curiously, Regina has little interest in replacing its courier delivery service with either the scanning technology New Brunswick and Alberta are using, or telefacsimile (perceived as very time-consuming for ILL staff and costly if commercial telephone lines are used): it is satisfied with the performance and costs of the present delivery system.

"Subscribing" to Other Collections

These arrangements are really a variation on the "miniature consortium" theme; the central difference is that, here, money changes hands, as smaller institutions pay fees to larger ones for access to their collections. The agreements included here offer different levels of access to the host collection, and access is not unfettered. In some cases it is limited by the numbers of items to be supplied during a given time frame; in others, a particular list of journals is specified; format can also be the governing factor (an agreement may include only books or only journals). Both host and guest institutions report that their arrangements are equitable and cost-effective.

California State University (CSU) at Chico, with the University of California (UC) at Berkeley

Almost every program in which one library "subscribes" to the collections of another is the acknowledged foster child of the Chico-Berkeley agreement. This California program was the first, and its motives and design merit a close look. CSU-Chico is geographically remote from other major universities; faculty and students cannot drive or take the bus across town to a research library—the nearest significant collection is ninety miles away. Facing a reduction in its journal budget of 25 percent, Chico identified three resource sharing goals:

> Providing faster service than we enjoyed with interlibrary loan; being able to demonstrate to faculty that the Library could support research notwithstanding the size of the collection or funding limitations; and keeping the cost of such support to a minimum.[12]

Although Chico is part of CSU's systemwide twenty-campus ILL agreement (enriched by a contract with the University of California to obtain whatever CSU does not own), it found that resource availability alone was not enough: the library also wanted delivery speed much greater than traditional interlending could provide. In their paper that rationalizes and describes the Chico experience, Carolyn Dusenbury and William Post write, "We needed a strategy that did not depend on the kindness of strangers or the good will of the library community. We needed to get quick and ready access to a research collection."[13] Appending telefacsimile to the traditional ILL process was not especially appealing because, while it increased delivery speed, it did nothing to reduce the supplying library's processing time. Similarly, commercial document services were not attractive because of the many different vendors needed to supply the depth and breadth of coverage the library required. Further, many vendors' charges for faxed documents seemed prohibitive.

So Chico decided to define the sort of collection that would make an ideal extension of its own. Interested in extending research capability in all fields, it sought "a large, deep and broad collection . . . located in Northern California."[14] Berkeley seemed to fill the bill and showed interest in developing an article delivery service. Chico obtained about $20,000 to fund the program's first year by submitting a proposal to the campus lottery fund whose purpose is to underwrite demonstration projects that (when they prove successful) will subsequently be absorbed by the unit's regular operating budget. The money paid for telefacsimile machines for the two libraries' ILL offices and student staff at Berkeley who would fill Chico's requests. Berkeley contributed both the telecommunications charges and the supervision of the student.

The project's parameters were simple. A goal of twenty-four-hour turnaround time was established, for up to twenty-five transactions per week, not to exceed ten per day; a transaction was defined as an item of thirty-five or fewer pages. In 1990 Chico requested 587 articles from Berkeley, which filled all but 63 or 10.7 percent of them. The 524 fills came from 370 journals, so that 71 percent were requests for unique titles, and 29 percent represented titles for which multiple requests were made. The unit cost for each article was $10.16; this cost would have been reduced to less than $5 per article had Chico requested the full twenty-five articles for fifty-two weeks (a total of thirteen hundred per year). Comparing its costs to the minimum charge available at the time through commercial services ($17.75 for a faxed document), Chico was pleased. Median turnaround time was an acceptable three days, and the library enjoyed "one stop shopping," rather than dealing with a confusing array of commercial document vendors. The total cost of the program in 1990–91 was $6,068.

Another factor confirmed Chico's decision to "subscribe" to Berkeley's collections. To the library's surprise, the median publication year for journal articles supplied through the program was 1985, and the average was 1981.6 (presumably, June or July of that year), indicating that few if any document vendors could have provided much of what Chico obtained from Berkeley. One quarter of the requests came from undergraduates, not surprising considering the impact of CD-ROM journal indexes; the average article was a relatively brief 8.5 pages, a figure probably affected by undergraduate volume. Dusenbury and Post sum up Chico's program (which continues to flourish) in this way:

> Is this everyone's solution? Probably not. Research libraries, by definition, will continue to purchase relatively broad and deep comprehensive collections. Research libraries cannot rely on another single collection to fill their extended needs, so the ability to borrow from many collections, or a selected group of collections, will continue. For small and medium sized institutions with research mandates or desires that their libraries are not funded to meet, an agreement to cover the costs of using a larger collection on a regular basis is certainly feasible.[15]

James Madison University (JMU), with the University of Virginia (UVA) and Virginia Polytechnic Institute (Virginia Tech)

The *New York Times* described Document Express (three Virginia universities' article delivery project) as "a new joint program in which students and faculty members obtain journal articles from one another's libraries by way of overnight facsimile."[16] Conceived at James Madison University (JMU) and patterned on the Chico-Berkeley program described above, Document Express debuted on September 1, 1991; JMU has borne the project's entire budget ($43,115 in the first year), believing as it does that its students and faculty members make the greatest use of the service. Indeed, early in the project JMU's library was logging around sixty requests a day, to Virginia Tech's and UVA's average of thirty each. JMU and Virginia Tech each make good use of UVA's general collections, while Virginia Tech's science and technical collections are of great interest to the other two institutions.

The project had its genesis in a familiar setting: a faculty panel chaired by JMU's librarian was invited to develop a list of journals to which the library should provide access. In an interesting twist, the panel was also asked to recommend how the library might acquire these titles. The use of commercial document suppliers was rejected, because of the University's concern about spending large sums of money outside the state of Virginia. When the panel's list (four hundred journals JMU did not own and one hundred it wished to cancel) was completed, library staff checked to see what other libraries owned them. Between them, UVA and Virginia Tech held 435 titles, indicating that a three-way arrangement would largely solve JMU's problem; Document Express was begun.

The project's first-year budget included three telefacsimile machines (high-end equipment with electronic memory), paper and other supplies, and the salaries of students who staff the project; because start-up costs were factored in, during the first year an article cost $12.68; the projected second-year cost-per-document is $7.88. The libraries use the OCLC ILL subsystem to send requests to one another; articles are faxed, and books are sent by UPS. While there is no shared catalog, the three have access to each other's holdings through OCLC and also work from printed lists of serials and holdings. JMU's librarian estimates that the subscription costs for the five hundred journals that form the project's core are around $123,000. This makes the service seem very cost-effective.[17]

Loyola Marymount University, with the University of California at Los Angeles (UCLA)

Loyola Marymount is a small Jesuit institution about ten miles from UCLA. Not long ago Loyola used $50,000 to purchase a "library car" (painted on the vehicle in large letters), employ a driver, and establish a fee-based borrowing program with the larger institution, to whose "friends" group it pays an annual flat fee of $4,000. The agreement provides for book loans, with limits of twenty books per trip and three trips per week.

When a faculty member requests a book Loyola does not own, first the ILL unit asks reference staff to check the UCLA catalog. The courier drives to UCLA where he or she retrieves and withdraws books that faculty want; all materials are charged to Loyola's library director, who also receives any fine notices; as a result of this arrangement, Loyola's interlending volume has dropped 50 to 60 percent. When the car is not being used for resource sharing with UCLA, library staff use it for errands such as picking up gifts of materials.

For several reasons, journals are not covered by the program. UCLA is concerned about copyright compliance: unintentionally, Loyola's courier could make too many copies from certain journals. And, managing photocopying costs might be difficult for the host library. UCLA is considering a commercial document delivery service for journal articles, in which Loyola could perhaps participate.

The UCLA library is an open one; Loyola's faculty may visit it and borrow free of charge or make photocopies at the same nominal cost UCLA readers pay. However, even though the drive is a short one, parking is difficult; under the present resource sharing program, Loyola's faculty are making much greater use of UCLA's collections than ever before. For its part, UCLA likes the idea of serving the "single institutional borrower," versus a number of individual Loyola readers. After the first six months, Loyola faculty were pleased, and UCLA reported no noticeable negative impact on its services or collections. Presumably, it also enjoyed the $4,000.

University of Southern California (USC) Electronic Library Consortium

USC says that, through the Electronic Library Consortium, it has "accepted a community responsibility to assist smaller academic institutions through access to our collections." The consortium's chief goal is to give faculty at small, neighboring liberal arts colleges access to research materials. Fewer than a dozen colleges belong, and there is a "nominal" annual membership fee, which gives them access to USC's online catalog and other electronic databases. After locating wanted materials in USC's catalog, librarians in participating institutions submit requests to USC Doheny Express for delivery.[18]

Reciprocal Reading and Borrowing

In these examples, readers affiliated with member institutions enjoy reciprocal on-site access to the collections of other participants. In some cases fees are paid, in others access is gratis. Other examples of reciprocal borrowing are described above (TRLN (Shared Catalogs); The University of Michigan (UM) and Michigan State University (MSU) (The Miniature Consortium); and below (LIBRAS (College and University Libraries); and the Search and Delivery Project (Multitype Library Systems)).

Bentley College, with Brandeis University and the Massachusetts Institute of Technology (MIT)

Bentley College is a sixty-five-hundred-student school with five masters programs in business and related subjects. Recently it purchased access to the libraries of MIT and Brandeis for faculty and graduate students. Bentley pays approximately $250 per year for each borrowing card, and views the program as a "safety valve" for readers frustrated with the limited resources of a small library (190,000 volumes), as well as a way to alleviate some of the pressures on interlibrary loan.

Brandeis (where Bentley purchased four cards) is a ten-minute drive, and MIT (two cards) is a half-hour away by car. At MIT, Bentley paid the local "flat rate" for borrowing cards; at Brandeis, a price was negotiated between the two library directors. Funding for the cards was taken from the materials budget. The cards are monitored in the director's office, where interested faculty and graduate students go to "check out" a card and sign a form indicating which card number they have and how long they plan to keep it (cards are typically lent for one week).

There are no limits on the number of books faculty and graduate students may borrow, and readers return books and pay fines themselves. Evaluation of the program will be informal, chiefly faculty feedback. Bentley and Brandeis also engage in a reciprocal interlending program, but Bentley pays a fee on the rare occasion that it borrows from MIT.

WILL (Walk-In InterLibrary Loan) (Massachusetts)

The twenty-nine Massachusetts Public Higher Education Libraries sponsor WILL—Walk-In InterLibrary Loan—a program that permits all faculty, staff, and students affiliated with member institutions to borrow at no charge from other participants. A reader presents a validated identification card from his or her local campus and agrees to follow the host library's policies. Each library is responsible for its own readers' delinquencies and lost materials. In the last two years, WILL has averaged 725 to 750 loans each year. Readers are usually students who live within a five- to ten-mile radius of the host library, and most borrowing takes place on weekends and holidays.

College and University Libraries

Years ago, university and research libraries began joining together for resource sharing; systems like the Research Libraries Group and the Association of Research Libraries are among the best-known cooperative arrangements in the nation. Today, other academic libraries whose size, mission, or governance is similar are succeeding in resource sharing, despite the absence of a shared catalog or even geographic proximity. This section describes both a successful statewide and local system, as well as a loosely federated library network whose members are scattered from coast to coast; in most cases, members also belong to larger systems, such as OCLC, the Research Libraries Group, and state or regional programs.

Network of Alabama Academic Libraries (NAAL)

Founded in 1984, the Network of Alabama Academic Libraries is a consortium of twenty colleges and universities, five research institutions not affiliated with educational institutions, and the Alabama Commission of Higher Education; by all accounts, it is one of the country's most successful academic library systems. The NAAL Resource Sharing Program began in 1985; members agree to waive all fees, give priority to each other's interlending requests, make their resources available to other members on the same basis as to their own readers, use telefacsimile to transmit journal articles, and ship books by UPS. The network funds the UPS service, telefacsimile maintenance contracts, and the monthly telephone charge for each fax line (members pay their own long-distance charges).

Net lenders are reimbursed for their net loans (in 1991, $7.50 per transaction). In a unique approach to encouraging interlending, NAAL also reimburses every library for its share of total ILL traffic, both borrowing and lending. Each library belongs to OCLC/SOLINET, and many use DOCLINE as well; OCLC and DOCLINE reports are the bases for determining reimbursements.[19]

NAAL ILL traffic (lending and borrowing) increased from 9,401 transactions in 1985–86 to 38,364 in 1990–91, some 400 percent. In 1990–91 expenditures included $50,000 for reimbursements, $17,297 for telefacsimile, and $38,339 for UPS.[20] An impressive 62.2 percent of all borrowed items were obtained from other NAAL libraries, and 85.5 percent of the remaining fills came from other SOLINET libraries. The cooperative's Statewide Collection Development Program has helped improve the NAAL fill rate. Each year members document deficiencies in a given subject area that supports graduate studies; between 1985 and 1991 the network awarded $2.6 million to address these inadequacies and help raise the general rate of acquisition.[21]

The Resource Sharing Program is largely supported with state money; LSCA funds reimburse members for lending to public libraries. In 1988 NAAL received a Title II-D grant to establish its telefacsimile network, and in 1989 to extend the network to branch libraries.[22] Telefacsimile improved the network's average request-to-receipt time from 9 days to 5.7 days. The addition of daily UPS service in 1989 for everything that could not be transmitted by telefacsimile reduced turnaround time further, to 5 days, despite the great increase in ILL volume.[23]

LIBRAS (Illinois)

LIBRAS (capitalized, though not an acronym) is a consortium of seventeen smaller college libraries in the Chicago suburbs. Each has its holdings in OCLC and many, though not all, use the same online catalog and circulation system (ILLINET Online, in which a number of non-LIBRAS libraries also participate). As might be expected, libraries participating in the shared catalog tend to borrow more from one another than from other LIBRAS members.

LIBRAS does not have or need its own delivery service, because each member has access to the Illinois statewide delivery system, which provides materials four days a week. Most LIBRAS members use telefacsimile to transmit articles; no charge is made, regardless of the number of pages. There is no standard request form; instead, readers complete local forms that are faxed to other LIBRAS libraries. Very little use is made of the OCLC ILL subsystem. Lenders promise to "initiate processing of requests within one working day of receipt and . . . complete the transaction within three working days of receipt."[24]

Reciprocal borrowing is another important component of LIBRAS; any student or faculty member with a valid local campus ID can borrow from another LIBRAS library; similarly, materials may be returned to any LIBRAS site. LIBRAS and another library cooperative, the Suburban Library System, jointly produce a union list of serials, which is updated annually. One LIBRAS member, Concordia University, receives all ERIC documents; in exchange for a fiche-to-fiche copier (provided by LIBRAS) and a modest charge of $.10 per exposure, it supplies copies of ERIC materials to all other members. In the 1990–91 academic year, Concordia supplied more than one thousand ERIC documents to other LIBRAS libraries.

The Oberlin Group

The Oberlin Group is made up of some seventy libraries of selective liberal arts colleges, nationwide. At the beginning of the 1991–92 academic year, the group established a cooperative interlending arrangement; this included establishing itself as a GAC (Group Access Capability) on OCLC (for details on this program, see chapter 5) and developing a union list of serials. All participants provide free loans and photocopies to each other; however, because group members are scattered across the country, each first exhausts its local and regional cooperative arrangements, then approaches another Oberlin Group library as a second or third step in seeking to borrow. There are no agreements for priority shipping, but members agree to handle each other's requests with dispatch; when partners both have telefacsimile capability, this is used.

Multitype Library Systems

Academic libraries have also found happiness in multitype library systems where provisions are made for effective resource sharing. Such systems can be particularly useful in less densely populated parts of the country. This section describes multistate, state, and regional multitype arrangements that succeed.

MINITEX (Minnesota, North Dakota, and South Dakota)[25]

MINITEX is a publicly supported network of more than two hundred academic, state agency, and other special libraries working cooperatively in resource sharing. During 1990–91, MINITEX received and processed more than 270,000 interlending requests from libraries in its three-state region (Minnesota, North Dakota, and South Dakota), with an 85 percent fill rate; 61 percent of the requests were filled within three working days, 85 percent within five working days. MINITEX has a valuable reciprocal arrangement with Wisconsin Library Services (WILS, described immediately below) to which it turns for requests that cannot be filled within the consortium.

Participants send loan requests to the MINITEX office electronically, by courier, or through the U.S. mail. There, central staff retrieve items from the University of Minnesota at Twin Cities libraries, the Minneapolis Public Library, or the Minnesota State Board of Health. Requests that cannot be filled from these sources are referred to other institutions in the cooperative, using the Minnesota Union List of Serials (MULS), OCLC, and local automated library systems as location finders. WILS is the court of next resort when regional sources fail. MINITEX operates a ground-based delivery system among sixty-five of its member libraries, located in cities throughout the region.

In the spring of 1992 MINITEX began to transmit documents through the Internet, using Ariel scanning technology. In addition to the MINITEX central office, the libraries at St. Cloud State University, the University of Minnesota at Twin Cities, the University of Minnesota at Duluth, and the Minnesota State University/PALS office have the same type workstation and communications capability. MINITEX has submitted a Title II-D grant proposal, "Strengthening Higher Education Programs through Just-In-Time Information Delivery"; if successful, it will place forty Ariel workstations in libraries in its region.

Wisconsin Library Services (WILS)

Wisconsin Library Services (WILS) is a multitype membership organization that promotes and supports resource sharing in the state of Wisconsin. In many ways, it acts to libraries in Wisconsin as the British Library Document Supply Centre (BLDSC) acts to libraries in the United Kingdom. Every academic library in the state belongs to WILS, and each pays an annual fee based on its projected volume of ILL requests. During the 1991–92 academic year, WILS charged $3.70 for each fill from the collections of the University of Wisconsin at Madison, and an additional $4 for requests that were referred elsewhere. "Elsewhere" includes other libraries, University Microfilms (UMI), and the BLDSC. Considering the prices charged by the last two suppliers, $7.70 is quite a good rate for the borrower to pay. WILS operates an electronic ILL bulletin board, and about half its members transmit borrowing requests in this way. The remainder use OCLC's ILL subsystem or telefacsimile. The system receives some eighty-five thousand requests annually, well over half of them from academic libraries. In 1990–91 the fill rate was over 90 percent.

Wisconsin libraries also borrow from and lend to each other directly, and WILS facilitates and monitors this program (there is concern that no one library be inundated with requests). First libraries are to verify that the desired item is unavailable from the University of Wisconsin at Madison; when Madison does not own it, the requester can go directly to any library in the state that can supply the item. Supplying libraries receive reimbursement (generally in the form of WILS "credits") for requests they fill for other institutions.

The State of North Carolina

North Carolina was the second state in the union to adopt a statewide GAC (Group Access Capability) through OCLC (for details on this program, see chapter 5). The GAC approach was judged to be the cheapest method of creating a statewide union catalog and union list of serials. In a county where unemployment was particularly high and jobs were needed, LSCA monies were used to fund a massive retrospective conversion project for the catalog records of public libraries throughout the state; similarly, the bibliographic records of academic libraries were converted in a special state-run workshop for mentally impaired adults.

In five years, North Carolina's OCLC database has grown from between five and six million records to thirteen million records. The retrocon staff were so efficient that, at a certain juncture, the state was scrambling to get more libraries to volunteer their shelf lists to keep the projects going. Unlike New York and some other states, North Carolina did not prioritize collections for retrospective conversion: rather, the emphasis was on getting everyone's records into OCLC as quickly as possible.

North Carolina's GAC goes beyond state boundaries; libraries can also see the holdings of other institutions in the Southeast. No "protections" for large libraries like the University of North Carolina at Chapel Hill or North Carolina State University at Raleigh have been established, but Howard McGinn, the director of the State Library, believes that the state's relatively even distribution of state colleges and universities naturally protects the larger research libraries, since GAC selective users go first to the nearest academic institution, not the biggest. North Carolina, a state with a strong sense of "community," does not reimburse net lenders. A side benefit of the GAC project is that every library in North Carolina now has a PC with a modem and a fax machine, which it can use for many purposes.

Search and Delivery Project (Washington and Idaho)

This small cooperative is coordinated by the Interlibrary Loan Department at Washington State University (WSU); its members include the Whitman County (Washington) Library System, the University of Idaho, Moscow-Latah County (Idaho) Library, and Neill Public Library (Washington). The Search and Delivery Project employs work-study students to search the WSU collections, locate materials wanted by the other participants, and deliver them to the requesting library. The costs of the "shuttle" service are totalled annually, and each member pays a share based on its percentage of total use. In one recent year, the total costs divided among the participants were $5,200; the fill rate was 70 percent, and same-week delivery was usual.[26]

Search and Delivery is now more than ten years old. Its modest costs include fuel (student messengers drive their own vehicles) and some part of the project supervisor's salary. Requests are sent through OCLC; the University of Idaho now includes WSU's holdings in its catalog and submits twenty to sixty requests a day through the Search and Delivery Project. Some of the participating libraries are only a few blocks away from WSU; materials are delivered daily to these sites. Other members, at distances of between twenty-two and thirty-six miles, round-trip, receive books and journal articles twice a week. Affiliates of member institutions are also free to borrow in person from WSU.

Notes

1. Blair, "Library," 71–76.
2. "Multitype Library Database Completed in Ohio," *Library Hotline* 21 (Feb. 3, 1992): 3.
3. William H. Mischo, and others, "University of Illinois at Urbana-Champaign," in *Campus Strategies for Libraries and Electronic Information*, ed. Caroline Arms, EDUCOM Strategies Series on Information Technology (Bedford, Mass.: Digital Press, 1990), 121.
4. David Bretthauer, "System Design for the Consortium Environment," *LITA Newsletter* 12 (Fall 1991): 21.
5. Nitecki, "Impact," 8.
6. "Defining the New Academic Library," *EDU Magazine*, no. 57 (Winter 1992): 3.
7. Center for Research Libraries, "User Membership in the Center for Research Libraries," Descriptive material, Apr. 10, 1991, 1.
8. Center for Research Libraries, *Handbook* (Chicago: CRL, 1990); "Associate Membership in the Center for Research Libraries," Descriptive material, Apr. 25, 1991; "Lending/Photocopy Service Policies (Effective 1 July 1990)," Memorandum from the Circulation Department to non-CRL member institutions June 26, 1990.
9. Much of this information comes from Phillips's "IRIS."
10. Carol MacDonald, "Services to Remote Users: Realities and Possibilities: REGLIN Consortium," Paper presented before program session no. 38, NOTIS Users' Group Meeting, Oct. 2, 1991, Chicago, Ill., 7.
11. Carol L. Adams and Marion Lake, "Stand and Deliver: An Assessment of the FAX Link, University of Alberta/University of Regina, September 1988-February 1989: Report to the University Librarian," Unpublished report, Main Library, University of Regina, Mar. 1989.
12. Dusenbury and Post, "Subscribing," 2.
13. Ibid., 5.
14. Ibid., 6.
15. Ibid., 11–12.
16. "Libraries Share Scholarly Work, Overnight, by Fax," *New York Times*, Oct. 27, 1991, "Campus Life," 39–40.
17. Mary Ann Chappell, "Meeting Undergraduate Literature Needs with ILL/Document Delivery," *Serials Review* 19, no. 1 (1993): 81–86, 94.

18. Margaret L. Johnson, Peter Lyman, and Philip Tompkins, "University of Southern California," in *Campus Strategies on Libraries and Electronic Information*, ed. Caroline Arms, EDUCOM Strategies Series on Information Technology (Bedford, Mass.: Digital Press, 1990), 188.
19. Medina, "Improving," 7–14.
20. "Network of Alabama Academic Libraries Resource Sharing Program," Chart, 1992.
21. Medina, "Tracking," 1–2.
22. Sue O. Medina, "Effective Governance in a State Academic Network: The Experience of the Network of Alabama Academic Libraries," *Library Administration & Management* 6 (Winter 1992): 15–20.
23. Medina, "Improving," 7–14.
24. LIBRAS Inc., "LIBRAS Administrative Handbook," 8–5.
25. Much of this information is drawn from MINITEX Library Information Network, "1991 Annual Report."
26. Gail P. Warner, "The Interlibrary Loan Fee Dilemma," *Collection Building* 8, no. 1 (1986): 33–34.

BIBLIOGRAPHY

Articles

Allen, Bryce, and Kathy Corley. "Information Brokers in Illinois Academic Libraries." *Illinois Libraries* 72 (Nov. 1990): 596–600.

American Library Association. Reference and Adult Services Division. Interlibrary Loan Committee. "Guidelines and Procedures for Telefacsimile Transmission of Interlibrary Loan Requests." *RQ* 30 (Winter 1990): 266–67.

———. Subcommittee on Continuing Education and Training. Barbara Beaton, chair, "Interlibrary Loan Training and Continuing Education Model Statement of Objectives." *RQ* 31 (Winter 1991): 177–84.

Anand, Havelin. "Interlibrary Loan and Document Delivery Using Telefacsimile Transmission: Part I. Preliminary Study." *Electronic Library* 5 (Feb. 1987): 28–33.

———. "Interlibrary Loan and Document Delivery Using Telefacsimile Transmission: Part II. Telefacsimile Project." *Electronic Library* 5 (Apr. 1987): 100–107.

Ardis, Susan B., and Karen S. Croneis. "Document Delivery, Cost Containment and Serial Ownership." *College & Research Libraries News* 48 (Nov. 1987): 624–27.

Arms, William, and Thomas J. Michalak. "Carnegie Mellon University." In *Campus Strategies for Libraries and Electronic Information*, edited by Caroline Arms, 243–73. EDUCOM Strategies Series on Information Technology. Bedford, Mass.: Digital Press, 1990.

Association of College and Research Libraries. Library Access Task Force. "ACRL Guidelines for the Preparation of Policies on Library Access." *College & Research Libraries News* 51 (June 1990): 548–56.

Atkinson, Hugh C. "Atkinson on Networks." *American Libraries* 18 (June 1987): 432–39.

———. "Policies and Controversies." In *Prospects for Improving Document Delivery: Minutes of the 101st Meeting, October 13–14, Arlington, Virginia*, edited by Nicola Daval, 16–21. Washington, D.C.: ARL, 1983.

"Auto-Graphics Introduces New Version of Electronic ILL Module." *Library Hi Tech News*, no. 90 (Mar. 1992): 7.

Bailey, Charles W. "Network-Based Electronic Serials." *Information Technology and Libraries* 11 (Mar. 1992): 29–35.

Battin, Patricia. "Research Libraries in the Network Environment." *Journal of Academic Librarianship* 6 (May 1980): 68–73.

Belanger, David. "Interlibrary Loan via Electronic Mail: Improving the Process." *Wilson Library Bulletin* 63 (Mar. 1989): 62–63.

Bell, Jo Ann, and Susan Speer. "Bibliographic Verification for Interlibrary Loan: Is it Necessary?" *College & Research Libraries* 49 (Nov. 1988): 494–500.

Billings, Harold. "The Bionic Library." *Library Journal* 116 (Oct. 15, 1991): 38–42.

Blair, Joan. "The Library in the Information Revolution." *Library Administration & Management* 6 (Spring 1992): 71–76.

Bleeker, Ans, and others. "Analysis of External and Internal Interlibrary Loan Requests: Aid in Collection Management." *Bulletin of the Medical Library Association* 78 (Oct. 1990): 345–52.

Bonham, Miriam. "Library Services through Electronic Mail." *College & Research Libraries News* 48 (Oct. 1987): 537–38.

Bonk, Sharon. "Interlibrary Loan and Document Delivery in the United Kingdom." *RQ* 30 (Winter 1990): 230–40.

Boss, Richard W. "The Procurement of Library Automated Systems." *Library Technology Reports* 26 (Sept.-Oct. 1990): 719–25.

Boss, Richard W., and Hal Espo. "The Use of Telefacsimile in Libraries." *Library Hi Tech* 5 (Spring 1987): 33–42.

Boss, Richard W., and Judy McQueen. "Interlibrary Document Delivery: The Options." In *Prospects for Improving Document Delivery: Minutes of the 101st Meeting, October 13–14, Arlington, Virginia*, edited by Nicola Daval, 112–17. Washington, D.C.: ARL, 1983.

———. "Interlibrary Document Delivery: The Options." In *Crossroads: Proceedings of the First National Conference of the Library and Information Technology Association, September 17–21, 1983, Baltimore, Maryland*, edited by Michael Gorman, 137–41. Library and Information Technology Series, no. 1. Chicago: American Library Association, 1984.

Boucher, Virginia. "The Interlibrary Loan Librarian." *Interlending and Document Supply* 17 (Jan. 1989): 11–15.

Boyer, Janice S., and John Reidelbach. "Document Delivery Pilot Project at UNO." *Nebraska Library Association Quarterly* 21 (Spring 1990): 7.

Brander, Linda. "Montana Faxnet Project." *Library Hi Tech* 5 (Summer 1987): 70–75.

Bretthauer, David. "System Design for the Consortium Environment." *LITA Newsletter* 12 (Fall 1991): 20–22.

Britten, William A., and Judith D. Webster. "Comparing Characteristics of Highly Circulated Titles for Demand-Driven Collection Development." *College & Research Libraries* 53 (May 1992): 239–48.

Brown, Barbara. "Interlibrary Loan in the Research Libraries Group." In *Prospects for Improving Document Delivery: Minutes of the 101st Meeting, October 13–14, Arlington, Virginia*, edited by Nicola Daval, 90–92. Washington, D.C.: ARL, 1983.

Brown, Steven A. "Telefacsimile in Libraries: New Deal in the 1980s." *Library Trends* 37 (Winter 1989): 343–56.

Budd, John M. "Interlibrary Loan Service: A Study of Turnaround Time." *RQ* 26 (Fall 1986): 75–80.

———. "It's Not the Principle, It's the Money of the Thing." *Journal of Academic Librarianship* 15 (Sept. 1989): 218–22.

Burroughs, Carol. "Who Can Stop the Lemmings? Fees for Resource Sharing: An Overview and an Option." *PNLA Quarterly* 52 (Spring 1988): 5–7.

Casorso, Tracy M. "The North Carolina State University Libraries and the National Agricultural Library Joint Project on Transmission of Digitized Text: Improving Access to Agricultural Information." *Reference Services Review* 19 (Spring 1991): 15–22.

———. "Research Materials: Now Only Keystrokes Away." *College & Research Libraries News* 53 (Feb. 1992): 128.

Cawkell, A. E. "Progress in Documentation: Electronic Document Delivery Systems." *Journal of Documentation* 47 (Mar. 1991): 41–73.

Chang, Amy. "Computerizing Communication for Interlibrary Loan." *College & Research Libraries News* 50 (Dec. 1989): 992–94.

———. "Developing an Electronic Information Service in an Academic Library." *College & Research Libraries News* 52 (Apr. 1991): 237–39.

———. "Interlibrary Loan Automation: An Implementation Guide." *Library Software Review* 8 (Mar.-Apr. 1989): 58–63.

Chappell, Mary Ann. "Meeting Undergraduate Literature Needs with ILL/Document Delivery." *Serials Review* 19, no. 1 (1993): 81–86, 94.

Clark, Marsha S. "Fees for Library and Information Services in Libraries: A Bibliography." *Collection Building* 8, no. 1 (1986): 57–61.

Coffman, Steve, and Helen Josephine. "Doing It for Money." *Library Journal* 116 (Oct. 15, 1991): 32–36.

Cohen, David. "A National Networked Solution to Improving Access to Journal Articles." *Journal of Academic Librarianship.* 15 (May 1989): 79–82.

Comeaux, Elizabeth A., and Susan Wilcox. "Automating Interlibrary Loan Statistics." *Technical Services Quarterly* 8, no. 3 (1991): 35–57.

"ContentsFirst, ArticleFirst Debut September 14." *OCLC Reference News,* no. 12 (Sept.-Oct. 1992): 1, 5.

Dalrymple, Prudence W., and others. "Measuring Statewide Interlibrary Loan among Multitype Libraries: A Testing of Data Collection Approaches." *RQ* 30 (Summer 1991): 534–47.

Davis, Erik. "CYBERLIBRARIES: Do Librarians Dream of Electric Books?" *Lingua Franca* 2 (Feb.-Mar. 1992): 47–51.

Deekle, Peter. "Document Delivery Comes of Age in Pennsylvania." *Wilson Library Bulletin* 65 (Oct. 1990): 31–33.

"Defining the New Academic Library." *EDU Magazine,* no. 57 (Winter 1992): 2–8.

De Gennaro, Richard. "From Monopoly to Competition: The Changing Library Network Scene." *Library Journal* 104 (June 1, 1979): 1215–17.

———. "The Libraries in Transition." *University of Pennsylvania Almanac* (Feb. 10, 1976): 305.

———. "Resource Sharing in a Network Environment." *Library Journal* 105 (Feb. 1, 1980): 353–55.

Denton, Barbara. "E-Mail Delivery of Search Results via the Internet." *Online* 16 (Mar. 1992): 50.

Dickson, Stephen P., and Virginia Boucher. "A Methodology for Determining Costs of Interlibrary Lending." In *Research Access through New Technologies,* edited by Mary E. Jackson, 137–59. New York: AMS Press, 1990.

"Document Ordering Debuts on FirstSearch." *OCLC Newsletter,* no. 201 (Jan.-Feb. 1993): 28.

Dorsey, James. "What Federal Libraries Need to Know about Internet." *Fedlink Technical Notes* 10 (Apr. 1992): 3, 5–6, 8.

Dougherty, Richard M. "A Conceptual Framework for Organizing Resource Sharing and Shared Collection Development Programs." *Journal of Academic Librarianship* 14 (Nov. 1988): 287–91.

Dowd, Sheila T. "Library Cooperation: Methods, Models to Aid Information Access." *Journal of Library Administration* 12, no. 3 (1990): 63–81.

Downes, Robin. "Resource Sharing and New Information Technology—An Idea Whose Time Has Come." *Journal of Library Administration* 10, no. 1 (1989): 115–25.

Dutcher, Gale A. "DOCLINE: A National Automated Interlibrary Loan Request Routing and Referral System." *Information Technology and Libraries* 8 (Dec. 1989): 359–70.

Eichelberger, Susan. "Using dBase III for Interlibrary Loan Journal Request File." *Library Software Review* 6 (July-Aug. 1987): 178–79.

Eichhorn, Sara. "The Making of MELDOC." *College & Research Libraries News* 51 (May 1990): 441–44.

Epple, Margie, and Carol Paszamant. "Providing a Statewide Citation/Location Service in New Jersey." *College & Research Libraries News* 50 (Dec. 1989): 997–1000.

Everett, David. "Interlibrary Loan Fees: A Different Perspective." *Journal of Academic Librarianship* 12 (Sept. 1986): 232–33.

Finnigan, Georgia. "Review of Private Sector Involvement in Document Supply." In *Interlending and Document Supply: Proceedings of the First International Conference Held in London, November, 1988*, edited by Graham P. Cornish and Alison Gallico, 80–83. Boston Spa, Eng.: IFLA Office for International Lending, 1989.

Finnigan, Georgia, and Sue Rugge. "Document Delivery and the Experiences of Information Unlimited." *Online* 2 (Jan. 1978): 62–69.

Flanders, Bruce. "Interlibrary Loan in Kansas: A Low Cost Alternative to OCLC." *Wilson Library Bulletin* 61 (Mar. 1987): 31–34.

Forsythe, David N. "Acquisitions or Access: A Changing Pattern." *SOL: Messages from SUNY/OCLC Network* 4 (May-June 1991): 2.

Galvin, Thomas J., and Allen Kent. "Use of a University Library Collection: A Progress Report on the Pittsburgh Study." *Library Journal* 102 (Nov. 15, 1977): 2317–20.

Gherman, Paul M. "Vision and Reality: The Research Libraries and Networking." *Journal of Library Administration* 8, no. 3–4 (1987): 51–57.

Gherman, Paul M., and Lynn S. Cochrane. "Developing and Using Unit Costs: The Virginia Tech Experience." *Library Administration & Management* 3 (Spring 1989): 93–96.

Gillikin, David P. "Document Delivery from Full-Text Online Files: A Pilot Project." *Online* 14 (May 1990): 27–32.

Greenberg, Evelyn. "Book Express: Meaningful Access." *College & Research Libraries News* 48 (Oct. 1987): 539–40.

Grycz, Czeslaw Jan, ed. "Special Issue on Economic Models for Networked Information." *Serials Review* 18, no. 1–2 (1992).

Hardesty, Larry. "Use of Library Materials at a Small Liberal Arts College." *Library Research* 3 (Fall 1981): 261–82.

Hearty, John A., and Valerie K. Rohrbaugh. "Current State of Full Text Primary Information Online, with Recommendations for the Future." *Online Review* 13 (Apr. 1989): 135–40.

Heath, Fred M. "An Interview with Thomas J. Michalak." *Library Administration & Management* 6 (Spring 1992): 62–65.

———. "Library Cooperative Activity: Common Characteristics of Successful Efforts." In *Operations Handbook for the Small Academic Library*, edited by Gerard B. McCabe, 29–48. New York: Greenwood Press, 1989.

Henshaw, Ron. "Library to Library." *Wilson Library Bulletin* 60 (Sept. 1985): 54–55.

Hewitt, Joe A. "Interlibrary Cooperation." In *Academic Librarianship Yesterday, Today, and Tomorrow*, edited by Robert D. Stueart, 97–117. New York: Neal Schuman, 1982.

Hewitt, Joe A., and John S. Shipman. "Cooperative Collection Development among Research Libraries in the Age of Networking: Report of a Survey of ARL Libraries." In *Advances in Library Automation and Networking*, vol. 1, edited by Joe A. Hewitt, 189–232. Greenwich, Conn.: JAI Press, 1987.

Higginbotham, Barbra B. "Telefacsimile: The Issues and the Answers." *Journal of Interlibrary Loan & Information Supply* 1, no. 1 (1990): 67–86.

Holicky, Bernard H. "Collection Development vs. Resource Sharing: The View from the Small Academic Library." *Journal of Academic Librarianship* 10 (July 1984): 146–47.

Holton, Janet E. "Document Delivery Services in a Special Library: How to Get What You Haven't Got!" *Colorado Libraries* 16 (Dec. 1990): 36–37.

Hurd, Douglas P., and Robert E. Molyneux. "An Evaluation of Delivery Times and Costs of a Non-Library Document Delivery Service." In *Energies for Transition: Proceedings of the 4th National Conference of the Association of College and Research Libraries, Baltimore, Maryland, 1986*, edited by Danuta A. Nitecki, 182–85. Chicago: ACRL, 1986.

Jackson, Mary E. "Library to Library." *Wilson Library Bulletin* 63 (Apr. 1989): 88–89.

———. "Library to Library." *Wilson Library Bulletin* 64 (Dec. 1989): 89.

———. "Library to Library [Ariel]." *Wilson Library Bulletin* 65 (Apr. 1991): 84–87.

———. "Library to Library [Pennsylvania Interlibrary Loan Code]." *Wilson Library Bulletin* 63 (Dec. 1988): 84–85.

———. "Library to Library [Telefacsimile Agreements]." *Wilson Library Bulletin* 63 (June 1989): 94–95, 141.

———. "Trends in Resource Sharing." *Wilson Library Bulletin* 64 (Apr. 1990): 54–55, 128.

———. "Trends in Resource Sharing." *Wilson Library Bulletin* 64 (June 1990): 99–100.

Johnson, Margaret L., Peter Lyman, and Philip Tompkins. "University of Southern California." In *Campus Strategies for Libraries and Electronic Information*, edited by Caroline Arms, 176–92. EDUCOM Strategies Series on Information Technology. Bedford, Mass.: Digital Press, 1990.

Keder, Jan. "Using the Campus Network for Interlibrary Loan and Book Orders." *Library Software Review* 8 (Sept.-Oct. 1989): 250–52.

Kelsey Ann L., and John M. Cohn. "The Impact of Automation on Interlibrary Loan: One College Library's Experience." *Journal of Academic Librarianship* 13 (July 1987): 163–66.

Kennedy, Sue. "The Role of Commercial Document Delivery Services in Interlibrary Loan." *Interlending and Document Supply* 15 (July 1987): 67–73.

———. "The Role of Commercial Document Delivery Services in Interlibrary Loan." In *Research Access through New Technology*, edited by Mary E. Jackson, 66–81. New York: AMS Press, 1989.

Kent, Allen. "The Goals of Resource Sharing in Libraries." In *Library Resource Sharing: Proceedings of the 1976 Conference on Resource Sharing in Libraries, Pittsburgh, Pennsylvania*, edited by Allen Kent and Thomas J. Galvin, 15–32. New York: Marcel Dekker, 1977.

Kibbey, Mark, and Nancy H. Evans. "The Network Is the Library." *EDUCOM Review* 24 (Fall 1989): 15–20.

Kjaer, Kathryn. "Current Access to Scientific Journals: An Alternative Strategy." *Colorado Libraries* 16 (Mar. 1990): 20–22.

Lahmon, Jo Ann. "Using Interlibrary Loan Data in Collection Development." *OCLC Micro* 7 (Oct. 1991): 19–22.

"Late Bulletins." *Library Journal* 117 (Apr. 1, 1992): 15.

Lee, Joel M. "Telecommunications Applications." In *Information Technology: Design and Applications*, edited by Nancy D. Lane and Margaret E. Chisolm, 41–82. Boston: G. K. Hall, 1991.

"Libraries Share Scholarly Work, Overnight, by Fax." *New York Times*, Oct. 27, 1991, "Campus Life," 39–40.

Line, Maurice B. "Interlending and Document Supply in a Changing World." In *Interlending and Document Supply: Proceedings of the First International Conference Held in London, November, 1988*, edited by Graham P. Cornish and

Alison Gallico, 1–4. Boston Spa, Eng.: IFLA Office for International Lending, 1989.

———. "Measuring the Performance of Document Supply Systems." *Interlending and Document Supply* 16 (July 1988): 81–88.

———. "Universal Availability of Publications in an Electronic Age." *IATUL Quarterly* 3 (Dec. 1989): 214–33.

Lingle, Virginia A., and Dorothy L. Malcom. "Interlibrary Loan Management with Microcomputers: A Descriptive Comparison of Software." *Medical Reference Services Quarterly* 8 (Summer 1989): 41–64.

Lowry, Charles B. "Resource Sharing or Cost Shifting: The Unequal Burden of Cooperative Cataloging and ILL in Network." *College & Research Libraries* 51 (Jan. 1990): 11–19.

Lucker, Jay K. "Document Delivery and Research Libraries." In *Prospects for Improving Document Delivery: Minutes of the 101st Meeting, October 13–14, Arlington, Virginia*, edited by Nicola Daval, 83–88. Washington, D.C.: ARL, 1983.

———. "Electronic Journal Publishing and Libraries." In *Prospects for Improving Document Delivery: Minutes of the 101st Meeting, October 13–14, Arlington, Virginia*, edited by Nicola Daval, 11–15. Washington, D.C.: ARL, 1983.

Lynch, Clifford A. "The Development of Electronic Publishing and Digital Library Collections on the NREN." *Electronic Networking* 1 (Winter 1991): 6–21.

Lynch, Clifford A., and Cecilia M. Preston. "Internet Access to Information Resources." In *Annual Review of Information Science and Technology*, vol. 25, edited by Martha E. Williams, 263–312. Amsterdam: Elsevier, 1990.

MacDougall, A. F., H. Wheelhouse, and J. M. Wilson. "Academic Library Cooperation and Document Supply: Possibilities and Considerations of Cost-Effectiveness." *Journal of Librarianship* 21 (July 1989): 186–99.

Mackey, Terry. "Interlibrary Loan: An Acceptable Alternative to Purchase." *Wilson Library Bulletin* 63 (Jan. 1989): 54–56.

Martin, Noelene P. "Information Transfer, Scholarly Communication, and Interlibrary Loan: Priorities, Conflicts, and Organizational Imperatives." In *Research Access through New Technology*, edited by Mary E. Jackson, 1–21. New York: AMS Press, 1989.

Martin, Susan K. "Delivery Systems: Hurry Up and Wait." In *Online Catalogs, Online Reference: Converging Trends: Proceedings of a Library and Information Technology Association Preconference Institute, June 23–24, 1983, Los Angeles,* edited by Brian Aveney and Brett Butler, 165–77. Chicago: American Library Association, 1984.

———. "Technology and Cooperation: The Behaviors of Networking." *Library Journal* 112 (Oct. 1, 1987): 42–44.

McKay, Sharon C. "The Internet: Its Origins, Uses, and Future." *At Your Service*, no. 20 (Mar. 1992): 9–11.

Medina, Sue O. "Effective Governance in a State Academic Network: The Experience of the Network of Alabama Academic Libraries." *Library Administration & Management* 6 (Winter 1992): 15–20.

———. "Improving Document Delivery in a Statewide Network." *Journal of Interlibrary Loan & Information Supply* 2, no. 3 (1992): 7–14.

Metz, Paul, and Paul M. Gherman. "Serials Pricing and the Role of the Electronic Journal." *College & Research Libraries* 52 (July 1991): 315–27.

Michalak, Sarah C. "Visions for the Future on Resource Sharing." *PNLA Quarterly* 52 (Spring 1988): 3–4.

Miller, Connie, and Patricia Tegler. "An Analysis of Interlibrary Loan and Commercial Document Supply Performance." *Library Quarterly* 58 (Oct. 1988): 352–66.

Miller, Marilyn E., and Patricia R. Guyette. "Interlibrary Loan." In *Operations Handbook for the Small Academic Library*, edited by Gerard B. McCabe, 109–20. New York: Greenwood Press, 1989.

Mischo, William H., and others. "University of Illinois at Urbana-Champaign." In *Campus Strategies for Libraries and Electronic Information*, edited by Caroline Arms, 117–41. EDUCOM Strategies Series on Information Technology. Bedford, Mass.: Digital Press, 1990.

Mosher, Paul H., and Marcia Pankake. "A Guide to Coordinated and Cooperative Collection Development." *Library Resources & Technical Services* 27 (Oct.-Dec. 1983): 417–31.

Mulroy, Kathleen C., and Mary Page. "Who is NJQ and Why Do They Borrow So Much? A Library Network Success Story." *Journal of Interlibrary Loan & Information Supply* 2, no. 1 (1991): 9–24.

"Multitype Library Database Completed in Ohio." *Library Hotline* 21 (Feb. 3, 1992): 3.

Munn, Robert F. "Collection Development vs. Resource Sharing." *Journal of Academic Librarianship* 8 (Jan. 1983): 352–53.

———. "Cooperation Will Not Save Us." *Journal of Academic Librarianship* 12 (July 1986): 166–67.

National Commission on Libraries and Information Science. "The Role of Fees in Supporting Library and Information Services in Public and Academic Libraries." *Collection Building* 8, no. 1 (1986): 3–17.

Newsome, Karen L. "Changing Strategies: Interlibrary Loan in the 1990s." *Illinois Libraries* 72 (Nov. 1990): 636–39.

Nitecki, Danuta A. "Impact of an Online Circulation System on Interlibrary Services." *Special Libraries* 73 (Jan. 1982): 6–11.

———. "Online Interlibrary Loan Services: An Informal Comparison of Five Systems." *RQ* 21 (Fall 1981): 7–14.

Ochs, Mary, and Bill Fenwick. "Macintosh Management for Interlibrary Loan." *Library Software Review* 9 (Dec. 1990): 372–73.

Okerson, Ann. "The Electronic Journal: What, Whence, and When," *Public-Access Computer Systems Review* 2, no. 1 (1991): 5–24.

Pagell, Ruth A. "Primary FTDs for the End User: New Roles for the Information Professional." *Online Review* 13 (Apr. 1989): 143–54.

Palmour, Vernon E., and Nancy K. Roderer. "Library Resource Sharing through Networks." In *Annual Review of Information Science and Technology*, vol. 13, edited by Martha E. Williams, 147–77. White Plains, N.Y.: Knowledge Industry Pubs., 1978.

Parravano, Ellen A. "Use and Management of Multiple Bibliographic Utilities in an Interlibrary Loan Referral Operation." In *Research Access through New Technology*, edited by Mary E. Jackson, 22–46. New York: AMS Press, 1989.

Peguese, Charles. "Telefacsimile, the Pennsylvania Experience: A State Library's Perspective." In *Research Access through New Technology*, edited by Mary E. Jackson, 82–102. New York: AMS Press, 1989.

Peters, Paul E. "Networked Information Resources and Services: Next Steps." *CAUSE/EFFECT* 14 (Summer 1991): 27–29, 33–39.

Potter, William G. "Creative Automation Boosts ILL Rates." *American Libraries* 17 (Apr. 1986): 244–46.

———. "Readers in Search of Authors: The Changing Face of the Middleman." *Wilson Library Bulletin* 60 (Apr. 1986): 20–23.

Quint, Barbara. "Connect Time: Wars, Roses, and Standards." *Wilson Library Bulletin* 65 (Feb. 1991): 108–10.

———. "Connect Time: Where's Your Parachute?" *Wilson Library Bulletin* 66 (Apr. 1992): 85–86.

Racine, Drew. "Access to Full-Text Journal Articles: Some Practical Considerations." *Library Administration & Management* 6 (Spring 1992): 100–104.

Regazzi, John J. "Designing the Ei Reference Desk." In *National Online Meeting: Proceedings, 1990*, edited by Martha E. Williams, 345–47. Medford, N.J.: Learned Information, Inc., 1990.

Rogers, Michael. "Library Searching Powers Attract Private Firms." *Library Journal* 117 (Apr. 1, 1992): 36.

Rogers, Sharon J., and Charlene S. Hurt. "How Scholarly Communication Should Work in the 21st Century." *College & Research Libraries* 51 (Jan. 1990): 5–6, 8.

Roth, Gisela A. "Online Document Ordering Systems of Online Vendors." *Online Review* 6 (June 1982): 243–51.

Rottman, F. K. "To Buy or to Borrow: Studies of the Impact of Interlibrary Loan on Collection Development in the Academic Library." *Journal of Interlibrary Loan & Information Supply* 1, no. 3 (1991): 17–27.

Russell, Dorothy W. "Interlibrary Loan in a Network Environment: The Good News and the Bad News." *Special Libraries* 73 (Jan. 1982): 21–26.

Saffady, William. "Six Bibliographic Utilities: A Survey of Cataloging Support and Other Services." *Library Technology Reports* 24 (Nov.-Dec. 1988): 727–839.

Saldinger, Jeffrey. "Full Service Document Delivery: Our Likely Future." *Wilson Library Bulletin* 58 (May 1984): 639–42.

Savage, Lon. "The Journal of the International Academy of Hospitality Research." *Public-Access Computer Systems Review* 2, no. 1 (1991): 54–66.

Schmidt, Karen A. "Electronic Publishing and the Library." In *Crossroads: Proceedings of the First National Conference of the Library and Information Technology Association, September 17–21, 1983, Baltimore, Maryland*, edited by Michael Gorman, 181–88. Library Information and Technology Series, no. 1. Chicago: American Library Association, 1984.

Selth, Jeff, Nancy Koller, and Peter Briscoe. "The Use of Books within the Library." *College & Research Libraries* 53 (May 1992): 197–205.

Simpson, Donald B. "Library Consortia and Access to Information: Costs and Cost Justification." *Journal of Library Administration* 12, no. 3 (1990): 83–97.

Sloan, Bernard G. "Resource Sharing in Times of Retrenchment." *Library Administration & Management* 6 (Winter 1992): 26–28.

"Special Section on Network-Based Electronic Journals." *Public-Access Computer Systems Review* 2, no. 1 (1991). Contains eight articles about the e-journal, present and future. PACS-R is sent free of charge to participants of the Public Access Computer Systems Forum (PACS-L), a computer conference on BITNET. To join PACS-L, send an electronic mail message to LISTSERV@UHUPVM1 that says: SUBSCRIBE PACS-L First Name Last Name.

Stevens, Rolland E. "A Study of Interlibrary Loan." *College & Research Libraries* 35 (Sept. 1974): 336–43.

Stevenson, Marsha J. "Design Options for an On-Campus Document Delivery Program." *College & Research Libraries News* 51 (May 1990): 437–40.

"Subscription Pricing for FirstSearch," *OCLC Reference News*, no. 13 (Nov.-Dec. 1992): 1–2.

Sweetland, James H., and Darlene E. Weingand. "Interlibrary Loan Transaction Fees in a Major Research Library: They Don't Stop the Borrowers." *Library and Information Science Research* 12, no. 1 (1990): 87–101.

Thompson, James C. "Journal Costs: Perception and Reality in the Dialogue." *College & Research Libraries* 49 (Nov. 1988): 481–82.

Turner, Fay. "The Interlibrary Loan Protocol: An OSI Solution to ILL Messaging." *Library Hi Tech* 8, no. 4 (1990): 73–82.

Tuttle, Marcia. "Journal Information: Ownership and Access." *Library Issues* 10 (Sept. 1989): 1–2.

"Value of METRO Membership 1987–88." *For Reference*, no. 187 (Sept. 1988): 3–5.

Waldhart, Thomas J. "The Growth of Interlibrary Loan among ARL University Libraries." *Journal of Academic Librarianship* 10 (Sept. 1984): 204–8.

———. "Patterns of Interlibrary Loan in the U.S.: A Review of Research." *Library and Information Science Research* 7 (July 1985): 209–29.

Walters, Edward M. "The Issues and Needs of a Local Library Consortium." *Journal of Library Administration* 8, nos. 3–4 (1987): 15–29.

Warner, Gail P. "The Interlibrary Loan Fee Dilemma." *Collection Building* 8, no. 1 (1986): 33–34.

Weber, Robert. "The Clouded Future of Electronic Publishing." *Publishers Weekly* 237 (June 29, 1990): 76, 78–80.

Wessling, Julie E. "Benefits from Automated ILL Borrowing Records: Use of ILLRKS in an Academic Library." *RQ* 29 (Winter 1989): 209–18.

White, Herbert S. "Interlibrary Loan: An Old Idea in a New Setting." *Library Journal* 112 (July 1987): 53–54.

Williams, Brian W., and Joan G. Hubbard. "Collection Management Uses of an Interlibrary Loan Database." In *The Best for the Patron: Proceedings of the Research Forum, Academic Library Section, Mountain Plains Library Association*, edited by Randy J. Olsen and Blaine H. Hall, 31–49. Emporia, Kans.: Emporia State University Press, 1990.

Williams, James G. "Performance Criteria and Evaluation for a Library Resource Sharing Network." In *Library Resource Sharing: Proceedings of the 1976 Conference on Resource Sharing in Libraries, Pittsburgh, Pennsylvania*, edited by Allen Kent and Thomas J. Galvin, 225–77. New York: Marcel Dekker, 1977.

Wilson, David. "Researchers Get Direct Access to Huge Data Base." *Chronicle of Higher Education* (Oct. 9, 1991): A24–A25, A28.

Wilson, Mark. "How to Set Up a Telefacsimile Network—The Pennsylvania Libraries' Experience." *Online* 12 (May 1988): 15–25.

Wood, James L. "Private Sector, Non-Library Document Delivery Services." In *Prospects for Improving Document Delivery: Minutes of the 101st Meeting, October 13–14, Arlington, Virginia*, edited by Nicola Daval, 93–95. Washington, D.C.: ARL, 1983.

Monographs

Adams, Roy. *Communication and Delivery Systems for Librarians*. Brookfield, Vt.: Gower, 1990.

Arms, Caroline, ed. *Campus Strategies for Libraries and Electronic Information*. EDUCOM Strategies Series on Information Technology. Bedford, Mass.: Digital Press, 1990.

Association of Research Libraries. *The Directory of Electronic Journals, Newsletters and Academic Discussion Lists*. 2nd ed. Washington, D.C.: ARL, Office of Scientific and Academic Publishing, 1992.

———. *Prospects for Improving Document Delivery: Minutes of the 101st Meeting, October 13–14, Arlington, Virginia*, edited by Nicola Daval. Washington, D.C.: ARL, 1983.

Boucher, Virginia. *Interlibrary Loan Practices Handbook*. Chicago: American Library Association, 1984.

Center for Research Libraries. *Handbook*. Chicago: CRL, 1990.

Coffman, Steve, ed. *The FISCAL Directory of Fee-Based Information Services in Libraries.* Norwalk, Calif.: FYI/County of Los Angeles Public Library, 1990.

Dewey, Patrick R. *FAX For Libraries.* Westport, Conn.: Meckler, 1990.

———. *101 Software Packages to Use in Your Library: Descriptions, Evaluations, and Practical Advice.* Chicago: American Library Association, 1987.

Directory of Online Databases, vol. 10, no. 1. New York: Cuadra/Elsevier, 1989.

Dougherty, Richard M., and Carol Hughes. *Preferred Futures for Libraries: A Summary of Six Workshops with University Provosts and Library Directors.* Mountain View, Calif.: Research Libraries Group, 1991.

Engle, June L., and Sue O. Medina, eds. *Issues in Cooperative Collection Development, SOLINET Resource Sharing and Networks Support Program, March 11, 1986.* Atlanta, Ga.: SOLINET, 1986.

Information Systems Consultants, Inc. *Document Delivery in the United States: A Report to the Council on Library Resources.* Washington, D.C.: ISCI, 1983.

Josephine, Helen. *Fee-Based Services in ARL Libraries.* SPEC Kit 157. Washington, D.C.: ARL, Office of Management Studies, 1989.

Kehoe, Brendan P. *Zen and the Art of the Internet: A Beginner's Guide.* Englewood Cliffs, N.J.: Prentice Hall, 1992.

Kent, Allen, and others. *Use Study of Library Materials: The University of Pittsburgh Study.* New York: Marcel Dekker, 1979.

Klinger, Marcia Henry, Linda Keenan, and Michael Reagan. *Search Sheets for OPACs on the Internet.* Westport, Conn.: Meckler, 1992.

Kranich, Karen. *Copyright Policies in ARL Libraries.* SPEC Kit 102. Washington, D.C.: ARL, Office of Management Studies, 1984.

Krol, Ed. *The Whole Internet User's Guide and Catalog.* Sebastapol, Calif.: O'Reilly & Associates, 1992.

Lancaster, F. W. *The Measurement and Evaluation of Library Services.* Washington, D.C.: Information Resources Press, 1977.

LaQuey, Tracy L. *User's Directory of Computer Networks.* Bedford, Mass: Digital Press, n.d.

Morgan, Bradley J., ed. *Information Industry Directory.* 11th ed. Detroit: Gale Research, 1991.

Morris, Leslie R., and Sandra C. Morris. *Inter-Library Loan Policies Directory.* 4th ed. New York: Neal-Schuman, 1991.

New York Metropolitan Reference and Research Library Agency. *The METRO Handbook and Directory of Members, 1991-92.* New York: METRO, 1991.

Patrick, Ruth J. *Guidelines for Library Cooperation: Development of Academic Library Consortia.* Santa Monica, Calif.: System Development Corporation, 1972.

Quarterman, John S. *The Matrix: Computer Networks and Conferencing Systems Worldwide.* Bedford, Mass.: Digital Press, 1990.

Tenopir, Carol, and Jung Soon Ro. *Full Text Databases.* New York: Greenwood Press, 1990.

Universal Serials and Book Exchange. *Your Guide to USBE Services.* Cleveland: USBE, 1990.

Weaver-Meyers, Pat, and others. *Interlibrary Loan in Academic and Research Libraries: Workload and Staffing.* ARL Occasional Pub. OP15. Washington, D.C.: ARL, 1989.

Young, Heartsill, ed. *The ALA Glossary of Library and Information Science.* Chicago: American Library Association, 1983.

Unpublished Material

Adams, Carol L., and Marion Lake. "Stand and Deliver: An Assessment of the FAX Link, University of Alberta/University of Regina, September 1988-February 1989: Report to the University Librarian." Unpublished report, Main Library, University of Regina (15 p. + appendices, Mar., 1989).

Allen, David B., and Johanna Alexander. "A Document Delivery Alternative for the CSB Library: Using Commercial Suppliers to Supplement Conventional Interlibrary Loan." 123 p. ED 275 330 (July 1986). Available from Educational Resources Information Center, 1600 Research Blvd., Rockville, MD 10850.

American Library Association. MARBI. "Providing Access to Online Information Resources: Discussion Paper No. 54." Unpublished paper (11 p., Nov. 22, 1991).

Bloomberg, Marty. "Serial Costs." Letter to William Aguilar (1 p. + 2 charts, Feb. 11, 1992).

Boss, Richard W., and Judy McQueen. "Document Delivery in the United States: A Report." 84 p. ED 244 626 (Oct. 1983). Available from Educational Resources Information Center, 1600 Research Blvd., Rockville, MD 10850.

Butler, John. "Collection Building vs. Document Delivery: An Evaluation of Methods to Provide NTIS Documents in an Academic Engineering Library." 82 p. ED 286 510 (June 1987).

Available from Educational Resources Information Center, 1600 Research Blvd., Rockville, MD 10850.

Center for Research Libraries. "Associate Membership in the Center for Research Libraries." Descriptive material (5 p., Apr. 25, 1991). Available from CRL, 6050 South Kenwood Ave., Chicago, IL 60637.

———. "Lending/Photocopy Service Policies (Effective 1 July 1990)." Memorandum from the Circulation Department to non-CRL member institutions (2 p., June 26, 1990). Available from CRL, 6050 South Kenwood Ave., Chicago, IL 60637.

———. "User Membership in the Center for Research Libraries." Descriptive material (3 p., Apr. 10, 1991). Available from CRL, 6050 South Kenwood Ave., Chicago, IL 60637.

Chambers, Joan. "Surveys on Interlibrary Loan." Letter to directors of ARL libraries (2 p., Feb. 20, 1992).

City University of New York. Consortium of Educational Communications and Technology. "By-Laws."

Columbia University Libraries. "Searching Library Catalogs over the Internet." Guide (4 p., Oct. 1991). Available from the Library Information Office, Butler Library, Columbia University, New York, NY 10028.

Currie, Jean. "Document Delivery: A Study of Different Sources." 10 p. ED 262 786 (May 1985). Available from Educational Resources Information Center, 1600 Research Blvd., Rockville, MD 10850.

Cutright, Patricia J., and Terry Edvalson. "Online Reference and Document Delivery Service Library Network." 37 p. ED 306 926 (Dec. 1988). Available from Educational Resources Information Center, 1600 Research Blvd., Rockville, MD 10850.

DIALOG Information Services, Inc. "DIALOG Full-Text Sources, Alpha List." Documentation (Aug. 1991).

Dusenbury, Carolyn, and William Post. "Subscribing to a Research Collection." Unpublished report (13 p., Apr. 1991). Available from Director of Library Services, Meriam Library, California State University, Chico, CA 95929-0295.

Faibisoff, Sylvia G. "A Study of Multitype Library Cooperatives: Including Developments in the Southwest Michigan Library Network, Michigan, California, and Texas, with References to New York State and Illinois." 96 p. ED 257 458 (July 1984). Available from Educational Resources Information Center, 1600 Research Blvd., Rockville, MD 10850.

"The FISCAL Primer." Packet. Available from Gelman Library Information Center, George Washington University, Gelman Library, 2130 H. St. N.W., Room B07, Washington, DC 20052.

Grycz, Czeslaw Jan. "Models for Networked Scholarly Information." Unpublished material (5 p., Mar. 18, 1991). Available from the Coalition for Networked Information to Advance Scholarship and Intellectual Productivity, 1527 New Hampshire Ave., N.W., Washington, DC 20036.

Halsey, Kathleen F. "An Evaluation of Document Delivery Service to Interlibrary Loan: A Commercial Firm and a Traditional Library Source." Master's thesis, Cardinal Stritch College. 78 p. ED 302 261 (Dec. 1988). Available from Educational Resources Information Center, 1600 Research Blvd., Rockville, MD 10850.

Heath, Fred M. "An Assessment of Education Holdings in Alabama Academic Libraries: A Collection Analysis Project." Unpublished report (25 p. + tables, Apr. 1990). Available from Network of Alabama Academic Libraries, Alabama Commission on Higher Education, One Court Square, Suite 221, Montgomery, AL 36104–3584.

Holmes, Glenda B., and others. "Mississippi Interlibrary Loan: Protocol and Procedures Manual." Documentation (Nov. 1988). Available from Mississippi Library Commission, Information Services Branch, 1221 Ellis Ave., P.O. Box 10700, Jackson, MS 39289-0700.

Information Systems Consultants, Inc. "Resource Sharing among Michigan's Publicly Assisted University Libraries." Unpublished report (28 p., Jan. 18, 1991).

Library of Congress. Network Development Office. "Document Delivery—Background Papers Commissioned by the National Advisory Committee." 84 p. ED 221 214 (1982). Available from Educational Resources Information Center, 1600 Research Blvd., Rockville, MD 10850.

"Library Technology Watch Program." Packet. Available from Room 130, Main Library, University of California at Berkeley, Berkeley, CA 94720.

LIBRAS Inc. "LIBRAS Administrative Handbook." Available from LIBRAS Inc., Barat College, 700 E. Westleigh Road, Lake Forest, IL 60045.

MacDonald, Carol. "Services to Remote Users: Realities and Possibilities: REGLIN Consortium." Paper presented before program session no. 38, NOTIS Users' Group Meeting, Oct. 2, 1991, Chicago, Ill. (9 p.). Available from NOTIS, 1007 Church St., 2nd Floor, Evanston, IL 60201–3622.

MacLeod, Murdo J., and Casimir Barkowski. "Report on the Study of Library Use at Pitt by Professor Allen Kent, et al. (A Pittsburgh Reply)." 49 [i.e., 51] p. ED 178 100 (July 1979). Available from Educational Resources Information Center, 1600 Research Blvd., Rockville, MD 10850.

Medina, Sue O. "Tracking Success in a Statewide Academic Network." Unpublished paper (3 p., 1992). Available from Network of Alabama Academic Libraries, Alabama Commission on Higher Education, One Court Square, Suite 221, Montgomery, AL 36104–3584.

Michalak, Thomas J. "The Impact of Table of Contents on Document Delivery in Libraries." Address, New Approaches to Document Delivery, a seminar sponsored by the Interlibrary Loan Roundtable of the Library Association of the City University of New York, (LACUNY), New York City, Apr. 10, 1992.

MINITEX Library Information Network. "1991 Annual Report." (36 p., 1991). Available from MINITEX Library Information Network, C/O S–33, Wilson Library, University of Minnesota, 309 19th Avenue S., Minneapolis, MN 55455–0414.

National Research and Education Network. "Fact Sheet." Broadside (Apr. 1991). Available from ALA Washington Office, 110 Maryland Ave., N.E., Washington, DC 20002.

"Network of Alabama Academic Libraries Resource Sharing Program." Chart (1 p., 1992). Available from Network of Alabama Academic Libraries, Alabama Commission on Higher Education, One Court Square, Suite 221, Montgomery, AL 36104–3584.

Neumann, Joan. "Enhanced METRO Cards to Provide Subject Referral." Letter to directors of METRO libraries (2 p., Feb. 13, 1991). Available from New York Metropolitan Reference and Research Library Agency, 57 E. 11th St., New York, NY 10003.

North Carolina State University. The Libraries. "NCSU Digitized Document Transmission Project: Electronic Document Delivery Service: A Pilot Service." Press release (2 p., Jan. 8, 1992). Available from Project Manager—DDTP, The Libraries, NCSU, Box 7111, Raleigh, NC 27695–7111.

———. "NCSU Digitized Document Transmission Project: Improving Access to Agricultural Libraries." Press release (3 p., Oct. 11, 1991). Available from Project Manager—DDTP, The Libraries, NCSU, Box 7111, Raleigh, NC 27695–7111.

NOTIS Systems, Inc. "PACLink and Z39.50 Implementation." Press release (5 p., Apr. 23, 1991). Available from NOTIS, 1007 Church St., 2nd Floor, Evanston, IL 60201–3622.

———. "PACLink ILL Patron Interface." Press release (23 p., June 18, 1991, revised Sept. 25, 1991). Prepared by Sara Randall. Available from NOTIS, 1007 Church St., 2nd Floor, Evanston, IL 60201–3622.

NYSERNET, "Beyond the Walls Instructional Workshop Package." Packet. Available for $99 (includes postage and handling) or $49 (NYSERNET affiliates and Interest Group Members) from NYSERNET, Inc., BEYOND THE WALLS, 111 College Place, Rm. 3–211, Syracuse, NY 13244–4100.

OCLC. "Interlibrary Loan Discussion Panel: Final Report." Unpublished report (11 p., Oct. 1990). Available from OCLC, Marketing & User Services Division, 6565 Frantz Road, Dublin, OH 43017–0702.

———. "A Summary of OCLC's Strategic Plan." (1991). Available from OCLC, 6565 Frantz Road, Dublin, OH 43017–0702.

"The Ohio State University Network Fax Project." Press release (6 p., July 1991). Available from Academic Computing Services, The Ohio State University, 1971 Neil Avenue, Columbus, OH 43210.

Phillips, Linda L. "IRIS: University of Tennessee, Knoxville/Vanderbilt University Joint-use Program, October 1988–December 1990: Final Performance Report." Available from Cooperative Information Services, University Libraries, University of Tennessee, Knoxville, TN 37996–1000.

Ra, Marsha. "A Centrally Supported Direct On-Line Document Delivery Service for the City University of New York: Planning Grant Request to the Council on Library Resources." Grant proposal (17 p., Aug. 28, 1991).

Research Libraries Group, Inc. "Ariel—An Introduction." Broadside (n.d.). Available from RLG, 1200 Villa St., Mountain View, CA 94041–1100.

———. "CitaDel." Folder (1992). Available from RLG, 1200 Villa St., Mountain View, CA 94041–1100.

———. "Research Libraries Group Interlibrary Loan Cost Study." Introductory material and worksheets (18 p., July, 1991). Available from RLG, 1200 Villa St., Mountain View, CA 94041–1100.

Sheffner, Ralph M., and others. "Interlibrary Loan in New York State. Recommended Redesign. Results of a Study: Redesign of Interlibrary Loan in New York State." Beaverton, Ore.: Ringgold Management Systems, 1986. 339 p. ED 274 351 (Jan. 1986). Available from Educational Resources Information Center, 1600 Research Blvd., Rockville, MD 10850.

Stubbs, Kendon. "Supply and Demand in ARL Libraries, 1985–86—1990–91." Graph (1 p., 1992). Available from ARL, 1527 New Hampshire Ave., N.W., Washington, DC 20036.

Wainer, Margaret A. "An Evaluation of the Facsimile Transmission Project among Multitype Libraries in West-Central Illinois (1983, 1984, 1985)." Unpublished report (12 p., Mar.

1986). Available from Illinois State Library, Centennial Building, Springfield, IL 62756.

Wiggins, Gary D. "Factors Which Influence the Choice of Document Delivery Mechanisms for Serials by Selected Scientific and Technical Special Librarians." Ph.D. diss., Indiana Univ., 1985.

H. W. Wilson Co. "Wilson and UMI Announce Product Link." Press release (2 p., Jan. 25, 1992). Available from H. W. Wilson Co., 950 University Ave., Bronx, NY 10452.

Wright, A. J. "No More Free Lunch: Commercial Fee-Based Information Services—Past, Present and Future." 23 p. ED 221 163 (May 1982). Available from Educational Resources Information Center, 1600 Research Blvd., Rockville, MD 10850.

INDEX

AAAS *See* American Association for the Advancement of Science
ACLCP *See* Associated College Libraries of Central Pennsylvania
ACRL *See* Association of College and Research Libraries
ALA *See* American Library Association
"ACRL Guidelines for the Preparation of Policies on Library Access" 86
ADONIS project 146
AMIGOS 36
ARL *See* Association of Research Libraries
Abstracting and indexing services *See* Indexing and abstracting services
Academy of Hospitality Research 313–14
Access model 19, 21, 277, 294–96, 318–19
Access program 249–89
  Administration 250–51
  Balance 4, 85, 190, 280
  Budgeting for 263, 270–71
  Communication with readers 283
  Costs and cost centers 5–6, 137–38, 222, 250, 252–54, 258–59, 261, 274–75, 280, 326
  Deciding when to use which option 259–61, 283–84
  Definition 2–3
  Dolimiting 250–52
  Evaluation 4, 250, 275–83
  Expansion 4–5
  Fees
    Charging local readers 264–68, 271, 296
    Charging other institutions and their readers 264–65, 268–72
  Fill rate 276–77, 281
  Funding 20, 82, 167, 189–90, 250, 270–74, 289, 325, 347, 351
  Locations 12
  Organizational issues 179, 184, 287–89
  Policies 260–61
  Potential demand 279–80
  Privileges 250–51
  Procedures 17
  Public relations 190, 276, 278, 280, 285–87
  Reader satisfaction 279–81
  Space 285–86
  Speed 6, 259, 277–80, 282
  Verification 12, 268
  Volume 275–76, 279, 281
  Workflow 183, 195, 240, 275
    See also individual elements, such as Interlibrary loan, Commercial document supply services
Acquisitions *See* Collection development
Adams, Roy 304, 322
Alabama Commission of Higher Education 352
Alabama libraries 11, 36, 40–41, 57, 117, 215, 218, 272, 340, 352–53
Alaskan libraries 36
Alexander, Johanna 153, 187
Allen, David B. 153, 187
American Association for the Advancement of Science 314
American Library Association 234, 284
Anand, Havelin 295
Andrew W. Mellon Foundation 217
Apple Computer 241, 340
Ariel 176, 184, 239–43, 245, 297, 337, 342, 354–55
  See also Scanning technology
Arms, Carolyn 302–3, 326
Arms, William 13

379

Article Clearinghouse *See* University Microfilms Incorporated
ArticleFirst *See* OCLC: ContentsFirst and ArticleFirst
Assets *See* Collection development; Purchasing versus borrowing
Associated College Libraries of Central Pennsylvania 214, 227, 234
Association of College and Research Libraries 177
Association of Research Libraries 10–11, 130, 209, 257–58, 277, 282, 301, 311, 336, 351
Atkinson, Hugh C. 11, 14, 40, 46–47, 51, 55, 63, 296
Audio information formats 12, 113, 116
Auto-Graphics *See* Electronic mail messaging systems
Automated integrated library systems 45, 61, 81, 109, 175, 270, 332–39, 353 *See also* Multiple database systems; Online catalogs; Shared catalogs; names of individual systems
Automation 4, 6, 40–41, 79–80, 94–109, 147–48
   See also Automated integrated library systems; Bibliographic utilities; CD-ROM catalogs; CD-ROM indexes; Consortia: Telecommunications capabilities; Electronic mail messaging systems; Electronic information formats; Electronic information networks; Interlibrary loan: Software; Interlibrary loan: Statistics; Multiple database systems; Online bibliographic searching; Online catalogs; Scanning technology; Shared catalogs; Table of contents services; Telecommunications costs;

Telefacsimile transmission; names of individual organizations and systems
Autonomy *See* Self-sufficiency

BAKER (Document delivery service) *See* University of California (Berkeley)
BITNET 98, 313, 316, 323
BLDSC *See* British Library Document Supply Centre
BRS 148, 161, 167, 170, 178, 180–81, 184, 288
Bailey, Charles W. 311, 316–17, 322, 326
Balance of trade 6, 11, 46, 53, 55–59, 63–64, 83, 87–88, 91, 105, 107, 132, 153–54, 194, 197, 252, 254, 260–62, 268, 271, 280–81, 343, 355–56
   See Also Interlibrary loan: Capping; Mutual benefit
Baruch College (New York) 335
Battin, Patricia 8, 10, 19, 33, 63
Belanger, David 102
Bentley College (Massachusetts) 342, 350–51
BiblioData 146
Bibliographic instruction 111, 131, 250
Bibliographic Retrieval Services, Inc. *See* BRS
Bibliographic utilities 4, 6, 12, 39, 41, 49, 79, 85, 92, 126, 128, 130, 138, 147–48, 202, 284–85, 297, 299–300, 323, 334
  Interlibrary loan subsystems 12, 38, 81–82, 87, 92, 95–99, 110, 112, 115, 133, 135, 137, 153, 156–58, 170, 183, 193, 197, 203, 234, 254, 262, 275, 281, 296, 338, 354
  Public accessibility 12, 131
  Statistical reports 122–24
    See also names of individual utilities
Bibliothèque Nationale (Paris) 183
Billings, Harold 9, 15, 274, 301–2, 319
Binding 15, 60, 310, 339
Biological Abstracts 156

Blair, Joan 294, 332
Bloomberg, Marty 26
Books *See* Monographic literature
Boss, Richard W. 41, 107, 203–5, 209–10, 212, 219, 232
Boucher, Virginia 5, 69, 83, 117, 257, 284
Bradley University (Illinois) 126
Brander, Linda 235
Brandeis University (Massachusetts) 342, 350–51
Brigham Young University (Utah) Computer Assisted Research Services 146
Briscoe Library *See* University of Texas Health Science Center (San Antonio)
British Library Document Supply Centre 164–65, 174, 183–84, 355
Brooklyn College (New York) 335
Brown, Barbara 212
Brown, Steven A. 218–19, 221, 229, 231
Browsing 20, 22–23, 172, 295
Budd, John M. 85
Budgets and budgeting 8–10, 12, 18–19, 27, 32, 34, 48–49, 78, 89, 111, 113, 116, 119, 197, 206, 244, 252, 256–57, 263, 270–74, 325–26, 333, 336, 339–40, 348–49, 351
   See also Access program: Budgeting for; Commercial document supply services: Budgeting for
Bush, George 300
Buying *See* Purchasing versus borrowing

CARL 41
  UnCover and UnCover2 22, 59, 164, 173–74, 186–87, 193, 238, 263
CAS *See* Chemical Abstracts Services Online
CAUSE 301
CCC *See* Copyright Clearance Center
CCLA *See* College Center for Library Automation (Florida)
CD-ROM catalogs 13, 41, 92, 103, 106, 130, 214, 275, 297, 299, 334
CD-ROM full-text 306–7, 310–11, 323
  See also Electronic journals
CD-ROM indexes 176, 179, 273, 287
  Impact on interlibrary loan 13, 14, 79, 348
  Impact on commercial document supply services 147
CIC *See* Committee for Institutional Cooperation
CICNET 238
CLS *See* Washington Research Library Consortium (Washington, D.C.)
CNI *See* Coalition for Networked Information
CONTU *See* National Commission on Technological Uses of Copyrighted Works
COPEMAL *See* Co-Operative Project East Midlands Academic Libraries (England)
CRL *See* Center for Research Libraries
CTRC *See* Colorado Technical Reference Center
CTW Library Consortium 50, 215–16, 333, 342
CUNY+ *See* City University of New York
California libraries 22–23, 26, 37, 41–42, 50, 107–9, 206, 216, 238, 257, 262–66, 269, 273–74, 299, 340, 346–50
California State University
  Chico 22–23, 50, 273–74, 340, 346–48
  San Bernardino 26, 206, 262–64
Campus mail 134, 136, 208, 283
Canadian libraries 36, 43, 50, 72, 139, 333, 341–42, 345–46
Carnegie Foundation for the Advancement of Teaching 217
Carnegie-Mellon University (Pennsylvania) 13, 206
Casorso, Tracy M. 309

Cataloging 11, 15, 36, 60, 89, 95, 252, 258, 281, 310, 318, 323–25, 332
  See also Retrospective conversion
Catalogs See CD-ROM catalogs; Online catalogs; Shared catalogs
Cawkell, A. E. 205, 217, 306
Center for Electronic Texts in the Humanities (Rutgers University) 306
Center for Research Libraries 183, 195, 332, 339–40
Chairman software See Electronic mail messaging systems
Chambers, Joan 257
Chang, Amy 108, 121
Chase Manhattan Bank, N. A. Library (New York) 146
Chemical Abstracts Services Online (CAS) 146, 151, 183
Circulation and circulation systems 11, 13, 15, 23–25, 41–42, 61, 70, 72–73, 75, 80, 92, 95–96, 106–7, 137, 207, 256, 276, 280–81, 287–88, 332–34, 337–39
CitaDel 176
City College (New York) 335
City University of New York 17–18, 37, 42, 87–88, 104, 207, 218–19, 228, 243, 266, 299, 334–35
Clark, Marsha S. 265
Clemson University (South Carolina) 109
Coalition for Networked Information (CNI) 301, 313
Cochrane, Lynn S. 254
Cohen, David 298
Cohn, John M. 126
Collection assessment 39–40
Collection development 8, 10–13, 15–16, 20–21, 23–26, 36, 88–90, 111, 117, 119–20, 124–25, 152, 250, 252, 256, 258, 262–64, 270, 273, 287–89, 294–95, 298, 318, 324, 339, 348
  See also Cooperative collection development; Journal literature; Monographic literature; Purchasing versus borrowing
Collection use studies 20, 23–26, 262–63, 274, 325
  DePauw study 25–26
  Pittsburgh study 20, 23–26
College Center for Library Automation (Florida) 42, 104, 332
College libraries 1–2, 11, 15–16, 21, 25, 253, 300, 312, 332–35, 350–54
Colorado Academic Research Libraries See CARL
Colorado College 109
Colorado libraries 109, 127, 178
  See also CARL
Colorado State University Libraries 127
Colorado Technical Reference Center 178
Columbia University (New York) 43, 71, 215, 286
Comeaux, Elizabeth A. 125
Commercial document supply services 17–18, 20, 27, 47, 60, 62, 108, 114, 144–97, 202, 207–8, 250, 252, 259, 271, 287–89, 295, 312, 326, 347–50
  Benefits 153–54
  Bibliographic verification 155–56, 159, 170, 178, 184, 188, 193, 268
  Billing 153, 157, 161, 163, 166, 188–89, 194
  Budgeting for 263
  Charging local readers 152, 186, 190–92, 264–68, 271, 296
  Checking account 161, 188, 190
  Clearinghouses 168–69
  Collection-based services 155–57, 159–68, 170–71, 189, 194–95
    General-interest services 161–65, 183
    Material-specific services 167–68
    Subject-specific services 165–67, 183

Confirmation 152, 156, 195
Costs and cost centers 4, 137–38, 146, 148–52, 154–59, 161–65, 167–71, 174–76, 178–83, 186–87, 192–94, 216, 253–54, 257–59, 261–63, 271, 347–49
Coverage 152, 161–63, 173–74, 180–81, 194–95, 348
Credit card charges 152, 159, 161, 171, 174–75, 189
Customer service support 159, 166, 170, 174, 196
Definition 2–3, 145–46
Deposit accounts 138, 152, 158–59, 161, 163–64, 166, 169–70, 175, 187–90, 340
Discounts 154, 158–59, 161, 163, 166, 170, 187–88, 196
Document quality 149, 162–63, 166, 172–73, 192–93, 195–96, 279
Ease of use 150–51, 192, 195, 279
Evaluation 158–59, 168, 190, 192–96
Expectations 150, 276
Experimenting with commercial document suppliers 158, 189–92
Fill rate 145, 149, 151, 162–63, 165, 168, 174, 190, 192, 195, 276, 281
Forms 156, 159, 161, 175, 181, 194, 279
Fulfillment 157
Funding sources 190, 325, 334
Geographic issues 150, 332, 346
Growth 11, 80, 146–49, 152, 276, 281, 319, 326
Handling fees 187–88
Information-on-demand services 146, 155, 169–71, 183, 194–95
Location verification 155, 159, 168, 184, 196, 275
"No fills" 155–56, 165, 171, 188, 193–96
Notifying readers 158, 168, 208–9
Order transmission 147–48, 155–56, 159, 179, 182–87, 193
Packaging 157
Performance 153–54
Pricing structures 152, 187–89
Privileges 190–91
Public relations 145, 191, 285–87
Reports 156–57, 159, 166, 170, 192
Rush orders 152, 157, 159, 161, 163–64, 168, 170, 178, 186, 268, 278
Selecting commercial document suppliers 152, 155–59, 183
Service charges 170, 174, 188, 193–94
Special materials 150–51, 155–56
Speed 4, 17, 150–52, 154, 157, 159, 161, 163, 165, 170–71, 174, 190, 193, 202–3, 260–61, 277–79
Telephone orders 146, 152, 156, 159, 161, 166–67, 170, 175, 182, 184, 193
Turnaround time 145, 149–50, 152, 159, 161–63, 165, 167–68, 170–71, 174, 178, 183, 281
When to use 154, 259–61, 263–64
Workflow 261
   See also Access program; Bibliographic utilities: Interlibrary loan subsystems; Copyright compliance; Electronic mail messaging systems; Fee-based services; Invoicing; Telefacsimile transmission
Commission on Preservation and Access 2
Committee for Institutional Cooperation 344
Communications costs *See* Telecommunications costs
CompuServe 178
Computer space costs 16
Concordia University (Illinois) 353
Conference proceedings 145, 161, 164, 193
Connecticut College *See* CTW Library Consortium
Connecticut libraries 44, 50, 212, 215–16, 333, 342
Consortia 31–64, 147, 234, 250, 285

Agreements 296, 332
Benefits 33, 35, 39, 47, 52, 53–55, 59–60, 63, 215, 228
Case studies 331–57
Collection overlap 40, 61
Cost-effectiveness 51–55, 59–62
Definition 2–3, 34
Document delivery systems 44, 45, 48–49, 51, 59, 61, 87, 212–17, 243, 298, 300, 333, 335–37, 343, 353–55
Evaluation 33, 39–49, 51–52, 87, 114, 116–17. See also Value of membership
Fees 38, 41, 45, 51–52, 59–60, 87, 138, 215, 336, 339–40, 355
Finances 45
Formation 33, 62–63
Function 36
Funding 333, 336, 339–40, 352–53
Geographic issues 35–36, 43–44, 49, 332, 352
Goals 38
Governance 35, 45, 82, 87
Interlibrary loan programs 11, 46, 48, 54, 59. See also Interlibrary loan
Library type 35–36, 332–37, 339–42, 351–54
Local 33, 37, 285, 351
Materials type 37
Miniature 49–51, 57, 92, 114, 261, 274, 296, 333–37, 341–51
Multitype 35, 37, 63, 136, 213, 217, 333–34, 350, 354–57
National 33, 36
Political structure 33–37
Political value 32, 54, 55
Reciprocity 38–39, 45–46, 55–59, 269, 296
Regional 33, 36–37, 95, 96, 351, 354–57
Responsibilities of membership 45–46, 63
State 33, 36, 338–42, 351, 354–56
Telecommunications capabilities 40–41, 60–61, 99–103
Value of membership 53–55, 59–62, 154

See also Cooperative collection development; Reciprocal access; Shared catalogs; Telefacsimile transmission: Networks; names of individual consortia
Consortium of Educational Communications and Technology (City University of New York) 87–88
Consortium Loan System See Washington Research Library Consortium (Washington, D.C.)
ContentsFirst See OCLC: ContentsFirst and ArticleFirst
Cooperative collection development 5, 33, 36, 43, 46–49, 60, 87, 234, 325, 337, 352
Co-Operative Project East Midlands Academic Libraries (England) 164–65
Cooperatives See Consortia
Coordinated collection development See Cooperative collection development
Copyright Clearance Center 119, 178,
Copyright compliance 4–5, 57, 80, 86, 90, 107, 113–14, 117–22, 125–27, 146, 153–54, 156, 161, 163–64, 166–67, 170, 175, 178, 188, 193, 197, 233–35, 242, 301, 304, 312, 316, 349
Cornell University (New York) 44, 170
Corporate libraries See Special libraries
Cost centers 4–6
See also individual cost centers
Cost savings 4, 52, 60
See also Consortia: Cost-effectiveness
Council on Library Resources 202, 207
Coupons 91, 138, 159, 164
See also Regional Medical Library System
Courier services 17, 27, 44, 49, 80, 136, 138, 156–57, 159, 175, 185, 209, 211–19, 221, 254, 344, 349, 353–54

Air 161, 164, 211–12, 341, 345
Cost structures and centers 193, 213–16, 218–19, 253–54
Evaluation 216–17
Messenger services 215–16, 349–50, 356
Regional delivery systems 38, 44, 48–49, 51, 61, 87, 93, 103, 136–37, 211–16, 219, 234, 258–59, 333, 335–37, 343, 354
See also Consortia: Document delivery systems; names of individual services
Currency exchange rates 9, 12
Current Contents 59, 165
Currie, Jean 170

DIALOG 96, 146–48, 151, 161, 164, 167, 178, 180–81, 184, 186, 236, 288
DOCLINE 94, 125, 178, 234–35, 260, 352
DRA 106
Dalhousie University (Nova Scotia) See NOVANET
Danish Loan Center 183
Dartmouth College (New Hampshire) 342–43
Dartmouth Dante Project 305
DataTimes 180
Davis, Erik 302, 321, 324
dBASE 119, 124, 126, 181
Defiance College (Ohio) 334
De Gennaro, Richard 7, 32, 269
Delaware County Library System 102
Denton, Barbara 186
Dickson, Stephen P. 257
Dissertations 108, 161, 167
DePauw University (Indiana) See Collection use studies: DePauw study
Dewey, Patrick R. 221, 225
Digital Research Associates See DRA
Document delivery 20, 27, 44–45, 48–49, 51, 57–58, 61, 82, 86–87, 92–93, 113, 116, 129, 154–56, 159–60, 185–86, 202–45, 250, 252, 260, 262, 287, 297, 325

Campus delivery service 208–9, 265–66, 268
Choices 203–5, 282
Cost structures and centers 114, 117, 136, 138, 185–88, 193, 204, 206, 209–17, 244, 253, 257
Definition 2–3, 202
Direct to reader 134, 158–59, 175–76, 207–8, 241–42, 314, 320–22
Discounts 211
Document quality 244, 279, 282
Ease of use 244, 279
Electronic 179–82, 186, 202, 205–6, 292–327, 340–42
Evaluation 243–44, 275
Experimenting 244–45
Funding 216–17
Predictability 206, 244, 260–61, 278
Rush service 204, 206, 268, 278
Speed 6, 12, 17, 50, 112, 116, 127, 136–37, 148, 185, 202–8, 214, 242–43, 245, 269, 277–79, 282, 297, 346
See also Commercial document supply services; Courier services; Electronic file transfer; Scanning technology; Telefacsimile transmission; United States mail; names of individual companies and systems
Document vendors See Commercial document supply services
Dougherty, Richard M. 11, 17–18, 21, 46–47, 55, 129, 277, 294, 298
Dow Jones News/Retrieval 180
Dowd, Sheila T. 14, 34, 252
Downes, Robin 9, 301, 312
Duke University (North Carolina) 43, 50, 337
Dusenbury, Carolyn 22–23, 266, 304, 347–48
Dynix 106

Ei Page One 175–76
E-mail See Electronic mail messaging systems

EDDIE (E-mail Document Delivery and Information Exchange) *See* Electronic mail messaging systems
EDUCOM 301
EL-MAIL *See* Electronic mail messaging systems
ERIC 160, 179, 183, 288, 353
ESL *See* Engineering Societies Libraries
Eastern Oregon State College 102
Educational Research Information Center *See* ERIC
Electronic books 305–6, 309, 322, 326
Electronic file transfer 148, 236–37, 242, 323
  See also Document delivery: Electronic; Scanning technology; Telefacsimile transmission
Electronic information formats 5, 12–13, 79, 148–49, 153, 155, 157, 159, 175, 179–82, 184–86, 191, 196, 205, 236–37, 244, 287, 299–300, 305, 322–24
  See also Electronic books; Electronic journals; Electronic publishing; names of individual formats
Electronic information networks 13–14, 33, 300–304, 307–8, 314–15, 318–19, 322
  See also BITNET; Internet; names of other individual networks
Electronic journals 180–81, 304, 306–20, 322–24, 326
 Acceptance 314, 317
 Access 322–24
 Backfiles 314, 317, 324, 326
 Copying 307, 316
 Costs and cost structures 307, 309–11, 315–17, 326
 Distribution 311–15
 Identifying 311
 Licensing 307, 313–17
 Purchasing individual articles 307–8, 311–13, 319–20, 326
 Speed of delivery 308–9
 Speed of publication 308–9
 Subscriptions 307–8, 312–15, 323
 Textual limitations 314, 318
 Use 309–311, 314–16
Electronic Library *See* National Library of Medicine
Electronic mail messaging systems 4, 17, 80, 92, 98, 99–103, 105, 107–109, 112, 115, 127, 130, 133–34, 137–38, 146, 154, 157, 170, 175–76, 184, 186, 204–205, 209, 234, 236, 242, 252, 254, 265, 283, 297, 309, 322–23, 333–34, 341–42, 355
  See also BITNET; Internet
Electronic publishing 304–22, 324–26
  See also Electronic books; Electronic information formats; Electronic journals; Scholarly publishing
Elsevier 314–15
Engineering Information, Inc. 175
  See also Ei Page One
Engineering Societies Libraries 178
Equipment 4, 15–16, 57, 61–62, 87, 100–101, 121, 123, 129, 138, 181, 190, 194, 228, 235, 239–40, 244, 258, 260, 271, 285, 304–5, 307, 310, 316, 323, 345, 353, 356
  See also Scanning technology: Equipment; Scholar's workstations; Telefacsimile transmission: Equipment
Equity *See* Balance of trade; Information ethics; Mutual benefit
Espo, Hal 219, 232
Ethics *See* Information ethics
Evans, Nancy H. 302–3
Everett, David 91
Express Mail *See* United States mail

FEDLINK 36
FILLS (Fast Interlibrary Loan and Statistics) 127
FTP *See* Electronic file transfer
Facts Found Fast 146

Faculty 1, 3, 7, 10, 14–19, 32, 36, 38, 45, 48–49, 62, 69, 71–72, 104, 108–9, 111, 119–20, 126, 179, 191, 208–9, 231, 242, 250–52, 259, 262–63, 267–68, 272, 274, 276, 310, 320, 322, 327, 336, 339, 344, 346, 348–51, 353
   Attitudes 19–20, 21–23, 24–25, 48–49, 190–91, 206–7, 273, 277, 284, 286, 295, 308, 317
Fair use *See* Copyright compliance
Federal Express 44, 93, 163, 185, 211–12
Federal Libraries Information Network *See* FEDLINK
Fee-based services 80, 147, 173–74, 177–78, 234–35, 265–66
   See also Commercial document supply services; names of individual services
Fee-versus-free *See* Information ethics
Fees 264–70
   See also Access program: Fees; Commercial document supply services: Charging local readers; Commercial document supply services: Handling fees; Consortia: Fees; Copyright compliance; Interlibrary loan: Fees; Reciprocal access: Fees; Telefacsimile transmission: Charging local readers; Telefacsimile transmission: Charging other libraries
Fenwick, Bill 125
Find/SVP 170
Finnigan, Georgia 158
Flanders, Bruce 101–2
Florida libraries 42, 104, 332
4th Dimension software 125
Free information *See* Information ethics
Full-text *See* Electronic information formats
Future 138–39, 293–94, 320–22, 325–27

GPO *See* Government Printing Office
Galvin, Thomas J. 23–24, 26
Gateways *See* Electronic information networks
Genuine Article *See* ISI
George Washington University Library (Washington, D.C.) 105
Georgetown University (Washington, D.C.) 336
Gherman, Paul M. 9, 52, 254, 273, 308, 310, 312, 315, 317
Gifts 25
Global (Commercial document supply service) 151
Government Printing Office 160
Government publications 113, 116, 145, 160–61, 167–68, 180, 193, 272
Greenberg, Evelyn 209
Guyette, Patricia R. 15, 36

H. W. Wilson Company 163, 263
Halsey, Kathleen F. 152, 162
Hardesty, Larry 23, 25–26
Harvard University (Massachusetts) 269
Health Sciences Libraries Consortium (Philadelphia) 243
HealthLink 243
Hearty, John A. 182
Heath, Fred M. 36, 38, 41, 44, 54–55, 86
Herstand, Jo Ellen 255
Hewitt, Joe A. 19, 22–23, 33, 38, 41, 47–48, 202, 284
High-Performance Computing and Communications Act 300
Holicky, Bernard H. 23, 25–26, 32, 274
Holton, Janet E. 178
Housing collections *See* Space costs
Houston Area Research Library Consortium 35, 48
Hubbard, Joan G. 119–20
Hughes, Carol 294
Hurd, Douglas P. 146
Hurt, Charlene S. 324

IAC *See* Information Access Company
IDS *See* Interlibrary Delivery Service (Pennsylvania)
ILDS *See* Intersystems Library Delivery Service (Illinois)
ILLINET/LCS system 41–42, 88, 106, 297, 338, 353
ILLRKS (Interlibrary Loan Record Keeping System) 127
IMPACT *See* CD-ROM catalogs
IRIS project 42, 344
ISCI 68–70, 72, 129, 163, 202, 210–11, 214, 217, 220, 252, 277–78, 282
ISDN *See* Integrated Services Digital Network
ISI 165–67, 171, 183
Idaho libraries 356
Illinois libraries 11, 40–42, 44, 50–51, 57, 88, 106, 126, 150, 212, 215, 228, 235, 297, 305, 338, 352–53
Illinois State Library 228
In-house collection use 25
Indexing and abstracting services 20, 22, 79, 159, 172, 274, 296–97, 303, 320, 325–26
    See also CD-ROM indexes; Commercial document supply services; Multiple database systems; Table of contents services
Indiana libraries 25–26, 70, 104, 159, 335–36
Indiana State University 335
Indiana University 335
Inflation 8–10, 12, 255, 273
Info-Mart 170
InfoQuest 146
Information Access Company 181
Information brokers *See* Commercial document supply services
Information delivery models 27, 273, 294, 301–3, 326
    See also Electronic journals
Information ethics 5–6, 16–17, 52–53, 149–50, 172, 177–78, 264, 266–69, 313

Information formats 12–13, 323
    See also Electronic information formats; names of individual formats
Information on Demand 118, 170–71, 183
Information policy 16
Information proliferation *See* Scholarly publishing
Information Store 146, 183
Information Systems Consultants, Inc. *See* ISCI
Information Unlimited 158
Institute for Scientific Information *See* ISI
Integrated library systems *See* Automated integrated library systems; Online catalogs
Integrated Services Digital Network (ISDN) 238–39
Interdependence *See* Consortia; Cooperative collection development; Resource sharing
Interlibrary Delivery Service (IDS) (Pennsylvania) 136, 206, 212–15, 219
Interlibrary loan 5, 18, 26, 33–36, 38–39, 47, 49, 53, 58, 63, 77–139, 145, 147–48, 150–55, 157, 162–63, 167, 175, 179, 207, 250, 258–60, 263–64, 300
    American Library Association policy 85
    Barriers 81–83, 129, 138–39
    Bibliographic verification 80, 83, 87, 90–91, 95, 120, 128–31, 134–36, 154–55, 172, 261, 268, 336, 338
    Borrowing operation 128–34, 254, 275–80, 282
    Borrowing locally owned items 40, 84–85, 287, 336
    Capping 254, 260–62, 271, 281
    Clearinghouses 61, 82, 94–95, 110, 297
    Codes and agreements 40, 80–81, 83–88, 94, 128, 187, 251, 261, 284, 299, 332, 334–36, 343, 346, 354
    Combatting abuses 251, 266, 320
    Communication with readers 108–10, 129–30, 134, 283

Confirmation 112, 115, 129, 132, 134–35, 155
Cost models 253–59
Costs 59–60, 81, 91, 96–99, 101, 103, 108, 114, 120–24, 127, 129, 132, 137–38, 147, 149, 152, 187, 193–94, 197, 252–54, 261, 282, 341, 343–49, 352, 355
Definition 2–3, 83–84
Efficiency 79, 81, 85, 93, 95, 112, 114–17, 128–37, 171, 254, 281–83
Evaluation 110–28, 190, 275–83
Fees 4, 59–60, 80, 86–88, 90–92, 98, 114, 117, 129, 132, 134, 137–38, 149–50, 154, 170, 258, 162
  Charging local readers 134, 138, 190–91, 251, 264–68, 271, 296
  Charging other institutions and their readers 138, 243, 254, 256, 258, 262, 264, 268–72, 296, 339–41, 349–51, 353, 355
Fill rate 38, 91–93, 122, 276–77, 281–83, 344, 352, 354–56
Forms 80, 82, 92, 95, 98–101, 104, 108–9, 112, 115, 123, 126–27, 129–30, 133, 138, 171, 261, 279, 345, 353
Forwarding requests 92, 95, 96, 103, 107, 115, 132, 134–35, 184, 262, 281
Fulfillment 135–36, 157
Future 138–39, 325–26
Geographic issues 83, 93, 97, 106, 132, 332, 357
Growth 10–15, 79–80, 107, 121, 212, 269, 281, 285, 345
Hierarchies 83, 85–86, 103, 354
Lender strings See Forwarding requests
Lending operation 128–29, 134–37, 254, 260, 275, 281–82
Loan periods 86
Location verification 80, 83, 87, 90–91, 92, 109–10, 115, 128–33, 136, 155–56, 172, 275, 343, 345, 353–54
Loss 129, 280, 282

"No fills" 115, 154, 171, 189, 281
Notifying readers 106, 108, 112–13, 129, 134, 155, 158, 208–209
Organizational issues 287–89
Overdues 91, 107, 113, 116, 121, 129, 137, 280, 338
Packaging 91, 93–94, 135–36, 138, 219, 240, 282–83
Partners 42, 49–50, 57, 113–14, 116, 122–23, 131, 152, 154–55, 171, 186, 244, 263, 275, 282, 325
  "Best" partners 90–94, 107, 192, 262
Photocopies 60, 87, 91, 94, 101, 114, 116–20, 122, 126, 134, 138, 150, 164, 207, 220, 244, 258, 341, 345
Point to point transmission of requests 85, 95, 110, 297, 355
Policies 115, 125, 132, 135, 287, 352
Privileges 86, 109, 251, 268–69, 342
Processing time 68
Protocols 82
Public relations 285–87, 341, 346
Reader-initiated requests 14, 41–42, 51, 88, 104–7, 125, 130, 297–98, 332, 335–36, 338
Reader satisfaction 58, 81, 131, 207, 221, 244, 279–80, 346
Recalls 338
Referral centers See Clearinghouses
Reimbursement of net lenders 56–57, 81, 87–88, 95, 97, 110, 138, 254, 269, 272, 352, 355–56
Renewals 108, 116, 129, 338
Request transmission 92–109, 112, 115, 128, 133, 202, 334–35, 340, 345
Restricted materials 38, 86, 87–88, 94, 112, 115, 132–33, 156
Rush requests 88, 90, 92–93, 133, 206, 220, 268, 278, 334
Satisfaction time 129, 277–78, 282, 344
Software 56, 80, 99, 101–2, 119–121, 123–28, 134, 138, 271

Space 136, 187, 279, 285–86
Speed 4–5, 18, 79, 89–90, 154, 193, 203–4, 206, 221, 267, 277–79, 282, 337, 342, 346
Statistics 86, 88, 94, 99–100, 107, 110–29, 133, 192, 244
  Borrowing 111–14
  Lending 115–17
Supplies 136, 138, 253, 258, 271, 344
Telephone requests 92, 110, 182, 265, 268, 283, 338, 340
Turnaround time 38, 61, 81, 86, 91, 93, 97, 103, 136, 152, 221, 243, 245, 263, 281, 283, 344, 353–54, 356
Volume 220, 224, 226, 275–76, 279, 281, 349, 351–52, 354–55, 357
Workflow 83, 94, 99, 128–37, 283
  See also Access program; Balance of trade; Bibliographic utilities: Interlibrary loan subsystems; Consortia: Interlibrary loan programs; Copyright compliance; Electronic mail messaging systems; Invoicing; Mutual benefit; Telefacsimile transmission; names of individual bibliographic utilities, consortia, and automated integrated library systems
Interlibrary Loan Protocol 138–39
Interlibrary Software and Services 127
International Conference on Interlending and Document Supply (1988) 78
Internet 11, 13–14, 42–43, 98–99, 157, 173, 176, 178, 180, 186, 206–7, 217, 219, 229, 232, 236–38, 240–43, 284, 299–301, 305, 311, 313, 316, 319, 323, 339–41, 344, 354
  Protocols 43, 300
  See also Electronic mail messaging systems; names of individual nodes

Intersystems Library Delivery Service (Illinois) 106, 212, 215, 353
Invoicing 60, 89, 91, 121, 125, 134, 158, 187–89, 256–57, 267, 270, 349–50
Iowa State University 166–67

Jackson, Mary E. 79, 240
James Madison University (Virginia) 50, 340, 348–49
Journal literature 8–10, 13, 15, 50, 58–59, 90, 109, 111, 116–20, 122, 126, 135, 146, 156, 161–62, 164, 180, 193, 204, 207, 216, 220, 233–35, 252, 256, 262–63, 265, 273–74, 276, 287, 289, 295–96, 301, 304, 306–310, 313–20, 325–26, 339, 343, 346, 348–50, 353
  Cancellations 22, 26, 32, 41, 47, 60, 151–54, 166–68, 172–73, 189–90, 192, 197, 206, 234, 262–63, 266, 273–74, 307, 325, 341, 349
  See also Collection use studies; Electronic journals
Journal of the International Academy of Hospitality Research (*JIAHR*) 313–14, 318

KIC See Kansas Information Circuit Interlibrary Loan Network
Kansas Information Circuit Interlibrary Loan Network (KIC) 100–101, 103
Kansas libraries 88, 100–101, 103
Kansas State Library 101
Keder, Jan 109
Keene State College (New Hampshire) 342–43
Kehoe, Brendan P. 238
Kellogg Foundation See W. K. Kellogg Foundation
Kelsey, Ann L. 126
Kennedy, Sue 148, 255, 259
Kent, Allen 19, 21, 23–26, 34, 53
Kibbey, Mark 302–3
King Research, Inc. 255

Kresge Foundation 217
Krol, Ed 238

LANs *See* Local area networks
LCS *See* ILLINET/LCS system
LEXIS 180
LIBRAS 43, 50, 338, 350, 353
LITA *See* Library and Information Technology Association
LOANet *See* Electronic mail messaging systems
Lahmon, Jo Ann 119
Lancaster, F. W. 276, 279
LaQuey, Tracy L. 238
Lending Library for Science and Technology *See* British Library Document Supply Centre
Librarians 2–4, 6–10, 12, 20, 147, 274, 283–84, 311
　Attitudes 12, 17–19, 82–83, 105, 149–52, 240, 263, 273, 279, 284–85, 295
　Roles 27, 88–89, 120, 129–30, 179, 196, 283–84, 295–96, 318–27, 336
　See also Staff
Library and Information Technology Association 203
Library associations *See* Consortia
Library budgets and budgeting *See* Budgets and budgeting
Library consortia *See* Consortia
Library Consortia System *See* ILLINET/LCS system
Library cooperatives *See* Consortia
Library networks *See* Consortia
Library of Congress 33, 117, 148, 196
Library staff *See* Staff
Library systems *See* Consortia
Library Systems & Services 103
Library Technology Watch Program (University of California, Berkeley) 238
Line, Maurice B. 78, 81, 204, 209, 253–55, 275–79, 305–6, 310–11
Lingle, Virginia A. 121
Linked catalogs *See* Shared catalogs

Load balancing *See* Balance of trade
Local area networks 307, 314–15, 323
　See also Electronic information networks
Louisiana libraries 40, 103
Louisiana State Library 103
Lowry, Charles B. 52, 54, 255–58
Loyola Marymount University (California) 216, 349–50
Lucker, Jay K. 15, 204, 304
Lynch, Clifford A. 11, 299–301

MARC records 95, 103, 323
MC^2 177
MCI Mail 178
MELVYL 41, 108–9
METRO (New York) 36, 44, 54, 58–59, 72, 110, 213, 215, 219
MIDNET 238
MINITEX Library Information Network 212, 340, 354–55
MULS *See* Minnesota Union List of Serials
Mackey, Terry 85
MacNeil Hospital (Berwyn, Illinois) 127
Madaus, Richard 332
Malcom, Dorothy L. 121
Martin, Noelene P. 82, 283, 285
Martin, Susan K. 11, 37, 159, 205–6, 218, 286, 302, 321
Marx, Karl 53
Maryland libraries 215
Massachusetts Institute of Technology 342, 350–51
Massachusetts libraries 269, 342, 350–51
McGinn, Howard 356
McQueen, Judy 148, 203–5, 209–210, 212
Measuring library quality 18–19, 111, 280, 293–95
Meckler Corporation 176
Medina, Sue O. 299
Medline 314
Mellon Foundation *See* Andrew W. Mellon Foundation
Metz, Paul 9, 273, 308, 310, 312, 315, 317

Michalak, Thomas J. 8, 13, 197, 206, 270
Michigan libraries 41, 50, 69, 129, 136–37, 210, 214, 217, 257, 269, 343–44, 350
Michigan State University 50, 343–44, 350
Microforms 15, 103, 161, 167–68, 202, 228, 314, 324, 334, 340, 353
Military libraries 36
Miller, Connie 147, 150, 153
Miller, Marilyn E. 15, 36
Minneapolis Public Library 354
Minnesota libraries 212, 354–55
Minnesota State Board of Health 354
Minnesota State University/PALS Office 355
Minnesota Union List of Serials 354
Mississippi Library Commission 103
Molyneux, Robert E. 146
Monographic literature 10, 13, 15, 89–90, 113, 116, 202–204, 220, 243, 256, 265, 276, 295–96, 298, 301, 304–306, 318–19, 326, 343, 346, 349, 351
See also Electronic books
Montana libraries 235
Moscow-Latah County (Idaho) Library 356
Mosher, Paul H. 33–34
Mount Saint Vincent University (Nova Scotia) See NOVANET
Multiple database systems 14, 43, 79, 176, 179, 263, 287, 297–98, 300, 334, 336
Munn, Robert F. 1–2, 8, 16
Mutual benefit 54–59, 63–64, 86
See also Balance of trade

NAAL See Network of Alabama Academic Libraries
NCSU DDTP See North Carolina State University Digitized Document Transmission Project
NEWSNET 180
NEXIS 180
NISO See National Information Standards Organization
NLM See National Library of Medicine
NORTHWESTNET 238
NORWELD (Ohio) 333–34, 342
NOTIS Systems Inc. 263
 PACLink and PACLoan 14, 42, 105–6, 297
NOVANET (Nova Scotia) 50, 72, 333, 342
NREN See National Research and Education Network
NSFNet See National Science Foundation Network
NTIS See National Technical Information Service
NYSERNET 238
Nassau County Library System 88
National Agricultural Library 218, 239, 241–42, 340
National Commission on Technological Uses of Copyrighted Works (CONTU) 117–18
National Coupon System 165
National Information Standards Organization 106, 127
National Legal Research Group 146
National Library of Canada 139
National Library of Medicine 94, 181, 205, 234–35, 314
National Periodicals Center 32–33, 81, 165
National Science Foundation Network (NSFnet) 236
National Research and Education Network (NREN) 11, 299–301
National Technical Information Service (NTIS) 151, 160, 167–68, 183
National Union Catalog 81
Nebraska libraries 171
Neill Public Library (Washington) 356
Net borrowing See Balance of trade
Net lending See Balance of trade

Network of Alabama Academic
   Libraries 11, 36, 40–41, 57,
   117, 215, 218, 272, 340, 352–
   53
Networks See Consortia;
   Electronic information
   networks
New Hampshire libraries 305,
   342–43
New Jersey libraries 44, 110, 306
New Jersey OCLC Access Center
   110
New-York Historical Society 257
New York Metropolitan Reference
   and Research Library Agency
   See METRO
New York libraries 41, 44, 58–59,
   85, 87–88, 136, 170, 178, 206,
   212, 216, 257, 272, 356
   See also City University of
      New York; Columbia
      University; METRO; New
      York University
New York University 71, 215
Newspapers 161, 169, 180–81,
   184, 340
Nitecki, Danuta A. 95
Nola Regional Library System
   (Ohio) 333–34
North Carolina libraries 37, 41,
   43, 50, 88, 337, 342, 350, 355–
   56
North Carolina State Library 356
North Carolina State University
   43, 50, 337, 356
  Digitized Document
      Transmission Project (DDTP)
      37, 208, 239, 241–42, 297,
      309, 340–41
  Electronic Document Delivery
      Service (EDDS) 208, 241–42,
      341
North Dakota libraries 354
Northwest Technical College
   (Ohio) 334
Nova Scotia College of Art and
   Design See NOVANET

OCLC 49, 85, 88, 95, 104, 119–20,
   125, 127–28, 138–39, 146, 166,
   236, 314, 332, 338, 342–43,
   352–54
  ContentsFirst and ArticleFirst
      174–75
  Group Access Capability (GAC)
      95–96, 98, 161, 297, 353,
      355–56
  ILL subsystem 11–12, 17, 56, 81–
      82, 92–93, 95–97, 110, 134,
      147, 155, 161, 164, 175, 183–
      84, 218, 241, 255–56, 262,
      269, 297, 335, 337, 340–41,
      343, 353, 355, 357
  Interlibrary Loan Discussion
      Panel 12, 56, 81, 203, 253,
      268, 297
  Statistical reports 122
OPACs See Online catalogs
ORBIT 181
OSI See Open Systems
   Interconnection Reference
   Model
Oberlin Group 36, 353–54
Ochs, Mary 125
Ohio libraries 36, 237, 333–34,
   338–39, 342, 353–54
Ohio State Library 338
The Ohio State University 237
OhioLINK 338–39
Okerson, Ann 307–8, 311–12,
   315–16, 325
Online Computer Library Center
   See OCLC
Online bibliographic searching 13,
   15, 79, 128, 147–48, 153, 156,
   159, 170, 176, 178–79, 184–85,
   274, 287–88
   See also names of individual
      services
Online catalogs 13–14, 16, 41–42,
   106, 130, 139, 147, 159, 163–
   64, 172, 175, 191, 236, 263,
   265, 296–99, 301, 305, 323,
   331–39, 350, 354
*Online Journal of Current Clinical
   Trials* 314
Online public access catalogs See
   Online catalogs

On-demand services *See*
 Commercial document supply
 services; Information-on-
 demand services
On-site access *See* Reciprocal
 access
Open Systems Interconnection
 Reference Model 106, 138–39
Optical scanning *See* Scanning
 technology
Oregon libraries 102
Ownership
 Benefits 22–23
 Costs 15, 20–21, 60, 252
  See also Collection
   Development; Purchasing
   versus borrowing
Ownership model 19, 21, 294–95,
 325
Ownership/access model *See*
 Access model

PACLink *See* NOTIS
PACLoan *See* NOTIS
PAIS '80+ 176
PALINET 82
PC-Loan *See* Interlibrary loan:
 Software
Pagell, Ruth A. 181
Palmour, Vernon E. 34, 60
Pankake, Marcia 34
Parapsychology Sources of
 Information Center 146
Parravano, Ellen A. 99
Patrick, Ruth J. 33, 35, 51, 62, 69–
 70, 212
Pennsylvania Interlibrary Loan
 Code 85
Pennsylvania libraries 13, 20, 23–
 26, 44, 82, 85, 136, 206, 212–
 15, 219, 227, 234, 243, 257,
 269
Pennsylvania Library Information
 Network *See* PALINET
Pennsylvania State Library 213–
 14
Pennsylvania State University 44
Periodical literature *See* Journal
 literature
Peters, Paul E. 10, 15, 23, 298,
 301, 311, 317

Pew Charitable Trusts 217
Polytechnic University (Brooklyn,
 N. Y.) 58–59, 216, 272
Post, William 22–23, 266, 304,
 347–48
Postage *See* United States mail
Potter, William G. 106
Preservation 15, 33, 36, 47, 60, 89,
 270, 308–10, 313, 317–18,
 324–26
 See also Interlibrary loan:
  Packaging
Preston, Cecilia M. 299–301
Princeton University (New Jersey)
 44
Priority Mail *See* United States
 mail
Project Gutenberg 305
Publishers *See* Electronic books;
 Electronic journals; Electronic
 publishing; Scholarly
 publishing
Publishing output *See* Electronic
 books; Electronic journals;
 Electronic publishing; Journal
 literature; Scholarly publishing
Purchasing versus borrowing 5,
 60, 88–90, 113
 Journals 90, 118–20, 252
 Monographs 89–90
Purdue University (Indiana) 159,
 335
Purolater 214

Quarterman, John S. 238
Queens College (New York) 335
Quint, Barbara 149, 264, 294

RLG *See* Research Libraries Group
RLIN *See* Research Libraries
 Information Network
Reciprocal access 27, 33–35, 38,
 45–46, 48–49, 56, 58–59, 68–
 75, 87, 118, 130, 250, 259–60,
 333, 336–37, 342, 344, 350–51,
 353, 357
 Cost-effectiveness 69–70
 Definition 68–69
 Eligibility 39, 71
 Evaluation 72–73, 75

Fees 69, 74–75, 138, 350–51
Fines 75, 349, 351
Geographic issues 44, 69, 260, 332, 337, 346, 350–51
Overdues 73, 351
Privileges 39, 71–72, 74–75
Promotion 73–74
Valuable materials 70, 112
See also Subscribing to collections
Reference 11, 111, 129, 263, 325
Reference and Adult Services Division (ALA) 234
Regional Medical Library system 54, 81, 94, 235
Research libraries 1–2, 19, 24–25, 32, 37, 84, 118, 262, 324, 331–32, 339–40, 347–48, 351–52, 356
Research Libraries Group 44, 46, 49, 71, 176, 212, 239–40, 243, 282, 294, 297, 302, 318, 332, 342, 344, 351–52
Interlibrary Loan Cost Study 60, 212, 255, 257–59, 275, 277, 282
Research Libraries Information Network (RLIN) 12, 98, 125–27, 138, 146, 175–76, 239, 306
ILL subsystem 81, 97–98, 110, 122, 164, 171, 183–84, 255, 340
Resource sharing 10, 14, 17, 19–21, 27, 32, 34, 38–39, 41, 43, 46–53, 55, 62, 63–64, 79, 81, 84, 86, 88, 100, 147–48, 202, 206, 213–14, 220, 228, 239, 242–44, 264, 274, 281, 295–96, 299–301, 325–26
Case studies 331–57
Costs 5–6, 54, 222, 273
Definition 3, 34–35
Efficiency 19
Partners 40
See also Consortia; Interlibrary loan; Reciprocal access
Retrospective conversion 12, 41, 300, 356
Roderer, Nancy K. 34, 60
Rogers, Sharon J. 324
Rohrbaugh, Valerie K. 182
Rottman, F. K. 120

Royalty fees See Copyright compliance
Rugge, Sue 158
Russell, Dorothy W. 82, 95
Rutgers University (New Jersey) 306

SAIL See National Library of Medicine
SAVEIT statistical software package 127–28
SDC 148, 167
SOLINET 36, 97, 352
SRIM See National Technical Information Service
STN International 180–81
SULAN See State University Library Automation Network (Indiana)
SUNY/OCLC 11
St. Cloud State University (Minnesota) 355
St. Mary's University (Nova Scotia) See NOVANET
Saldinger, Jeffrey 169
Satellite transmission 164
Savage, Lon 318
Scanning technology 27, 36, 43–44, 49, 57, 62, 127, 148, 171, 175, 184, 202–3, 206, 217, 224–25, 237, 239–43, 245, 297, 299, 340–41, 346, 354
Costs and cost centers 240, 242–43
Direct-to-reader delivery 241–42, 303, 309
Document quality 239–41, 279, 282
Equipment 194, 239–42, 271, 341, 355
Needs assessment 242–43
Partners 4, 186, 217, 242–44
Turnaround 242, 341
When to use 260
See also Ariel; North Carolina State University Digitized Document Transmission Project
Schmidt, Karen A. 318, 324
Scholarly communication 301, 308

Scholarly publishing 8–10, 12–13, 27, 78, 172, 197, 302, 308–9, 311, 313–14, 316–17
  See also Electronic books; Electronic journals; Electronic publishing
Scholar's workstations 302–5, 319, 322
Scientific publishing *See* Electronic journals; Electronic publishing; Scholarly publishing
Search and Delivery Project *See* Washington State University Search and Delivery Project
Selected Research in Microfiche *See* National Technical Information Service
Selection *See* Collection development
Self-sufficiency 3, 8, 16, 19, 21, 32, 46, 48, 52, 78, 325
Serial literature *See* Journal literature
Shared catalogs 13, 39, 41–42, 45, 49, 51, 61–62, 79, 92, 103–7, 130–33, 287, 299–300, 319, 331–39, 342, 344, 349–50, 352–53, 357
Sheffner, Ralph M. 85
Sherman H. Masten Learning Resource Center (Randolph, N.J.) 127
Shelving *See* Space costs
Shipman, John S. 38, 48, 202
Simpson, Donald B. 33, 45, 52, 252
Singapore Institute of Standards and Industrial Research 146
Sonoma Internet Library Access Software 322
South Carolina libraries 109
South Dakota libraries 354
Southern Library Information Network *See* SOLINET
Space costs 15, 60, 89, 121, 252, 256, 258, 310, 313, 325
Special libraries 147, 152, 170, 177, 179, 184, 259–60, 319, 326, 354
SprintNet 176

Staff 61, 244
  Attitudes 132, 279, 284–85
  Roles 121, 175, 179
  Time 4, 16, 54, 59, 112, 115–16, 121, 124, 129, 137, 154–55, 190, 194, 226, 229–32, 235, 242, 253, 258, 260, 270–71, 275, 277, 280–84, 338, 341–43, 347
  Training 81, 99, 123, 128–29, 135, 176, 179, 182–85, 190, 225, 283, 285
Stanford University (California) 257
State University Library Automation Network (Indiana) 104, 335–36
State University of New York (Albany) 257
State University of New York/OCLC *See* SUNY/OCLC
Stevens, Rolland E. 84
Stevenson, Marsha J. 209
Storage cabinets *See* Space costs
Storage centers 5, 116, 336–37
Students 10, 14–16, 18–19, 21–22, 25, 36, 38, 49, 62, 69, 71–72, 104, 108–109, 111, 120, 126, 179, 206–9, 216, 242, 250, 262–63, 267–68, 272, 295, 320, 322, 327, 332, 334, 336, 339, 342, 346, 351, 353, 356
  Undergraduates 10, 16–17, 25, 38, 73, 111, 130, 205, 250–51, 262, 276, 295, 298, 306, 345, 348
  Graduate students 1, 7, 17, 71, 111, 250–51, 259, 334, 351
Subscribing to collections 274, 340, 342, 346–50
Suburban Library System (Illinois) 353
Supplies 59, 271
Susquehanna University (Pennsylvania) 219
Sweeney, Richard 59
System Development Corporation *See* SDC
System for Automated Interlibrary Loan (SAIL) *See* National Library of Medicine

TOCs *See* Table of contents services
TRLN *See* Triangle Research Libraries Network (North Carolina)
TULIP (The University Licensing Program) 314–15
Table of contents services 20, 22, 79, 166–67, 171–76, 183, 191, 193–94, 204, 298, 300, 326, 335
  Definition 171
  Reader-initiated requests 172–76, 297–98
    See also Commercial document supply services; names of individual services
Tanzania National Documentation Centre 146
Tear sheets 166
Technical University of Nova Scotia *See* NOVANET
Technology *See* Automated integrated library systems; Automation; Bibliographic utilities; CD-ROM catalogs; CD-ROM indexes; Consortia: Telecommunications capabilities; Electronic file transfer; Electronic mail messaging systems; Electronic information formats; Electronic information networks; Future; Interlibrary loan; Multiple database systems; Online bibliographic searching; Online catalogs; Shared catalogs; Scanning technology; Table of contents services; Telecommunications costs; Telefacsimile transmission; names of individual organizations and systems
Tegler, Patricia 147, 150, 153
Telecommunications costs 4, 15–16, 97–99, 101, 147, 156, 182, 194, 220, 223, 228–29, 231–33, 237, 242, 253, 258, 284, 300, 302, 344, 352

Telefacsimile transmission 27, 36, 43–44, 49, 57, 59, 62, 80, 86, 100, 147–48, 154, 156, 171, 185–86, 202–4, 206–7, 209, 214–15, 217–39, 243–45, 254, 299, 303, 333, 337, 340, 344–46, 348–49, 352, 354
  Agreements and policies 88, 91, 133, 221, 228, 234–35, 352
  Benefits 219
  Charging local readers 191, 296
  Charging other libraries 229, 258, 268–70, 353
  Commercial document supply services's use 148–49, 161–64, 166, 170, 174–76, 178, 193, 220, 347
  Cost-effectiveness 220
  Costs and cost centers 137, 157, 217–20, 222, 227–33, 235, 239, 242, 254
  Cover sheets 232
  Direct-to-reader delivery 218, 237, 303, 309, 314, 336
  Document quality 217–18, 221, 229–30, 233, 239, 279, 282
  Equipment 129–30, 194, 196, 217, 219, 222–28, 231, 233, 237–39, 271, 284, 334, 345, 347, 349, 352
  Feasibility studies 219
  Funding 228, 334, 345, 347, 349
  Geographic factors 219
  Group IV equipment 238–39
  Memory 223, 225–26
  Microcomputer as fax machine 225, 237
  Needs assessment 219–21
  Networks 234–36
  Paper 196, 218, 221–23, 230, 233
  Partners 4, 133, 184, 186, 217, 221, 259, 263
  Reports 226
  Request transmission 88, 92, 110, 185, 218, 234, 265, 334, 340–41, 344–45, 353, 355
  Rush requests 133, 217, 219–20, 268, 278, 334
  Site preparation 230
  Speed 17, 217–21, 239, 263, 282, 347
  Standards 222

Supplies 138, 230–33, 349
Turnaround time 88, 221, 344, 347, 353
When to use 206, 218–19, 221, 259–60, 335
Workflow 135, 220, 229–30
Telephone answering machines 134, 209, 218, 283
Telex 161, 164
Temporary acquisition 2, 89, 273, 289, 296
Tennessee libraries 23, 26, 42, 104, 181–82, 230, 232, 344
Texas libraries 35, 48, 108–9, 125, 151–52, 167–68, 255, 257, 301
Texas Tech University 108–9
Theses 161, 164, 167, 193
Thompson, James C. 311
Toledo-Lucas Public Library (Ohio) 333–34
Triangle Research Libraries Network (North Carolina) 337, 342, 350
Trinity College (Connecticut) See CTW Library Consortium
Turner, Fay 139
Tuttle, Marcia 15, 18

UMI See University Microfilms Incorporated
UPS See United Parcel Service
USBE See Universal Serials and Book Exchange
UTLAS 110
Union catalogs See Shared catalogs
United Parcel Service 44, 136–37, 185, 211, 213–15, 344, 349, 352–53
United States Book Exchange See Universal Serials and Book Exchange
United States Department of Education 336
United States mail 17, 27, 44, 59, 91, 99, 108, 133–34, 136, 146, 157, 161, 163, 166, 170, 175–76, 178, 182–86, 193, 202, 208–211, 214, 218–19, 221, 253, 265, 283, 334, 340, 344, 354
United States Patent and Trademark Office 160
Universal access See Information ethics
Universal document supply services See Commercial document supply services; Information-on-demand services
Universal Serials and Book Exchange 90, 118, 168–69, 195
University College of Cape Breton (Nova Scotia) See NOVANET
University Microfilms Incorporated (UMI) 59, 118, 147, 152, 157, 161–64, 167, 169, 171, 175–76, 178, 183, 355
University of Alabama School of Law 117
University of Alberta (Canada) 36, 43, 50, 341–42, 345–46
University of California 37, 41, 107–8, 346
  Berkeley 22–23, 42, 50, 238, 257, 265–66, 269, 274, 299, 340, 346–48
  Irvine 109
  Los Angeles 216, 349–50
  Riverside 23, 26
University of Colorado (Boulder) 178
University of Evansville (Indiana) 335
University of Findlay (Ohio) 334
University of Houston 301
University of Idaho 356
University of Illinois 305
  Chicago 150
  Urbana-Champaign 11, 40–42, 338
University of King's College (Nova Scotia) See NOVANET
University of Michigan 50, 257, 269, 343–44, 350
University of Minnesota
  Duluth 355
  Twin Cities 354–55
University of Nebraska (Omaha) 171
University of New Brunswick (Canada) 36, 43, 50, 341–42

University of New Hampshire
(Manchester) 342–43
University of North Carolina
(Chapel Hill) 43, 50, 337, 356
University of Notre Dame
(Evansville, Indiana) 335
University of Pennsylvania 44,
257, 269
University of Pittsburgh *See*
Collection use studies:
Pittsburgh study
University of Regina (Canada) 36,
50, 342, 345–46
University of Southern California
Electronic Library Consortium
350
University of Texas
Austin 151–52, 167–68, 255
Health Science Center (San
Antonio) 125
McKinney Engineering Library
(Austin) 167–68
University of Tennessee
(Knoxville) 23, 26, 42, 104,
181–82, 230, 232, 344
University of Toronto Library
Automation Systems *See*
UTLAS
University of Virginia 50, 340,
348–49
University of Wisconsin
Madison 85, 355
Stevens Point 162–63
Utah libraries 146

VU/TEXT 180
Vanderbilt University (Tennessee)
42, 104, 230, 232, 344
Video information formats 12,
202, 243
Vincennes University (Indiana)
335
Virginia libraries 50, 57, 254, 256,
340, 348–49
Virginia Polytechnic Institute
(Virginia Tech) 50, 256, 313–
14, 323, 340, 348–49

W. K. Kellogg Foundation 217

WESTLAW 180
WESTNET 238
WILL (Walk-In InterLibrary Loan)
(Massachusetts) 351
WILS *See* Wisconsin Library
Services
WLN *See* Western Library
Network
WRLC *See* Washington Research
Library Consortium
(Washington, D.C.)
Wainer, Margaret A. 235
Waldhart, Thomas J. 81
Walters, Edward M. 37
Washington Research Library
Consortium (Washington, D.C.)
36, 105, 297, 336–37
Washington, D.C., libraries 36,
105, 297, 336–37
Washington state libraries 98, 212,
356–57
Washington State University
Search and Delivery Project
356–57
Wayne State University
(Michigan) 343
Weber, Robert 304–5
Wesleyan University
(Connecticut) *See* CTW Library
Consortium
Wessling, Julie E. 127
Western Library Network 12, 96,
98, 122, 127
White, Herbert S. 18, 53, 252, 264,
266, 294
Whitman County (Washington)
Library System 356
Wiggins, Gary D. 152, 203
Wilcox, Susan 125
Williams, Brian W. 119–20
Williams, James G. 53, 56, 60
Wisconsin libraries 85, 110, 162–
63, 355
Wisconsin Library Services
(WILS) 110, 162–63, 354–55

Yale University (Connecticut) 44